D1482202

Restorative Community Justice

Repairing Harm and
Transforming Communities

Edited by

Gordon Bazemore - Florida Atlantic University
Mara Schiff - Florida Atlantic University

anderson publishing co.
2035 Reading Road
Cincinnati, OH 45202
800-582-7295

Restorative Community Justice:
Repairing Harm and Transforming Communities

Copyright © 2001
    Anderson Publishing Co.
    2035 Reading Rd.
    Cincinnati, OH 45202

    Phone 800.582.7295 or 513.421.4142
    Web Site www.andersonpublishing.com

Library of Congress Cataloging-in-Publication Data

Restorative community justice : repairing harm and transforming communities / edited by
Gordon Bazemore, Mara Schiff
    p.   cm.
Includes bibliographical references and index.
ISBN 1-58360-506-1 (pbk.)
1. Restorative justice. 2. Vicitms of crimes. 3. Community-based corrections. I. Bazemore, S. Gordon.
II. Schiff, Mara.

HV8688 .R47   2000
364.6'8--dc21

                                                            00-040577

Cover digital composition and design by Tin Box Studio, Inc.   EDITOR Ellen S. Boyne
                                                ACQUISITIONS EDITOR Michael C. Braswell

Transferred to Digital Printing 2010

Contents

Part I
Introduction

GORDON BAZEMORE
MARA SCHIFF

What's Going On?

- In New Zealand, government officials, representatives of community groups, and researchers meet to "take stock" following 10 years of a national experiment in applying restorative justice principles to the country's youth court. This reform moved juvenile offender dispositions out of the adversarial setting of the court and into the informal context of a "family group conference." These conferences, in which offenders, crime victims, and their families work with juvenile justice professionals to craft sanctions focused on holding offenders accountable and repairing harms their crimes have caused, represents the largest-scale implementation of restorative justice decisionaking in the world to date.

- In Deschutes County, Oregon, "community justice officers" (formerly called probation officers) meet with a citizen advisory board to discuss their progress in moving toward neighborhood duty assignments rather than individual offender caseloads. In the meeting, they and community corrections administrators also hear recommendations from the advisory board about how surplus funds formerly allocated to juvenile offender residential beds in a state facility will be committed to local prevention activities and victim services.

- In a predominantly African-American neighborhood in Minneapolis, a mixed-race group of community members share refreshments after completing a highly emotional community reentry circle in which a black teenager who had been incarcerated for pointing a pistol at a white neighbor in an attempted robbery was being welcomed back into the neighborhood. The victim and his wife, who had considered moving out of the neighborhood following this incident, embraced the young man and his parents at the conclusion of the circle and congratulated him on his progress while away from the community and his willingness to accept responsibility and make amends for what he had done.

• In several European countries, an estimated 750 victim-offender mediation programs facilitate dialogue between victims and offenders and negotiate reparative plans that are aimed at giving victims input and information about the crime and the opportunity to meet face-to-face with offenders. In these and some 500 programs in the United States and Canada, practitioners are beginning to include a broader range of more chronic and serious offenders in a nonadversarial alternative to court sentencing, as well as traditional diversion, now also employed at other stages of the criminal justice process.

• In Pittsburgh, Pennsylvania, young offenders assigned to a day-treatment facility in an inner-city neighborhood as an alternative to incarceration work side-by-side with neighbors on housing restoration, community clean-up, voter registration, odd-jobs for the elderly, community gardens, and other community service projects as a core component of their supervision plan. Some offenders also learns mediation and conflict-resolution skills and act as mentors to younger offenders and those new to the program.

• In Canberra, Australia, police officers direct family group conferences in which offenders, crime victims, and their families or supporters meet to develop restorative justice solutions to crimes ranging from shoplifting to felony assault to drunk driving. Similar programs in the United States and Canada utilize police-facilitated family group conferences generally in response to misdemeanor crime by juveniles as a diversion option.

• In Denver, Colorado, members of a local neighborhood accountability board sponsored by the district attorney's office listen to citizen concerns about juveniles drinking after hours in local parks. One result of this meeting is a series of problem-solving measures that include expanded treatment and educational opportunities for young people with substance abuse problems, discussion with young people in the neighborhood about alternative recreational opportunities, and restrictions on use of parks after hours.

• In Dakota and Washington Counties in Minnesota, community corrections managers and staff complete qualitative agency audits designed to gauge changes in staff attitudes and transformation in organizational culture consistent with an ongoing three-year restorative justice initiative. In one of the state's prisons, a guard embraces a young inmate facing release in a few weeks who he had on several occasions told that his chances of not coming back were 20 to 1. The two had just completed a "reentry circle" in which the guard expressed the view that sitting in on circle discussions with inmates and staff had changed his entire outlook on offenders.

- In Austin, Texas, the District Attorney's office sponsors meetings in which local African-American ministers and other community leaders and interested citizens meet with jailed drug traffickers in circle sentencing sessions in which the offenders discuss the harms their crimes have caused to neighborhoods, and citizens consider alternative sanctions that may be recommended as an alternative to the traditional plea-bargaining process.

- In shopping centers and malls in the United States and parts of the United Kingdom, police facilitate meetings between owners or representatives of retail establishments and young shoplifters to develop informal sanctions that may require apologies, restitution, community service, or other measures as an alternative to formal court processing.

- In New York, New York, the Midtown Community Court offers social services, community service referrals, tutoring, and childcare as a supplement to traditional court services at the neighborhood level. In other community courts and "community justice centers" around the country, citizens are invited to discuss local concerns about crime and disorder and to develop new initiatives designed to "build the capacity" of neighborhood organizations to prevent and control crime.

- In South St. Paul, Minnesota, two students recently involved in a fist fight in the gymnasium sit in a circle with teachers, other students, school resource officers, parents, and a restorative conferencing facilitator, to discuss the harm this incident had caused to the school environment and the student themselves. This and similar meetings in this middle-school are held to consider alternatives to suspension that increase staff and student skill in problem-solving and conflict resolution.

- In several U.S. states, community-based victim support groups assist those injured by violent crimes in a healing journey that may involve talking about the impact of crime on their lives with groups of offenders, meeting with their own offender, supporting other victims of crime, or working with delinquency prevention programs.

- Throughout the state of Vermont, and increasingly in other jurisdictions in the United States, volunteers meet with offenders and
victims in reparative boards, accountability panels, and neighborhoods boards to develop plans for offenders to redress the
harm they have caused to victims and their communities.

- In Edmonton, Alberta (Canada), local police officers meet regularly with local citizen groups who have taken responsibility for conducting community restorative conferences with offenders involved
in a wide range of crimes. While police officers themselves initially
facilitated most restorative conferences and employ a variety of
problem-solving conferencing approaches "on the street," they now
refer more serious cases to these neighborhood restorative conferencing groups and act primarily in a sponsorship and support role.

- In Tallahassee, Florida, African-American ministers, local police
officers, and staff of the Neighborhood Justice Center conclude a
meeting on improving race relations in police encounters with
black citizens. After adjournment, several participants in this
meeting move to another room for a box supper prior to an early
evening community conference in which some of the group will
facilitate a neighborhood accountability conference with juveniles
referred by the state's attorney's office.

In much of the world today, citizens and criminal justice professionals are engaged in new and distinctive conversations about how to
respond to crime. Though traditional concerns with crime control,
punishment, and offender surveillance and treatment continue to dominate the mainstream criminal justice agenda, this new discourse goes
well beyond the legal issues associated with lawbreaking and is concerned with something more complex than the problems presented by
individual lawbreakers. As indicated by the examples above, those
involved in these new conversations seem to be looking at crime and disorder in a different way—through a "new lens" (Zehr, 1990). This lens
focuses our attention on the harm crime causes to individuals, communities, and relationships and on problems that, if not resolved, will
result in future crime and a weakening of community life. The new lens
also seems to bring into focus the strengths and assets in individuals and
communities that may become resources in resolving these problems.

It is certainly possible that some of the rhetoric associated with what
appears to be an emerging new justice movement is simply an attempt
to "repackage" traditional criminal justice programs, policies, and
philosophies. Indeed, some of the practices and agency policies now
being called "restorative justice" will be difficult to distinguish from
long-standing offender diversion programs or alternative dispute resolution processes. And some of what is being labeled "community jus-

tice" may look scarcely different from the community corrections or team policing experiments of the 1970s. Yet, those who listen closely to the new conversations—and observe some of the best practices—will soon notice that a distinctive shared vision may be guiding advocates of a new way of responding both to individual offenses and to the conditions believed to cause them.

This value-based vision is less about creating larger, tougher, or even more efficient criminal justice agencies and systems, and more about building local citizen and neighborhood efficacy to respond to crime and these conditions in ways that create safer, more peaceful, and more just community environments. It is less about punishing offenders on behalf of the state in ways that are more threatening, and more about holding lawbreakers accountable for the harm caused to their victims and communities in ways that "make things right" by repairing this harm. It is less about building more treatment programs for young offenders, and more about building new relationships between offenders and their communities. It is less about simply following the letter of the law in victims' rights statutes—that at times seem more focused on hurting offenders than helping victims—and more about attending to victim needs and involving crime victims and their supporters as active participants in justice decisionmaking. Finally, it is less about increasing the uniformity of punishment and promulgating more legislation to protect the rights of offenders in an adversarial process, and more about developing community-focused responses to crime and conflict that seek to rebuild the capacity of citizens and community groups to mobilize informal social control and socialization processes.

For skeptics, much of the apparent consensus among the diverse groups and individuals actively engaged in the new dialogue is viewed as being based on a shared opposition to the status quo. However, even among critical observers, there is growing acknowledgement of a significant alignment around general core themes, such as the return to community as the locus of problem-solving and a questioning of the capacity of formal criminal justice agents to prevent crime or respond effectively to it in isolation from citizens and neighborhood groups. In these as well as more specific themes of community-building, addressing the needs of crime victims, strengthening relationships, and prioritizing new forms of accountability and new strategies for achieving public safety and offender reintegration, there is an important break with the treatment-versus-punishment and crime control-versus-rights debates that have frequently been associated with criminal justice in the past half-century. Yet, beyond this common ground lies a vast area of unsettled territory.

The diversity of policy and practice examples, as represented in the limited set listed at the beginning of this introduction, makes more complex any attempt to describe a movement in which even the choice of

terminology used to identify it is contested ground. The wide array of
names being used to describe what some have referred to as a "new paradigm" include, for example, "restorative justice," "community justice," "restorative community justice," "indigenous justice," "responsible justice," "transformative justice," and "balanced and restorative
justice"—to mention a few.

Ultimately, we maintain that serious dialogue about values and principles is currently more important to identifying the common ground
in this movement—and to its ultimate success—than are labels or
packaging. In this volume, we will use the term "restorative community justice" (see also Bazemore and Schiff, 1996; Young, 1995) to
describe what is by any assessment a diverse and evolving array of policies, practices, and ideological tendencies. Provisionally, we believe this
term captures the essence of what is both distinctive and important
about what appears to be an emerging new justice vision. It also
allows practitioners and scholars to build continuously on the diversity that is vital to creativity in both discourse and practice. Especially at the practice level, we view this diversity as a strength that can unite
a broad group of constituencies who share a sense of need to minimize
the trend toward bigger and more complex justice systems that seem
to produce less satisfying results.

In doing so, it may be helpful to view the movement around
restorative and community justice as a large "tent." The occupants of
this tent are threatened, on the one hand, by the possible limitations
on growth and creativity that would result from overly restrictive
admission criteria. On the other hand, there is equal danger in an open-
entrance policy that allows so many into the tent that it leaks and/or
produces unmanageable conflict between occupants. In order to open
admission to new and emerging practices that reflect the values inherent in the new discourse, while excluding those simply attempting to
repackage old interventions and concepts, we suggest that principles,
rather than programs, must ultimately be the gatekeeper. Although a
principle-based definition would allow one to rank various practices
along multiple dimensions based on their potential to meet a variety
of restorative community justice objectives, such a definition (unlike
black and white distinctions) would not imply the existence of any pure
program models. No practice or policy is inherently "restorative" or
representative of "community justice," and some practices and policies not currently thought to be part of the restorative- or community-
justice framework may become so by incorporating certain principles.

Although we argue that there is now enough convergence in the
ideas and practice of restorative justice and community justice to justify an attempt to explore a common vision (see Chapter 1), it is
important not to gloss over the considerable differences that may
remain between these two frameworks that have emerged somewhat

independently. Although Chapter 1 provides a detailed discussion of similarities and differences between these two terms, we offer the following as general definitions and brief descriptions of the concerns of each perspective.

The term "community justice" has been used generally to describe a preference for neighborhood-based, more accessible, and less formal justice services that, to the greatest extent possible, shift the locus of justice intervention to those most affected by crime (Barajas, 1995; Clear and Karp, 1999). According to one definition, community justice includes:

> . . . all variants of crime prevention and justice activities that explicitly include the community in their processes. Community justice is rooted in the actions that citizens, community organizations, and the criminal justice system can take to control crime and social disorder. Its central focus is community-level outcomes, shifting the emphasis from individual incidents to systemic patterns, from individual conscience to social mores, and from individual goods to the common good. (Clear and Karp, 1999:25)

Practices most often associated with community justice include: community policing, community prosecution, community courts, community corrections, and a variety of related initiatives (National Institute of Justice, 1996). Community justice programs and initiatives seek to be explicitly preventive and attempt to employ a problem-solving focus to intervention (Goldstein, 1990).[1] A community-justice mission for criminal justice agencies and systems is grounded in a commitment to the community as primary client or "customer" of the justice system. Regarding overall normative orientation, proponents of community justice have argued, for example, that it is critical to pay serious attention to neighborhood concerns for disorder, fear of crime, and quality-of-life issues that may seem unrelated or only vaguely related to the crime rate or to formal criminal justice functions (Boland, 1998; Kelling and Coles, 1996; Wilson and Kelling, 1982).

Restorative justice is a new way of thinking about crime that emphasizes one fundamental fact: crime is a violation of individuals, communities, and relationships. If crime is important because of the harm it causes, "justice" must amount to more than punishing or treating those found guilty of lawbreaking. Crime "creates obligations to make things right" (Zehr, 1990:181), and restorative justice therefore includes all responses to crime aimed at doing justice by repairing the harm, or "healing the wounds," that crime causes (Van Ness and Strong, 1997). Restorative justice practices focus on informal decisionmaking in the response to crime, such as victim-offender mediation or dialogue, family group conferencing, and a range of other processes designed to include victim, offender, and community in developing a plan for repairing this harm. The restorative justice framework also encompasses the reparative sanctions or obligations such as restitution and community service that may result from these processes or from court (or other formal) sentencing procedures, such as restitution and community services, as well as a variety of policy strategies that flow out of a commitment to victim, offender, and community as primary "stakeholders" in the justice process.

Purpose and Goals of this Volume

This volume presents a snapshot of an early but important stage of the restorative community justice movement. Our goal is to capture some of the essence of this evolving creative change in the response to crime. Hence, rather than to seek to define and categorize practices and initiatives, we consider what are for the most part ongoing and unresolved debates over practice, theory, and implementation in the context of core principles of restorative community justice. Therefore, we cannot claim that this book provides the reader with a complete, definitive picture of the restorative and community justice movements.[2] Rather, chapters consider critical and unresolved issues and attempt to break new ground in what is clearly an evolving set of practices and philosophies.

Students and scholars new to restorative and community justice will learn much about the theory and practice associated with these frameworks. However, the volume should not be viewed as introductory. While the book should not be considered a how-to guide or even a general blueprint for implementation, criminal justice professionals will benefit from the critical examination of the movement, its practice, and its philosophy. In addition, several chapters present straightforward descriptions of some of the leading restorative and community justice practices, and also provide a strong grounding in the value framework and normative theories that inform ongoing reform efforts. We believe these descriptions and conceptual overviews will be of interest to both scholars and criminal justice professionals, as well as more general policy audiences.[3] Although the book clearly has a Western focus, indigenous experiences with community and restorative justice practices are briefly considered by several authors. The collection of essays is therefore international in scope but is by no means representative of the range of societies and cultures experimenting with restorative community justice. Our somewhat limited sampling of countries—which includes the United States, Canada, Australia, New Zealand, the United Kingdom, and several European countries—was driven by an effort to address critical themes and issues, offer case studies that raise theoretical and implementation concerns, and ensure that we selected the most capable authors to accomplish these objectives.

By far, the greatest attraction of this book is the range of authors we have assembled as contributors. A unique feature in this regard is the inclusion of several outstanding practitioners of restorative justice as well as leading researchers and theorists. Notably, several chapters were assigned specifically as collaborations between a leading criminal justice professional working in community restorative justice and a researcher/scholar noted for his or her work in this area. Interestingly, several of the practitioners writers are also noted for their critical scholarship on restorative community justice, and several of those primarily known for their research and theoretical contributions to this emerging field have also been on the front line of policy and program development and implementation.

By inviting contributions from authors who represent a wide range of perspectives, including essentially critical ones, we run the risk that the reader who is looking for a fully developed, coherent new philosophy of justice will be confused, if not disappointed.[4] This book is clearly not a marketing tool for advocates of restorative community justice. Although we include authors who make strong value statements about the potential for certain practices, or the restorative community justice philosophy generally, readers will not find irrefutable rationales for supporting these new approaches, or for persuading others to do so. Some may view this critical perspective as unfair or unkind to those who are taking risks in experimenting with promising new approaches. Our perspective, however, is that it is through such critical examination that reformers ultimately refine practice. Moreover, the most effective critical examination is one that ultimately leads toward solutions to persistent problems. Because some of these solutions, we believe, can be found within the principles of restorative community justice, this critical perspective should be viewed as a strength of this book, with the potential to improve emerging policy and practice. To put these criticisms in context, these authors are at least equally critical of "business as usual" in criminal justice. While it is important to avoid caricatures of the current system, we remind readers that attacks on restorative and community justice must be seen in the context of problems and dysfunctional features of current criminal justice practice rather than against some ideal standard.

In addition to providing a critical perspective, several essays were prepared to consider themes outside the normal range of issues discussed by restorative and community justice advocates. These include the connection to social justice, the linkage to other theories in criminology and other social sciences, the connection to the political and economic context, and implications for offender reintegration. As we will discuss in more detail in Chapter 1, the challenge of any effort to integrate restorative and community justice is to merge practice and theory between macro and micro, informal and formal, and prevention and intervention. We believe several chapters effectively bridge these domains. One important, though implicit, theme in several of the chapters is the need for greater collaboration and dialogue between practitioner and researcher. Until very recently, restorative community justice had not gained the interest of criminologists and other social scientists. Practice, with the notable exception of the now widely studied victim-offender mediation model (Umbreit, 1999), has generally proceeded without benefit of much research evidence. Precisely because restorative justice and community justice are so different than what has come before, researchers need to become more immersed in the nuances of practice before attempting to impose evaluation models on interventions in which participants are likely to be seeking very different outcomes than those prioritized in traditional criminal justice interventions (Bazemore, 2000; Clear and Karp, 1999).

We believe each contribution in this volume invites scholars to look critically and with an open mind at the restorative community justice agenda. Although several chapters offer important theoretical breakthroughs in a movement that has been accused of having little theory, there is ample opportunity for critique and expansion of existing or emerging theoretical models. For administrators and practitioners, these contributions provide an opportunity for an introspective examination of what it is they are trying to accomplish in restorative community justice interventions and how their practice is actually related to these desired outcomes. The mix of chapters primarily authored by practitioners (e.g., judges, probation administrators, community workers) and by academics/researchers should provide an excellent context for this cross-fertilization of theory and practice. Given the dynamic nature of the restorative community justice movement at this time, we have sought as editors to avoid adherence to a strictly defined script for this volume that might place restrictions on the creativity of these authors. Generally, we selected each contributor because of his or her expertise in a specific arena of restorative and community justice, assigned each a topic within a general thematic area, and then allowed substantial leeway in the development of each contribution.

Primary themes of the emerging restorative and community justice discourse have guided our efforts to organize this book around what we view as key components of the new movement. These themes include the general turn away from an individualized, offender-oriented focus for criminal justice intervention that is concerned primarily with treatment and punishment and toward a more holistic approach focused on repair and community building. A second theme, regarding victim, offender, and community involvement in these efforts to repair and strengthen communities and relationships, is a primary consideration informing the development of new strategies and process- es for involving these stakeholders. A third, overarching theme for those implementing and evaluating restorative community justice is the new emerging role for justice systems and justice professionals that is needed to support such stakeholder involvement and the new relation- ship between government and community that is suggested by these.

These themes mirror the three core principles of restorative justice defined by Van Ness and Strong (1997). This suggests that if crime is to be viewed as more than lawbreaking, the justice response must focus on repair and involve in decisionmaking those harmed by the crime. To accomplish both, the response must develop new configu- rations of roles and responsibilities for justice systems and the com- munity. The themes also parallel principles of community justice, although proponents of the latter tend to argue that community jus- tice is focused on community building for preventive purposes rather than simply repair (Clear and Karp, 1999; for other differences and sim- ilarities in these frameworks, see Chapter 1).

Structure of the Book

Based on consideration of these three themes, the contributions in Part One, which we label the *foundation*, consider core principles and theoretical underpinnings of restorative and community justice. Specifically, the essays in this section address specific meanings of concepts of repairing harm or making things better for communities. The section begins with a general consideration of differences and sim- ilarities between the restorative and community justice frameworks. In this introductory chapter, the editors also discuss the origins and scope of the modern restorative community justice movements, con- sider these new practices and ideas in the context of other related social movements, and briefly address the question "why now?" in light of the more dominant trends in criminal justice toward system expansion and punitiveness. Next, in Chapter 2, restorative justice pioneer Daniel Van Ness and researcher Mara Schiff consider the utility of stakeholder satisfaction as a primary indicator of the extent to which restoration has occurred. Their premise is that clarifying the concept of satisfac- tion may go a long way toward helping practitioners and researchers develop and refine standards for gauging success in restorative inter- ventions. Finally, in Chapter 3, Australian criminologists John Braith- waite and Declan Roche elaborate on the accountability or responsi- bility component of repair and restoration. Their distinction between active and passive responsibility for crime invites us to consider that a major benefit of repairing harm and relationships as an objective of justice intervention is that it encourages offenders to *actively* seek to meet their obligations to others. The state-versus-community role in the response to crime is also further clarified in Braithwaite and Roche's discussion.

In Part Two, the authors address what we view as the new *context* for restorative community justice. This new context is a function of the active involvement in justice decisionmaking of three new stakeholders: victim, offender, and community. Authors in this section generally consider the meaning and implications of repair for meeting the specific needs of these three stakeholders and then explore, to a somewhat lesser extent, the challenges involved in engaging them in the justice process. Although crime victims must be primary stakeholders in a restorative community justice agenda, years of victim exclusion and insensitive treatment by criminal justice systems mean that restorative justice proponents have to work harder to win the support of victims and their advocates than of other constituencies. In the first chapter of this section, United States victim advocate Mary Achilles and groundbreaking restorative justice philosopher and practitioner Howard Zehr make it clear that victims are often traumatized not only by offenders but by their treatment in the justice process itself. In doing so, they provide a practical but rarely discussed assessment of the needs of crime victims in the aftermath of crime. On the positive side, these authors suggest that the promise of restorative community justice is one that has already won initial support among a number of victim advocates, and many of the latter are indeed becoming leaders in restorative justice reform efforts. Yet, past mistakes in seeking to involve crime victims in new programs and processes, coupled with the legacy of negative experiences in the traditional system, indicate that restorative community justice practitioners must continue to reexamine their values and intervention protocols if they hope to strengthen this often fragile alliance.

Next, in Chapter 5, researcher Gordon Bazemore and corrections practitioner Michael Dooley consider the role of the offender as a stakeholder and outline a restorative community justice perspective on rehabilitation and reintegration. Beginning with the assertion that restorative justice proponents have often been unspecific about their view of rehabilitation and of the offender as well as a critical examination of the practical and conceptual limits of existing rehabilitation models, these authors explore what the concept of repair could mean for a more holistic model of reintegration and rehabilitation based on the idea of building and/or strengthening social relationships.

In Chapter 6, United Kingdom researcher Adam Crawford and United States corrections and community justice scholar Todd Clear consider the community as a stakeholder in restorative community justice. The community's role has probably been least well defined, and these authors provide an insightful critique that raises questions about the capacity of restorative and community justice practice to actually define and engage "community" and meet its needs. In doing so, these authors consider the limitations placed on restorative justice by structural injustice and question the motives of some government agencies in efforts to devolve justice to communities in which these injustices have not been addressed. Finally, in Chapter 7, corrections administrator Mark Carey examines the criminal justice agency as a different kind of "stakeholder" whose role and mandate will necessarily change if victims, offenders, and community members and groups are to become involved in justice decisionmaking. Carey views the practical problem of organizational culture as a barrier to reform that may hinder restorative community justice efforts and suggests general strategies for cultural change consistent with the new agenda.

In Part Three of the book, authors address the *content* (or practice) of intervention in restorative community justice. More specifically, they discuss three types of restorative decision-making processes aimed at engaging stakeholders in decisions about how to repair the harm. [5] In Chapter 8, New Zealand criminologists Gabrielle Maxwell and Allison Morris consider family group conferencing as a case study in the implementation of an increasingly popular restorative justice process. Drawing upon their extensive body of research on the New Zealand experience with family conferencing as the primary dispositional strategy in juvenile court, these researchers contrast theoretical and practical assumptions of this model with other conferencing approaches and realistically assess the ability of conferencing to accomplish some of the objectives advocates have set for this process.

In Chapter 9, researcher and community justice theorist David Karp and corrections practitioner Lynn Walther describe Vermont's reparative boards as a somewhat more structured, though still informal, restorative community justice decisionmaking technique. In neighborhoods throughout Vermont, volunteer citizen board members meet regularly to determine sanctions for nonviolent felony offenders that aim to repair harm to victims and communities as an alternative to court sentencing. Although they have been somewhat controversial among advocates of more "traditional" and more consensus-based restorative processes, such as victim-offender mediation, Vermont's reparative boards represent the most institutionalized form of restorative community justice decisionmaking in North America, and have been adapted widely as diversion-level "accountability boards" and "neighborhood youth panels" in several jurisdictions in the United States. While they list several shortcomings of boards, including difficulties thus far in involving crime victims regularly in board hearings, Karp and Walther suggest that boards seek to operationalize community justice principles, and attempt to "build community" by encouraging citizen norm affirmation and practical support for offenders and other stakeholders in the crime.

In Chapter 10, Canadian Judge Barry Stuart, who has worked with aboriginal communities for a number of years to expand and improve the use of circle sentencing (and more generally, the circle model of decisionmaking), presents core principles in a four-step process for conducting "peacemaking circles." Stuart suggests that circles are designed to balance condemnation of the criminal incident with the need to acknowledge the value of the offender as a community member, to attend to the needs of victims, and to build community capacity to respond to crime in the future. Building on Christie's idea of crime and conflict as an opportunity for transformative change (Christie, 1978), the author considers difficulties in following a consensus process that is truly inclusive, while also insisting that such a process is essential for viable and sustainable resolutions to crime and conflict. Because, in Stuart's view, it is the process itself that is transformative, community and restorative justice advocates are urged to be flexible in adapting techniques and structural program designs to a process that fits the needs of stakeholders rather than the reverse.

In Part Four of this book, contributors consider the *future* of restorative community justice in the context of both limitations and the potential to bring about broader transformation. Here, authors present explicitly critical discussions of what seems to be wrong or missing in some current efforts to implement restorative community justice and include responses to criticisms from the vantage point of a broader vision. In this section, authors consider challenges to implementation and explore possibilities for expanding the restorative community justice vision. In Chapter 11, researchers Evelyn Zellerer and Chris Cunneen draw on their extensive experience in Canada and Australia, respectively, with restorative community justice efforts involving indigenous populations and the application of these approaches to women as both victims and offenders. Although many restorative processes draw heavily on the insights of indigenous decisionmaking (e.g., Stuart, 1996; this volume), implementation efforts have, according to these authors, often involved heavy-handed and insensitive attempts to impose a restorative process on aboriginal communities that is inconsistent with their own settlement traditions, and have often ignored the special needs of women and girls in the process. Although many of the abuses described by Zellerer and Cunneen were perpetrated primarily by traditional criminal justice agencies in their respective countries rather than by restorative justice reformers, these examples of less-than-thoughtful restorative implementation efforts should serve as a caution for proponents of community justice who seek to engage indigenous communities in ways that are also sensitive to the special needs of females in these contexts.

From a very different perspective, Australian criminologist Kenneth Polk argues in Chapter 12 that the restorative agenda is incomplete in its limited focus on the criminal justice process. He notes the framework's failure to address the practices of formal socializing institutions and, especially, the problems at the level of the political economy that have resulted in a "crisis of abandoned youth." Beginning with a vital historical perspective on how, until recent decades, most Western societies managed to absorb most young people into the political economy and a conventional lifestyle, Polk argues that the restorative community justice focus on *reintegrating* young offenders must begin by confronting the current reality that large numbers of young people have simply never been *integrated*. Though restorative and community justice theorists are increasingly engaging more macro issues of structural discrimination and inequality at the community level (e.g., Braithwaite, 1998; Clear and Karp, 1999), Polk reminds us that few have addressed the arenas of school and work as targets for either prevention or intervention.

Yet, restorative and community justice principles certainly *could* be adapted to such arenas. As Kay Pranis notes in Chapter 13, restorative justice interventions have an important role in more general efforts to promote social justice. Pranis is a Minnesota corrections practitioner whose experience has been focused primarily at the neighborhood level, working with citizens and community groups seeking to develop alternative responses to crime. For her, the key in engaging social justice issues is the democratization of criminal justice through participatory decisionmaking. In a reflective, highly personal account of her experiences at the "cutting edge" (or "healing edge") of restorative community building in Minnesota and elsewhere, she acknowledges that community restorative justice alone cannot resolve political and economic dilemmas of social justice. However, it can result in an important kind of power-sharing that opens doors to engaging broader community problems through a consensus process based more on personal connections than confrontation. While the process of engaging citizens is focused on rather micro, yet concrete problems in the lives of citizens, when viewed through the restorative community justice lens, these problems can be seen as connected to community-level social justice issues rather than as isolated incidents.

In Chapter 15, the editors consider possible futures for restorative community justice. In doing so, we look back on the various contributions of our collaborators in this volume for signs of optimistic visions for restorative community justice in the next century, while taking account of the dangers raised about emerging practices in the new framework as well as the path of expansion that appears likely for the current criminal justice enterprise.

Endnotes

[1]   Though the term is most widely associated with these practices in the United States, in Canada, "community justice" seems to have been more associated with efforts to devolve justice functions to local communities (especially aboriginal communities) and is also used by some to describe a variety of decision-making processes, such as circle sentencing, that are often associated with restorative justice (Bazemore and Griffiths; 1998; Shaw and Jane, 1998, Stuart, 1996).

[2]   We use the term "movement" very loosely here and throughout this volume to refer to a generally unorganized coalition of groups who share an interest in promoting further development of restorative and community justice practice, theory, philosophy, and policy. In this sense, organization in the sense of oppositional movements in other sectors (e.g., the environment, civil rights) is virtually nonexistent, and organization in the sense of professional associations is fragmented into groups having a special interest in one aspect of restorative practice or in theory and research. Examples of the former include the Victim Offender Mediation Association (VOMA) and the International Network for Research on Restorative Justice for Juveniles.

[3]   One of the interesting features of the restorative community justice movement thus far, as Kay Pranis suggests in her chapter, is that researchers and scholars lag far behind community members and professionals in the most advanced practices. Though influenced by scholarly writings and by research and theory, the field seems to be several steps ahead of those who seek to document and synthesize these practices. The good news at this stage of the restorative community justice movement is that it has been practitioners who are demanding rigorous research, and researchers who are asking for more explicit statements of practice and implementation protocols.

[4]   For a more complete and less equivocal statement of restorative and community justice, see Van Ness and Strong, 1997.

[5]   Decision-making alternatives such as restorative justice conferencing are only one of several categories of practice in restorative community justice. At a minimum, these categories also include offender sanctions or obligations, community building, initiating victim support and service interventions, and offender reintegration approaches (Bazemore and Walgrave, 1999; Clear and Karp, 1999). Changes in the decision-making process are, however, one of the most significant innovators in the new model, and they are currently receiving most of the attention, especially in restorative justice circles.

References

Barajas, E., Jr. (1995). "Moving Toward Community Justice." In *Topics in Community Corrections*. Washington, DC: National Institute of Corrections.

Bazemore, G. (2000). "Community Justice and a Vision of Collective Efficacy: The Case of Restorative Conferencing." In *Criminal Justice 2000*, edited by The National Institute of Justice. Washington, DC: National Institute of Justice.

Bazemore, G., and M. Schiff (1996). "Community Justice/Restorative Justice: Prospects for a New Social Ecology for Community Corrections." *International Journal of Comparative and Applied Criminal Justice* 20:311-334.

Boland, B. (1998). "Community Prosecution: Portland's Experience." In *Community Justice: An Emerging Field*, edited by D. Karp, 253-278. Lanham, MD: Rowman and Littlefield.

Braithwaite, J. (1998). "Restorative Justice." In *The Handbook of Crime and Punishment*, edited by M. Tonry, 343-344. New York: Oxford University Press.

Christie, N. (1978). "Conflicts as Property." *British Journal of Criminology* 17:1-15.

Clear, T., and D. Karp (1999). *The Community Justice Ideal: Preventing Crime and Achieving Justice*. Boulder, CO: Westview Press.

Goldstein, H. (1990). *Problem-Oriented Policing*. New York: McGraw-Hill.

Kelling, G., and C. Coles (1996). *Fixing Broken Windows*. New York: Free Press.

National Institute of Justice. (1996). *Communities: Mobilizing Against Crime: Making Partnerships Work*. Washington, DC: National Institute of Justice.

Pranis, K, and D. Bussler (1998). "Achieving Social Control: Beyond Paying!" Minneapolis: Minnesota Department of Corrections.

Stuart, B. (1996). "Circle Sentencing: Turning Swords into Ploughshares." In *Restorative Justice: International Perspectives*, edited by B. Galaway and J. Hudson, 193-206. Monsey, NY: Criminal Justice Press.

Umbreit, M. (1999). "Avoiding the Marginalization and McDonaldization of Victim Offender Mediation: A Case Study in Moving Toward the Mainstream." In *Restoring Juvenile Justice: Repairing the Harm of Youth Crime*, edited by G. Bazemore and L. Walgrave. Monsey, NY: Criminal Justice Press.

Van Ness, D., and K. Strong (1997). "Restorative Justice Practice." Monograph. Washington, DC: Justice Fellowship.

Wilson, J., and G. Kelling (1982). "Broken Windows: The Police and Neighborhood Safety." *The Atlantic Monthly* 249(3):29-38.

Young, M. (1995). *Restorative Community Justice: A Call to Action*. Washington, DC: National Organization for Victim Assistance.

Zehr, H. (1990). *Changing Lenses: A New Focus for Crime and Justice*. Scottdale, PA: Herald Press.

Part II
Foundations of Restorative Community Justice

1

Understanding Restorative Community Justice: What and Why Now?

GORDON BAZEMORE
MARA SCHIFF

Definitions and illustrative practices associated with community justice and restorative justice such as those presented in the introduction to this book suggest very different sets of focal concerns in what may appear to be distinct frameworks. Indeed, initial statements of both community and restorative justice, as well as some of the best known practices associated with each, suggest three apparent differences. First, as Crawford and Clear (this volume) observe, until recently most restorative justice practice has been at the more micro level of primarily informal responses to individual incidents of crime, while community justice has been more concerned with larger units of intervention and collective outcomes. Second, the restorative justice emphasis on repairing harm has generally been perceived as a way of intervening in *reaction* to observed crimes (Bazemore and Walgrave, 1999), while community justice has been explicitly focused also on the prevention of crime (Barajas, 1995; National Institute of Justice, 1995). Third, restorative justice since its earliest origins in community mediation (Bianchi, 1994) has had an informal, community-based focus, generally operating outside the formal system and at times distrusting of its motives. Community justice, by contrast, was largely a creation of the formal criminal justice system in the United States. It appears to have grown directly out of the community policing movement in the 1980s as an attempt by its academic supporters and U.S. Department of Justice advocates to design a more comprehensive policy framework to support a system-wide movement to adapt core principles of community policing to courts, corrections, prosecution, and so on (National Institute of Justice, 1996; Robinson, 1996).

In this chapter we consider the importance of these differences and examine common themes that suggest that recent trends are moving these frameworks more toward convergence. To do so, we first briefly examine common and unique origins of community and restorative justice. We then contrast the two perspectives and consider indicators of this convergence in theory and practice. Finally, we briefly address the question "why now?" in the context of social and cultural movements as well as current dominant trends in criminal justice.

Origins of Restorative and Community Justice: A North American Historical Overview

Practices and settlement processes that are now referred to as "restorative justice" have roots in virtually all ancient human societies. Ancephelous societies generally preferred reparative and often ritualistic responses to crime that sought to restore community peace and harmony as an alternative to blood feuds, which generally had devastating consequences for community life (Weitekamp, 1999). The emphasis on vengeance later became more formalized, more predominant, and also somewhat moderated in the late middle-ages, as feudal lords and kings consolidated the response to crime and social control through the power of the state, in essence "inventing" retributive punishment (Speirenberg, 1985). Van Ness et al. (1989) argue that the Norman invasion of Britain marked the beginning of a paradigm shift, a turning away from the understanding of crime as a victim-offender conflict within the context of community toward the concept of crime as an offense against the state. William the Conqueror (1066) and his descendants saw the legal process as one effective tool for centralizing their own political authority. Eventually, anything that violated the "king's peace" was interpreted as an offense against the king and offenders were thus subject to royal authority. Under this new approach, the king—and, gradually, "the state"—became the paramount victim, while the actual victim was denied any meaningful place in the justice process. As this occurred, the emphasis on reparation to crime victims was gradually replaced with the emphasis on punishment of the wrongdoer by the state, what is now referred to as "retributive justice" (e.g., Zehr 1990).

Moving ahead to seventeenth- and eighteenth-century England and the American colonies, we may find the roots of what is now being called "community justice" in the use of unpaid constables—and, later, part-time sheriffs—in small towns and neighborhoods, which employed informal mechanisms of social control, order maintenance, and peacemaking (Critchley, 1978). The debate about whether policing should become a state function with full-time law enforcement officers was hotly contested in early nineteenth-century England (Emsley, 1983), at a time when virtually all social control was local and predominantly citizen-based. The prominent role of the citizen, rather than paid professional, as primary keeper of both peace and order was perhaps most clearly illustrated by the individual most credited with making policing a state function, Sir Robert Peel. Peel saw the prevention of crime as the primary goal of policing and suggested that the police officer's role should be viewed as an extension of the role every citizen must play in keeping communities safe (Emsley, 1983).

Modern Origins of Community Justice

The rise of community justice in the 1990s can be attributed primarily to efforts to extend the concepts and practice of community policing to other components of the criminal justice system. Essentially, a nostalgic image of the small-town sheriff and the neighborhood beat cop became the symbolic role model for the community police officer (Skolnick and Bayley, 1986; Wilson and Kelling, 1982). In addition, the approach developed as a direct response to the critique of the professional model of policing in which the detached officer in a squad car responded to 911 calls (Sparrow, Moore, and Kennedy, 1990).

Community justice advocates in the 1990s proposed an alternative to the isolated criminal justice "expert" who was seemingly more concerned with case processing than serving citizens and communities. Community corrections and prosecution strategies offered distinct alternatives to approaches in which tasks are managed and processed in centralized offices that are out of touch with community needs (Boland, 1998; Clear and Corbett, 1998). In any case, we suggest that the modern history of community justice—at least in its most prominent form in the United States—can be traced most directly to the 1980s experimentation with community policing.[1] Specifically, research assessments of what did not work about the professional model of policing (Goldstein, 1990; Wilson and Kelling, 1982), and new conceptualizations of a holistic vision of what a new community policing could become (Skolnick and Bayley, 1986; Sparrow, Moore, and Kennedy, 1990) created a framework that translated with relative ease to community corrections, courts, prosecution, and defense (National Institute of Justice, 1996).

Although the details of how community *policing* grew into community *justice* are sketchy at best, there appear to be three probable tracks of influence in the United States, and possibly the United Kingdom and Canada. First, at the practice level, there has been a genuine cross-fertilization of strategic emphases. "Beat probation," for example, appears to be an almost direct application of neighborhood policing to the community corrections context. Police/probation partnerships illustrate both the collaborative theme in community policing and a growing range of shared professional values (Corbett et al., 1996). The notion of prosecutors adopting a neighborhood rather than a caseload (Boland, 1998) is similarly an application of community policing ideas to the prosecution function, while the problem-solving and accessibility emphases of community courts are analogous to the pragmatic problem-oriented and service-provision emphases of many community policing advocates (Goldstein, 1990; Skolnick and Bayley, 1986).

Second, academic interpretations of community justice seem to borrow heavily from "deeper" conceptualizations of community policing as a potentially comprehensive reform (Moore and Stephens, 1991). The implications for organizational reform in corrections and courts (Bazemore, 1998; Clear and Karp, 1998), for example, seem to have borrowed heavily from those who challenged the mandate and organizational hierarchies of policing. Such bureaucratic restructuring, as well as efforts to redesign police officer roles, was a prelude to engaging communities as partners in community policing reform (Moore and Stephens, 1991; Rosenbaum, 1994).

Third, in the United States, and in the United Kingdom and Canada (Crawford, 1997; Shaw and Jane, 1998), federal justice department administrators learned much from community policing experiments about how to make the "community" a target and partner in various criminal justice interventions. These bureaucrats and politicians began to understand the power and political resiliency of rhetoric involving appeals to the community (Crawford, 1997). They also learned (and continue to learn) about successful and unsuccessful efforts of community policing initiatives to overcome resistance to organizational restructuring, and especially to engage and sustain community involvement successfully (Rosenbaum, 1994; Skogan, 1998).

Today, community policing is a widespread phenomenon that has influenced most of the Western world (Crawford, 1997; National Institute of Justice, 1996). Community courts, prosecution, defense, revitalized community corrections, and neighborhood justice centers are becoming increasingly common in the United States (Clear and Karp, 1998; Karp, 1997).[2] "Community justice" is not a widely used term outside of North America (Crawford and Clear, this volume). Yet, in the United States and some Canadian provinces, a great deal of funding has been made available to breathe life into the community justice agenda. It remains to be seen whether community prosecution and other practices associated with community justice will take hold internationally in the way that community policing has.

Modern Origins of Restorative Justice

Although reparation in the form of restitution and community service had been used occasionally by United States courts in this century (Schafer, 1970), these sanctions did not become widely popular as sentencing options until the 1970s. Restitution and community service—and to a lesser extent, victim-offender mediation—have been used since the 1970s with increasing regularity in criminal and juvenile courts and are often administered by probation and community diversion programs (Hudson and Galaway, 1977; Umbreit, 1994).

The 1980s saw great expansion in victim-offender mediation programs (Umbreit, 1999), in part as a result of a great interest in restitution and community service programs as a means of institutionalizing reparative sanctions in juvenile courts. This period brought an emphasis on programmatic alternatives to both disposition and diversion and a proliferation of local alternative diversion projects that included mediation and/or reparative sanctions (Schneider, 1985; 1986).

In the 1990s, these and other reparative sanctions and processes are again generating considerable interest as part of a broader international movement (Bazemore and Umbreit, 1995; Hudson et al., 1996; Zehr, 1990). This broader movement has given greater emphasis to restorative decision-making processes such as victim-offender mediation or dialogue, family group conferencing, and circle sentencing, in addition to reparative sanctions such as restitution, community service, and victim service, while also seeking to frame the latter within a restorative framework (Bazemore and Maloney, 1994).[3]

Although much that is interesting and exciting about restorative justice today seems to be "in the air" in creative community planning and "visioning" sessions, restorative justice policies and practices are clearly "on the ground" in local communities, states, provinces, and even entire countries. In some cases, such as New Zealand, disposition of all delinquency cases (with the exception of murder and rape) are handled in community family group conferences. Additionally, in the state of Vermont, where most nonviolent felons and misdemeanors are sentenced by community boards to make reparation to the victims, restorative justice plays a dominant role in criminal justice policy (Belgrave, 1995; Dooley, 1995). Significant state and local impact can also be seen, for example, in Minnesota, Ohio, Colorado, and Maine, and other states that have adopted restorative justice as the mission for their corrections departments. State juvenile justice systems in 35 states (including Pennsylvania, Colorado, Illinois, California, Idaho, and Montana, among others) have adopted restorative justice principles in policy or statute (O'Brien, 1999). In Minnesota, restorative principles are becoming a common feature of policy discussion in virtually all criminal justice sectors, and restorative practices can be observed in schools and the workplace in some communities.

Attention to victim interests, which increased in North America as the victims' movement gained influence in the 1990s (Seymour, 1977; Young, 1996), along with changes in the practice of victim-offender mediation designed to better accommodate victim needs for information, input, reparation, and healing, all contributed to the emphasis on the individual stakeholder in restorative justice. The focus on repair and "healing" as a primary outcome of intervention—also influenced by faith community and feminist supporters who have viewed restorative justice as an alternative to punishment and a means of restoring balance between offender and victim (Bazemore and Umbreit, 1995; Zehr, 1990)—has directed restorative justice to concentrate on the aftermath of crime. Until recently, this has distanced restorative practices and philosophy from the arena of crime prevention. Ties to the faith community (Shaw and Jane, 1998) and the alternative dispute resolution movement—as well as the influence of the women's movement and the feminist critique of patriarchal, depersonalized justice (Bowman, 1994; Harris, 1990)—have also helped to keep restorative justice informal, inclusive, and interpersonal, focusing on resolution and dialogue between victims and offenders.

The level of interest and activity at a systems level in what have traditionally been viewed as marginal, informal diversion programs would not have been predicted even five years ago. Most restorative justice initiatives today remain limited to relatively small experiments and are often lacking in a vision of systemic reform (e.g., Bazemore and Walgrave, 1999; Van Ness and Strong, 1997). Although victim-offender mediation programs (and, to a lesser extent, other forms of restorative conferencing experiments) appear to be flourishing in Europe as well as other parts of the world, they seem to remain as ancillary components of justice systems dominated by more mainstream policies.

Although community justice and restorative justice have common ancient roots, their more modern origins seem somewhat different. There is much overlap, and the above account is in no way meant to diminish the complexity of the modern evolution of the components of community justice or various tendencies within the restorative justice movement. Moreover, in part because of the predominantly North American use of the term "community justice," our account here by no means captures the complexity of similar practices and philosophies in the rest of the world.

Community Justice and Restorative Justice:
Differences and Convergence

Restorative justice's focus on *repairing harm* to individual victims, with a concern for respectful treatment of the offender, is a response to the perceived failure of criminal justice systems and agencies to pay adequate attention to these needs (Zehr, 1990). Victim-offender mediation, which is by almost any measure the most widely implemented restorative justice technique in the world (Umbreit, 1999), until very recently has been a process primarily focused on dialogue between the individual victim and the offender, mediated by a third party and aimed particularly at meeting victims' needs for information, input, reparation, and healing. In some restorative justice circles, especially among some advocates of community mediation and victim-offender dialogue, admonitions to work within, or to attempt to reform, the formal system were historically received with responses ranging from outright opposition to skepticism. Community justice, in contrast, seems to have inherited the neighborhood (macro) focus from the community and problem-oriented policing movements. This was in many ways a direct response to dissatisfaction with the "incident-driven" arrest emphasis that is associated with the professional model of policing (Wilson and Kelling, 1982).

In a similar way, the preventive agenda of community policing was posed as an alternative to the "reactive" focus of "911 policing" (Sparrow, Moore, and Kennedy, 1990), and it included a promise to "solve problems rather than simply process cases." It was not long before community corrections, courts, and prosecutors began to embrace neighborhoods as clients and targets of intervention and also began to adopt a "problem-solving" model of prevention in their respective domains (Bazemore and Schiff, 1996; Boland, 1998; Chavis, 1998; Corbett, 1996; Kelling and Coles, 1998). Whereas restorative justice advocates have continued to emphasize informal programs and processes, the implementation agenda of community and problem-oriented policing (Goldstein, 1990; Trojanowicz and Carter, 1988), and now community justice itself, has been *system-focused*—giving priority to relocating court, prosecution, police, and defense agencies closer to neighborhoods and making them generally more accessible (National Institute of Justice, 1996). The newest part of this discussion on system change has been focused on actual change in the roles of justice professionals to facilitate community participation in justice processes (Corbett, 1996; Dooley, 1998; Maloney, 1998).

Despite these apparent differences in focus, a practical convergence—with theoretical implications—is already at work between community and restorative justice. Notably, key distinctions based on case versus community, prevention versus intervention, and formalism versus informalism now appear to be breaking down.

Case versus Community

With regard to the case/community distinction, some observers suggest that restorative justice in the 1990s clearly entered a "community phase" (Shaw and Jane, 1998). The almost singular emphasis on a
dyadic mediation process of the previous two decades was supplemented
by a broader concern with citizens and communities as entities suffering
harm and thereby also requiring healing and repair.[4] Citizens and
neighborhood groups are now seen as resources in facilitating restorative processes *and* as targets of intervention in capacity-building
efforts. The latter emphasis can be seen most clearly in Vermont's
involvement of citizens in neighborhood reparative boards (Karp,
this volume), in the rise of family group conferencing in Australia, and
circle sentencing and various revitalizations of indigenous justice in
Canada and the United States (Melton, 1995; Stuart, 1996). All have
provided a practical grounding to the movement away from the dyadic,
more individualized focus of restorative justice.[5]

This expansion of new and important roles for citizen volunteers
and neighborhood organizations in restorative justice (Braithwaite,
1998; McCold, 1996) has brought what some see as a needed, if challenging, corrective in restorative policy and practice (Achilles and
Zehr, this volume; Bazemore and Griffiths, 1997). In addition, the linkage between restorative justice and broader theories of social control
(Braithwaite, 1989; 1998), and the sometimes tenuous connection
between restorative justice and the communitarian movement (Bazemore, 1999b; Etzioni, 1998), helped to move the normative theory of
restorative justice further away from speculation about the impact of
victim and offender on each other, toward more broadly framed etio-
logical theories (e.g., Braithwaite, 1998) that are more consistent
with holistic statements of the restorative vision (Van Ness and Strong,
1997; Van Ness et al., 1989).

On the community justice side, the community building and general quality-of-life emphasis of community-oriented policing was not
a framework that easily incorporated the needs and involvement of individual crime victims and offenders. Based in part on the aggressive critique of some victims' advocates (Herman, 1998) and on a more
thoughtful analysis of who should be viewed as the clients of criminal
justice agencies, many community justice advocates are now embracing the individual victim as a primary customer of service (Barajas,
1995; Clear and Karp, 1998; Maloney, 1998). It seemed more difficult
to incorporate the offender into community justice except in broad
statements about personal accountability (Barajas, 1995; Klein, 1997).
However, the suggested inclusion of asset building or competency
development into the community justice agenda (Bazemore and Schiff,
1996; Bazemore and Terry, 1997; Clear and Karp, 1998; Maloney,

1998) combined with an emerging critique of harm to community life and efficacy caused by current offender intervention approaches (Bazemore, 1999a; Rose and Clear, 1998) points the way toward a community justice for the offender that is different from the punitive and traditional rehabilitative perspectives. In general, much emerging community justice practice and literature seems to be moving toward a more micro emphasis for individual victims and offenders, in conjunction with the more macro focus on community building (see especially Dunlap, 1988; Barajas, 1995; Clear and Karp, 1998; Maloney, 1999).

Formal versus Informal

As a system-based reform, community justice was primarily concerned with modifying formal organizational structures and intervention protocols. For example, much discussion in community policing focused on changing the organizational mission and the role of line officers to allow them to do a better job of engaging the community (Moore and Trojanowicz, 1988). The limited hypothesis that community justice could simply result in an expansion of the current system by changing the *location* and *user-friendliness* of criminal justice services (Bazemore and Griffiths, 1997; Clear, 1996) has led to an emphasis on the need to bring citizens to the forefront in some community justice circles.

Although it has always been implicit in community policing efforts to engage citizens in various partnership activities (e.g., Moore and Stephens, 1991; Moore and Trojanowicz, 1988; Skolnick and Bailey, 1986), the citizen role in the response to crime was seldom explicitly defined (Rosenbaum, 1994) beyond one-on-one contacts focused on providing information to police officers and participating in community meetings and marches.

Today, however, community police officers in some jurisdictions facilitate restorative conferences as a way of institutionalizing informal problem-solving. Such problem-solving can also empower individual citizens and primary stakeholders in a "front-end" response to crime and local conflict. Moreover, some community prosecutors and judges involved in "community courts" are embracing informal decisionmaking by initiating and sponsoring restorative community boards, community conferences, and even circle sentencing. As part of a community justice strategy, such processes explicitly take decisionmaking out of the adversarial context and share discretion over sanctioning with community members (Earle, 1996; Gerard et al., 1999; Denver District Attorney's Office, 1999).

Although restorative justice advocates will almost always prefer an informal process to a system-driven formal one, systemic and organizational agendas in restorative justice are explicit in Van Ness and

Strong's third core restorative justice principle, which addresses the need to transform the roles of government and community, and the relationship between the two in the response to crime. Their contention is that government is responsible for preserving order but the community is responsible for establishing peace (Van Ness and Strong, 1997; Van Ness et al., 1986)

The formal system is often a target of change in restorative justice initiatives (Bazemore and Walgrave, 1999). Conceptually, some have posited the need for value-driven change in justice systems to allow for the new focus on repairing harm and stakeholder participation in a different type of justice decision-making process (Bazemore, 1999a; Carey, this volume). More practically, concrete change in roles and resource allocation—as well as intraorganizational cultural transformation to improve the fit between justice agencies and the restorative focus—is clearly on the agenda of restorative justice practitioners. Some of these professionals are now in positions of power with various justice system agencies rather than being simply outsiders (Dooley, 1998; Perry and Gorcyzyk, 1997; Maloney, 1998).

Prevention versus Reaction

Prevention has been an explicit primary focus of community justice. While some would argue that the emphasis on repair necessarily makes restorative justice a reactive model (Bazemore and Walgrave, 1999; Van Ness and Strong, 1997), many restorative justice practitioners also seek to pursue preventive goals (Pranis, this volume; Stuart, 1996). As Hudson et al. observe in their assessment of the community-building potential of restorative conferencing processes:

> (Restorative) Conferences help to illustrate the responsibility of citizens to participate in community affairs. The reciprocity evident in the family group conference process helps emphasize the point that people can benefit from the challenge and opportunities of helping others. Receiving help can actually weaken one's self-esteem but giving help as well as receiving it empowers people and strengthens their sense of self-worth. (Hudson et al., 1996:3)

The line between prevention and intervention is difficult to draw when practical examples of restorative and community justice intervention are considered at face value. For example, would minor offenses dealt with in a school-based restorative conflict resolution process such as family group conferencing be viewed as prevention or intervention? Is not the community-building emphasis of reparative boards (Karp, this volume) both an outcome of the effort to repair harm and a necessary requirement if citizen board members are to sustain their reparative activity. On the community justice side, is not community-building activity aimed explicitly at prevention in its essence but also about repairing and/or strengthening relationships between individuals and parochial groups damaged or weakened by crime? Are police diversion practices, in which officers choose to work with minor offenders in their neighborhoods by intervening with their families and schools, reactive or preventive in nature?

Consistent with many of the practical examples presented in the introduction of this book, the most persuasive theoretical statements on "community justice" now clearly incorporate restorative justice in a way that makes it difficult to determine where one begins and the other ends (Clear and Karp, 1999; Earle, 1996; Perry and Gorcyzck, 1998; Denver District Attorney's Office, 1999). Similarly, restorative justice advocates are emphasizing community building, prevention, and system-change themes that are more consistent with community justice, or perhaps simply more consistent with some of the more holistic statements of restorative justice (Van Ness and Strong, 1997). Although it is possible that advocates of a more micro and informal restorative justice will distance themselves from community justice advocates who wish to pursue a more macro and system-change focus, we think it unlikely that community justice advocates will want to pay less attention to the needs and involvement of victims, communities, and offenders as primary stakeholders or deny the need for informal, interpersonal problem solving processes that have been the hallmark of restorative justice. Similarly, we believe that few restorative justice advocates will deny the desirability of making neighborhood and community-level impacts. Many are already working toward justice system reform in one way or another. While "product differentiation" may lead some to align with one term or another, it appears that most of the often-confusing diversity at this level is occurring at the *program* level rather than at the level of agency administration or conceptualization.[6] At this level, there is (ironically) probably as much dispute over best practice within the restorative justice movement as between restorative and community justice proponents.[7]

Finding Common Ground

Most likely, the adoption of one term or another by criminal justice systems and community-based programs will be based on political or marketing considerations. In the United States, for example, the term "restorative" has met with opposition among groups as diverse as victims' advocates (who resent the implication that crime victims can be "restored" by some justice system intervention) to crime prevention specialists (who view the term as reactive rather than proactive by its very nature) to government officials (who believe it may send a "soft on crime" message to communities). For their part, restorative justice advocates may fear that use of the term "community justice" may diminish the priority given to the very informal processes they have worked so hard to develop—in part because these approaches do not come naturally to most system professionals—and, more significantly, because they fear an erosion of the normative theory and principles that now inform the best restorative practices. Our view, however, is that if current trends continue, there will be so much cross-fertilization in both the practice and the theory of community and restorative justice that it will be impossible to distinguish between these approaches—despite the fact that practitioners and administrators will continue to choose different labels to describe their intervention agendas. Ultimately, if principles indeed are most important, it is encouraging that both restorative justice and community justice scholars, working closely with practitioners, who for pragmatic reasons have chosen one term or another to describe their new agenda, are now developing rather parallel sets of normative statements that may eventually result in a more completed alternative justice model (e.g., Clear and Karp, 1999; Van Ness and Strong, 1997; Zehr and Mika, 1998).

Essentially, the common ground between restorative and community justice can be found in concerns that require a rethinking of performance outcomes, priorities for practice, justice processes, and appropriate roles for both justice professionals and community members. Intervention objectives, for example, shift from a sole concern with conviction, incapacitation, and reduced recidivism to a focus on such outcomes as enhancing community capacity to prevent crime (Chavis, 1998), fear reduction (Kelling and Coles, 1998), victim satisfaction, conflict resolution, and restoration of loss and "healing" (Van Ness and Strong, 1997). Because these objectives demand more than change in offender behavior, the "target" of intervention is also broadened to include communities, crime victims, other citizens, and interpersonal relationships (Bazemore, 1998b; Buerger, 1994; Byrne, 1989). Intermediate objectives tend to be focused on meeting the needs of individual victims, offenders, and citizens affected by crime in a way that finds common ground between apparently conflicting interests but moves toward the larger goal of strengthening community and rebuilding relationships. Practices to accomplish these goals vary widely from what have now become mainstream (such as community policing) to processes such as circle sentencing and new community conflict resolution approaches. Intervention strategies move beyond arrest, treatment, punishment, surveillance, and risk management to include such approaches as problem-solving, restitution, community service, mediation, and reform in school disciplinary procedures. Decisionmaking about the response to crimes and offenders changes from an emphasis on formal procedures (such as court sentencing hearings directed by justice professionals) to community courts and nonadversarial processes (such as mediation and conferencing) that allow for maximum involvement of victims, offenders, and community members in setting the terms of accountability for sanctioning. Finally, although the implications for justice professionals remain the least discussed aspect of the restorative and community justice vision, the aforementioned changes in practice and process would seem to require a transition away from the "expert" role to a role of facilitator and supporter of community-driven justice responses (Bazemore, 1998; Boland, 1996; Pranis, 1996). Together, the emerging common vision is one that suggests that the outcome of justice intervention—whether formal or informal—should be a solution that aims toward repairing what is harmed by crime and, in doing so, strengthens the ability of participants in the justice process.

Given this convergence, why then should we not simply settle on one term: "restorative justice" or "community justice"? While we might agree with proponents of community justice that the concerns of restorative justice can be incorporated into a complete community justice model, at present "community justice" does not appear to have as much international currency as "restorative justice" (Braithwaite, 1998; Braithwaite and Roche, this volume; Crawford, personal communication). In Europe, for example, the term may simply not resonate, perhaps because the concept of "community" is viewed in a different way than in North America and other more recently settled countries, and because their justice systems have tended to be viewed as more representative of the community than in the North America (Bazemore and Walgrave, 1999; Weitekampe, 1998).

In the United States, some restorative justice advocates are concerned with the lack of a value framework in early statements of community justice (Pranis, 1997). Such a framework is needed precisely to check the expansion and further encroachment of the criminal justice system (albeit in more benign forms) on community collective efficacy (Bazemore, 1999b; Rose and Clear, 1998) as well as to divert primary attention from the much needed focus on the interests of individual crime victims (Achilles and Zehr, this volume; Herman, 1998). We may agree with restorative justice advocates that more complete statements specifically addressing the new role and relationship between the community and the criminal justice system (Van Ness and Strong, 1997) could incorporate all the concerns of community justice. However, we must also acknowledge that despite these statements, many continue to view restorative justice (primarily, if not exclusively) as a programmatic response focused on individual victims via the technique of victim-offender mediation. For now, at least, the term "restorative community justice" may be most likely to focus attention on the broader picture while retaining the micro emphasis.

Why Now?

There are no easy explanations for the growing interest in restorative justice at a time when criminal and juvenile justice systems in most states appear to be embracing a punitive model. Much of this interest seems to have emerged during a unique period of convergence between diverse justice philosophies and political, social, and cultural movements. Broadly, modern restorative justice appears to have been directly influenced by new developments in the victims' rights movement and an expanded role for victims in a community justice process (Young, 1996); the community and problem-oriented policing philosophy and movement (Goldstein, 1990; Rosenbaum, 1994; Skogan and Hartnett, 1997; Sparrow, Moore, and Kennedy, 1990); and renewed interest in indigenous dispute-resolution, settlement processes—at times accompanied by political efforts, especially in Canada, to "devolve" criminal justice responsibilities to local communities (Griffiths and Hamilton, 1996; Melton, 1995).

Although it has been suggested that restorative justice may be simply another strategy for "getting tough" with offenders (Levrant et al., 1999), there is no evidence for this assumption either in practice or in the philosophical statements of restorative justice advocates. While restorative justice is in no way a lenient approach, it is, if anything, grounded in a strong critique of punishment generally, and retributive justice, specifically (Bazemore and Walgrave, 1999; Zehr, 1990). Criticism of both rights-based, adversarial perspectives, as well as of social welfare models (Braithwaite and Petit, 1992; Bazemore and Umbreit, 1995; Walgrave, 1995), also has affected the evolution of the new restorative justice movement. Some faith communities have been both supporters and practitioners of restorative justice, and several denominations appear to be expanding their involvement (Braithwaite, 1998; Shaw and Jane, 1998).[8] In another way, the women's movement and feminist critique of patriarchal justice (Bowman, 1994; Harris, 1990) has probably influenced the restorative justice tendency toward inclusiveness, as well as its related challenges to hierarchical decisionmaking.[9]

To put the restorative community justice movement in context, it is important to raise larger questions that address political, economic, and ideological influences. Although a thorough consideration of political and economic influences is beyond the scope of this paper, it can be said that there are competing views about the motivation

behind government interest in restorative justice. Some have emphasized the association of restorative justice with cost-savings and fiscal
"get tough" polices (Daly and Immarigeon, 1998). On the political
side, some have emphasized that community and restorative justice must
be viewed in the context of the legitimacy crisis facing former welfare-
state post-industrial governments such as the United Kingdom, Canada, and New Zealand (Crawford, 1997). In Canada, in particular, the
response to this crisis has seemed to be "devolving" justice, as well as
social welfare functions, to local communities—especially aboriginal
communities.

In the United States, the conservative movement mounted an attack
on social services in the 1990s. However, criminal justice expansion has
proceeded at an unprecedented pace, and restorative community justice has been championed by advocates across the political spectrum
(Colson and Van Ness, 1989; Pepinksy and Quinney, 1991; Morris,
1994). Moreover, political and economic influences on restorative
justice do not lend themselves to easy categorization as conservative,
liberal, or otherwise. In New Zealand, for example, though cost-sav-
ing was certainly on the agenda in that country's movement to insti-
tutionalize family group conferencing (Daly and Immarigeon, 1998),
there was also evidence of ideological leadership in search of a more
progressive, less punitive, and more culturally appropriate response to
youth crime (McElrae, 1996). The dominance of this more progressive
vision, moreover, has been most clearly illustrated by recent opposition on the part of those more supportive of the incapacitative and
deterrence-focused policies that preceded restorative justice reforms in
that country (Ministry of Justice, 1998). In Canada, the devolution of
justice functions has been accompanied by relatively large amounts of
funding to local communities—a policy that has itself been criticized for
its top-down approach that provided support for new staff positions in
the *name* of community justice and empowerment (Griffiths and Corrado, 1999). Similarly, although there are also many valid concerns about
cultural imperialism, as illustrated by efforts to impose specific conferencing models on indigenous communities in Australia (Bargen,
1996; Cunneen, 1997), it is interesting that the New Zealand reforms
were viewed as importing concepts and techniques from indigenous cultures into existing Western justice systems (McElrae 1993).

Although proponents of restorative community justice show a
tendency toward over-hyping new interventions and the overuse of anti-
court and anti-system rhetoric (Daly, 1996; Harrington and Merry,
1988), there is also danger in deconstructing or oversimplifying reform
movements and failing to recognize complexity and uniqueness in
goals and motivation. While there is certainly some truth to arguments
that restorative justice has become popular because it has met certain
needs of political economies, virtually all reform movements that

have implications for power-sharing and community participation could also be analyzed this way (e.g., Cohen, 1985). A competing hypothesis is that the motivation behind recent efforts to implement restorative policies was neither primarily economic nor political but more akin to a "muddling through" approach. At the ideological level, a more constructive critical approach can be taken that is useful in understanding different tendencies and theories-in-use that become apparent as one examines conferencing in practice. Harrington and Merry's (1988) analysis of neighborhood justice and mediation in the 1970s and 1980s may provide a useful protocol for assessing the movement around restorative conferencing. Their emphasis on "multiple ideological projects"—often defined primarily in opposition to an assumed status quo—points to competing objectives within the mediation movement. These objectives were based on three frames of reference: social transformation, personal growth, and social service delivery. As will be described later, parallel struggles are apparent within the modern restorative justice movement, but there are new and distinctive emerging ideological and theoretical tendencies.

Although the quest for a proactive community may be viewed as nostalgic (Crawford, 1997), the restorative justice movement also seems to build upon an element of anxiety about the loss of the community's capacity to address youth crime, trouble, and conflict. Related to this is a legitimate concern about the growth and expansion of the criminal justice system, its increasing consumption of resources, and the fear that this expansion has itself diminished community capacity to manage conflict (Bazemore 1999a; McKnight 1995; Rose and Clear 1998). There also appears to be something appealing about the restorative orientation that may rise above (or at least sidestep) two long-standing strands of discourse in criminal and juvenile justice policy reform. Specifically, the restorative focus on repairing harm seems to challenge the terms of the punishment-versus-treatment and crime-control-versus-libertarian debates. In the discourse of restorative and community justice, the repair of harm, the building of community, and the capacity to respond to crime and conflict thereby replace punishment and treatment as a new continuum for intervention (Bazemore, 1998; Van Ness and Strong, 1997). In addition, distinctive new concerns of restorative and community justice suggest a new continuum for *reform,* focused neither on expanding government crime control nor on simply ensuring the protection of rights and limiting intervention. Restorative justice advocates will ultimately stand with libertarians on many issues, because they question the value of much government intervention and are especially critical of the professionalization and expansionism of criminal justice that has individualized the response to what are in fact collective troubles of victims, offenders, and communities (Bazemore, 1999; Christie, 1977). The new vision, however, is not anti-intervention, and it is much more than a *government hands-off* approach. Restorative community justice instead seeks to promote a *community "hands on"* approach and to do so partly through government action in a significantly different role.

Endnotes

[1]   For a similar, albeit more critical, analysis of the emergence of community policing and a community focus for criminal justice in the United Kingdom, see Crawford, 1997, Chapter 2.

Given the widespread agreement on failures in the implementation of community policing—despite remaining commitment to the viability of the conceptual model—it is probably more important to look at community policing as a case study in what can go wrong in implementing reforms as comprehensive in scope as those proposed by restorative and community justice advocates.

[2]   A range of preventive initiatives are now also included under the community justice umbrella (National Institute of Justice, 1996). In some instances, a community justice initiative may be inclusive of a restorative justice focus; in other cases, the two may be highly compatible, if not indistinguishable. In Denver's community prosecution initiative, for example, restorative conferencing is a fundamental feature of a larger initiative aimed at the overall goal of building community capacity to respond to crime.

[3]   Restitution, community service, and other reparative sanctions are probably in more widespread use but are not necessarily implemented as part of a fully restorative agenda and may even be used as a punishment add-on rather than an obligation to repair harm that might serve as an alternative to other punishments (Bazemore and Maloney, 1994; Umbreit, 1999). A recent survey of VOM programs in the United States suggests that a majority may be moving toward at least occasional inclusion of parties other than offender and victim, such as a family member (Umbreit and Greenwood, 1998). Shaw and Jane suggest that the modern origins of restorative justice actually began in the 1960s and 1970s with community mediation and dispute resolution (Bianchi, 1994), as influenced by Christie's conceptualization of crime as conflict that has been "stolen" from citizens and communities by the state (Christie, 1977). They argue that the dyadic/mediation phase of restorative justice is actually Phase 2 in a three-stage movement that began with, and is now returning to, a community emphasis.

[4]   In the best statements of community justice, the more radical vision of community policing as a way to empower citizens and community groups was captured, though often statements and policy initiatives of the early 1990s seemed to be primarily a prescription for simply improving the accessibility of prosecution, corrections, and courts by locating these in neighborhoods with more user-friendly focus rather than changing the role and relationship (National Institute of Justice, 1996; also see Bazemore and Griffiths, 1998). Moreover, the gaping discrepancy between implementation of community policing and the vision of community-building and problem-solving no doubt created skepticism about the ability of prosecutors and judges to do anything other than place their staff in neighborhood setting. Therefore, too often, practice devolved to the lowest common denominator (e.g., school-based probation officers, teen courts as the primary component of community prosecution).

⁵   Several books and edited volumes are now available that focus exclusively on
restorative justice (Bazemore and Walgrave, 1999; Hudson and Galoway, 1996;
Van Ness and Strong, 1997) Our decision to combine restorative and community justice runs the risk of alienating those who find significant differences between
them. There are some strongly held disagreements about principles, strategy,
and implementation.

⁶   Nowhere is product differentiation more apparent than in the rise of restorative
conferencing—including several varieties of family group conferencing, victim-
offender dialogue, circle sentencing, and (depending on one's definition) community
conferencing and neighborhood reparative boards. In Australia alone, there are
probably a dozen variations of family group conferencing (Daly, 1998). In United States jurisdictions such as Minnesota, where restorative conferencing programs
seem to sprout up almost daily, there are probably 20 distinct restorative or community conferencing models in the Minneapolis/St.Paul area alone. There are clearly ideological and practical reasons for this differentiation based on emerging theories-in-use (Bazemore, 2000). However, there is also a great deal of guarding of
specific program models against incursion by other models, as well as attempts
to market one program or another as the "real" restorative justice alternative. The
other side of this differentiation is a tremendous creativity, as local restorative programs appear to adopt core elements of a certain model and a hybridization begins
to combine what appear to be the best elements of several models.

Beyond these terms, an even larger group of corollary criminal justice innovations, such as therapeutic jurisprudence, drug courts, peer mediation, youth
development, strength-based intervention, and alternative dispute resolution,
suggest that other criminal justice professionals and their allies seem to champi-
on themes similar to those illustrated in the examples presented above. Beyond
the boundaries of criminal justice, the phrase "it takes a village to raise a child"
has now become almost a part of the popular culture in the United States and a
key symbolic component of a new public policy discourse that emphasizes
rebuilding human connections and strengthening community as a solution to problems in education, health care, child rearing, the environment, and so on. In fields
as diverse as industry, labor relations, education, environmental regulation, hos-
pitals, organized religion, and family dispute resolution, various restorative conferencing models (including circles and family group conferencing) have been used
as conflict resolution techniques. Some have noted that the movement is linked
to much broader changes in the way decisions are being made and conflict is being
resolved in a variety of institutional contexts. The use of restorative conferencing in schools, for example, has implications for making conferencing and
restorative values a part of the broader culture and repertoire of responses to harmful behavior, and such applications may ultimately increase the resilience and sustainability of these approaches (Shaw and Jane, 1998:4). There are also even more
opportunities for alliances with parallel reform movements in criminal justice that
have not been fully exploited in the restorative movement in the United States.
These include other nonadversarial approaches, such as drug courts, therapeutic
jurisprudence, peer mediation, and some teen courts.

Discussion Questions

1. Discuss several alternative explanations for why the restorative justice movement arose when it did. Which reasons are the most convincing?

2. What are some ways restorative and community justice differ? How are they similar? Do you agree that these are more similar than different or do you think the distinctions are important to maintain?

3. What are some possible limitations and some possible strengths of a restorative justice model? How do these contrast with the traditional retributive model?

References

Barajas, E., Jr. (1995). "Moving Toward Community Justice." In *Topics in Community Corrections*. Washington, DC: National Institute of Corrections.

Bargen, J. (1996). "Kids, Cops, Courts, Conferencing and Children's Rights—A Note on Perspectives." *Australian Journal of Human Rights*, University of New South Wales 2:3.

Bazemore, G. (1998). "Restorative Justice and Earned Redemption: Communities, Victims and Offender Reintegration." *American Behavioral Scientist* 41:768-813.

Bazemore, G. (1999a). "The Fork in the Road to Juvenile Court Reform." *The Annals of the American Academy of Political and Social Science* 564:81-108.

Bazemore, G. (1999b). "In Search of a Communitarian Justice Alternative: Youth Crime and the Sanctioning Response as a Case Study." In *To Promote the General Welfare: A Communitarian Legal Reader*, edited by D. Carney. Willamsburg, VA: Lexington Books.

Bazemore, G. (2000). "Community Justice and a Vision of Collective Efficacy: The Case of Restorative Conferencing." In *Criminal Justice 2000*, edited by National Institute of Justice. Washington, DC: National Institute of Justice.

Bazemore, G., and C. Griffiths (1997). "Cirles, Boards, Conferences and Mediation: Scouting the New Wave in Community Justice Decision-Making." *Federal Probation* LXI(2):25-37.

Bazemore, G., and D. Maloney (1994). "Rehabilitating Community Service: Toward Restorative Service in a Balanced Justice System." *Federal Probation* 58:24-35.

Bazemore, G., and M. Schiff (1996). "Community Justice/Restorative Justice: Prospects for a New Social Ecology for Community Corrections." *International Journal of Comparative and Applied Criminal Justice* 20(2):311-335.

Bazemore, G., and C. Terry (1997). "Developing Delinquent Youth: A Reintegrative Model for Rehabilitation and a New Role for the Juvenile Justice System." *Child Welfare* 74(5):665-716.

Bazemore, G., and M. Umbreit (1995). "Rethinking the Sanctioning Function in Juvenile Court: Retributive or Restorative Responses to Youth Crime." *Crime & Delinquency* 41:296-316.

Bazemore, G., and L. Walgrave (1999). *Restorative Juvenile Justice: Repairing the Harm of Youth Crime.* Monsey, NY: Criminal Justice Press

Belgrave, J. (1995). *Restorative Justice: A Discussion Paper.* Monograph. Wellington, New Zealand: New Zealand Ministry of Justice.

Bianchi, H. (1994). *Justice as Sanctuary: Toward a New System of Crime Control.* Bloomington: Indiana University Press.

Boland, B. (1996). "What Is Community Prosecution?" *National Institute of Justice Journal* 231:35-40.

Boland, B. (1998). "Community Prosecution: Portland's Experience." In *Community Justice: An Emerging Field*, edited by D. Karp, 253-278. Lanham, MD: Rowman and Littlefield.

Bowman, C.G. (1994). "The Arrest Experiments: A Feminist Critique." In *Taking Sides: Clashing Views on Controversial Issues in Crime and Criminology*, edited by R. Monk, 186-191. Gilford, CT: Dushkin Publishing Group.

Braithwaite, J. (1989). *Crime, Shame and Reintegration.* Cambridge, England: Cambridge University Press.

Braithwaite, J. (1998). "Restorative Justice." In *The Handbook of Crime and Punishment*, edited by M. Tonry, 323-344. New York: Oxford University Press.

Braithwaite, J., and C. Parker (1999). "Restorative Justice is Republican Justice." In *Restorative Juvenile Justice: Repairing the Harm of Youth Crime*, edited by G. Bazemore and L. Walgrave. Monsey, NY: Criminal Justice Press.

Braithwaite, J., and S. Mugford (1994). "Conditions of Successful Reintegration Ceremonies: Dealing with Juvenile Offenders." *British Journal of Criminology.* 34(2):139-171.

Braithwaite, J., and P. Petit (1992). *Not Just Deserts: A Republican Theory of Criminal Justice.* Oxford, England: Clarendon Press.

Buerger, M.E. (1994). "A Tale of Two Targets: Limitations of Community Anticrime Actions." *Crime & Delinquency* 40:411-36.

Byrne, James M. (1989). "Reintegrating the Concept of Community into Community-Based Corrections." *Crime & Delinquency* 35:471-99.

Chavis, D. (1998). "Building Community Capacity to Prevent Violence through Coalitions and Partnerships." In *Community Justice: An Emerging Field*, edited by D. Karp, 81-94. Lanham, MD: Rowman and Littlefield.

Christie, N. (1977). "Conflict as Property." *The British Journal of Criminology* 7(1):1-14.

Clear, T.R. (1996). "Toward a Corrections of 'Place': The Challenge of 'Community' in Corrections." *National Institute of Justice Journal* 8:52-56.

Clear, T., and D. Karp (1998). "The Community Justice Movement." In *Community Justice: An Emerging Field*, edited by D. Karp, 3-30. Lanham, MD: Rowman and Littlefield.

Clear, T., and D. Karp (1999). *The Community Justice Ideal: Preventing Crime and Achieving Justice.* Boulder, CO: Westview Press.

Clear, T., and R. Corbett (eds.) (1998). *The Community Corrections of Place.* Washington, DC: Office Department of Justice.

Cohen, S. (1985). *Visions of Social Control: Crime, Punishment, and Classification.* Cambridge, England: Polity Press.

Colson, C., and D. Van Ness (1989). *Convicted: New Hope for Ending America's Prison Crisis.* Westchester, IL: Crossway Books.

Corbett, R. (1996). "Amazing Grace and Then Some: Reflections on the Boston Strategy." In *Community Justice: Concepts and Strategies,* edited by the American Probation and Parole Association, 165-179. Lexington, KY: American Probation and Parole Association.

Crawford, A. (1997). *The Local Governance of Crime: Appeals to Community and Partnerships.* New York: Oxford University Press.

Critchley, T.A. (1978). *A History of Police in England and Wales.* London: Constable.

Cunneen, C. (1997). "Community Conferencing and the Fiction of Indigenous Control." *Journal of Criminology* 30:292-311.

Daly, K. (1996). "Diversionary Conferences in Australia: A Reply to the Optimists and Skeptics." Paper presented at the annual meeting of the American Society of Criminology, Chicago, IL.

Daly, K., and R. Immarigeon (1998). "The Past, Present and Future of Restorative Justice: Some Critical Reflections." *Contemporary Justice Review* 1(1):21-45.

Denver District Attorney's Office (1999). "Community Prosecution in Denver." *Denver District Attorney's Community Prosecution Division Newsletter* 6:1-3.

Dooley, M. (1995). "Reparative Probation Program." Monograph, Vermont Department of Corrections.

Dooley, M. (1996). "Reparative Probation Boards." In *Restoring Hope through Community Partnerships the Real Deal in Crime Control,* edited by B. Fulton, 185-192. Lexington, KY: American Probation and Parole Association.

Dooley, M. (1998). "The New Role of Probation and Parole: Community Justice Liaison." In *Community Justice: Concept and Strategies,* edited by American Probation and Parole Association, 195-208.

Dunlap, K. (ed.) (1998). *Community Justice: Concepts and Strategies.* Lexington, KY: American Probation and Parole Association.

Earle, R. (1996). "Community Justice: The Austin Experience." *Texas Probation* 11:6-11.

Emsley, C. (1983). *Policing and Its Context, 1750-1870.* London: Macmillan.

Etzioni, A. (1998). "Community Justice in a Communitarian Perspective." In *Community Justice: An Emerging Field,* edited by D. Karp, 373-378. Lanham, MD: Rowman and Littlefield.

Ezell, M. (1992). "*Juvenile Diversion: the Ongoing Search for Alternatives.*" In *Juvenile Justice and Public Policy,* edited by I. Schwartz, 45-58. New York: Lexington Books.

Garafalo, J., and K. Connelly (1980). "Dispute Resolution Centers, Part I: Major Features and Processes." *Criminal Justice Abstracts* 12:46.

Gerard, G., R. Paulson, and H. Burns (1999). *CCNP Community Conferencing Internal Evaluation Report*. Minneapolis: Minnesota Department of Corrections.

Goldstein, H. (1990). *Problem-Oriented Policing*, New York: McGraw-Hill.

Gordon, D.R. (1991). *The Justice Juggernaut*. New Brunswick, NJ: Rutgers University Press.

Griffiths, C., and R. Corrado (1999). "Implementing Restorative Youth Justice: A Case Study in Community Justice and Dynamics of Reform." In *Restorative Juvenile Justice: Repairing the Harm of Youth Crime*, edited by G. Bazemore and L. Walgrave, 237-263. Monsey, NY: Criminal Justice Press.

Griffiths, C., and R. Hamilton (1996). "Spiritual Renewal, Community Revitalization and Healing. Experience in Traditional Aboriginal Justice in Canada." *International Journal of Comparative and Applied Criminal Justice* 20(1):285-310.

Harrington, C.B., and S. Merry (1988). "The Ideology of Community Mediation." *Law and Society Review* 22:709-35.

Harris, M.K. (1990). "Moving Into the New Millenium: Toward a Feminist Vision of Justice." In *Criminology as Peacemaking*, edited by H. Pepinsky and R. Quinney, 83-97. Bloomington: Indiana University Press.

Herman, S. (1998). "Viewing Restorative Justice Through Victims' Eyes." Paper presented at the International Conference on Restorative Justice for Juveniles, Ft. Lauderdale, FL.

Hudson, J., and B. Galaway (eds.) (1977). *Restitution in Criminal Justice*. Lexington, MA: Heath and Company.

Hudson, J., B. Galaway, A. Morris, and G. Maxwell (eds.) (1996). *Research of Family Group Conferencing in Child Welfare in New Zealand*. Monsey, NY: Criminal Justice Press.

Karp, D. (1997). "Community Justice." Research Seminar on Community, Crime, and Justice. Monograph. George Washington University/National Institute of Justice.

Kelling, G., and C. Coles (1996). *Fixing Broken Windows*. New York: Free Press.

Kelling G., and C. Coles (1998). "Disorder and the Court." In *Community Justice: An Emerging Field*, edited by D. Karp, 233-252. Lanham, MD: Rowman and Littlefield.

Klein, A.R. (1997). *Alternative Sentencing, Intermediate Sanctions and Probation*, Second Edition. Cincinnati: Anderson.

LaPrairie, C. (1994). "Community Justice or Just Communities: Aboriginal Communities in Search of Justice." Ottawa: Ottawa Department of Justice. Unpublished paper.

Levrant, S., F. Cullen, B. Fulton, and J. Wozniak (1999). "Reconsidering Restorative Justice: The Corruption of Benevolence Revisited? *Crime & Delinquency* 45(1):3-27.

Lofquist, W.A. (1983). *Discovering the Meaning of Prevention: A Practical Approach to Positive Change*. Tucson, AZ: AYD Publications.

Maloney, D. (1998). "The Challenge of Restorative Community Justice." Address at the annual meeting of the Juvenile Justice Coalition, Washington, DC.

Maxwell, G., and A. Morris (1993). *Family Participation, Cultural Diversity and Victim Involvement in Youth Justice: A New Zealand Experiment*. Wellington, New Zealand: Victoria University.

McElrae, F.W.M. (1993). "A New Model of Justice." In *The Youth Court in New Zealand: A New Model of Justice*, edited by B.J. Brown, 1-14. Auckland, New Zealand: Legal Research Foundation.

McElrae, F.W.M. (1996). "The New Zealand Youth Court: A Model for Use with Adults." In *Restorative Justice: International Perspectives*, edited by B. Galaway and J. Hudson, 69-83. Monsey, NY: Criminal Justice Press.

McCold, P. (1996). "Restorative Justice and the Role of the Community." In *Restorative Justice: International Perspectives*, edited by B. Galoway and J. Hudson. Monsey, NY: Criminal Justice Press

McCold, P., and B. Wachtel (1998). *Restorative Policing Experiment: The Bethlehem Pennsylvania Police Family Group Conferencing Project*. Pipersville, PA: Community Service Foundation.

McKnight, J. (1995). *The Careless Society: Community and Its Counterfeits*. New York: Basic Books.

Melton, A. (1995). "Indigenous Justice Systems and Tribal Society," *Judicature* 70(3):126-133.

Michalowski, R.J. (1995). *Order, Law, and Crime*. New York: Random House.

Ministry of Justice (1998). "Restorative Justice: The Public Submissions." Auckland, New Zealand: Ministry of Justice.

Moore, D.B., and T. O'Connell (1994). "Family Conferencing in Wagga Wagga: A Communitarian Model of Justice." In *Family Group Conferencing and Juvenile Justice: The Way Forward or Misplaced Optimism?*, edited by C. Adler and J. Wundersitz, 45-86. Canberra, ACT: Australia Institute of Criminology.

Moore, M. (1997). "Looking Backward to Look Forward: The 1967 Crime Commission Report in Retrospect." *National Institute of Justice Journal* 12:24-30.

Moore, M., and D. Stephens (1991). *Beyond Command and Control: The Strategic Management of Police Departments*. Washington, DC: Police Executive Research Forum.

Moore, M., and R. Trojanowicz (1988). "Policing the Fear of Crime." In *Perspectives on Policing*. Washington, DC: National Institute of Justice.

Morris, R. (1994). *A Practical Path to Transformative Justice*. Toronto: Rittenhouse.

National Institute of Justice (1996). *Communities Mobilizing Against Crime: Making Partnerships Work*. Washington, DC: National Institute of Justice.

O'Brien, S. (1999). "Restorative Justice in the States: A National Survey of Policy and Practices." Paper presented at the annual meeting of the Academy of Criminal Justice Sciences, March, Orlando, FL.

Pepinsky, H.E. , and R. Quinney (eds.) (1991). *Criminology as Peacemaking*. Bloomington: Indiana University Press.

Perry, J.G., and J.F. Gorcyzyk (1997). "Restructuring Corrections: Using Market Research in Vermont." *Corrections Management Quarterly* 1(3):2-35.

Pittman, K., and W. Fleming (1991). "A New Vision: Promoting Youth Development." Testimony to House Select Committee on Children, Youth and Families, Academy for Education, Development, Washington, DC (September).

Polk, K. (1984). "When Less Means More." *Crime & Delinquency* 30:462-480.

Polk, K. (1994). "Family Conferencing: Theoretical and Evaluative Questions."In *Family Group Conferencing and Juvenile Justice: The Way Forward or Misplaced Optimism?*, edited by C. Adler and J. Wundersitz, 155-168. Canberra: Australia Institute of Criminology.

Polk, K., and S. Kobrin (1972). *Delinquency Prevention Through Youth Development.* Washington, DC: Office of Youth Development.

Pranis, K. (1996). "Communities and the Justice System—Turning the Relationship Upside Down." Paper presented before the Office of Justice Programs, U.S. Department of Justice.

Pranis, K. (1997). "From Vision to Action: Church and Society." *Presbyterian Church Journal of Just Thoughts* 87(4):32-42.

Pranis, K., and D. Bussler (1998). "Achieving Social Control: Beyond Paying!" Monograph, Minnesota Department of Corrections.

Robinson, J. (1996). "Research on in Child Welfare in New Zealand." In *Family Group Conferences: Perspectives on Policy and Practice*, edited by J. Hudson, B. Galaway, A. Morris, and G. Maxwell, 49-64. Monsey, NY: Criminal Justice Press.

Rose, O., and T. Clear (1998). "Incarceration, Social Capital and Crime: Implications for Social Disorganization Theory." *Criminology* 36(3):471-479.

Rosenbaum, D. (1988). "Community Crime Prevention: A Review and Synthesis of the Literature." *Justice Quarterly* (1)5:323-395.

Rosenbaum, D. (1994). *The Challenge of Community Policing: Testing the Promise.* Beverly Hills, CA: Sage.

Sampson, R. (1995). "The Community." In *Crime*, edited by J.Q. Wilson and J. Petersilia, 193-216. San Francisco: Institute for Contemporary Studies.

Sampson, R., and W.B. Groves (1989). "Community Structure and Crime: Testing Social Disorganization Theory." *American Journal of Sociology* 94:744-802.

Sampson, R., S. Rodenbush, and F. Earls (1997). "Neighborhoods and Violent Crime: A Multi-level Study of Collective Efficacy." *Science Magazine* (August):277.

Sampson, R., and W.J. Wilson (1998). "Toward a Theory of Race, Crime and Urban Inequality." In *Community Justice: An Emerging Field*, edited by D. Karp, 97-118. Lanham, MD: Rowman and Littlefield.

Schafer, S. (1970). *Compensation and Restitution to Victims of Crime.* Montclair, NJ: Patterson Smith.

Seymour, A. (1977). "Looking Back, Moving Forward—Crime Victims and Restorative Justice." *ICCA Journal* 8(1):13-17.

Shaw, M., and F. Jane (1998). *Restorative Justice and Policing in Canada: Bringing the Community into Focus.* Ontario, Canada: Royal Canadian Mounted Police and the Ontario Provincial Police.

Sherman, L., and H. Strang (1997). "Restorative Justice and Deterring Crime." RISE Working Paper # 3, Australia National University.

Skogan, W. (1990). *Disorder and Decline: Crime and the Spiral of Decay in American Neighborhood.* New York: Free Press.

Skogan, W. (1998). "Crime and Racial Fears of White Americans." In *Community Justice: An Emerging Field,* edited by D. Karp, 118-136. Lanham, MD: Rowman and Littlefield.

Skogan, W., and S. Hartnett (1997). *Community Policing, Chicago Style.* New York: Oxford University Press.

Skolnick, J., and D. Bayley (1986). *The New Blue Line: Police Innovation in Six American Cities.* New York: Free Press.

Sparrow, M., M. Moore, and D. Kennedy (1990). *Beyond 911.* New York: BasicBooks.

Spierenburg, P. (1984). "The Spectacle of Suffering." In *Correctional Contexts, Contemporary and Classical Readings*, edited by J. Marquart and J. Sorenson, 3-16. Los Angeles: Roxbury Press.

Stuart, B. (1995). "Sentencing Circles—Making 'Real' Differences." Unpublished paper. Territorial Court of the Yukon.

Stuart, B. (1996). "Circle Sentencing: Turning Swords into Ploughshares." In *Restorative Justice: International Perspectives*, edited by B. Galaway and J. Hudson, 193-206. Monsey, NY: Criminal Justice Press.

Sullivan, M. (1989). *Getting Paid: Youth Crime and Work in the Inner City.* Ithaca, NY: Cornell University Press.

Trojanowicz, R., and D. Carter (1988). *The Philosophy and Role of Community Policing.* East Lansing: Michigan State University Press.

Umbreit, M. (1994). *Victim Meets Offender: The Impact of Restorative Justice and Mediation.* Monsey, NY: Criminal Justice Press.

Umbreit, M. (1999). "Avoiding the Marginalization and McDonaldization of Victim Offender Mediation: A Case Study in Moving Toward the Mainstream." In *Restoring Juvenile Justice—Repairing the Harm of Youth Crime*, edited by G. Bazemore and L. Walgrave. Monsey, NY: Criminal Justice Press.

Umbreit, M., and R. Coates (1993). "Cross-Site Analysis of Victim-Offender Conflict: An Analysis of Programs in These Three States." *Juvenile and Family Court Journal* 43(1):21-28.

Umbreit, M., and J. Greenwood (1997). *National Survey of Victim Offender Mediation Programs in the United States.* St. Paul, MN: Center for Restorative Justice and Mediation.

Umbreit, M., and S. Stacy (1996). "Family Group Conferencing Comes to the U.S.: A Comparison with Victim Offender Mediation." *Juvenile and Family Court Journal* 29-39.

Van Ness, D. (1986). *Crime and Its Victims: What We Can Do.* Grove, IL: Intervarsity Press.

Van Ness, D. (1993). "New Wine and Old Wineskins: Four Challenges of Restorative Justice." *Criminal Law Forum* 4:251-76.

Van Ness, D., D. Carlson, T . Crawford, and R. Strong (1989). *Restorative Justice Practice*. Washington, DC: Justice Fellowship.

Van Ness, D., and K.H. Strong (1997). *Restoring Justice*. Cincinnati: Anderson.

Walgrave, L. (1993). "Beyond Retribution and Rehabilitation: Restoration as the Dominant Paradigm in Judicial Intervention against Juvenile Crime." Paper presented at the International Congress on Criminology, Budapest, Hungary.

Walgrave, L. (1995). "Restorative Justice: Just a Technique or a Fully-Fledged Alternative?" *Howard Journal of Criminal Justice* 34(3):228-249.

Weiss, C. (1997). "How Can Theory-Based Evaluation Make Greater Headway?" *Evaluation Review* 21(4):501-524.

Weitekamp, G.M. (1999). "The History of Restorative Justice." In *Restoring Juvenile Justice: Repairing the Harm of Youth Crime*, edited G. Bazemore and L. Walgrave. Monsey, NY: Criminal Justice Press.

Weitekamp, E. (1995). "'Community' in European and American Contexts." Paper presented at the Second International Conference on Restorative Justice for Juveniles, Ft. Lauderdale, FL.

Wilson, J. (1967). *Varieties of Police Behavior: The Management of Law and Order in Eight Communities*. Cambridge, MA: Harvard University Press.

Wilson, J., and G. Kelling (1982). "Broken Windows: The Police and Neighborhood Safety." *The Atlantic Monthly* 249(3):29-38.

Yazzie, R. (1993). "Life Comes From It: Navajo Justice Concepts." *New Mexico Law Review* 24:175-190.

Young, M. (1996). *Victim Assistance in the Juvenile Justice System: A Report on Recommended Reforms*. Washington, DC: Office for Victims of Crime, U.S. Department of Justice.

Zehr, H. (1990). *Changing Lenses: A New Focus for Crime and Justice*. Scottdale, PA: Herald Press.

Zehr, H., and H. Mika (1998). "Fundamental Concepts of Restorative Justice." *Contemporary Justice Review* 1:47-55.

2
Satisfaction Guaranteed?
The Meaning of Satisfaction in Restorative Justice

DANIEL W. VAN NESS
MARA F. SCHIFF

Restorative justice is a relatively new movement and one that is far broader in scope than other criminal justice movements. Unlike desert theory, for example, which is limited to sentencing theory, restorative justice addresses the entire response to crime, including its impact on victims and communities as well as offenders (Bazemore and Griffiths, 1997; Bazemore and Schiff, 1996). As a result of these factors, the restorative justice movement has not yet developed a consistent and well-defined vocabulary that would lend specificity and precision when discussing restorative values. Words such as "healing," "reparation," "fairness," and "satisfaction" are all commonly used in restorative literature, but most of these are ill-defined conceptually, especially in empirical research literature. This has made studying and measuring the impacts of restorative interventions difficult.

In this chapter we will examine one of these key concepts: *satisfaction*. Our purpose is to bring a measure of analytical rigor to a term that many people intuitively recognize as central to restorative thinking. We hope that this will contribute to greater common understanding and agreement about the meaning and importance of this concept. We will begin by setting out three attributes that effective restorative justice terminology should have. Second, we will show that the concept of satisfaction is sufficiently central to restorative justice theory that it needs to possess those three attributes. Third, we will propose a definition of satisfaction that incorporates all three, drawing on key elements in restorative justice theory as well as the use of the term in law and in social science research. Finally, we will present a strategy for empirically testing the validity of our definition.

Meaning and Language in Restorative Justice

Language is a tool for expressing the value and meaning of complex concepts. It is therefore necessary that the vocabulary used to discuss such abstract ideas be both precise and suggestive. It must *denote* and *connote* essential meanings about those ideas. We believe that one of the problems in communicating about restorative justice has been the use of language that is powerfully suggestive but not adequately precise. Those who "get it," or who have made the "paradigm shift," are left without a sufficiently precise vocabulary with which to communicate with those who remain unpersuaded. Or worse, they attempt this communication using "old paradigm" language with its nonrestorative definitions and connotations.

Furthermore, the lack of such precision can mask disagreement about the meaning and nature of key concepts within the restorative justice movement itself (McCold, 1996). The lack of precise and specific terms conveying commonly shared meanings hinders genuine communication within and outside the restorative movement. This makes establishing and implementing consistent restorative principles and policies difficult, and impedes efforts to measure their effectiveness. We propose that three attributes should be present in the terms given to key concepts in restorative justice: *metaphor*, *meaning*, and *measurement*.

First, the terminology assigned to key concepts must be evocative. Certain words can be metaphors or symbols for the conceptual values and principles they express. For example, *proportionality* conveys symbolic meaning as a core principle of desert theory. It conjures up images of balancing and measuring that are central to that concept of sentencing. While metaphors alone do not constitute a theory, they provide significant symbols for communicating fundamental aspects of the theory. In addition to being a symbol, an effective metaphor must also be simple enough to become the identifying mark by which people understand and support the philosophy. Postmodern literature refers to "symbolic referents" as those components of a philosophy or ideology through which people come to identify the concept itself. For example, a flag is the symbolic referent of patriotism; an olive branch is the symbolic referent of peace. While words do not have the physically tangible quality of a dove or a flag, they do convey important intangibles that are key in shaping perceptions about the theory.

Second, in addition to being evocative, the terminology must also be conceptually clear. It must be defined clearly enough that proponents and opponents alike both understand its meaning and acknowledge that it expresses something fundamental about the theory. Returning to a previous example, proportionality in desert theory is commonly understood to mean that the severity of the punishment should be proportionate to that of the crime; there is little disagreement about this or about its relevance to the theory. Similarly, the terms used for key concepts of restorative justice should express some unique and defining aspect of the theory and be sufficiently precise to assure us that we are talking about the same thing.

Third, the language used to describe and characterize the key concepts of restorative justice should lend itself to measurement. If satisfaction, fairness, or healing is an essential aspect of a restorative response to crime, then those terms need to be analyzed sufficiently to enable researchers to evaluate the extent to which that outcome occurs. Researchers must be able to consistently and reliably measure the concepts those words convey. The term should lend itself to empirical testing and evaluation.

In sum, language used in restorative justice will derive power from three critical attributes: (1) *metaphor*—it should offer symbolic content that conveys the essence of restorative justice, (2) *meaning*—it should describe with precision something important about the conceptual basis of restorative justice, and (3) *measurement*—it should lend itself to evaluation.

The Importance of Satisfaction in Restorative Justice

Certain terms appear regularly in theoretical and research literature on restorative justice. It has been said, for example, that restorative justice involves fairness (Umbreit and Coates, 1992), accountability (Bazemore, 1996; Braithwaite and Roche, this volume), and healing (Boers, 1992; Van Ness and Strong, 1997; Zehr, 1990). The term "satisfaction" also appears frequently, and like the other terms, it seems to capture something essential about restorative processes (see, for example, Morris and Maxwell, 1998). Of interest is its use to indicate the extent to which a restorative intervention has been successful. In particular, it has often been used to measure the impact of an intervention on the participants.

Umbreit is one of the few researchers who has specifically examined satisfaction, primarily in relation to victims. In an early study (1988), he posits that satisfaction to victims means that the "restitution was fair," the victim was "treated fairly in mediation," the "mediator was fair," and the "mediation was helpful." His explanation for offender satisfaction is somewhat tautological—he reports that satisfaction means that the restitution agreement was fair, the offender was "satisfied with the mediation session," "satisfied with the services of the case manager," and the process resulted in a "more positive opinion about the victim." More recently, Umbreit (1998) has found that victim satisfaction with mediation is a result of the victim's attitude toward the mediator, perception of the fairness of the restitution agreement, and the importance of meeting the offender. In this research, Umbreit does not examine offender, community, or government satisfaction.

Morris and Maxwell (1998) found that for parents, satisfaction seemed to hinge on whether the young person "got off too lightly" or whether treatment or help was offered. For young people, it was more about how the outcome compared with that of their co-offenders or with their notion of appropriate penalties. Young people receiving more severe sanctions reported levels of dissatisfaction almost three times as high as those receiving less severe penalties. Victim satisfaction seemed related to whether the outcome was either too harsh or too soft or, more frequently, because agreements made by young offenders were not kept.

Other studies suggest additional components of satisfaction. Among them are fairness (Hughes and Schneider, 1990; Umbreit and Bradshaw, 1998; Umbreit and Coates, 1992; Warner, 1991), effectiveness (Hughes and Schneider, 1990), having a positive experience (Marshall, 1990), the opportunity to express and understand feelings (Smith, Blagg, and Derricourt, 1985), completion of the agreement (Warner, 1991), participation (Umbreit and Coates, 1992), attitude toward the mediator (Umbreit and Bradshaw, 1998), meeting the offender (Umbreit and Bradshaw, 1998), and input into the decision-making process and outcome (Coates and Gehm, 1985).

Umbreit (1996) suggests that satisfaction is linked to getting answers from the offender (for victims), being able to communicate about the circumstances and impact of the crime, making and receiving an apology, and negotiating restitution. Netzig and Trenczek (1996) suggest (without explicitly stating) that satisfaction is linked to overcoming fears resulting from the incident, coming to terms with what happened, and being able to meet the offender/victim face-to-face. Some research suggests that satisfaction with outcomes for offenders is linked to the belief that they are given meaningful work to do, learn useful skills, and feel that their service benefits others (McIvor, 1991; Varah, 1981). Moore and O'Connell (1994) suggest that victims participating in family group conferencing are more satisfied when they believe sufficient attention has been placed on meeting their needs.

Some researchers have intimated the content of satisfaction by describing what results in *dissatisfaction*. Clairmont (1994) states that victim dissatisfaction in aboriginal community justice programs in Canada resulted from lack of sufficient involvement, reservations about the fairness and effectiveness of the process, and that offenders were not held sufficiently accountable for their actions. In mediation and family group conferencing, dissatisfaction has resulted from agreements that were not kept (Maxwell and Morris, 1998; Umbreit and Coates, 1992), and the perception that offenders are not remorseful also influences how victims feel about the process.

Drawbacks of Emphasizing Satisfaction in Restorative Justice

While satisfaction is clearly an important theme in the literature of restorative justice, there may also be some potential drawbacks to emphasizing its importance. The objections include the following:

1. An overemphasis on satisfaction may lead to minimization of other important goals of restorative justice. If programs focus principally on achieving satisfaction, they may neglect other important restorative aims, such as inclusion, fairness, accountability, or healing. While we think this an unlikely scenario, it is possible that in the face of scarce resources and lack of community and justice system support, programs may need to make hard choices about where to concentrate attention. In such circumstances, important restorative objectives may be overlooked.

2. One criticism of restorative justice has been its inattention to broader social justice concerns (see Pranis, this volume). Such arguments have been grounded in the assumption that it is not possible to address crime and its impact on individuals as separate from the broader social inequalities that result in crime (e.g., Karp, 1997). A restorative focus on satisfaction of the parties who are most directly affected by the crime (the victim, the offender, the surrounding community) may not adequately reflect the broader societal costs of crime and the social framework within which crime occurs. Hence, concentrating on individual criminal events and the parties directly affected by them may leave important structural inequities unaddressed.

3. The expectations of the parties when engaging in a restorative process may have a great deal to do with their level of satisfaction at its conclusion. In other words, if expectations were initially low, participants may report high degrees of satisfaction when they are pleasantly surprised. If their expectations are initially high, then they may report dissatisfaction when the same process fails to

deliver its anticipated benefits. This inability to account for pre-intervention differences may bias the extent to which satisfaction is a valid and reliable indicator of "restorativeness."

4. Finally, why should we even care about satisfaction? To the extent that "justice" is about righting wrongs, punishing wrongdoers, and equalizing power imbalances, is the satisfaction of the participants truly necessary? The retributive framework that currently informs our justice system asserts that criminal wrongs are corrected when culpable individuals are punished. Under this approach, there is no particular need for individual parties to be satisfied with the process or the outcome—it is, in fact, irrelevant. It is possible that even under a restorative model, satisfaction is not paramount—but rather a welcome by-product of some other feature that better characterizes the fundamental values of restorative justice.

However, we suspect that those limitations can be overcome by careful planning and program design. Further, we think that it is worth the effort to do so. There are a number of reasons why it would be useful to embrace satisfaction as a critical element in restorative justice.

1. At a fundamental level, satisfaction is (or at least should be) a requirement for any justice system; it keeps people from taking the law into their own hands, it preserves the authority of the justice system, and it increases likelihood that decisions will be followed voluntarily.

2. Designing responses to crime that are satisfying to all parties reduces the likelihood that crime and its subsequent outcome can be "stolen" from the parties, as Christie argues the current criminal justice system has done (Christie, 1977). This is important when we consider the criticism that some programs once seen as community-based and responsive have been overtaken by bureaucratic and formal requirements [e.g., see Elias's (1992) critique of the victims' movement].

3. The focus on satisfaction provides a constraint on predictable efforts to increase the efficiency of the justice response to crime at the cost of decreasing concern for the interests of the parties. While the parties themselves will have an interest in efficiency, it should not come at the cost of other important concerns that have a critical impact on the future—both in terms of the behavior of the parties involved and the behavior of the justice system response to crime.

In conclusion, then, we suggest that three things—(1) the frequency with which the term *satisfaction* appears in evaluation literature, (2) the conceptual congruity of the term with key values and principles of restorative justice, and (3) the programmatic and policy benefits of using the term in communications about restorative justice—all suggest that it is a key concept within restorative justice.

Defining Satisfaction

In many ways, *satisfaction* seems to be an intuitively appealing term because it underscores the personal and relational aspect of restorative justice (we are interested in how all the parties *feel* about the result) and it permits the parties to decide for themselves what is essential in responding appropriately to crime. Furthermore, satisfaction is potentially a compelling term to use in policy debate on responses to crime. Rather than resorting to old notions of toughness or proportionality, restorative justice advocates could argue for a response to crime that results in *satisfaction* of the parties. Visions of satisfied parties evoke an image of the participants being at peace with one another and themselves, suggesting that this term may meet at least one of the three important characteristics of restorative language mentioned earlier, that is, metaphor.

It is not immediately clear, however, whether satisfaction can address the other two attributes of meaning and measurement. In order to determine that, it is necessary to articulate a precise definition for satisfaction that simultaneously retains its personal dimensions but is sufficiently objective to permit conceptual analysis and development of evaluative measures.

One of the problems with defining *satisfaction* is that it is a subjective term. What is satisfactory to one victim may not be satisfactory to another. What is satisfactory to an offender one day may not be satisfactory a year later. What is satisfactory to members of a community that is perceived to be relatively safe may not be satisfactory after that community experiences a rise in fear of crime, nor may it be satisfactory to a community plagued by constant violent crime. While this subjectivity is important in understanding the restorative perspective, it also presents difficulties for recognizing it, communicating clearly about its meaning and importance, and fostering the conditions necessary to produce stakeholder satisfaction.

However, these limitations need not prevent us from assigning a technical definition that adds objective structure to an otherwise subjective term. One area in which this has occurred has been in the field of law. In the common law of contracts, the term *satisfaction* has been used for centuries to require one party to perform to the other's contentment (DiMatteo, 1995). Courts have needed to decide what to do when the performing party argues that the other party has unreasonably withheld satisfaction to avoid paying for service provided. Courts have traditionally resolved this by interpreting satisfaction clauses using an objective standard: would a reasonable person have been satisfied?

Even when contracts have involved fancy, taste, or particular judgment (as in satisfaction with a work of art, for example) and courts could not inject a "reasonable person" standard, judges have attempted to provide some objectivity. Recognizing that such genuinely subjective clauses could lend themselves to capriciousness and arbitrariness, judges have applied a modified version of the "reasonable person" standard. The view of most jurisdictions is that subjective satisfaction can be withheld only in good faith, and good faith is determined by using an objective standard (would a reasonable person have made this good-faith objection?).

In other words, courts have narrowed the inherent subjectivity of satisfaction by applying objective tests whenever possible: Would reasonable people have been satisfied, and has satisfaction been withheld in what a reasonable person would deem to be good faith? Satisfaction's subjectivity can be made sufficiently objective by understanding more fully what would satisfy reasonable persons in the positions of the particular parties.

Based on this, we can begin to articulate a definition of satisfaction:

> *Satisfaction refers to the state of mind of reasonable persons in the position of specific victims, offenders, their families, and other affected community members who have experienced a fully restorative response to crime.*

So what then is a fully restorative response to crime? Van Ness and Strong (1997) propose four values as characteristic of restorative processes and outcomes: (1) encounter, (2) reparation, (3) reintegration, and (4) participation. We suggest that when all four take place fully, reasonable persons in the position of the various parties will experience satisfaction. In other words, satisfaction in a restorative intervention is a measure of the extent to which the parties experience encounter, reparation, reintegration, and participation. It results when parties to a crime encounter the other parties, give and/or receive reparation for harm done, are reintegrated into safe communities, and are provided the opportunity to participate fully in the justice process.

The empirical research cited previously supports the contention that encounter, participation, reparation, and reintegration are important components of a satisfactory restorative process, but no study has directly examined or tested that assertion. Consequently, our definition, while supported by existing research, should be considered more a hypothesis for further empirical research than a definitive statement on what constitutes satisfaction in restorative processes. Research that could validate this hypothesis is described below.

Subjective and Objective Measurements of Satisfaction

Morris and Maxwell (1998) acknowledge the difficulty in distinguishing exactly what people mean when discussing *satisfaction* with family group conferences in New Zealand. They state:

> Understanding what people actually mean when they answer such questions [about satisfaction] has proved problematic for researchers but this is, by definition, the most important measure of how participants view the processes in which they participate. The failure to deconstruct the concept of "satisfaction" almost certainly reflects the fact that people vary in both their level of expectation and the type of outcomes they view as appropriate; hence, their "satisfaction" cannot be predicted from examining outcomes alone.

This underscores the subjective element of satisfaction, and the importance of both process and outcome in achieving it. The most obvious way to measure the presence of satisfaction, then, is to ask people whether they are satisfied. This kind of research on restorative interventions has been ongoing for the past decade, but is there a way to predict when participants will be satisfied? We have just argued that satisfaction in a restorative intervention is a measure of the extent to which the parties experience encounter, reparation, reintegration, and participation. It results when parties to a crime encounter the other parties, give and/or receive reparation for harm done, are reintegrated into safe communities, and are provided the opportunity to participate fully in the process.

Van Ness and Strong (1997) have broken down each of these concepts into specific elements that can lend themselves to empirical investigation.

1. **Encounter** is a *meeting or series of meetings*, usually face-to-face, with the other parties. The meeting will be characterized by *narrative* (each party telling the story from his or her own perspective), expression of *emotion*, growing *understanding* of the others, and a concluding *agreement* that is particular to the situation and achievable by the parties.

2. **Reparation** is the process by which the *responsible party makes amends* for, or repairs, the harm he or she has caused the other party(ies). Reparation will be made first to the *parties directly injured* by the offense, reflecting both the *seriousness of the injury* and the *seriousness of the offense*, and it will be tailored to the capabilities of the offender so that completion in a timely fashion is *feasible*.

3. **Reintegration** is the re-entry of each party into community life as "whole, contributing, productive persons." It involves *creation of relationships* between the parties and members of the community that are *characterized by mutual respect, mutual commitment,* and *shared values* that lead to a shared understanding of intolerance for deviant behavior.

4. **Participation** means the opportunity for *direct and full involvement of each party* in the encounter, reparation, and reintegration. It requires processes that make the involvement of each party *relevant* and that increase the likelihood that such participation will be *voluntary* and not coerced.

Each of the italicized characteristics above might be formulated as empirically testable variables. We suggest that the extent to which these attributes are present will determine how much satisfaction occurs within a restorative intervention.

Testing the Definition

The first step in a future research project would be to identify the extent to which people agree that satisfaction is critical in restorative interventions. One method might be to survey victims, offenders, community members, program administrators, local justice system personnel, and local policymakers about their knowledge of, and experiences with, restorative and nonrestorative programs.

Second, assuming there was agreement about the importance of satisfaction in restorative justice, it would be necessary to identify, measure, and test its most salient indicators. The definition we have offered incorporates four key concepts (encounter, reparation, reintegration, and participation). For each, we have suggested specific indicators (e.g., face-to-face meetings with narrative and expression of emotion; all the parties directly injured by the offense are involved; the outcome reflects both the seriousness of the injury and the seriousness of the offense; there is direct and full involvement of each party in the encounter; such participation is voluntary; and so forth).

Analytically, this formulation of satisfaction would be well suited to factor analysis and structural equation modeling. The primary value of these analytic techniques is that they allow abstract and unobservable ideas (e.g., "encounter", "reintegration," "satisfaction") to be measured through directly observable characteristics. To perform such tests, observable variables are identified (Was there a face-to-face meeting? Was a relationship created? Did the offender complete his or her agreement?) that represent aspects of the intangible concept being studied. Factor analysis then tests whether these observable indicators are statistically related to one another in predictable ways. From these tests, the analyst can then conclude whether such tangible indicators are reliable measures of the abstract concept being tested.

Structural equation modeling then allows the analyst to test whether the intangible variables, or factors, are indicators of a deeper level of abstraction (in this case, satisfaction). In our example, the analyst would take this first level of abstractions—encounter, reparation, reintegration, and participation—and determine whether they constitute elements of satisfaction. Figure 2.1 presents a graphic model of how this might look.

Figure 2.1
Elements of Satisfaction

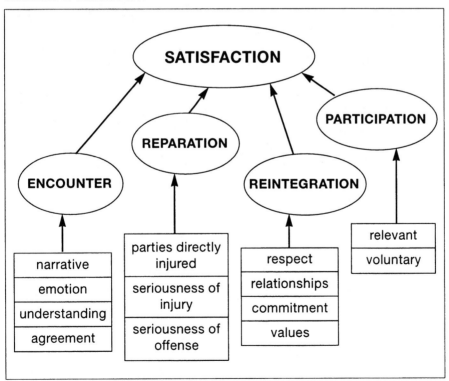

The assumption underlying this research would be that if victims, offenders, and community members participate in a program that provides high levels of encounter, reparation, reintegration, and participation, their levels of satisfaction with the program/process will be high. This further presupposes that if satisfaction is high, restorative justice is present. Note, however, that this research would *not* determine whether restorative justice is present, only whether the components of satisfaction are. The extent to which satisfaction is a valid indicator of restorative justice would depend on the level of agreement that satisfaction signifies the presence of restorative justice.

Research of this nature would have a number of benefits. First, it would test the definition we have proposed, confirming or refuting our hypotheses about the importance and nature of satisfaction.

Second, it might suggest ways that definition might be refined to incorporate the research findings. If the research indicates either that satisfaction is not an important component of restorative interventions or that our constructs are not significant predictors of satisfaction, then the next step would be to either: (1) reconsider the theoretical propositions on which the research was based, (2) identify other possible explanations of the relationships found, and/or (3) reconsider what indicators of satisfaction have not been adequately accounted for.

Third, research should help us construct a programmatic model that incorporates those components most likely to result in high participant satisfaction which would lead in turn to highly restorative programs. In other words, research should be used to create and generate programs that will reliably produce highly restorative outcomes. While satisfaction is not the only indicator of "restorativeness," we believe that understanding its components would go a long way toward identifying those program elements that must be present in order for a program to be considered restorative.

Finally, this research could lead to a set of program evaluation tools. By clarifying what programmatic components lead to high levels of satisfaction, it would be possible to determine the extent to which programs meet some critical tests of restorativeness. Truly restorative programs should be characterized by high degrees of encounter, reparation, reintegration, and participation, which should result in high degrees of satisfaction with the process and the outcome. Programs incorporating many or most of these elements would be more likely to be restorative than programs with little or none of these attributes.

Areas Needing Further Development

This chapter has not considered several areas that need further development. First, it is simpler to think of and measure satisfaction of the victim and offender than of the community and the government. This raises the question of whether the definition of satisfaction presented here is sufficient for all four parties or if additional conceptual work is necessary to delve into the importance and elements of satisfaction for those two parties. For example, how would an emphasis on satisfaction affect current governmental responsibilities in deciding legal issues such as due process limitations and constraints on use of force?

Second, what is the nature and role of proportionality in achieving satisfaction? What happens when a restorative process concludes and the offender or victim finds that the agreement reached was significantly different from the "going rate" for such offenses and circumstances? Should there be upper and lower proportionality constraints, even in a restorative system? If so, how would this affect the nature of the process? If the lack of proportionality seems to result in consistent and/or long-term dissatisfaction among parties to restorative interventions, should steps be taken to incorporate such concerns into restorative processes, and how should this be approached?

Third, can satisfaction be used as a method of critiquing non-restorative approaches to criminal justice, or is its utility limited to restorative approaches? The broader its application, the more likely its value for understanding both the principles of restorative justice and the differences between restorative and contemporary criminal justice approaches.

Conclusion

The intent of this chapter has been to explore the meaning of satisfaction as a key concept in restorative justice. In so doing, we have discussed why we believe the vocabulary of restorative justice must be carefully selected to express its key concepts adequately. We argued that satisfaction is indeed one of those key concepts. Next, we proposed a definition of satisfaction that gives conceptual clarity to a word that is already evocative. We then suggested that that definition might be tested, including an analytic framework for investigation. Finally, we identified areas needing further exploration.

What is often lacking in discussions about restorative justice is agreement on the meaning of words used to name key organizing principles of the theory. We hope that this chapter moves us closer to a common understanding of satisfaction, thereby contributing to the eventual transformation of justice and justice systems.

Discussion Questions

1. Why do Van Ness and Schiff believe it is important to clarify the language used to express restorative concepts? What are the three key components from which restorative language derives its power?

2. What is important about the concept of satisfaction in restorative community justice and how is this different from what is seen to be most important in traditional retributive models?

3. What do the authors say are the components of satisfaction and why are these important?

4. Do you agree that satisfaction is a key concept in measuring the effectiveness of restorative interventions or do you think some other concept better characterizes the ultimate goal of restorative community justice?

References

Bazemore, G. (1996). "Three Paradigms for Juvenile Justice." In *Restorative Justice: International Perspectives,* edited by B. Galaway and J. Hudson, 37-68. Monsey, NY: Criminal Justice Press.

Bazemore, G., and C. Griffiths (1997). "Circles, Boards, Conferences and Mediation: Scouting the New Wave in Community Justice Decision-Making." *Federal Probation* LXI(2):25-37.

Bazemore, G., and M. Schiff (1996). "Community Justice/Restorative Justice: Prospects for a New Social Ecology for Community Corrections." *International Journal of Comparative and Applied Criminal Justice* 20(2):311-335.

Boers, A.P. (1992). *Justice that Heals: A Biblical Vision for Victims and Offenders.* Newton, KS: Faith and Life Press.

Bradshaw, W., and M. Umbreit (1998). "Crime Victims Meet Juvenile Offenders: Contributing Factors to Victim Satisfaction with Mediated Dialogue in Minneapolis." *Juvenile and Family Court Journal* 49(1):17-25.

Braithwaite, J., and D. Roche (2001). "Responsibility and Restorative Justice," this volume.

Christie, N. (1977). "Conflict as Property." *British Journal of Criminology* 17(1):1-15.

Claimont, D. (1994). *Community Assessment of Crime, Justice and Diversion.* Halifax, Nova Scotia: Tripartite Forum on Native Justice.

Coates, R., and J. Gehm (1985). *Victim Meets Offender: An Evaluation of Victim Offender Reconciliation Programs.* Valparaiso, IN: PACT Institute of Justice.

DiMatteo, L.A. (1995). "The Norms of Contract: The Fairness Inquiry and the "Law of Satisfaction: A Nonunified Theory." *Hofstra Law Review* 24:349-405.

Elias, R. (1992) "Which Victim Movement? The Politics of Victim Policy." In *Victims of Crime: Problems, Policies and Programs*, edited by A.J. Lurigio, W.G. Skogan, and R.C. Davis. Newbury Park, CA: Sage.

Hughes, S., and A. Schneider (1990). *Victim Offender Mediation in the Juvenile Justice System*. Washington, DC: Office of Juvenile Justice and Delinquency Prevention.

Karp, D. (1997). "Community Justice," *Research Seminar on Community, Crime, and Justice Monograph*. George Washington University: National Institute of Justice.

Marshall, T. (1990). "Results From British Experiments in Restorative Justice." In *Criminal Justice, Restitution and Reconciliation*, edited by B. Galaway and J. Hudson. New York: Willow Tree Press.

McCold, P. (1996). "Restorative Justice: Variations on a Theme." Paper presented to the Conference on Restorative Justice for Juveniles: Potentialities, Risks and Problems for Research, Leuven, Belgium, May 12-14.

McIvor, G. (1991). *Sentenced to Serve*. Aldershot, England: Avebury.

Moore, D.B., and T. O'Connell (1994). *"Family Conferencing in Wagga-Wagga: Communitarian Model of Justice."* In *Family Conferencing and Juvenile Justice: The Way Forward or Misplaced Optimism?*, edited by C. Alder and J. Wundersitz. Canberra: Australian Institute of Criminology.

Morris, A., and G. Maxwell (1998). "Restorative Justice in New Zealand: Family Group Conferences as a Case Study." *Western Criminology Review* 1:1. See: *http://wcr.sonoma.edu/v1n1/morris.html*

Netzig, L., and T. Trenczek (1996). "Restorative Justice as Participation: Theory, Law, Experience and Research." In *Restorative Justice: International Perspectives*, edited by B. Galaway and J. Hudson. Monsey, NY: Criminal Justice Press

Pranis, K. (2000). "Restorative Justice, Social Justice, and the Empowerment of Marginalized Populations." In *Restorative and Community Justice: Cultivating Common Ground for Victims, Offenders and Communities,* edited by G. Bazemore and M. Schiff. Cincinnati: Anderson.

Smith, D., H. Blagg, and N. Derricourt. (1985). "Victim-Offender Mediation Project." Report to the Chief Officers' Group, South Yorkshire Probation Service. Cited in T. Marshal and S. Merry (1990). *Crime and Accountability: Victim Offender Mediation in Practice*. London: Home Office.

Umbreit, M. (1988). "Mediation of Victim-Offender Conflict." *Journal of Dispute Resolution* 31:85-105.

Umbreit, M. (1996). "Restorative Justice Through Mediation: The Impact on Programs in Four Canadian Provinces." In *Restorative Justice: International Perspectives*, edited by B. Galaway and J. Hudson. Monsey, NY: Criminal Justice Press.

Umbreit, M. (1998). "Restorative Justice Through Victim-Offender Mediation: A Multi-Site Assessment." *Western Criminology Review* 1(1).

Umbreit, M. (1999). "Restorative Justice Through Juvenile Victim Offender Mediation." In *Restoring Juvenile Justice: Changing the Context of the Youth Crime Response*, edited by G. Bazemore and L. Walgrave. Monsey, NY: Criminal Justice Press.

Umbreit, M., and R.B. Coates (1992). "The Impact of Mediating Victim-Offender Conflict: An Analysis of Programs in Three States." *Juvenile and Family Court Journal* 43(1):21-28.

Van Ness, D., and K.H. Strong (1997). *Restoring Justice*. Cincinnati: Anderson.

Varah, M. (1981). "What About the Workers? Offenders on Community Service Orders Express Their Opinions." *Probation Journal* 120-123.

Warner, S. (1991). Reparation, Mediation and Scottish Criminal Justice. In *Restorative Justice on Trial: Pitfalls and Potentials of Victim-Offender Mediation— International Research Perspectives,* edited by H. Messmer and H. Otto, 197-210. The Netherlands: Kliewer Academic Publishers.

Wright, M. (1991). *Justice for Victims and Offenders.* Milton Keynes, England: Open University Press.

Zehr, H. (1990). *Changing Lenses: A New Focus for Crime and Justice.* Scottdale, PA: Herald Press.

3

Responsibility and Restorative Justice

JOHN BRAITHWAITE
DECLAN ROCHE

Restorative justice owes part of its growth in popularity to its broad political appeal, offering something to politicians of varying stripes. In particular, "getting offenders to take responsibility for their actions" has been part of the political appeal of restorative justice. So has "getting families to take responsibility for their kids." While it may seem appropriate to exploit such political appeal, restorative justice must have a more meaningful sense of responsibility than this. Restorative justice cannot sell itself in these terms yet simultaneously distance itself from similar sounding neoconservative ideas of responsibility, without clearly articulating its own conception of responsibility. As O'Malley says, "Discourses of responsibility for crime and crime prevention are . . . not possessions of the political Right, and they do not imply only a punitive response to offending" (O'Malley, 1994:22). Responsibility is a fundamental and contestable part of any scheme of justice, including restorative justice.

The purpose of this chapter is to explore the concept of responsibility within a restorative justice framework. As a starting hypothesis, let us see if restorative responsibility might be conceived as that form of responsibility most likely to promote restoration—of victims, offenders, and communities. Given that framework, we will first find a useful distinction between active responsibility and passive responsibility. Then we show how that distinction maps onto distinctions between active and passive deterrence, rehabilitation, and incapacitation. We then seek to develop the rudiments of a jurisprudence of active responsibility. Finally, we consider some worries about the restorative conception of responsibility we have developed.

Active and Passive Responsibility

Carol Heimer (1999:18) makes a distinction between being held accountable for the wrong one has done in the past and taking responsibility for the future. Mark Bovens (1998:27) makes a similar distinction between passive responsibility and active responsibility. Twentieth-century Western retributive justice has been mostly concerned with passive responsibility. Restorative justice, we will argue, shifts the balance toward active responsibility.

Bovens says that in the case of passive responsibility "one is called to account after the event and either held responsible or not. It is a question of who *bears* the responsibility for a given state of affairs. The central question is: 'Why *did* you do it?'" (Bovens, 1998:27). Bovens sees passive responsibility as requiring transgression of a norm, a causal connection between conduct and damage, blameworthiness, and sometimes a special relationship of obligation toward the person(s) harmed (Bovens, 1998:28-31). The literature is full of debates about the best way to conceive of passive responsibility (see, for example, Mulgan, 1997; Thomas, 1998). We will not add to those debates here. While we have some doubts about Bovens's conception of passive responsibility, we will not discuss them, as our interest is to move on to the special appeal for restorative justice theory of his concept of active responsibility.

First, however, it must be said that restorative justice cannot do without some concept of passive responsibility. For example, a restorative justice conference is held after the commission of a crime ("after the event," in Boven's terms) and in light of the admission of guilt by the offender (which determines "who bears responsibilty"). Furthermore, a conference, at least in its early stages, will often involve asking the offender why he or she did it. Our argument is not that restorative justice abandons passive responsibility, but that restorative justice uses passive responsibility to create a forum in which active responsibility can be fostered. Restorative justice, then, is about shifting the balance from passive responsibility toward active responsibility.

So what is active responsibility, according to Bovens? He sees active responsibility as a virtue, the virtue of taking responsibility when something needs to be done to deal with a problem or put things right: "[T]he emphasis lies much more on action in the present, on the prevention of unwanted situations and events . . . The central question here is: 'what *is* to be done?'" (Bovens, 1998:27).

To interpolate in a restorative justice frame, active responsibility entails seeking to take responsibility to repair harm, and especially to restore relationships. According to Bovens, active responsibility requires: (1) an adequate perception of threatened violations of a norm, (2) consideration of consequences, (3) autonomy, and (4) taking obligations seriously. Restorative dialogue, in which the problem rather than the person is put in the center of the circle (Melton, 1995), and in which respectful listening is a central value, seems well designed to cultivate Boven's virtue of active responsibility. As Heimer and Staffen (1998:369) put it, "it is the humanity of other people that inspires responsibility." Bovens also sees active responsibility as requiring "conduct based on a verifiable and consistent code"(Bovens, 1998:36). This seems to be an excessively positivist requirement; families can nurture active responsibility through restorative dialogue without codifying their norms.

We argue that restorative justice reconceptualizes responsibility, so that when people claim that restorative justice offers *better* responsibility than traditional court sentencing,[1] they are impliedly making a claim about what is accomplished by active responsibility.

Those who favor retribution are concerned with passive responsibility because their priority is to be just in the way that they hurt wrongdoers. The shift in the balance toward active responsibility occurs because the priority of restorative justice proponents is to be just in the way that they heal.

While it is clear that a backward-looking, deontological theory such as retributivism is clearly concerned more with passive than active responsibility, the influence of passive responsibility also permeates forward-looking, consequentialist theories. Utilitarians along the lines of Jeremy Bentham are equally preoccupied with hurting rather than healing, and with passive rather than active responsibility. We will argue that utilitarians have an inferior theory of deterrence, rehabilitation, incapacitation, and crime prevention to that of restorative justice theorists. At the root of this inferiority is the utilitarian's obsession with passive responsibility to the exclusion of active responsibility.[2] First, we will show how under the restorative alternative, while passive responsibility maps onto passive deterrence, active responsibility maps onto active deterrence—and the latter is more powerful. Then we will do the same for rehabilitation and incapacitation.

Passive and Active Deterrence

Deterrence is not an objective of restorative justice. In fact, to make deterrence of wrongdoing a value would destroy restorative justice for the same reason that making shaming a value would destroy it. As Kay Pranis (1998:45) puts it, "An intention to shame [we add deter] is not respectful. An intention to help a person understand the harm they caused and to support them in taking full responsibility for that harm is respectful."[3] However, this is not to deny that theories of shame and deterrence can help us understand why restorative processes might have more preventive potential than retributive/deterrent processes.

Most deterrence literature in criminology indicates that the severity level of punishment rarely has a significant deterrent effect. While a criminal justice system with no passive deterrence would clearly be one with a lot of crime, the data give utilitarians reason to be discouraged that increasing the quantum of passive deterrence will reduce crime (or that reducing passive deterrence will increase crime). Active deterrence, we will suggest, is a different story.

Ayres and Braithwaite (1992:19-53) have argued that deterrence theory in criminology is primitive compared to deterrence theory in international relations because it is excessively passive. When the United States seeks to deter a form of international behavior, it does not announce in advance that the punishment if states do X will be Y, if they do 2X, it will be 2Y, and so on with a passive deterrence tariff. Instead, its deterrence strategy is active in two important senses. First, the United States uses its power to persuade other states on whom the rogue state is dependent for some reason (for example, trade) to intervene (actively) to persuade the rogue state that it should refrain from the rogue action. What is being mobilized by this kind of active deterrence is a web of complex interdependency (Keohane, 1984). Second, the United States' strategic deterrence is active in the sense of being dynamic rather than passive. The deterrent threat does not just sit there as a passive promise of punishment; deterrence is escalated up and down an enforcement pyramid in response to the level of cooperative response and the concessions made by the rogue state. International relations theory has escaped the shackles of Benthamite thinking about certain response with punishments calibrated to be passively optimal.

Restorative Justice and Deterrence

How could restorative justice theory do better than legal deterrence theory? Let us illustrate with some restorative justice analogies to active webs of complex interdependence. Consider the restorative approach that has been developing in Australian business regulation. First, the regulator meets with the agents in the corporation who seem most passively responsible for the lawbreaking, along with some victims (where appropriate). Because the corporate actors most directly responsible have the most to lose from a criminal conviction of the corporation, they will be hard targets, difficult to deter. They are likely to fight passive deterrence by denial of responsibility. For Benthamite corporate crime fighters, that is the end of the story—another contested court case that they do not have the resources to fight, another defeat at the hands of those who control corporate power. However, what we know is that causal and preventive power over corporate crime is, as the philosophers say (Lewis, 1986), overdetermined. So what we do is move up the organization, widening the circle of dialogue, convening another conference to which the boss of the passively responsible agent of the corporation is invited. Often the boss will turn out to be a hard target as well. When that fails, we convene another conference and invite her boss. Fisse and Braithwaite (1993:230-232) have described one restorative justice experience in which the process led right up to the Chief Executive Officer, who was the "toughest nut" of them all. After that, though, the Australian Trade Practices Commission widened the circle to include the Chair of the Board, who was shocked at this recalcitrant unwillingness to restore the victims' losses and reform the corporation's compliance systems. The Chair actually fired the CEO. (Not very restorative! A case of active deterrence leading to passive deterrence.)

In other more extended treatments of the deterrence theory of restorative justice, Braithwaite (1997a, 1999) has argued that corporate crime is not different from common crime in that it is mostly a collective, or at least a socially embedded, phenomenon, in which there are many actors with preventive capabilities. For example, one interpretation for the success of whole-school anti-bullying programs in reducing bullying up to 50 percent (Olweus, 1993) is in these terms. Whenever a fourth grader is bullying another child, many children in the school (particularly from the fifth grade up) are in a position to intervene to prevent the bullying. From a deterrence theory perspective, therefore, whole-school anti-bullying programs work because the deterrence target shifts from the bully (a hard target to deter passively) to active deterrence of responsible peers of the bully.

One reason that empowerment is a central value of restorative justice is that it encourages people to take active responsibility—and active responsibility delivers, among other things, active deterrence. The environmentally conscious citizen of the corporation intervenes to stop the environmental crime even though she has no passive responsibility for causing it. A school friend intervenes to stop bullying even though she bears no passive responsibility for it. An ideal of the design of restorative institutions is to create democratic spaces for the nurturing of the virtue of active responsibility among citizens, young and old.

In the context of violence against women, Braithwaite and Daly (1994) have argued that restorative justice is more likely to be attempted, taken seriously, and to actually work, if it is located within a dynamic enforcement strategy in which the upshot of repeated failure of restorative conferences will be escalation to deterrence and incapacitation. This is not to advocate restorative justice transacted on the basis of threat. Rather it is to say that powerful criminals are more likely to succumb to the entreaties of restorative justice when deterrence is threatening in the background instead of threatened in the foreground (for the theory, see Ayres and Braithwaite, 1992:47-51). The idea is not that deterrence is there as an ever-present passive threat but that everyone knows it is democratically available as an active possibility if dialogue fails or is spurned. Because "everyone knows" this, there is no need to make threats; indeed, to do so is counterproductive. So an offender who chooses not to participate in a conference knows the alternative is an appearance in court, where he or she will be subject to passive responsibility.

The Restorative Justice Process and Responsibility

Conferences and circles provide opportunities to nurture active responsibility. If you empower citizens in a punitive society to decide how to put right a wrong, many choose to do so punitively against the wrongdoer. Kathleen Daly suggests that restorative justice does deliver a deal of retribution (Daly, 2000). Moreover, because restorative justice processes of confronting victims and their own families are often grueling even for hardened offenders, and because we know that "the process" in all systems is usually the greater part of punishment (Feeley, 1979), restorative justice also delivers a lot of process-related passive deterrence.

However, the empirical experience of restorative justice is that victims and other citizens are not as punitive as we expected they would be, and not as punitive as they are in the context of adversarial courtroom justice. When courts do intervene to overturn decisions of restorative justice conferences, it is rarely to make them less punitive; instead, it is usually to increase punishment (Maxwell and Morris, 1993). So it seems that while people have the opportunity to pursue punitiveness and passive responsibility, they choose to do so far less than we might expect.

A conference convened by one of the authors of this chapter provides an example. A middle-aged married couple came to the conference to meet the young person who had stolen and damaged beyond repair the car the husband had spent three years and thousands of dollars restoring. In the conference, it was explained to the offender that he had done great damage to the car, probably without realizing it. After the man explained that, his wife shared that her stoic husband had been privately shattered about the loss of the car that he had hoped to display at car shows—and that since the offense, he did not have the heart to start over. She also explained that their daughter was in the advanced stages of a difficult pregnancy and the loss of the car made it difficult to help with tasks such as collecting their grandchildren from school and doing grocery shopping. Yet, despite the harm, the couple declined offers of physical labor from the offender, insisting that the only outcome that would help them was one that helped him (in this case, taking small steps to resume his education). In Boven's terms, the couple was concerned that the young person exercise his active responsibility in respect to this incident in a way that nurtured the virtue of active responsibility in him for the future.

A process that allows victims to meet the offender and his or her family often generates compassion for the offender and a better understanding of his or her actions. Compassion contributes to the pursuit of restoration and active responsibility more than it does to the pursuit of punishment. However, there is not always compassion in conferences and there often is retribution. How can this be an alternative model of justice if citizens often choose to deter or seek revenge? One response is to draw an analogy to democracy. If you set up a democracy, citizens often vote for candidates with anti-democratic values. What is happening there is that we honor the institution (democracy) that conduces to a shift to democratic values rather than honoring the values themselves. To take democracy away from people as soon as they chose to manifest anti-democratic values would be not only perverse but a prescription for historically unsustainable democracy. What we do instead is write constitutions that put limits on anti-democratic action.

Likewise, restorative justice must be constitutionalized so that limits are placed on the pursuit of deterrence. Thus, people can (if they insist) pursue anti-democratic or anti-restorative aims to the extent to which those systems allow.[4] We think these limits should constrain restorative justice conferences against any incarcerative or corporal punishment, any punishment that is degrading or humiliating,[5] and any punishment in excess of that which would be imposed by a court for the same wrongdoing.[6]

Active and Passive Rehabilitation

> "Support without accountability leads to moral weakness. Accountability without support is a form of cruelty."
> —Harriet Jane Olsen, *The Book of Discipline of the United Methodist Church* (1996)

Having outlined in some detail the story of active and passive deterrence, we hope we can briefly state how to apply the same principles to active and passive rehabilitation (for more detail, see Braithwaite, 1998, 1999). There is much evidence that the least effective way of delivering rehabilitation programs is for the state to decide what is best and to require criminals to be passive recipients of that benevolence. In the most empowering restorative justice programs, such as one described by Burford and Pennell (1996), which is designed to deal with family violence, the victims, offenders, and their communities of care are not subjected to rehabilitative prescription but are empowered with knowledge. Experts come into the conference to explain the range of rehabilitative options available. State monopolies of provision of rehabilitative services are replaced by a plurality of service providers from civil society, private enterprise, and the state. More radically, resourcing can be available for professional help for communities of care to craft and operate their own rehabilitative interventions.

The two variables in play here that we know are associated with superior rehabilitative outcomes are: (1) active choice as opposed to passive receipt, and (2) embedding of that choice in networks of social support (Cullen, 1994) rather than choice by isolated individuals. We suspect that the reason for active rehabilitation being superior to passive rehabilitation goes beyond the documented effects of commitment and social support. We also suspect that communities of care empowered with good professional advice will actually make technically superior choices from among a smorgasbord of rehabilitative options, because of the richer contextual knowledge they have of the case (Bazemore, 1999; Bazemore and Dooley, this volume). This is particularly plausible in a world in which, for example, psychotherapy often seems to work but in which there is no consistent evidence showing that one school of psychotherapy works better than another. The hope is that contextually informed community-of-care choices (assisted by professional choice brokers) will be better on average than individual or state choices (Braithwaite, 1998).

Active and Passive Incapacitation

In Braithwaite and Daly's (1994) family violence enforcement pyramid, most of the options for escalation are in fact more incapacitative than deterrent. They include options like "a relative or other supporter of the woman moving into the household," "the man moving to a friend's household," and imprisonment. Once we move beyond a passive conception of incapacitation, which is statically linked to confinement in state prisons, we can see that *capacitation of victims* can be theoretically equivalent to *incapacitation of offenders*. Hence, in a family violence enforcement pyramid, giving a victim the capacity to leave by putting a bank account or funding for alternative accommodation at her disposal (victim capacitation) can be functionally equivalent to removing the offender from the home (offender incapacitation).

Court-ordered incapacitation is notoriously less effective than it would seem. Violent men continue to perpetrate assault and rape in prison. Drug dealers continue to entice vulnerable young people.

Judges incapacitate drunk drivers by canceling their licenses only to find that a majority of them continue to drive (Barnes, 1999).

By contrast, the active intervention of communities of care evokes alternative modalities of incapacitation. If the problem is that it is only on Friday and Saturday nights that the offender gets out on the town, Uncle Harry can take responsibility for holding the keys to the car on Friday and Saturday nights and ensuring that the car stays in the garage. Alternatively, the girlfriend can volunteer to call a taxi every time. Or the drinking mates can sign a designated driver agreement at the conference. Or the owner of the pub or club where the offender drinks can agree to train the staff to intervene so that someone else in the bar drives the offender home. We have seen all these forms of active incapacitation negotiated at restorative drunk driving conferences. All of them require cultivation of the virtue of active responsibility. We never see them in drunk driving court cases, which last an average of seven minutes in Canberra, compared with 90 minutes for conferences (Barnes, 1999).

Active Crime Prevention, Active Grace

Braithwaite (1998, 1999) has argued that crime prevention programs mostly fail for four reasons: (1) lack of motivation, (2) lack of resources, (3) insufficiently plural deliberation, and (4) lack of follow through. He argued that making restorative justice conferences a site of crime prevention deliberation in the community can help remedy those four reasons for the failure of crime prevention programs. Motivation, resources, and follow-through on crime prevention have more momentum when coupled to the mainstream processing of criminal cases than when ghettoized into specialized crime prevention units. We will not reiterate the four sets of arguments here, but one way of summarizing them is that they are concerned with the way restorative justice deliberation nurtures the virtue of active responsibility. Active responsibility does not come naturally in response to a plea to attend a Neighborhood Watch meeting. It comes more naturally in reply to a plea from a neighbor who has been a victim of crime to support them in a conference/circle. Similarly, an occupational health and safety poster in the workplace proclaiming "Reporting (accidents) is everyone's responsibility" does not foster a sense of active responsibility in the way that conferences held to discuss specific workplace injuries do.

Serious crime is an opportunity to confront evil with a grace that transforms human lives to paths of love and care. Desmond Tutu would want us to evaluate his Truth and Reconciliation Commission less in terms of how it prevents crimes of violence and more in terms of how its healing lays the foundation of a more humane South Africa.

While we can never expect restorative justice institutions to be the most important institutions of community building, they can play their part in the nurturing of active responsibility that is the indispensable ingredient of community development.

If we believe that reintegrative shaming is what is required to deal with the wrongdoing of a Winnie Madikizela-Mandela and a P.W. Botha alike,[7] no one is required to take active responsibility for saying "shame on you" for the killings and the racism under an evil regime. The testimony of the victims and the apologies (when they occur, as they often enough do) are sufficient to accomplish the necessary shaming of the evil of violence. However, there can never be enough citizens active in the reintegration part of reintegrative shaming. If is true that reintegrative shaming prevents crime, and if it is true that it is the reintegration part that is always in short supply, then the particular, if limited, kind of integration into communities of care that is transacted in restorative justice rituals has a special humanitarian significance.

Toward a Jurisprudence of Active Responsibility

So far, we have conceived of active responsibility as the essential element for securing restoration. At the same time, we have argued that without passive responsibility there is risk of injustice. For example, a minimum requirement for punishing an offender for doing wrong would be an inquiry to demonstrate causal responsibility for the wrong.

Now we will complicate this picture by arguing that while passive responsibility remains indispensable to justice in this way, restorative justice propels us to develop a more just notion of criminal liability, on which passive responsibility depends. That is, the emphasis on active responsibility is not only a matter of the jurisprudence of restoration but also of the normative theory of justice.

We turn to Brent Fisse's (1983) theory of reactive fault (further developed in Fisse and Braithwaite, 1993) for key insights here. All criminal justice systems incorporate notions of causal fault and reactive fault. Causal fault is about being causally responsible, while reactive fault is about how responsibly one reacts after the harm is done. The balance between the two varies enormously from system to system. Western criminal justice systems (such as that of the United States) are at the causal end of the continuum; Asian systems (such as that of Japan) tend to be at the reactive end. Yet, even in the West, reactive fault sometimes dominates causal fault, as evidenced in our intuition that with hit-and-run driving, the running is the greater evil than the hitting. Early guilty pleas in court and "remorse" also result in sentence reductions. In *Crime, Shame and Reintegration*, Braithwaite

(1989:165) told two stories to illustrate the extremes in the cultural balancing of causal and reactive fault, the first from Haley (1982:272), the second from Wagatsuma and Rosett (1986:486):

> The first is of two American servicemen accused of raping a Japanese woman. On Japanese legal advice, private reconciliation with the victim was secured; a letter from the victim was tabled in the court stating that she had been fully compensated and that she absolved the Americans completely. After hearing the evidence, the judge leaned forward and asked the soldiers if they had anything to say. "We are not guilty, your honor," they replied. Their Japanese lawyer cringed; it had not even occurred to him that they might not adopt the repentant role. They were sentenced to the maximum term of imprisonment, not suspended.

> The second story is of a Japanese woman arriving in the U.S. with a large amount of American currency which she had not accurately declared on the entry form. It was not the sort of case that would normally be prosecuted. The law is intended to catch the importation of cash which is the proceeds of illicit activities, and there was no suggestion of this. Second, there was doubt that the woman had understood the form which required the currency declaration. After the woman left the airport, she wrote to the Customs Service acknowledging her violation of the law, raising none of the excuses or explanations available to her, apologizing profusely, and seeking forgiveness. In a case that would not normally merit prosecution, the prosecution went forward *because* she has confessed and apologized; the U.S. Justice Department felt it was obliged to proceed in the face of a bald admission of guilt. (emphasis in original)

These are stories about how the United States justice system creates disincentives for reactive fault, while the Japanese justice system requires it. Fisse (1983) advocates "reactive fault" as the core criterion of criminal fault. In its most radical version, this would mean in a case of assault, the alleged assailant would go into a restorative justice conference not on the basis of an admission of criminal guilt but on the basis of admitting responsibility for the *actus reus* of an assault ("I was the one who punched her").[8] Whether the mental element required for crime was present would be decided reactively, on the basis of the constructiveness and restorativeness of his or her reaction to the problem caused by the act (Braithwaite, 1998). If the reaction were restorative, the risk of criminal liability would be removed; only civil liability would remain. However, if reactive criminal fault were found by a court to be present,[9] that would be insufficient for a conviction; the mental element for the crime would also have to be demonstrated before or during its commission.[10] However, reactive fault would be a more important determinant of penalty than causal fault.

This gives us an answer to the retributivist who says: "Where is the justice with two offenders who commit exactly the same offense: one apologizes and heals a victim who grants him mercy; the other refuses to participate in a circle and is punished severely by a court." The answer is that while the two offenders are equal in causal fault, they are quite unequal in reactive fault. Viewed in terms of passive responsibility, they might be equal; in terms of active responsibility, though, they are not.[11]

The Major Worry about Active Responsibility

In restorative justice conferences, sometimes victims say they are responsible for their own victimization or others blame them for it. This is not a worry when victims blame themselves for leaving open the window through which the burglar entered; indeed, it can be a good thing if it motivates victims to invest in target hardening to protect them from a repeat victimization.[12] Similarly, a victim of a schoolyard fight may reflect on the provocation of the offender that led to the assault. It is a different matter, though, if a girl who is a victim of sexual assault is blamed for wearing a short skirt. What is the difference? It is that this type of victim-blaming is connected to a history of subordination of young women, and the denial of their freedom, which has been much exacerbated by victim-blaming.

Restorative justice implies a grave risk of the occurrence of oppressive victim-blaming. The hope is that when it occurs, participants in the circle will speak up in defense and support of the victim—that there will be reintegrative shaming of victim-blaming. The fact that we cannot guarantee that this will occur is deeply troubling.

Defenders of formal legal processes might further protest that criminal trials do incorporate formal guarantees against victim-blaming. Most of these, however, come into play at the level of proving that sexual assault occurred—guarantees not relevant to normal restorative justice processes that are not concerned with the adjudication of guilt. In any case, it is hard to argue that victim-vilification does not occur in criminal trials.[13] As Hogg and Brown put it, "Police, lawyers and judges have often been derisory in their treatment of complainants who have acted in . . . 'sexually provocative' ways" (1998:65). Indeed, restorative justice advocates argue that the problem with the criminal trial is that it creates incentives for the prosecution to vilify defence witnesses, and vice versa. This is what puts the vulnerable most at risk of stigmatization. The problems that formal legal guarantees against victim-blaming seek to redress are in part problems created by the formal adversarial process.

In terms of the impact of victim-blaming on traditional adversarial justice, we should not confine our examination to trials and sentencing. Ngaire Naffine suggests that in light of the statistics on the extent of unreported rapes, rapes without active resistance (and we would suggest, rapes involving other types of victim-blaming) are "much less likely to find their way into a court of law . . . (and) are more likely to be filtered out of the criminal justice system" (Naffine, 1992:761). Hence, it is clear that victim-blaming is a problem at every level.

What can be said in favor of restorative justice is that while the criminal trial assembles in one room those capable of inflicting maximum damage on the other side, the restorative justice conference assembles in the room those capable of offering maximum support to their own side—be it the victim or the offender side. It is in this structural difference, and in the ethic of care and active responsibility that it engenders, that restorative justice places its hope against victim vilification.

It will be a hope that will continue to be disappointed from time to time, we fear. There are few higher priorities for research and development than to improve the micro-design of conferences/circles. Videos shown to participants before they go into their first conference could not only show how conferences work and how participants can be actively responsible citizens within them, but perhaps they could also warn against victim-blaming and urge a responsibility to speak out against victim-blaming should it occur. Training for convenors should also address this risk. For both court and conference processes, research should be able to test a variety of innovations in order to discover which procedures best protect victims from stigmatization.

Restorative Justice—Beyond Responsibilization

In its traditional criminological forms, utilitarianism tended to objectify and infantilize offenders. In contrast, many writers see newer crime prevention and community policing as involving a new form of subjectification and responsibilization (Crawford, 1997; Garland, 1997; O'Malley, 1992). Garland, for example, identifies a new mode of governing crime, which he characterizes as a "responsibilization strategy": "This involves the central government seeking to act upon crime not in a direct fashion through state agencies (police, courts, prisons, social work, etc.) but instead by acting indirectly, seeking to activate action on the part of non-state agencies and organizations" (Garland, 1996:452). Garland says that this is a response to the predicament that "having taken over control functions and responsibilites which once belonged to the institutions of civil society, the state is now faced with its own inability to deliver the expected levels of control over criminal conduct"(Garland, 1996:449). The recurring message of this approach, as Garland puts it, "is that the state alone is not, and cannot effectively be, responsible for preventing and controlling crime" (Garland, 1996). Clearly, it is possible to read our account of restorative justice in this frame.

There are some distinctions that must be drawn, however. Responsibilization strategies vary in their approaches to achieving responsibility. Foucault's work is the theoretical influence underlying the responsibilization literature. Subjects are "taught to become 'responsible'" (Garland, 1997:191) by "techniques of the self" for cultivating a security-conscious *homo prudens*. This Foucauldian interpretation is contrasted with one in which individuals are assumed to be "'naturally' capable" of responsible action (Garland, 1997:191). Our conception of restorative responsibility is closer to the end of the continuum that assumes a natural capability for responsibility. At least we assume that the simple process of human beings talking through the consequences that have been suffered as a result of wrongdoing is all that is needed to elicit spontaneous proffering of active responsibility. At the same time, though, however natural and unforced the dialogue within it, we must concede that the creation of the institution of a restorative justice conference is itself a regulatory move designed to cultivate this "natural capability" for responsibility.

There are many unattractive features of responsibilization trends from which restorative justice must keep its distance. We see the worst manifestation of responsibilization in laws that hold parents legally liable for the delinquencies of their children. The normative theory of restorative justice should make it clear that only individual actors who are passively responsible (causally responsible) for crime should be held legally or morally responsible for it. Active responsibility of all kinds, including offers of help and support, forgiveness, care, compassion, love, and participation—all the things on which restorative justice most depends for success, should be conceived as gifts rather than moral duties, and certainly not as legal duties. They are supererogatory,[14] to put the claim formally. The legal system rightly recognizes parents as having duties of care to their children. In the context of a restorative justice conference for a criminal offense, though, a decision by parents to refuse to attend (or do anything the conference asks) should not be viewed as a breach of any duty.[15] No one, including the offender, has a duty even to attend.[16]

Restorative justice works because people are prepared to assume an active responsibility (particularly when they have a personal involvement) beyond any allocated passive legal or moral responsibility. Active responsibility often involves an assumed collective responsibility that can provide restoration and crime prevention in ways that courts restricted to allocating passive responsibility (enforced responsibility) cannot. A more structural worry about responsibilization is that it pass-es gender-related burdens of care down to individuals. This worry is that what is going on is a move by the state to slough off some of its social welfare obligations. A comparable concern arises with using restorative justice to deal with regulatory offenses; it may be part of a state's strategy to walk away from its obligations to regulate in areas such as environment (where it has clear responsibilities) by del-egating them to civil society.

Christine Parker's (1999) work is a useful corrective here (see also Braithwaite and Parker, 1999). Parker sees a need for two-way com-munication. She wants institutions in which the justice of the law fil-ters down into the justice of the people as manifest in restorative jus-tice processes (so that, for example, respect for fundamental human rights constrains informal justice). Obversely, Parker wants a restora-tive justice that gives the justice of the people an opportunity to per-colate up to influence the justice of the law. In terms of active and pas-sive responsibility, we want the active responsibility to have an influence on the passive responsibility. The same theme is apparent in recent writings of Clifford Shearing (1995) and Jurgen Habermas (1996) on how the state can open itself up to "the input of free-float-ing issues, contributions, information, and arguments circulating in a civil society set apart from the state" (Habermas, 1996:183-184). According to Habermas (1996:442), the theory is clear:

> [T]he public sphere is not conceived simply as the back room of the parliamentary complex, but as the impulse-generating periphery that *surrounds* the political center: in cultivating normative reasons, it affects all parts of the political system without intending to conquer it. Passing through the channels of general elections and various forms of participation, pub-lic opinions are converted into a communicative power that authorizes the legislature and legitimates regulatory agencies, while a publicly mobilized critique of judicial decisions imposes more-intense justificatory obligations on a judicia-ry engaged in further developing the law.

The theory sounds fine, but it all seems rather romantic to imagine the day-to-day work of conferences bubbling up to influence the law. Cumulatively and potentially, though, this is not necessarily romantic. In communities in which conferencing is widespread, justice dilemmas that arise in conferences are discussed in civil society (at dinner par-ties, for example, including those attended by judges.)[17]

We can already cite specific conferences in New Zealand that have had an impact, albeit small, on the law. In the Clotworthy case, the deci-sion of a conference for community service and victim compensation to fund cosmetic surgery needed as a result of a vicious knife attack was overruled by the Court of Appeal.[18] To the disappointment of restorative justice advocates, the Court of Appeal ordered a custodial sentence. However, the sentence was reduced in response to the wishes of the victim as articulated in the conference. Moreover, the Court did recognize the principle that the demands of restorative justice can affect sentences in very serious cases. Put another way, conferencing is in a position not dissimilar to the routine processing of cases in the lowest courts. Although what happens in the lowest courts might be the bulk of the law in action (and therefore "is" the law), rarely does it have any impact on the law in the books, or formal law. In rare strategic cases, though, the Magistrates "bubble up" the Clotworthy case.

One can imagine how restorative justice processes might achieve this task in a variety of contexts. A conference for schoolgirls caught smoking marijuana could communicate to school principals that passive responsibility such as expulsion is excessive and inappropriate. Conferences can and do also "bubble up" community disapproval of certain investigative techniques by the police, which tend to be suppressed in court. This capacity can be reinforced by making an inquiry of how fairly participants have been treated by the police in this formal part of the restorative justice process. Where there is a concern, the police, as a signatory of the conference agreement, can commit to report back to the participants about the results of an internal or ombudsman investigation of their conduct.

Fisse and Braithwaite (1993:232-237) have documented how a series of conferences exposed the victimization of Australian Aboriginal people in remote communities through fraudulent practices by major insurance companies. One of the decisions of the meetings between offending companies, regulators, victims, and Aboriginal Community Councils was to call a press conference. The abuses exposed were so systemic and shocking that the Prime Minister asked to be briefed by the regulatory agency. Significant change to regulatory law and practice ensued.

While it would be overly optimistic to hope that conferences would often be the transmission vehicle to percolate the justice of the people into the justice of the law, such cases show this is a possibility that can be realized. The Aboriginal insurance cases show that just as restorative justice can serve to responsibilize individuals in a way that relieves the state of burdens, so is it possible for powerless individuals to use restorative justice to responsibilize the state when the state is failing in its regulatory or welfare obligations.

Restorative justice is empowering in that it takes a ball away from the feet of a judge and puts it at the feet of a group of citizens. The type of responsibilizing that then goes on depends on how those citizens decide to exercise their political imagination in the use of that little piece of power. To use a soccer analogy, many will kick their own goals by taking responsibility for awesome burdens of care for which the state should be giving them more help. Others will learn from the example of those Aboriginal Community Councils from far North Queensland and kick the goals of state responsibilization.

Conclusion

A neglected part of the restorative justice research agenda has been the development of a restorative conception of responsibility—the kind of responsibility that will maximise restoration of victims, offenders, and communities. We have seen that restorative responsibility will be very different from traditional conceptions of criminal responsibility. It will involve a balance between passive and active responsibility with a substantial shift toward the latter.

We have seen that restorative responsibility has:

1. An important political rationale;

2. A strong philosophical foundation in responsibility for action and responsibility as a virtue;

3. A promising jurisprudential future through development of Fisse's notion of reactive fault; and

4. Practical promise in its links to theories of crime prevention.

At the same time, there remain unsolved worries about responsibilization, such as the risks of blaming victims of sexual assault and foisting unreasonable expectations on single parents who already are expected to do too much with too little support.

Discussion Questions

1. Why is responsibility an important concept in restorative community justice? How does this model conceive of responsibilty differently than traditional justice models?

2. Distinguish between passive responsibility and active responsibility. How does restorative community justice engage active responsibility? Can you identify occasions when restorative justice might not do this?

3. How could the restorative community justice concept of responsibility change the focus of deterrence, incapacitation, and rehabilitation?

4. What is active deterrence? Compare and contrast active incapacitation and passive incapacitation.

Endnotes

[1]   The recent Canadian Supreme Court decision *R v. Glaude* (1999) provides an example of such a comparison: "Central to the (restorative justice) process is the need for offenders to *take* responsibility for their actions. By comparison, incarceration obviates the need to *accept* responsibility" (emphasis added) (at 72)

[2]   Some readers might question whether an approach that aims to prevent future events can be characterised as passive responsibility. After all, active responsibility is about the prevention of unwanted events. But it is our contention that one can seek to avoid future events using passive responsibility or active responsibility. At the heart of the difference between the active and passive forms of these theories is the distinction between people taking responsibility (the active form) and risking being held accountable (the passive form).

[3]   The normative force of Pranis's assertion arises in our view from the normative claim that respectfulness (Braithwaite, 1989) ranks beside non-domination (Braithwaite and Pettit, 1990; Pettit, 1997) and empowerment (Braithwaite, 1999b) as central restorative values.

[4]   Some critics might argue that punitiveness on one hand, and active responsibility and restorative justice on the other, are not mutually exclusive: that is, if active responsibility is the taking of responsibility to restore harm, and a punitive outcome is what is required to restore some victims' harm (by satisfying their desire to punish), then punitive outcomes can involve active responsibility. However we would say if a punitive outcome is imposed on an offender without their consent it in no way involves active responsibility. If an offender does seek or actively consent to a punitive outcome, then it may involve active responsibility, but we would nevertheless seek to impose limits on such outcomes.

[5]   For instance, the International Covenant on Civil and Political Rights prohibits inhuman or degrading treatment or punishment (Article 7).

6   For example, under the legislation governing one conferencing scheme in Australia, the outcome must "not (be) more severe than those that might have been imposed in court proceedings for the offence" (Section 52(6)(a) Young Offenders Act 1997 (NSW)).

7   The allegations against Winnie Madikizela-Mandela included the murder of a child in her pursuit of political objectives on behalf of the African National Congress. P.W. Botha was the South African head of state during a period when his Cabinet is alleged to have authorized murder and other atrocities against those opposed to Apartheid.

8   Functionally, New Zealand law already accomplishes this result by putting cases into family group conferences not on the basis of an admission of criminal guilt, but on the basis of formally "declining to deny" criminal allegations.

9   An example of this would be if a report from a conference said that the offender simply cursed the victim and refused to discuss restitution.

10 Brent Fisse takes the more radical view that if criminal liability is about punishing conduct known to be harmful and if failure to respond responsibly is harmful, then such reactive fault can be sufficient to establish criminal liability.

11 This is not the whole answer, however. The other part of it is that the just deserts theorist is seen as morally wrong to consider equal justice for offenders a higher value than equal justice for victims (Braithwaite, 1999).

12 Having just been a victim of burglary is the single biggest predictor of burglary victimisation (Pease)

13 In Victoria, Australia, a man who raped a woman received a sentence that took into account that the woman's experience as a prostitute meant it was reasonable to assume that she suffered less psychological harm than would have been suffered by other victims of sexual assaults [*Hakopian*, 1991, unreported, Victorian County Court (see Cass 1992 for case summary and comment)].

14 See Mellema, 1991; Heyd, 1982.

15 Of course, this would not be the position with care and protection as opposed to a criminal justice conference, where the legal subject of the conference is whether parents are meeting their legal duty to care for and protect their child.

16 The only duty here rests with the police and prosecutor, who have a duty to take sufficiently serious cases to court when the opportunity for voluntary acts of responsibility in a restorative framework are spurned.

17 Indeed judges will attend conferences during their lifetimes as supporters of victims or of their own children who get into trouble as offenders.

18 *The Queen v. Clotworthy* (CA 114/98, 29 June 1998, NZ Court of Appeal) allowing appeal from sentence of District Court Judge Thorburn, 24 April 1998

References

Ayres, I., and J. Braithwaite (1992). *Responsive Regulation: Transcending the Deregulation Debate*. Oxford, England: Oxford University Press.

Barnes, G. (1999). "Procedural Justice in Two Contexts: Testing the Fairness of Diversionary Conferencing for Intoxicated Drivers." Ph.D. dissertation, University of Maryland.

Bazemore, G. (1999). "After Shaming, Whither Reintegration: Restorative Justice and Relational Rehabilitation." In *Restorative Juvenile Justice: Repairing the Harm of Youth Crime*, edited by G. Bazemore and L. Walgrave. Monsey, NY: Criminal Justice Press.

Bazemore, G., and M. Dooley (2000). "Restorative Justice and The Offender: The Challenge of Reintegration," this volume.

Bovens, M. (1998). *The Quest for Responsibility*. Cambridge, England: Cambridge University Press.

Braithwaite, J. (1989). *Crime, Shame and Reintegration*. Cambridge, England: Cambridge University Press.

Braithwaite, J. (1997a). "On Speaking Softly and Carrying Sticks: Neglected Dimensions of Republican Separation of Powers." *University of Toronto Law Journal* 47:1-57.

Braithwaite, J. (1998). "Linking Crime Prevention to Restorative Justice." In *Conferencing: A New Response to Wrongdoing*. Proceedings of the First North American Conference on Conferencing, August 6-8, Minneapolis.

Braithwaite, J. (1999). "Restorative Justice; Assessing Optimistic and Pessimistic Accounts." In Michael Tonry (ed.) *Crime and Justice: A Review of Research.*

Braithwaite, J., and K. Daly (1994). "Masculinities, Violence and Communitarian Control." In *Just Boys Doing Business*, edited by T. Newburn, and E. Stanko. London and New York: Routledge.

Braithwaite, J., and C. Parker (1999). "Restorative Justice is Republican Justice." In *Restoring Juvenile Justice: Repairing the Harm of Youth Crime*, edited by Gordon Bazemore and Lode Walgrave. Monsey, NY: Criminal Justice Press.

Braithwaite, J., and P. Pettit (1990). *Not Just Deserts: A Republican Theory of Criminal Justice*. Oxford, England: Oxford University Press.

Burford, G., and J. Pennell (1996). "Family Group Decision Making: New Roles for 'Old' Partners in Resolving Family Violence." *Implementation Report Summary*. St. Johns, Newfoundland: Family Group Decision Making Project.

Cass, D. (1992). "Case and Comment: Hakopian." *Criminal Law Journal* 16:200-204.

Crawford, A. (1997). *The Local Governance of Crime: Appeals to Community and Partnerships*. Oxford, England: Clarendon Press.

Cullen, F.T. (1994). "Social Support as an Organizing Concept for Criminology: Presidential Address to the Academy of Criminal Justice Sciences." *Justice Quarterly* 11(4):527-559.

Daly, K. (2000) "Revisiting the Relationship Between Retributive and Restorative Justice." In *Restorative Justice: Philosophy to Practice*, edited by H. Strang and J. Braithwaite, 33-54. Aldershot, England: Dartmouth.

Eckel, M.D. (1997). "A Buddhist Approach to Repentance." In *Repentance: A Comparative Perspective*, edited by A. Etzioni and D.E. Carney. New York: Rowman and Littlefield.

Feeley, M. (1979). *The Process is the Punishment*. New York: Russell Sage.

Fisse, B. (1983). "Reconstructing Corporate Criminal Law: Deterrence, Retribution, Fault, and Sanctions." *Southern California Law Review* 56:1141-1246.

Fisse, B., and J. Braithwaite (1993). *Corporations, Crime and Accountability*. Cambridge, England: Cambridge University Press.

Garland, D. (1996). "The Limits of the Sovereign State: Strategies of Crime Control in Contemporary Society." *The British Journal of Criminology* 36(4):445-471.

Garland, D. (1997). "'Governmentality' and the Problem of Crime: Foucault, Criminology, Sociology." *Theoretical Criminology* 1:173-214.

Habermas, J. (1996). *Between Facts and Norms: Contributions to a Discourse Theory of Law and Democracy*. London: Polity Press.

Heimer, C. (1999). "Legislating Responsibility," unpublished manuscript.

Heimer, C., and L. Staffen (1998). *For the Sake of the Children: The Social Organization of Responsibility in the Hospital and the Home*. Chicago: The University of Chicago Press.

Heyd, D. (1982). *Supererogation: Its Status in Ethical Theory*. Cambridge, England: Cambridge University Press.

Hogg, R., and D. Brown (1998). *Rethinking Law and Order*. Sydney: Pluto Press.

Keohane, R. (1984). *After Hegemony: Cooperation and Discord in World Politics*. Princeton, NJ: Princeton University Press.

Lewis, D. (1986). "Causation" and "Postscript: Redundant Causation." In *Philosophical Papers*, Vol. II. Oxford, England: Oxford University Press.

Makkai, T., and J. Braithwaite (1994a). "Reintegrative Shaming and Regulatory Compliance." *Criminology* 32(3):361-385.

Maxwell, G.M., and A. Morris (1993). *Family, Victims and Culture: Youth Justice in New Zealand*. Social Policy Agency and Institute of Criminology, Victoria University of Wellington, New Zealand.

Mellema, G. (1991). *Beyond the Call of Duty: Supererogation, Obligation and Offence*. Albany: State University of New York Press.

Melton, A.P. (1995). "Indigenous Justice Systems and Tribal Society." *Judicature* 79:126-133.

Mulgan, R. (1997). "The Processes of Public Accountability." *Australian Journal of Public Administrion* 56(1):25.

Naffine, N. (1992). "Windows on the Legal Mind: The Evocation of Rape in Legal Writings." 18 *MULR* 741.

Olweus, D. (1993). "Annotation: Bullying at School: Basic Facts and Effects of a School Based Intervention Program." *Journal of Child Psychology and Psychiatry* 35:1171-1190.

O'Malley, P. (1992). "Risk, Power and Crime Prevention." *Economy and Society* 21:252-275.

O'Malley, P. (1994). "Responsibility and Crime Prevention: A Response to Adam Sutton." *The Australian and New Zealand Journal of Criminology* 27:21-24.

Parker, C. (1999b). *Just Lawyers*. Oxford, England: Oxford University Press.

Pease, K. (1998). "Repeat Victimization: Taking Stock." Crime Detection and Prevention Series, Paper 90. Police Research Group, London.

Pettit, P. (1997). *Republicanism*. Oxford, England: Clarendon Press.

Pranis, K. (1998). "Conferencing and the Community." In *Conferencing: A New Response to Wrongdoing*. Proceedings of the First North American Conference on Conferencing. August 6-8, Minneapolis.

Shearing, C. (1995). "Reinventing Policing: Policing as Governance." In *Privatisierung staatlicher Kontrolle: Befunde, Konzepte, Tendenzen. Interdisziplinare Studien zu Recht und Staat* 3:69-88.

Thomas, P. (1998). "The Changing Nature of Accountability." In *Taking Stock: Assessing Public Sector Reforms*, edited by G. Peters and D. Savoie. Montreal: McGill-Queen's University Press

Part III
The Context of Restorative Community Justice: Stakeholder and Organizational Roles

4

Restorative Justice for Crime Victims: The Promise and the Challenge

MARY ACHILLES
HOWARD ZEHR

Introduction

Rarely does the Western process of justice deliver good news for crime victims. A leading specialist on trauma, Judith Lewis Herman, has stated it plainly: "If one set out to design a system for provoking intrusive post-traumatic symptoms, one could not do better than a court of law" (Herman, 1992:72).

Over the past three decades, a variety of reform strategies have sought to improve the lot of victims within the criminal justice system. These have included increased victim services, self-help groups, and legally defined rights. Yet, for the majority of victims, the pursuit of justice remains an unsavory and unsatisfactory experience.

Perhaps the boldest initiative addressing the role of the victim in justice within the modern era is the movement often called *restorative justice*. Arguing that the definition of justice underlying the Western legal system is itself flawed, restorative justice seeks to refocus the conception of and approach to justice to one in which harm to victims is central to the definition of—and response to—crime. This centrality of harm implies that victims should have a central role in justice and that offender accountability should be defined in terms of these harms and the resulting obligations to victims. But can restorative justice deliver on this promise to victims? Is it likely to do so? What are the possibilities and challenges?

In the following chapter, we outline briefly some key needs of many crime victims, suggest ways that the emerging paradigm of restorative justice might address these needs, examine some of the dangers for victims, and make suggestions about what might be needed if restorative justice is to live up to its promise to victims.

What do Victims Need from Justice?

The sudden, random, and often violent nature of crime affects not only victims but their families, friends, and communities. It pushes victims out of their normal sense of order. The suddenness and the violence eludes normal coping mechanisms and may leave victims ill-equipped to process forthcoming events. Crime is often described in terms of three primary impacts: physical, financial, and emotional. Although crime can contain some, all, or any combination of these impacts, the most devastating—and often least attended to—is the emotional impact.

Marlene Young of the National Organization for Victim Assistance describes the array of emotions that plague victims in the aftermath of crime. These intense emotions can include anger, rage, fear, terror, frustration, confusion, guilt, self-blame, shame, humiliation, grief, and sorrow. Not all victims experience all of these emotions, but they are common themes in the natural human response to crime. Moreover, these emotions often leave victims feeling isolated and lonely (Young, 1993:3-5).

In short, the crisis of victimization is comprehensive and focused on a victim's identity, including his or her sense of self in relation to the world. This larger crisis can be categorized as three interrelated subcrises or traumas that force victims to confront three fundamental questions: (1) the crisis of self-image (who am I?), (2) a crisis of meaning (what do I believe?), and (3) a crisis of relationship (who can I trust?). The crisis of victimization is fundamental because it undermines three underlying assumptions upon which we build our sense of safety and wholeness: autonomy, order, and relatedness (Johnson, 1990:128-130).

A common experience for crime victims is the loss of their sense of autonomy. Victims are rendered powerless during the commission of the crime and often for long periods afterward. They may feel that their continued re-experience of the emotions and memories of the event is out of control for years. Such a loss of control is deeply dehumanizing and demoralizing. All of us need to feel that we control our own lives, so one of the most important intervention strategies is to assist victims in regaining some power and control over their lives.

Victimization leaves crime victims seeking a new sense of order and looking for rational reasons for the crime events. How and why did this happen? Was I responsible for this? Since we all seek order in our world, the absence of rational answers to such questions often leads victims into self-blame and doubt about their own responsibility for the event. Answers to these questions and the many others that surface can reduce the frustration and confusion that victims experience and can help to restore a new order in their lives.

Victimization leaves victims feeling isolated and alone. The uniqueness of their experience and the flood of emotions they experience separates them from those around them. Often those closest to them are not very helpful; as secondary victims, they often are trying to cope with their own needs. Thus, the primary victim tends to be alienated from those that he or she usually counts on most. Crime victims can become suspicious of strangers or even neighbors or others that remind them of the crime. They begin to question who they can trust. People need to be accepted by others and engage in healthy relationships. Relationships provide us with a mirror to ourselves; it is through interaction with others that we form and affirm our sense of identity. Crime victims are often forced to review and re-establish these primary relationships.

Crime is traumatic. The road of recovery and reconstruction may be long and circuitous, filled with pain and struggle; it is not a linear process. The journey requires victims to incorporate the event into the fabric of their being and to reconstruct a new order. It requires regaining a sense of identity, autonomy, and order, as well as the forging of new (and the reestablishment of old) relationships (Herman, 1992:51).

Given these experiences, there are many things that victims need from a justice process. While the community and the justice system cannot address all of their needs, they can have a profound impact on a victim's recovery. The justice system can and should provide an arena that contributes to a victim's sense of justice and healing.

Victims need and deserve a safe place in the immediate aftermath of crime. Safety—both physical and emotional—is crucial to recovery. Victims need long-term assurances that this will not happen again or at least that the system and the community are taking appropriate steps to minimize the possibility of reccurrence. They need a safe place to express a cataclysm of emotions without judgment or blame.

Victims need restitution. Restitution not only provides repayment by the offender for the damages incurred but it holds the offender accountable as the person responsible. Most importantly, it vindicates the victim. Vindication is important because it absolves the victim of responsibility and provides needed validation of the harm done.

Victims need answers to questions. They want to know what happened and why because answers restore an essential sense of order. They want answers that, to the extent possible, are real and not conjectured; they want answers that are as multi-layered as real life, not the simplistic, binary answers that emerge from the legal process. Some of these answers are interpretive and have to be discovered by the victims themselves (e.g. "Why did I react as I did? Why have I acted as I have since that time?") Others, however, are factual and most come from others (e.g., "What happened? Why did it happen? What is being done about it?").

Another area of need is what some call voice, truth-telling, or ventilation. Victims need to tell their story, a story will include not only the event but what has transpired in the immediate aftermath. Marlene Young describes it like this: "Victims need to tell their story over and over again. The repetitive process is a way of putting the pieces together and cognitively organizing the event so that it can be integrated into the survivor's life" (Young, 1993:17). This includes being able to tell their story to those that matter, including judges and sometimes the offender.

Finally, victims need to feel empowered. They need to recover the sense of autonomy and control that was taken away from them in the offense. Consequently, the justice process needs to be designed to re-empower victims. This means that the process should include as many opportunities for participation, voice, and choices for victims as possible.

Unfortunately, the criminal justice system does little to address the needs of victims. Despite landmark legislation and state constitutional amendments for victim rights, the role of the victim is still largely relegated to that of occasional participant or observer. Victims continue to have no legal standing, the absence of which relegates them to a lesser status; they are not viewed or treated as key stakeholders. Their experience in the criminal justice system often mirrors their status during the commission of the crime: that of involuntary participant. As a result, the criminal justice system does little for the victims' sense of justice. Their circumscribed roles are so confined that options and opportunities for healing are limited.

Crime represents a profound expression of disrespect for the victim as a person; it signifies a denial of the victim's personhood, a failure to value him or her as an individual. When the legal system ignores victims, the cycle of disrespect is again perpetuated.

What does Restorative Justice Offer Victims?

Restorative justice theory holds great promise for victims because it offers options that do not exist in the present system. The redefinition of crime as a violation that creates obligations provides much-needed recognition to crime victims by the community and by the justice system. As the individual harmed, he or she is considered a central stakeholder in a justice process. This stands in stark contrast to the present system, which sees the state as the entity offended and relegates the victim to the sidelines.

Elevating victims to the status of a key stakeholder provides them with validation of their worth as a member of the community—something that is often taken from them during the commission of the crime and rarely is restored by the present process of justice. The concept that violations create obligations identifies the victim as the person to whom the offender is first and foremost accountable and identifies the offender as the person accountable to their victim for the specific harm done.

Because it focuses on reparation of harm, restorative justice provides opportunities for greater and more meaningful participation by the victim in the identification of harms and needs, including what they believe they need from the offender, the community, and the system. By starting at the point of identification of harms, restorative justice emphasizes the importance of providing immediate, direct assistance to all victims in the aftermath of crime. This increases the likelihood of response to crime victims when there is no identified offender. Because the present system focuses primarily on the offender—what they did and what punishment they deserve—there is no opportunity for participation by victims when their assailant is not identified or apprehended.

A focus on identifying victim needs as the starting point of justice—and particularly what the victim needs from the community, the offender, and the system—is a significant and valuable change from the present system in which the processing of the offender takes precedence over the needs of victim recovery and reconstruction. Assisting victims in the identification of their needs is an essential beginning step in their journey to recovery and reconstruction.

Standard approaches to crisis and trauma intervention for victims emphasize reparation and prediction, ventilation and validation, safety and security (Young, 1993:13-24). Restorative justice theory parallels these standard crisis and trauma intervention theories. Identification of harms and corresponding needs (preparation and prediction), storytelling (ventilation) and recognition of the victim harm as a starting point for the justice process (validation), and safety and security—all of these fundamental elements of restorative justice reflect core elements of intervention services for crime victims. Restorative justice has potential to address the five victim needs articulated above: (1) a sense of safety, (2) answers to questions, (3) an opportunity to testify to their truth, (4) an opportunity to feel empowered, and (5) the possibility of restitution and, thus, vindication.

Restorative justice holds great potential to address a multitude of victim needs. The central promise that restorative justice makes to victims—that they will be stakeholders and that a key purpose of the process will be to address the harm done to them—is enticing to victims and victim advocates. There could be no greater elevation of

victims than to start the justice process from the point of the harm
caused and the question how to repair that harm. That victims would
no longer be on the sidelines but more centrally located on the playing field is in itself a far-reaching concept offering hope and comfort
to victims.

Will Restorative Justice Deliver on its Promise?

In spite of the promise of restorative justice, however, many victims,
victim advocates, and victim service providers remain ambivalent and
wary about restorative justice. While there is increasing dialogue
between victim groups and restorative justice advocates, for the most
part they remain in separate camps, with substantial misconceptions
about one another (Achilles and Amstutz, 1998:6-7).

Some concerns of victim groups grow out of a well-founded fear
of losing fragile and hard-won gains made by the victim movement in
the last several decades. Beyond that, however, serious concerns result
from the tendencies toward co-optation that inevitably occur when new
approaches are incorporated into old ones. Because restorative justice
approaches are for the most part operating within the traditional,
offender-oriented justice system, many are concerned that restorative
approaches will be distorted in such a way that victims will once
again be sidelined or misused. These dangers are magnified by the
naïveté of some restorative justice practitioners and by failures to
fully implement restorative values within this movement.

The history of justice reform in general has not been encouraging.
So-called reforms frequently (perhaps usually) have ended up being
reshaped to meet the needs of the "old" system and its practitioners
(Feeley, 1983; Rothman, 1980). Efforts to empower stakeholders have
often been taken over by professionals; witness, for instance, the
prominence of lawyers in parts of the mediation movement. Offender-oriented alternatives to incarceration at best have served as sup-
plements to prison and, at worst, as new ways to control and punish
offenders outside prisons. The same subversion of goals can be seen in
many victim-oriented reforms. Victim assistance programs, for example, all too often have been used as tools to strengthen prosecution
efforts rather than to empower and aid victims fundamentally.

The punitive focus of the criminal justice system, often critiqued
by restorative justice advocates, masks a reality that has important
implications for any effort to reshape the justice system: criminal justice is fundamentally designed to respond to offenders. Once a criminal event moves beyond investigation to arrest and prosecution, cases
are defined and processed around offender identities and issues. The
stated goal or rationale of the justice system has alternated between

helping, rehabilitating, and punishing offenders, but the motivating question of justice has remained the same: what does the offender deserve? Added to this is the offender-oriented backgrounds, job descriptions, and orientations of most justice (including restorative justice) practitioners as well as the general lack of knowledge of victim perspectives among justice practitioners. The result is a powerful impetus to ignore or misuse victims when restorative justice programs operate alongside or within that milieu.

Consequently, a significant pressure for restorative justice programs is to become primarily a diversionary program for offenders, even while claiming to service both victims and offenders. Vermont's Reparative Probation Program may be a case in point. After a public opinion survey and an extensive rethinking of the concept of probation, the Vermont Department of Corrections has developed a "reparative probation" track based on an explicitly restorative justice philosophy. In cases referred to this program, panels of community volunteers are to work with victims and offenders to determine appropriate sentences that hold offenders accountable while meeting victim and community needs. However, anecdotal and preliminary evidence suggests that so far victims have participated in a minority of cases, victim advocates do not play an intrinsic role in the process or the planning, and the guiding question often continues to revolve around what the offender deserves (compare Karp, 2000; Russell, 1999:95ff). Efforts are being made to address these deficiencies based on the standards implicit in the stated mission and values of the program. In the meantime, however, the model is being adopted elsewhere without the extensive attention to values and philosophy on which the Vermont model was based—and; thus, without the benchmarks of good practice implicit in a conscious restorative justice framework.

Another example of the way restorative justice practitioners have perpetuated this offender orientation may be seen in how these programs are advertised. One widely advertised restorative justice conference recently provided on its brochure an extensive list of potential audiences—but with no mention of victims or victim advocates. A restorative justice web site listed a series of suggested activities for those interested in applying restorative justice—again, with no mention of victim-related activities. Similarly, few restorative justice programs provide services to victims without an offender referral.

Not all of the dangers for victims can be attributed directly to the offender-oriented pressures of the justice system; restorative justice advocates and practitioners must accept responsibility for failing to take seriously the full implications of the philosophy and values they espouse and, in some cases, for naïvely attempting to apply restorative approaches in highly problematic areas (such as domestic violence) without adequate attention to complexities and safeguards.

At least four factors may contribute to the failures of restorative justice to live up to its promise:

1. As restorative justice has become more popular, it has often been viewed as a program or methodology rather than a philosophy with a set of underlying values and principles. As a concept, restorative justice places great emphasis on the roles and needs of victims and it address-es offender accountability first of all in terms of the harm done to victim. However, many programs have not adopted an explicit statement on values and philosophy. Without that framework and the benchmarks of good practice they imply, an offender orientation will almost certainly be perpetuated.

2. The focus on restorative justice as a methodology has been compounded by a tendency to assume that "one size fits all" rather than to have program shapes emerge out of community dialogues about values, philosophy, needs, and resources. Programs cannot be simply "plugged in" but need to reflect the community and community ownership, including that of the victim community.

3. Organizers of restorative justice programs have com-monly failed to include victim voices early on in the design and implementation of programs. A variety of reasons may be suggested; sometimes it may be naïve oversight, or a belief on the part of practitioners, or the assumption that they know what victims need and want. However, often it also reflects an unwillingness to engage in the difficult dialogue that is not only likely but essen-tial when victims and victim advocates are engaged. Without these voices at the table, it is unlikely that vic-tim interests and concerns will be addressed. Moreover, once the program is underway, it is unrealistic to assume that victim and victim advocates will join in with a full sense of ownership and engagement.

4. Restorative justice programs have failed to build in—and sometimes have even been hostile to—evaluation, espe-cially the kind that assesses practice and outputs against values, mission, and philosophy. Often this neglect is a result of financial concerns; evaluation can seem like a lux-ury when struggling to fund basic operations. However, this reluctance may also reflect fear of critique and/or skepticism about an activity that is seen as "academic" or abstract. Without evaluation against benchmarks of prin-ciples and values, however, programs may easily get off track, failing in practice to implement the philosophy they claim to espouse (and this is especially true for vic-tim issues).

A newly emerging area of concern in restorative justice has to do with the respective roles of victims and communities. In early conceptualizations of restorative justice, victims and offenders were seen as central "players," with communities having somewhat secondary supporting roles. Increasingly, however, restorative approaches such as circle processes are incorporating community members and are being advocated as new forms of community empowerment and participatory democracy. This is an important correction in restorative justice approaches, but it raises the old concern: Will community roles and concerns dominate over those of victims? Will practitioners assume that community and victim needs and roles are equivalent?

Restorative justice argues that crime has both a public and a private dimension but that these dimensions have been out of balance in the modern legal system. The public or community dimension has been predominant, but its place has been represented by the state; in practice, the community has been left out. Restorative justice seeks to bring a better balance by recognizing the private or interpersonal dimensions of crime while giving the community a genuine role. In doing so, however, it will need to ensure that it does not once again upset the balance in favor of the "public" dimension of crime.

What Can be Done?

An important safeguard against the subversion and co-optation of restorative justice is an ongoing emphasis on principles and values (Zehr, 1995:207-215). This will mean that as it moves from the visionary stages to the implementation stage, the movement as a whole will need to find ways to balance attention to practice with attention to principles. Education and training in the field must strike this balance, as must patterns of staffing and supervision. What is needed, in short, is an ongoing emphasis on what might be called value-based practice. Also essential are efforts to create a much fuller dialogue between victims and ex-offenders, victim advocates and service providers, offender advocates and service providers, and restorative justice advocates and practitioners.

To address the concern about victims specifically, we propose the following guidelines or signposts for restorative justice practice:[1]

We are working toward appropriate victim involvement in restorative justice programs when. . . .

>   1.   *. . . victims and victim advocates are represented on governing bodies and initial planning committees.*
>
>   If victims are central to the process of justice in restorative justice theory, then they and their advocates need to

be included in the early stages of program design. Their inclusion in the process of development highlights the programs' commitment to crime victims and the sensitivities that need to be addressed so as not to revictimize. Subtleties of program design that ensure safe and welcoming messages to injured crime victims can be offered by victims and their advocates. This important view can assist in enhancing the quality of a program and a sense of ownership in the program from the victims' perspective. It also sends a strong message of inclusion to the victim services community.

2.   *. . . efforts to involve victims grow out of a desire to assist them, not offenders. Victims are not responsible to rehabilitate or assist offender unless they choose to do so.*

The present system of justice is fundamentally a business designed for processing offenders. The concern for offenders is important, and it is appropriate for them to benefit by participation, but we must be careful never to use victims primarily as a way to benefit or otherwise deal with offenders. That should not be the reason for victim involvement in justice. (Conversely offenders should also never be used for the sole benefit of victims.) Similarly, victims should not be pressured to feel that rehabilitation of offenders is their responsibility. In reality, victims are often concerned to know that someone is taking responsibility for the rehabilitation and even the welfare of offenders, and some may choose to take on that concern themselves. However, it should not be presumed to be their responsibility.

3.   *. . . victims' safety is a fundamental element of program design.*

Whether working with crime victims in the immediate aftermath of an incident or years later, all interventions must first and foremost recognize victim's safety and security needs, both physical and emotional. The manner in which program services are delivered should reflect sensitivity to this and offer victims an opportunity to identify and articulate their personal safety needs. Victims must be free to express their natural human responses to the crime, including anger, rage, and need for vengeance without judgment and with understanding of their pain.

4. *. . . victims clearly understand their roles in the program, including potential benefits and risks to themselves and offenders.*

Victims must be prepared for program participation by providing them with as much information as possible on their role in the process, what to expect, and the known risks and benefits to themselves and to offenders. Victims should be informed of any benefits to the offender offered by the program and particularly what and if any benefits the offender will receive from the victim's participation. It is appropriate for the offender to benefit from the victim's participation, but efforts must be made to reduce, if not eliminate, any unwanted surprise outcomes for the victim.

5. *. . . confidentiality is provided within clear guidelines.*

A victim's right to privacy must always be protected: their experiences, including post-crime experiences, must be treated with sensitivity and respect because of the intense personal nature of the experience. Victims should choose when, what, and how information is disclosed about them and their experience. They should also be informed as to any rules and regulations regarding confidentiality under which the program operates.

6. *. . . victims have as much information as possible about their case, the offense, and the offender.*

To meet basic needs for information and to personalize the experience of justice for both victim and offender, restorative justice seeks to maximize the exchange of information between victim and offender, whether directly or indirectly. Victims may or may not choose to engage in face-to-face dialogue with the offender—or there may be other reasons why it is inappropriate or impractical—but victims usually have a variety of informational needs regarding the offender that can be addressed.

7. *. . . victims can identify and articulate their needs and are given choices.*

The opportunity to identify their own needs and make choices about how they are addressed can help to re-empower victims. Thus, opportunities for choices should be maximized; programs must be careful not to fall into a litany of rigid, scripted options. Certainly victims must be the gatekeepers regarding whether and when a direct encounter takes place.

8.   *. . . victims' opportunities for involvement are maximized.*

Because a core element of victim trauma is disempower-
ment, restorative justice programs should provide as
many opportunities as possible for victims to be involved
in their "case" as well as the program as a whole. There
should be as few limits on participation as possible.

9.   *. . . program design provides referrals for additional support and assistance.*

Crime victims may have additional needs that cannot be
met by the program. While they should not feel obligated to offer comprehensive services, programs ought to be
familiar with additional community services for victims
and routinely make those referrals. A strong working
relationship with other victim services in the community will make the transition for additional assistance for
the victims much smoother.

10. *. . . services are available to victims even when their
offenders have not been arrested or are unwilling or
unable to participate.*

If victims are central to the process of justice and their
needs are the starting point, then as a justice system we
cannot simply offer services only when offenders are
identified and or arrested; to the extent possible, we
must provide services and options for victims even when
the offender is not known. To do otherwise perpetuates
the offender-driven nature of the system.

Conclusion

We have argued that for restorative justice to live up to its claims,
it must remain grounded in principle and must not only listen to but
incorporate victims' voices. Beyond that, restorative justice advocates
and practitioners who do not come from victim-oriented backgrounds
will need to fine-tune their sensitivities to victim issues so that they can
share responsibility for monitoring the movement.

Victims and their spokespersons should not have to carry such a
burden alone, just as people of color should not have to carry the full
burden of monitoring and calling attention to the operation of race and
privilege in our society, nor should women be the only voices to speak
out on gender issues. Indeed, those with credentials gained from long
involvement with offender and restorative justice issues may need to
use their "social capital" to ensure that victims' perspectives and
needs retain their important place.

Restorative justice offers a hopeful vision of justice for victims, but good intentions and wonderful ideas are not enough. Substantial challenges must be met if this vision is to prove a reality rather than a mirage.

Discussion Questions

1. Why is extra effort needed to address the needs of crime victims in justice interventions? How and why have criminal justice systems failed to meet these needs in the past?

2. What are some potential dangers in the restorative justice approach from a victims' perspective? What might be some advantages?

3. How has the inflexibility of the "one size fits all" approach to intervention limited victim choice? Can restorative community justice overcome this? Should it?

Endnote

[1]   Also available as a bookmark from the Mennonite Central Committee: 21 South 12th St., P.O. Box 500, Akron, PA 17501-0500.

References

Achilles, M., and L.S. Amstutz (1998). "Working Together: Victim Services and Victim Offender Mediation Programs." *National Organization for Victim Assistance Newsletter* 18:5-6:6-7.

Feeley, M. (1983). *Court Reform on Trial: Why Simple Solutions Fail*. New York: Basic Books.

Herman, J.L. (1992). *Trauma and Recovery*. New York: Basic Books.

Johnson, R. (1990). *Death Work*. Pacific Grove, CA: Brooks/Cole.

Karp, D.R. (2000). "Harm and Repair: Observing Restorative Justice in Vermont." Unpublished paper.

Rothman, D.J. (1980). *Conscience and Convenience: The Asylum and Its Alternatives in Progressive America*. Boston: Little, Brown.

Russell, S.S. (1999). "Restorative Justice: An Innovative Criminal Justice Idea." Unpublished masters thesis. Norwich University.

Young, M. (1993) *Victim Assistance: Frontiers and Fundamentals*. Washington, DC: National Organization for Victim Assistance.

Zehr, H. (1995). "Justice Paradigm Shift? Values and Visions in the Reform Process." *Mediation Quarterly* 12:207-216.

5

Restorative Justice and the Offender: The Challenge of Reintegration

GORDON BAZEMORE
MICHAEL DOOLEY

The set of ideas known as restorative justice and community justice was not widely discussed as an alternative justice paradigm until the mid-1990s. It is therefore not surprising that these ideas have thus far been subjected to relatively little criticism. However, given the rapid spread of practice, policy, and implementation initiatives in the Western world in the past five years, many (including the editors of this volume) have now concluded that critical reflection is long overdue (Bazemore and Walgrave, 1999; Dooley, 1998).

Recent critical commentary, however, is somewhat disturbing, not because it raises issues that are difficult for this set of principles and practices but because the target of this criticism often seems to be something that scarcely resembles restorative justice. In recent writings, for example, restorative justice has been depicted as a kind of "lawless" process resembling a community tribunal without concern for due process or proportionality (Feld, 1999), "shaming ceremonies" akin to "Scared Straight" or similar confrontational approaches (Levrant et al., 1999), an extension of the victim's rights movement (Wilkinson, 1998); a decision-making process based on a "master-status" discourse that legitimizes the justice system and "marginalizes" young offenders (Arrigo and Schehr, 1998), and a new (less effective) treatment program model (Levrant et al., 1999).

Most puzzling has been criticism from some advocates of less punitive, humane approaches to the treatment of offenders (Arrigo and Schehr, 1998; Immarigeon, 1999; Levrant et al., 1999). Those assessments have been somewhat confusing to practitioners and policy-makers who have viewed treatment and restorative justice perspectives as at least compatible, if not mutually supportive (Crowe, 1998), and who imagined their proponents as probable allies in the fight against the rise of the "punitive paradigm" (Cullen and Wright, 1996; Walgrave and Bazemore, 1999). The most disturbing aspect of these critiques has been the suggestion that restorative justice is simply another way of "getting tough with offenders," and as such, is a component of an anti-progressive agenda (see especially, Arrigo and Schehr, 1998; Levrant et al., 1999), and from a very different perspective (Polk, 1994; compare Polk, this volume).

Of course, any intervention can be co-opted, and it is not difficult to find current examples of policy and practice in which terms like "community" and "restorative" are apparently being used to disguise business as usual, if not a clear expansion of crime control.[1] Describing interventions such as shaming and confrontation or "chain-gang" community service as part of a "get tough" movement, however, is very different from concluding that restorative justice has anything to do with such a movement. Moreover, doing so misrepresents restorative justice in the same way that presenting a weakly designed and poorly implemented counseling or cognitive restructuring program misrepresents effective treatment (e.g., Andrews et al., 1990).

The purpose of this chapter is to outline an explicitly *restorative* perspective on the offender. In addition, though restorative justice is not a treatment program, we explore implications of the restorative emphasis on the repair and rebuilding of social relationships for a more holistic approach to offender reintegration and rehabilitation. First, however, it is important to consider restorative perspectives on the offender in the light of other criminal justice philosophies and in the context of limitations inherent in currently dominant models of rehabilitative intervention.

Restorative Justice, Other Paradigms, and Perspectives on the Offender

To depict restorative justice advocates as anti-offender or supportive of the "get tough" movement is to ignore the bulk of published writings and certainly the classic works on this topic (e.g., Schneider, 1985; Zehr and Umbreit, 1982). This literature generally takes a pro-offender stand, and if anything, might lead critics to conclude that restorative justice advocates are overzealous in their opposition to retributive punishment (Walgrave and Bazemore, 1999). Moreover, much early restorative justice practice—for example, most victim-offender mediation (then referred to as victim-offender reconciliation) and most restitution in juvenile justice could be rightly accused by victim advocates as being highly offender-focused, and was indeed especially concerned with diverting offenders from more severe punishment—including incarceration (Schneider, 1985; Zehr, 1982). Today, restorative justice advocates are likely to present a portrait of victim and offender as equally powerless actors, both marginalized by the current retributive system (Wright, 1991). Discussions in the restorative justice literature of accountability to victims as a primary goal of intervention, the need for victim involvement, and an expansion of the menu of options directed at victim needs (Bazemore and Umbreit, 1995) have nothing to do with punishment in the retributive sense. Moreover, support for offender redemption and reintegration remains a primary theme in most restorative justice writing (Pranis and Bazemore, 2000; Van Ness and Strong, 1997).

Although much of the criticism of restorative justice that alleges a "get tough" focus seems oblivious to the literature, there are legitimate reasons for misunderstandings regarding the restorative justice outlook toward the offender. First, the temporal association between the rise of interest in restorative justice and that in "shaming" as an essentially retributive response—at least in the United States context—(Karp, 1998) has created some confusion. Shaming, in this sense, has no grounding in the restorative justice tradition. Although "reintegrative shaming" has been associated with a certain model of restorative justice conferencing (Braithwaite and Mugford, 1994), the strongest advocates of this model are clear about the lesser importance of shame in restorative sanctioning processes, relative to social support:

> The testimony of the victims and the apologies (when they occur, as they often do) are sufficient to accomplish the necessary shaming of the evil of violence. *But there can never be enough citizens active in the reintegration part* of reintegrative shaming (Braithwaite and Roche, this volume, emphasis ours).

Clearly, this statement is part of an intervention agenda that gives high priority to offender reintegration and support. Yet, as we will discuss later in this paper, this is support of a different nature than what. may emerge in the context of offender treatment programs. Note that the statement does not say, "there can never be enough *counselors* involved in reintegration."

Second, because the restorative justice literature has given attention to the role and needs of the crime victims as central to the restorative response, publications may often seem vague about the offender. The central focus on victims is essential, in part because it is the most difficult aspect of restorative justice for criminal and juvenile justice agencies to incorporate. However, the concern is that lack of clarity about the offender role—beyond meeting obligations to victim and victimized communities—may well compartmentalize restorative justice as simply another approach to sanctioning offenders or providing victim services. Because traditional criminal justice philosophies have not addressed the role and needs of the crime victim, one could presume that it is the victim emphasis that distinguishes restorative justice.

Certainly, each of the four dominant sanctioning paradigms— deterrence, retribution, incapacitation, and rehabilitation (e.g., Packer, 1968)—have a distinctive viewpoint on crime and the response to the offender. However, while these perspectives differ on the rationale for intervention (Packer, 1968; Von Hirsch, 1997), it may be said that there are a number of similarities in the view of the offender presented. In fact, the primary distinction may lie between those who view the offender as motivated by forces beyond his or her control, and thereby subject to change by treatment (rehabilitationists) or by the threat and/or execution of punishment (deterrence advocates), and those nonutilitarians who avoid issues of transforming offenders altogether by focusing only on the need to punish fairly (retributivists) or manage lawbreakers effectively to ensure public safety within acceptable limits of fairness and due process (incapacitationists). Ultimately, the only practical intervention choices are between those focused on helping, hurting, or controlling the offender.

Although it does not necessarily reject the objectives of other philosophies as secondary goals (Bazemore and Umbreit, 1995), restorative justice—with its emphasis on repairing harm—provides different choices. The vacuum left by the absence of discussion of a restorative view of the offender, however, leaves this model open to much speculation around at least four possibilities:

1. Restorative justice is essentially unconcerned or neutral about the offender once reparative obligations to the crime victim and community have been met (essentially a victim focus with an alternative sanctioning emphasis that is implicitly critical of punishment);

2. Restorative justice is anti-rehabilitation because to not be so allows offender treatment needs to overwhelm the focus on the need to repair victim harm and may jeopardize the proportionality and fairness of sanctioning as a result of the addition of treatment obligations (Walgrave, 1999);

3. Restorative justice is supportive of punishment and simply adds the reparative obligation to the victim and community to the list of punitive requirements; and

4. Restorative justice is supportive of offender rehabilitation but would need to make no statements beyond those affirming support for current treatment models and programs (e.g., Crowe, 1998).

We wish to suggest that none of the above depictions is an accurate portrayal of the restorative justice view of the offender. There is, of course, at least one other possibility that grows out of the more holistic, or "maximalist," vision of restorative justice. This vision is grounded in a principle-based, distinctively restorative *approach* to sanctioning crime, building safer communities, helping victims, and reintegrating offenders (Bazemore and Walgrave, 1999; Braithwaite, 1989; Stuart, 1996; Van Ness and Strong, 1997; Zehr, 1990). Advocates of restorative justice can no more neglect the rehabilitative needs of the offender than they can ignore how public safety issues are addressed. Hence, the fifth possibility is that restorative justice is supportive of the offender and of efforts to reintegrate both offender and victim (Van Ness and Strong, 1997). However, a normative theory of intervention based on restorative justice would seem to require a different way of thinking about and "doing" rehabilitation. Such an approach is needed, we argue, precisely because of practice and conceptual deficiencies in the individual treatment model.

The Limits of Individual Treatment

> Indeed, researchers have recognized that a major limitation of even the empirically-driven, well-conceived and carefully executed treatments for serious antisocial behavior is that they address at best a small subset of the factors that contribute to the problems experienced by these youths across several social contexts (e.g., Shoenwald et al., forthcoming).

There is a widely accepted approach to rehabilitative intervention generally known as the "what works" or "effective correctional treatment" paradigm (Andrews and Bonta, 1994; Gendreau et al., 1994; Levrant et al., 1999; Lipsey and Wilson, 1998). Formal correctional treatment is a critical component of the rehabilitative enterprise, and we do not question the need for appropriately targeted, effective clinical intervention provided by trained professionals (e.g., Andrews and Bonta, 1994). The problem arises when the effective correctional treatment (ECT) paradigm is presented as a monolithic response to rehabilitation, corrections, or *crime control* itself (Levrant et al., 1999:16, 19). Regarding crime control, implying that reducing recidivism rates for offenders referred to treatment programs is anything more than one small component of an approach to managing the risks to citizens presented by crime ignores the threat posed by offenders who never make it into correctional programs. As a mission for corrections agencies, effective treatment meets only one expectation of citizens who view overall public safety and sanctioning as key objectives of these agencies. Even rehabilitation itself, as we suggest below, demands more than just a focus on formal treatment programs.

We have previously argued that both punishment *and* treatment responses are driven by incomplete, "closed system" paradigms (Bazemore, 1999a; Bazemore and Umbreit, 1995). As one practitioner expresses it:

> Treatment and punishment standing alone are not capable of meeting the intertwined needs of the community, victim, offender and family. For the vast majority of the citizenry, juvenile justice is an esoteric system wrapped in a riddle. Support comes from understanding, understanding from involvement and participation. Community involvement and active participation in the working of a juvenile court is a reasoned response . . . (currently) community members are not solicited for input or asked for their resourcefulness in assisting the system to meet public safety, treatment and sanctioning. (Diaz, 1997)

Elsewhere we have drawn attention to a number of practical and conceptual limitations of the individual treatment model (Bazemore, 1999a; Bazemore and Terry, 1997). Essentially, most treatment programs are highly professionalized responses to crime that have proliferated in the past three decades as part of a general expansion of justice system intervention that appears to have widened and strengthened the net of system control. In the process, they have undercut informal and noncriminal justice community socialization and social control mechanisms, and in doing so, such programs send a clear message to communities to "leave crime to the experts" (Bazemore, 1999b; Braithwaite, 1994; McKnight, 1995). Grounded in the assumption of underlying disturbance and deficits that demand remedial and/or therapeutic approaches to intervention, programs based on the individual treatment model have generally failed to build upon potential strengths of offenders, their families, and their support groups, thereby limiting each to the role of "client" in need of service or surveillance (Benson, 1997; McKnight, 1995). The one-dimensional nature of treatment also reinforces a growing tendency in criminal justice toward specialization that further separates services provided for offenders from the obligations they have to communities and victims harmed by their behavior. The message to offender, victim, and community is thus a confused and inconsistent one that mitigates against a systemic, seamless, user-friendly, and inclusive approach to intervention (Dooley, 1999).

The great strength of the ECT, or "what works," literature is its empirical evidence demonstrating the relative potency of various offender treatment programs and strategies. Equally important is the clear documentation from meta-analytic assessments that many treatment programs do *not* work, or may actually increase recidivism (Lipsey, 1995). However, the scope of research findings and theoretical frameworks relevant to factors that appear to be responsible for the stopping or slowing down of criminal activity by offenders in treatment programs is highly constricted in ECT meta-analyses. Specifically, data from program evaluation studies is limited to populations of offenders known to criminal justice authorities who happen to have been referred to one or more treatment programs that have been evaluated by experimental or quasi-experimental methods. These offenders are compared with similar offenders in alternative criminal justice intervention programs. We have no information, therefore, on offenders who were not known to authorities, or on those who received no formal treatment. Therefore, a rather large body of findings on these hidden offenders who eventually desist from delinquent and criminal behavior without formal intervention (e.g., Elliott, 1994) is thereby excluded. As a result, we are unable to assess the value of these formal interventions compared with *no intervention* or with more naturalistic processes of social control and the provision of "social support" (Bazemore, 1999; Cullen, 1994; Sampson et al., 1997). Moreover, meta-analyses based on comparisons of competing treatments test the viability of a very limited set of generally clinically based theories of intervention and offender reform that are for the most part disconnected from broader theories of crime and delinquency (Gaes, 1998).

To develop a more holistic, theoretical, empirical, and practical framework for a complete model of reintegration, it is important to uncouple the notion of rehabilitation from formal treatment programs. Practically, a complete model of reintegration would acknowledge the importance of effective treatment programs but also emphasize the essential role of community support, the importance of strong relationships with law-abiding adults and with community institutions, and the need for a "lens" for intervention that can help practitioners envision the offender as a potential resource rather than simply a client (Bazemore and Terry, 1997).

Restorative Community Justice and Offender Reintegration: Building Relationships

Though it is not a model of crime control, corrections, nor even a complete approach to rehabilitation, restorative community justice is by definition multidimensional in its concern with all issues of harm caused by crime. Focused on the needs of victim, community, and offender as the primary stakeholders in the response to crime (Van Ness and Strong, 1997), restorative intervention is a distinctive way of "doing justice" that also has important implications for offender rehabilitation strategies as well as for how crime is sanctioned, what initiatives will enhance community safety and crime prevention, and a more satisfying response to crime victims (Bazemore and Walgrave, 1999). By addressing multiple interests and collective outcomes (Clear and Karp, 1999), restorative justice is also capable of avoiding the individualizing tendencies of both treatment and punishment paradigms.[2] As Sampson and Wilson (1995:54) observe, "the unique value of a community level perspective is that it leads away from a simple 'kinds of people' analysis to a focus on social characteristics of collectivities that foster violence (and crime)."

Repair, Offenders, and Obligations: How Can Restorative Justice Principles Inform Reintegrative Strategies?

A restorative justice approach to offenders and reintegration must be grounded in restorative principles. Based on the premise that crime is more than lawbreaking, Van Ness and Strong have suggested the following three core principles:[3]

1. Principle 1: Justice requires that we work to heal victims, offenders and communities that have been injured by crime.

2. Principle 2: Victims, offenders and communities should have the opportunity for active involvement in the justice process as early and as fully as possible.

3. Principle 3: We must rethink the relative roles and responsibilities of the government and the community. In promoting justice, government is responsible for preserving a just order and the community for establishing peace. (Van Ness and Strong, 1997:8-9)

A restorative justice approach to intervention, including activities aimed at rehabilitating offenders, begins with a normative focus on harm and repair. If behavior labeled as crime is characterized by the hurt or damage it causes to individuals, communities, and relationships, justice cannot be achieved through a focus on lawbreaking or by simply punishing or treating lawbreakers. Indeed, because crime "creates obligations to make things right," (Zehr, 1990:18), harm that is not addressed is likely to become a barrier to any long-term successful resolution (Van Ness and Strong, 1997).

Though repair is an important objective in its own right, it is also a prerequisite for (and a part of) achieving other justice objectives, such as public safety, fairness, victim satisfaction and repair, accountability in sanctioning, and in this case, rehabilitation. When harm is not addressed, other justice interventions become rather empty and meaningless, and may even exacerbate harm (Rose and Clear, 1998). From the perspective of the offender, the idea of repair focuses our attention first on the obligation that incurs when a crime is committed. Though generally not addressed in the standard treatment model (e.g., Andrews and Bonta, 1994), this obligation, according to citizen surveys indicating strong support for reparative sanctions (Doble and Immerwahr, 1997; Moon et al., 2000; Pranis and Umbreit, 1992; Schwartz et al., 1992), is part of a more naturalistic or "common sense" attitude toward crime and the offender. Essentially, the notion that a person who has hurt someone or the community is entitled to help without making amends for what has been damaged flies in the face of virtually universal norms of fairness. Precisely for this reason, we find it necessary to view this obligation to, in essence, "clean up the mess" caused by one's behavior as a necessary first step in any complete model of offender reintegration. As even critics of restorative justice acknowledge, purely rehabilitative models: "must confront a crucial weakness common to other progressive policy agendas: the charge that intervention is a form of entitlement to offenders . . . Given the principle of less eligibility, any provision of treatment services to offenders is open to attack because such social welfare is undeserved." Restorative justice approaches, on the other hand, "move away from the principle of entitlement to the principle of social exchange" (Levrant et al., 1999:22). In this way, restorative justice explicitly engages the community and victim side of the reintegration equation that has been missing from standard treatment models. Though reintegration is never automatic, the notion of community acceptance of the offender who has "made it right" with their stakeholders seems less far-fetched.

We and others have argued elsewhere that, while sanctioning as punishment is generally a counterdeterrent that works in opposition to the goal of true accountability, as well as reintegration, both formal and informal sanctions focused on repair are a critical part of a reintegrative strategy (Bazemore and Umbreit, 1995; Braithwaite and Mugford, 1994). Such sanctions may reinforce rather than hinder offender rehabilitation when: (1) accountability is defined as an obligation to victim and community, (2) offenders are asked to accept responsibility for their crime (cognitively and emotionally "own" the behavior), (3) offenders do something to make it right with those they have harmed (behavioral commitment), and (4) crime victims and community members have an active role in setting the terms of accountability and monitoring completion of the obligation (Bazemore and Umbreit, 1995; Claussen, 1996).

Although all three restorative justice principles provide an important core set of guidelines for determining what practices and processes are "restorative," repairing harm is the ultimate outcome sought. Without this focus for intervention, the second principle of involvement, for example, may be interpreted simply as an effort to engage stake-holders in efforts to punish or treat offenders. Instead, Principle 2 is important precisely because it defines the *methodology* for achieving repair: it is virtually impossible to repair harm without fully engaging those individuals and groups who have experienced the harm. If this principle of stakeholder involvement can be viewed as defining the nature of a justice *process* focused on the goal of healing or reparation (i.e., inclusive versus top-down and expert-driven), Principle 3 defines the specific roles and responsibilities of the justice system and community as well as the new relationship between justice professionals and citizens that is required to facilitate victim, offender, and citizen participation in a reparative response to crime.

Toward a Theory of Reintegration: The Social Relationship as an Integrating Concept

Taken seriously, the restorative justice focus on repair implies a distinctive way of thinking about "doing rehabilitation." To date, however, restorative justice proponents have not offered a complete theory of intervention to explain why one might expect the reparative act to bring about change in the offender. Inconsistency in the practice of emerging restorative justice programs is to be expected but often makes it difficult to identify the "independent variable" that is expected to produce the intended changes in the behavior of offenders as well as other stakeholders. Even in more established programs, such as victim-offender mediation, in which the intervention itself has become relatively stabilized, restorative justice practitioners are at times unclear about intermediate impacts they expect to achieve, and how these might be related to more long-term change in offender behavior.[4]

Restorative justice decision-making processes, such as victim-offender dialog and various other conferencing models, as well as reparative sanctions including community service and restitution, are not appropriately contrasted with treatment programs on offender outcome such as recidivism. Nonetheless, though restorative approaches target multiple outcomes for victims and community, they have been surprisingly impactful in reducing offending,[5] especially when compared to the usual court and diversion alternatives. We cannot easily explain why such short-term encounters might change behavior. The experience of offenders in these interventions clearly produces some initial change in attitude, behavior, and/or circumstances that may lead to something else that eventually impacts lawbreaking. If we are to learn how to focus restorative intervention for maximum impact on offenders without diminishing the emphasis on the needs of victims and community members, a theory of restorative intervention must articulate what that change, and that "something else" might be. There are, of course, many possibilities: for instance, increased empathy for one's victim leads to a generalized empathy for others; paying restitution provides a sense of accomplishment and a sense of fairness; or social support sends a message of community caring that makes the offenders want to conform in order to please those who care about him or her.[6] Because these and other intermediate impacts may imply distinct theories-in-use (Bazemore, 2000), it is often impossible to link even the same restorative intervention to a developmental theory of offender transformation.

Repair and Relationships Despite its conceptual richness, repair can remain a vague concept at the level of operationalizing an intervention response focused on offender reintegration. After dealing with the offender's obligation to others, we are left in something of a quandary unless we: (1) emphasize the harm to his or her family and loved ones, or (2) focus on remedying past harms to the offender. Although restorative practices need not necessarily avoid either and certainly should seek to repair harm to families, the focus on past victimization of the offender in the absence of clear boundaries may run the risk of erecting yet another treatment model, or reinforcing existing individual assessment protocols. In the worst case scenario, this emphasis may be seen as excusing the offender's behavior and minimizing the focus on current harms to the immediate victim(s).

Some restorative justice proponents and practitioners have given new life to the meaning of repair by focusing on the need to restore, strengthen, or build *relationships* between offenders, communities, and crime victims. Ultimately, rebuilding, strengthening, or establishing new relationships is a central long-term goal of the restorative process and, at least implicitly, a key component of what is meant by the notion of *repairing the harm* (Braithwaite and Parker, 1999; Van Ness and Strong, 1997).

Because crime is both a *cause* and a *result* of weak relationships, strengthening relationships at the level of neighborhood and parochial groups is a first step in healing that may also bring people together in a way that has preventive and reintegrative implications (Bazemore, 1999a; Pranis and Bazemore, 2000). For the offender, when reintegration occurs, it is often said that it is his or her relationships with law-abiding community members that work to prevent crime through both affective and instrumental constraints (Hirschi, 1969). Intervention aimed at preventing future crime must therefore focus not only on the offender's obligation to repair material and other harms to victim and community; it must also focus on mending weak or broken relationships between offender and community, victim and community, and (where appropriate) victim and offender.

As a concept that may link broader community processes to the problems presented by individual offenders, the social relationship is ultimately the mechanism for mobilizing both "social support" (Cullen, 1994; Cullen et al., 1999) and social control (Bazemore, 2000; Clear and Karp, 1999; Sampson et al., 1997). The provision of support seems unequivocally associated with a relationship between the provider and receiver, though the quality and quantity of support is related to our ties—through kinship, friendship, and instrumental affiliations—to individuals and social groups. Support is in part a function of the nurturing and socialization process, and both are dependent upon the level and quality of caring and concern, linked to the affective commitment of one or more caring adults (Rutter, 1985; Werner, 1986). Research on adolescents and young adults is consistent in its support of the critical role of affective and instrumental ties, both in preventing crime and in increasing the likelihood that young offenders will make the transition from criminal to conventional lifestyles (Elliott, 1994; Hirschi, 1969).

At a micro level, where reintegration actually occurs, personal relationships often act as both bridge and buffer between the offender and the community. The social relationship also smoothes the way for the development of additional connections between the offender, law-abiding citizens, and legitimate institutions. The bridge to such a connectedness is the "social capital" needed to allow for access to institutional roles (e.g., in work, education, and community groups) that provide the offender with a legitimate identity. Such social capital is garnered as the number and strength of relationship increase, and these relationships, in turn, provide access to additional legitimate roles that further build social capital.

Although the effectiveness of treatment is in part a function of the quality of the relationship between the therapist or counselor and the client of services (Andrews and Bonta, 1994; Lipsey, 1995),[7] more important from a restorative justice perspective are the relationships that offenders develop with law-abiding community members who are not paid to spend time with them (Pranis and Bazemore, 2000). These citizens, and the community groups they may be affiliated with, function as a support network for the offender, playing the roles of sponsor, teacher, guide, coach, and advocate (Bazemore, 1997; McKnight, 1995). Unfortunately, the current structural and cultural configuration of treatment programs and social service agencies is not set up to develop and promote such informal support networks. Nor is intervention geared toward advocacy for change in the organizational dynamics of socializing institutions (such as school and work) that might new make formal and informal roles available for offenders and young people in trouble (Polk, this volume). Although no one in the treatment community is likely to oppose such efforts, and some professionals no doubt seek to create and nurture such connections for their clients, advocacy and relationship-building are not part of the job description of the average counselor or social work professional working with offenders. Moreover, as service agencies and programs become more staff-intensive and client-dependent, treatment programs may actually create disincentives for staff to seek community participation. Unfortunately, as treatment agencies evolve from "cottage industries" to more complex service bureaucracies, the ultimate disincentive for citizen involvement (beyond such practical barriers as liability concerns) is that volunteer participation may raise questions about the need for new staff and thereby weaken the agency administrator's case for program and system expansion (Pittman and Fleming, 1991).

Roles and Relationships: Theory and Practice A reintegrative strategy based on strengthening connections and building meaningful relationships between young offenders and law-abiding adults includes several practical intervention components that should fit together as a seamless whole rather than as independent programmatic units. First, offenders need some minimal level of skill and social capital in order to develop and maintain strong relationships. They need assets that allow them to take advantage of the "connectedness" that can be experienced through good relationships with employers, teachers, friends, fellow church members, and the like (Bazemore and Terry, 1997; Benson, 1997). These assets cannot be built in a vacuum, however, nor are they likely to be fully developed in treatment or in "competency development programs" focused primarily or exclusively on remedial training or cognitive therapy. While these programs represent one component of an asset-building strategy (Benson, 1997) for many offenders, when they are not connected to roles that allow offenders to demonstrate competencies a way that strengthens a community connection, such programs run the risk of becoming yet another deficit-focused intervention that further isolates offenders from their communities.

Hence, a second practical component of a relationship-building strategy is to discover ways to change the context in which offenders are expected to develop the assets that will help them form and sustain relationships. Young people are most likely to learn such skills in settings in which they are connected naturally to positive adults and peers, and where the context for coming together is not primarily based on the offender's need for remedial training or treatment. The best context for such learning is one in which there is mutual commitment to a common task, through which there is opportunity for developing affective and instrumental ties to conventional adults and groups. The best historical examples are the classic apprenticeship models in craft and trade occupations, the master/student relationship in the arts, and the extended family business, all of which provided natural ties between young and old and a clear transition to adulthood.

While such possibilities (with the limited exception of the arts and sports) are less available to young people in today's political economy, there are ways to recreate such learning contexts. One of the easiest and least well exploited, for example, is the opportunity for meaningful service to others—in a setting in which meaningful work is accomplished by offenders working together with community members on projects such as Habitat for Humanity homes or doing chores for the elderly (Bazemore and Maloney, 1994). Such service can itself be linked to a new kind of "designed" paid work experience, that is in turn linked to new career tracks (Bazemore, 1991; Pearl et al., 1978). In addition to such structural linkages, new spaces for relationship building and skill development must also be designed to maximize possibilities for the development of affective as well as instrumental ties between young offenders and conventional groups and individuals. The community service examples illustrate the importance of the linkage between developing skills in offenders and providing opportunities to *practice* and *demonstrate* these skills in a context in which offenders are allowed to make a clear contribution to the common good or to individuals in need. Such a context makes it possible to send a message to offenders, and to their communities, that those who have harmed others but made amends also have something to offer and are worthy of further support and investment in their reintegration.

The Cycle of Relationships and Reintegration As may be apparent from the foregoing discussion, the relationship-building process cannot be depicted as a linear, recursive model. Indeed, to the extent that we have suggested that offenders need skills to develop and sustain relationships, and that these skills are acquired primarily through relationships with others, our argument may seem tautological. As Figure 5.1 suggests, however, the treatment and/or remedial focus on removing deficits and providing skills—even when redefined as providing competencies to make new relationships possible—is very much akin to the "receptacle model" of education that depicts students as passive vessels waiting to be filled up with knowledge. Instead of a linear, two-step path to reduced recidivism and social adjustment in which remediation is viewed as the independent variable, Figure 5.2 suggests that the social relationship and associated opportunities to contribute to the common good are the causal factors that provide the necessary context for competency-building. New assets, in turn, lead to more connections and stronger relationships, a greater repertoire of skills, and still more connections (and the opportunities these provide). In fact, this model is primarily nonrecursive in that there are anticipated feedback loops between skill-building, relationship-building, access to positive roles, and offender adjustment associated with a reduction in offending.

Figure 5.1
Treatment/Remedial Model

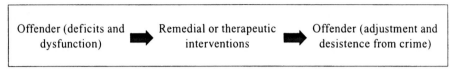

Figure 5.2
Restorative/Relational Model

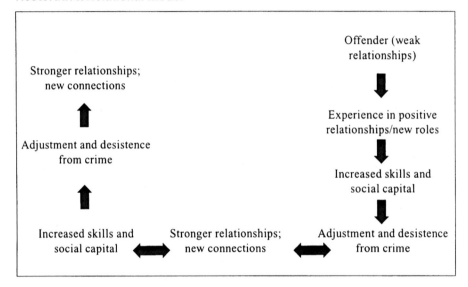

As part of a cyclical process, criminal activity is expected to decline until, at some point, the life space of the offender is simply too full of conventional activity and too committed to law-abiding others—by virtue of positive roles, and the restraints imposed by informal social controls centered around the offender's social relationships—to make offending a likely prospect. While the traditional intervention model generally leaves relationship-building to chance, a restorative *relational* model begins and ends with the social relationship as an independent, intervening, and dependent variable.

Because current treatment programs and agencies are unlikely to move naturally in this direction, new structures for social support are needed that can become new contexts for relationship-building at the individual/interpersonal, institutional (e.g., school, work), and community levels. Following the principle of organizational change that "you are what you measure," promoting such an agenda for intervention would require the development of new intermediate, theoretically derived performance outcomes for intervention (Bazemore and Washington, 1995; Osborn and Gaebler, 1992). Such outcomes would provide an alternative to the closed-system focus on treatment program completion rates and move justice agencies toward measuring the intermediate changes that are thought to lead to lower recidivism: stronger relationships, experience in new roles, enhanced skills, and social capital.

While it would undoubtedly provoke opposition from traditionalists, such an alternative receives support from research on how most lawbreakers cease or at least begin to limit their involvement in criminal behavior. What is demonstrated in the research on resiliency, for example, is the need for committed, sustained relationships between at-risk young people and adults with a long-term interest in their well being and successful development (Rutter, 1985; Werner, 1986).[8] What is demonstrated in research on maturational reform of delinquents and young offenders is that it is stable connections that flow from adult roles in family, work, and community that account for desistance from crime (Elliott, 1994). It is the lack of availability of such roles (e.g., family and work options) that characterizes underclass neighborhoods in which crime is sometimes the norm (Sampson and Wilson, 1995; Wilson and Kelling, 1982). Nonetheless, at a social ecological level, what is being demonstrated by the Chicago studies of collective efficacy (Sampson et al., 1997; Sherman et al., 1998) is that the impact of informal sanctions and social support may reduce community crime rates despite the presence of other risk factors (e.g., poverty) associated with underclass neighborhoods. A social justice strategy focused on developing new roles that connect individuals to social institutions and community life (Polk, this volume; Pranis, this volume), coupled with an intentional focus on mobilizing informal controls and supports through restorative intervention, is therefore an important part of a holistic reintegrative "recipe," and of a general strategy for more effective crime control.[9]

Discussion

In a recent critical assessment of the rise of punitive/retributive polices in United States juvenile justice, Moon et al. (2000) observe that:

> *Consistent with this shift in philosophy* [to a restorative justice model], Illinois has enacted legislation that increases the length of time that juveniles may be held in custody and detention, has provided for more extensive fingerprinting of youths, has created a statewide database to track young offenders, has placed limits on the number of station adjustments allowed for delinquents who are not officially cited by the police, and has removed special protective language from the juvenile court process (e.g., an "adjudicatory hearing" will now be referred to as a trial) (Dighton, 1999) [emphasis added].

We have argued in this chapter that such attributions of a linkage between restorative justice and "get tough" approaches indicate more of a misunderstanding or misrepresentation of the views of restorative justice proponents than any tendency in restorative justice literature or practice.

In summary, restorative justice writers and practitioners seek to support both victims and offenders. Restorative justice also has very clear implications for rehabilitative intervention and a more naturalistic model of offender reintegration. In this model, the social relationship is the vehicle for providing both formal and informal social support and control. Such support and control, in turn, provides the emotive components of attachment to conventional groups. It also provides the basis for instrumental commitment to conventional lines of action that is provided by roles in which offenders can demonstrate competency and their potential value to communities. The fact that such roles for young people seem to be in chronically short supply requires that an intervention model aimed at maximizing attachment and commitment must focus on the creation of new institutional roles as well as informal and quasi-formal support networks for facilitating reintegration and integration of offenders (Polk, this volume; Polk and Kobrin, 1972). Because relationship-building is more complex than simply creating new intervention programs, we have argued for the development of new models of reintegration and rehabilitation based essentially on strengthening offender competencies, and building connections between offenders, law-abiding adults, and socializing institutions (Bazemore, 1998; 2000). Just as restorative justice advocates have talked about creating the "spaces" for informal dispute resolution and inclusive decisionmaking about responses to crime that repair harm, advocates of a restorative approach to reintegration must envision new spaces for dealing with offenders in a context that builds upon the strengths of offenders and the communities surrounding them.

Restorative justice is clearly more than a "new correctional paradigm" (Levrant et al., 1999), but it is also less. Restorative justice advocates have never claimed that efforts to repair harm to all stakeholders (including efforts to build or rebuild relationships that will help offenders resist crime) and treatment interventions with offenders are either/or propositions. Appropriate treatment is required on a prescriptive basis for those offenders whose risk and need profiles indicate cognitive or behavioral patterns—including substance abuse or addiction—that limit their ability to form positive relationships. Therapeutic interventions for this portion of the offender population could therefore support the restorative goal of strengthening existing connections with positive peers and groups and building new ones.

Although many corrections practitioners seem to be merging restorative justice principles with effective treatment approaches (Carey, this volume; Crowe, 1998; Rhine et al., 1998) the problem among some advocates of effective treatment has been a failure to acknowledge that rehabilitation (and certainly crime control) is a bigger issue than changing the attitudes, thinking, and problematic behavior of offenders. Indeed, we have implied in this chapter that without the social support (and social control) imbedded in relationships, offenders may face barriers to reintegration regardless of the level of personal transformation. The question restorative justice might pose for advocates of the effective treatment paradigm is: What good is a change in thinking patterns if the offender's relationships with law-abiding peers are weak or nonexistent? And how can such relationships be strengthened without adopting an approach to "doing justice" and to intervention that moves beyond consideration of the needs and risks of offenders to address the interests of victim and community and the role of the latter in achieving true reintegration of those harmed by crime *and* those who have harmed others?

Discussion Questions

1. What problems in current treatment models make them incomplete, insular, and one-dimensional?

2. Has restorative justice neglected the offender? Has it ignored rehabilitation? Why has restorative justice been perceived as punitive?

3. How do restorative justice principles inform a new rehabilitation strategy? How would such a strategy be different from past rehabilitative approaches?

4. Discuss the potential common ground between offender treatment and restorative justice. How would treatment methods change under the influence of restorative principles? Is relational rehabilitation feasible? Why or why not?

Endnotes

[1]   Efforts to co-opt restorative justice should not be surprising given the history of other criminal justice reforms. Indeed, co-optation has also been a central feature of the history of the treatment movement itself (Mennel, 1974; Platt, 1977; Rothman, 1980). More recently, some have characterized implementation of just-deserts reforms as an effort to ensure proportionality and fairness in sentencing that ended in little more than an expansion of crime control and punishment (Tonry, 1997). In their recent critique of restorative justice, Levrant et al. (1999)

also imply that restorative justice is anti-progressive. They suggest that the restorative justice movement today has much in common with "the triumph of benevolence" that occurred at the turn of the twentieth century when corrections systems and juvenile courts gained power and credibility by adoption of an apparently benign rehabilitative model. Their implication that the "what works" or "effective correctional treatment" model is a central component of a new progressivism in criminal justice is indeed ironic, given the fact that it was the individual treatment paradigm that served in this earlier era as a cover for abuse that resulted, for example, in unprecedented increases in the incarceration of at-risk young people "in their best interests" associated with the rise of the juvenile court (Platt, 1977; Rothman, 1980).

2   With regard to reintegration and rehabilitation, the goal can never be simply a change in offender behavior. Because offender reintegration requires change in *multiple* stakeholders, restorative principles move us necessarily toward seeking transformation in communities, citizens, and crime victims as well as offenders. Though the victims' well-being and community interests are also primary concerns, restorative justice assumes that the needs of the three stakeholders are to some degree mutually intertwined rather than antagonistic.

3   Other ancillary principles of restorative justice have also been articulated (see Van Ness and Strong, 1997; Zehr and Mika, 1998) A number of underlying *values* of restorative justice, notably respect and inclusiveness, are also often discussed as principles in practice settings.

4   Most treatment programs are equally vulnerable to the charge that they lack a theory of intervention or logical linkage that connects the service with intended results (Gaes, 1998). Yet, if we may reasonably ask of treatment programs why six months of counseling would be expected to have any long-term impact on offenders, it is even more reasonable to ask why even the most meaningful community service experience or the successful completion of restitution or direct service to a victim would have any effect. Why would one expect a one-to-two-hour mediation session or family group conference to influence future offense behavior in conjunction with, or independent of, such reparative experiences?

5   Though these effects, which have an average magnitude of 32 percent reduction in recidivism in some reanalyses of findings from multiple evaluations (for example, Nugent et al., forthcoming), do not match those of the most effective, high-end, multimodal treatment programs (Andrews and Bonta, 1994), they perform significantly better than many other long-term treatment programs in common use (Lipsey, 1995). Recidivism reduction effects are not as strong, though positive, in the case of restorative sanctions such as restitution and community service (Butts and Synder, 1991; Schneider, 1990). Newer restorative conferencing programs are only beginning to be examined with regard to their impact on recidivism (Stuart, 1996). Unlike many clinical treatment programs, few, if any, restorative programs have yielded *negative* impacts on recidivism (Lipsey, 1995). Moreover, unlike multimodal treatment programs (Shoenwald et al., forthcoming), individual restorative program components, such as participating in a restorative conference, completing community service, or attending a victim impact panel, are generally evaluated independently rather than studied together as part of an integrated approach to rehabilitation, the *joint* impact of which might be expected to result in even larger reductions in recidivism.

6   Among the logical candidates for making the link between restorative practice and anticipated outcomes is John Braithwaite's work in providing a normative theoretical alternative to just deserts (Braithwaite, 1989; Braithwaite and Petit, 1992). Broadly concerned with the larger sociological issue of the absence of a common commitment to norm affirmation and to maintaining community tolerance limits (Braithwaite, 1989) in what Braithwaite (Braithwaite, 1989; Sampson et al., 1997) labels "high-crime" societies (or high-crime communities), reintegrative shaming theory has been adapted and applied primarily to a particular model of family group conferencing (Moore and O'Connell, 1994). Some of these applications seem to amount to a reduction of a macro normative theory about how communities produce and manage the process of social control, justice decisionmaking, and offender reintegration to a micro intervention aimed at confrontation and shaming of individual offenders. Although recent social psychological work on the role of shame in social control (Retzinger and Scheff, 1996; Tomkins, 1992) has implications for restorative practice and for theories of intervention, it is yet unclear how these perspectives can be linked to broader theories of crime.

7   There are, however, practical limits to this professional relationship, as well as competing agendas that may weaken its impact, at least over sustained intervals. Though important, such professional relationships take on a different connotation because offenders know that treatment providers are paid to spend time with them. Similarly, the focus on the strength and quality of social relationships cannot be operationalized as simply the creation of more "mentoring programs," because the influence of the mentor is almost by definition transient and may become artificial and staff-driven.

8   As may be apparent from the previous discussion, the relational approach to reintegration is indeed consistent with several important bodies of criminological theory and research (Bazemore, 1999). Social control perspectives (e.g., Hirschi, 1969; Polk and Kobrin, 1972) emphasize the importance of the "bond" individuals have to conventional groups. This bond can in turn be viewed as culturally and structurally fixed in the roles individuals assume in the context of community groups and socializing institutions (e.g., family, work, school). These roles thereby provide for informal constraints on deviant behavior based on affective ties to significant others (teachers, parents), as well as on a more rational "stake in conformity" that limits individual involvement in crime by the risk posed to the future conventional opportunities (Briar and Piliavin, 1965; Polk and Kolbrin, 1972).

9   Notably, at the micro level, numerous studies of decision-making processes, such as victim-offender dialog and other forms of restorative conferencing (Nugent et al., forthcoming; Sherman et al., 1998) provide growing empirical support for the potency of restorative processes in mobilizing and impacting stakeholders. The challenge is to connect those interventions with efforts to build collective efficacy in communities rather than treating these decision-making alternatives as isolated programs (Bazemore, 2000) The idea of relationship-building also provides a core linking concept between various intervention practices and theories of community and crime (e.g., Bursick and Grasmick, 1993; Skogan, 1990). More broadly, relationship-building is also linked to emerging theories that may challenge medical and public health perspectives on the capacity of communities to mobilize resources. Unlike the focus of these perspectives on community risks and deficits, these new frameworks emphasize resiliency and strength at the individual level, and community capacity at the social ecological level (Benson, 1997; McKnight, 1995).

References

Andrews, D.A., and J. Bonta (1994). *The Psychology of Criminal Conduct.* Cincinnati: Anderson.

Andrews, D.A., J. Bonta, and R.D. Hoge (1990). "Classification for Effective Rehabilitation: Rediscovering Psychology." *Criminal Justice and Behavior* 17:19-52.

Arrigo, B., and R. Schehr (1998). "Restoring Justice for Juveniles: A Critical Analysis of Victim-Offender Mediation." *Justice Quarterly* 14:629-666.

Bazemore, G. (1991). "New Concepts and Alternative Practice in Community Supervision of Juvenile Offenders: Rediscovering Work Experience and Competency Development." *Journal of Crime and Justice* 14(2):27-52.

Bazemore, G. (1997). "The 'Community' in Community Justice: Issues, Themes and Questions for the New Neighborhood Sanctioning Models." *The Justice System Journal* 19:193-228.

Bazemore, G. (1998). "Restorative Justice and Earned Redemption: Communities, Victims and Offender Reintegration." *American Behavioral Scientist* 41:768-813.

Bazemore, G. (1999a). "After Shaming, Whither Reintegration: Restorative Justice and Relational Rehabilitation." In *Restorative Juvenile Justice: Repairing the Harm of Youth Crime*, edited by G. Bazemore and L. Walgrave. Monsey, NY: Criminal Justice Press.

Bazemore, G. (1999b). "The Fork in the Road to Juvenile Court Reform." *The Annals of the American Academy of Political and Social Science* 564:81-108.

Bazemore, G. (1999c). "In Search of a Communitarian Justice Alternative: Youth Crime and the Sanctioning Response as A Case Study." In *To Promote the General Welfare: A Communitarian Legal Reader*, edited by D. Carney. Willamsburg, VA: Lexington Books.

Bazemore, G. (2000). "Community Justice and a Vision of Collective Efficacy: The Case of Restorative Conferencing." In *Criminal Justice 2000*, edited by the National Institute of Justice. Washington, DC: National Institute of Justice.

Bazemore, G., and S. Day (1995). "The Return to Family Intervention in Youth Services: A Juvenile Justice Case Study in Policy Implementation." *The Journal of Sociology and Social Welfare* 22:25-50.

Bazemore, G., and C. Griffiths (1997). "Conferences, Circles, Boards, and Mediation: The 'New Wave' in Community Justice Decisionmaking." *Federal Probation* 59:25-37.

Bazemore, G., and D. Maloney (1994). "Rehabilitating Community Service: Toward Restorative Service in a Balanced Justice System." *Federal Probation* 58:24-35.

Bazemore, G., and C. Terry (1997). "Developing Delinquent Youth: A Reintegrative Model for Rehabilitation and a New Role for the Juvenile Justice System." *Child Welfare* 74(5):665-716.

Bazemore, G., and M. Umbreit (1995). "Rethinking the Sanctioning Function in Juvenile Court: Retributive or Restorative Responses to Youth Crime." *Crime & Delinquency* 41:296-316.

Bazemore, G., and L. Walgrave. (1999). *Restorative Juvenile Justice: Repairing the Harm of Youth Crime*. Monsey, NY: Criminal Justice Press.

Bazemore, G., and C. Washington (1995). "Charting the Future of the Juvenile Justice System: Reinventing Mission and Management." *Spectrum: The Journal of State Government* 68:51-66.

Benson, P. (1997). *All Kids Are Our Kids*. San Francisco: Jossey-Bass.

Braithwaite, J. (1989). *Crime, Shame and Reintegration*. Cambridge, England: Cambridge University Press.

Braithwaite, J. (1994). "Thinking Harder about Democratising Social Control." In *Family Conferencing and Juvenile Justice: The Way Forward or Misplaced Optimism?*, edited by C. Alder and J. Wundersitz, 199-216. Canberra: Australian Institute of Criminology.

Braithwaite, J., and S. Mugford (1994). "Conditions of Successful Reintegration Ceremonies: Dealing with Juvenile Offenders." *British Journal of Criminology* 34:139-171.

Braithwaite, J., and C. Parker (1999). "Restorative Justice is Republican Justice." In *Restorative Juvenile Justice: Repairing the Harm of Youth Crime*, edited by G. Bazemore and L. Walgrave, 103-126. Monsey, NY: Criminal Justice Press.

Braithwaite, J., and T. Petit (1992). *Not Just Deserts: A Republican Theory of Criminal Justice*. Oxford, England: Clarendon Press.

Briar, S., and I. Piliavin (1965). "Delinquency, Situational Inducements, and Commitments to Conformity." *Social Problems* 13:35-45.

Bursick, R.J., and G. Grasmick (1993). *Neighborhoods and Crime: The Dimension of Effective Community Control*. New York: Lexington Books.

Butts, J., and H. Synder (1991). "Restitution and Juvenile Recidivism." Pittsburgh: National Center for Juvenile Justice.

Carey, M. (2001). "Infancy, Adolescence and Restorative Justice: Strategies in Promoting Organizational Reform," this volume.

Christie, N. (1978). "Conflicts as Property." *British Journal of Criminology* 17:1-15.

Claussen, R. (1996). "Restorative Justice—Fundamental Principles." New York: The Working Party on Restorative Justice (established by the United Nations Alliance of NGOs on Crime Prevention and Criminal Justice).

Clear, T., and D. Karp (1999). *The Community Justice Ideal: Preventing Crime and Achieving Justice*. Boulder, CO: Westview Press.

Crowe, A.H. (1998). "Restorative Justice in Offender Rehabilitation: A Meeting of the Minds." *Perspectives* 22:28-40.

Cullen, F.T. (1994). "Social Support as an Organizing Concept for Criminology." *Justice Quarterly* 11:527-559.

Cullen, F.T., and J.P. Wright (1996). "The Future of Corrections." In *The Past, Present and Future of American Criminal Justice*, edited by B. Maguire and P. Radosh. Dix Hills, NY: General Hall.

Cullen, F.T., J.P. Wright, and M.B. Chamlin (1999). "Social Support and Social Reform: A Progresive Crime Control Agenda." *Crime & Delinquency* 45:188-207.

Daly, K., and R. Immarigeon (1998). "The Past, Present and Future of Restorative Justice: Some Critical Reflections." *Contemporary Justice Review* 1(1):21-45.

Diaz, J. (1997). " Mission Statement." Pinal County Department of Juvenile Court Services, Florence, AZ.

Dighton, J. (1999). "Balanced and Restorative Justice in Illinois." *The Compiler: Illinois Criminal Justice Information Authority* (Winter):4-5

Doble, J., and S. Immerwahr (1997). "Delawareans Favor Prison Alternatives." In *Sentencing Reform in Overcrowded Times*, edited by M. Tonry and K. Hatlestad. New York: Oxford University Press.

Dooley, M. (1998). "The New Role of Probation and Parole: Community Justice Liaison." In *Community Justice: Concept and Strategies*, edited by American Probation and and Parole Association, 195-208.

Dooley, M. (1999). "Classification and Restorative Justice: Is There a Relationship?" *Topics in Community Corrections*. Longmont, CO: NIC Monograph.

Elliott, D. (1994). "Serious Violent Offenders: Onset, Developmental Course, and Termination." American Society of Criminology, 1993 Presidential Address. Reprinted from *Criminology* 32(1).

Feld, B. (1999). "Rehabilitation, Retribution and Restorative Justice: Alternative Conceptions of Juvenile Justice." In *Restorative Juvenile Justice: Repairing the Harm of Youth Crime*, edited by G. Bazemore and L. Walgrave, 17-44. Monsey, NY: Criminal Justice Press.

Gaes, G. (1998). "Correctional Treatment." In *The Handbook of Crime and Punishment*, edited by M. Tonry, 712-738. New York: Oxford University Press.

Gendreau, P., and D. Andrews (1990). "Tertiary Prevention: What the Meta-Analyses of the Offender Treatment Literature Tells Us About What Works." *Canadian Journal of Criminology* 32:173-84.

Gendreau, P., F. Cullen, and J. Bonta (1994). "Up to Speed: Intensive Rehabilitation Supervision the Next Generation in Community Corrections." *Federal Probation* 58:72-79.

Hirschi, T. (1969). *Causes of Delinquency*. Berkeley: University of California Press.

Hudson, J., B. Galaway, A. Morris, and G. Maxwell (eds.) (1996a). *Introduction*. Monsey, NY: Criminal Justice Press.

Hudson, J., B. Galaway, A. Morris, and G. Maxwell (eds.) (1996b). *Research of Family Group Conferencing in Child Welfare in New Zealand*. Monsey, NY: Criminal Justice Press.

Immarigeon, R. (1999). "Implementing the Balanced and Restorative Justice Model: A Critical Appraisal." *Community Corrections Report* (March/April):35-47.

Karp, D. (1998). "Judicial and Judicious Use of Shame Penalties." *Crime & Delinquency* 44:277-294.

Levrant, S., F. Cullen, B. Fulton, and J. Wozniak (1999). "Reconsidering Restorative Justice: The Corruption of Benevolence Revisited?" *Crime & Delinquency* 45:3-27.

Lipsey, M.W. (1995). "What Do We Learn from 400 Research Studies on Effectiveness of Treatment with Juvenile Delinquents?" In *What Works: Reducing Reoffending*, edited by J. McGuire. New York: Wiley.

Lipsey, M., and D. Wilson (1998). "Effective Intervention for Serious Juvenile Offenders: A Synthesis of Research." In *Serious and Violent Juvenile Offenders: Risk Factors and Successful Interventions*, edited by R. Loeber and D. Farrington, 313-366. Thousand Oaks, CA: Sage.

McKnight, J. (1995). *The Careless Society: Community and Its Counterfeits*. New York: BasicBooks.

Mennel, R. (1974). *Thorns and Thistles*. Chicago: University of Chicago Press.

Moon, M., J. Sundt, F. Cullen, and J. Wright (2000). "Is Child Saving Dead? Public Support for Rehabilitation." *Crime & Delinquency* 46:38-60.

Moore, D. (1998). "The Crisis of Abandoned Youth—Official Reaction." Unpublished manuscript.

Moore, D., and T. O'Connell (1994). "Family Conferencing in Wagga-Wagga: A Communitarian Model of Justice." In *Family Group Conferencing and Juvenile Justice: The Way Forward or Misplaced Optimism?*, edited by C. Adler and J. Wundersitz. Canberra: Australia Institute of Criminology.

Morris, A., and G. Maxwell (2001). "Restorative Conferencing," this volume.

Nugent, W.R., M.S. Umbreit, L. Wiinamaki, and J. Paddock (forthcoming). "Participation in Victim Offender Mediation and Re-Offense: Successful Replications." *Journal of Research on Social Work Practice*.

Osborn, D., and T. Gaebler (1992). *Reinventing Government*. Reading, MA: Addison-Wesley.

Packer, H. (1968). *The Limits of the Criminal Justice Sanction*. Palo Alto, CA: Stanford University Press.

Pearl, A., D. Grant, and E. Wenck (1978). *The Value of Youth*. Davis, CA: Dialogue Books.

Pittman, K., and W. Fleming (1991). "A New Vision: Promoting Youth Development." Testimony to House Select Committee on Children, Youth and Families, Academy for Education and Development, Washington, DC.

Platt, A. (1977). *The Child Savers: The Invention of Delinquency*. Chicago: University of Chicago Press.

Polk, K. (1994). "Family Conferencing: Theoretical and Evaluative Questions." In *Family Group Conferencing and Juvenile Justice: The Way Forward or Misplaced Optimism?*, edited by C. Adler and J. Wundersitz, 155-168. Canberra: Australia Institute of Criminology.

Polk, K., and S. Kobrin (1972). " Delinquency Prevention Through Youth Development." Washington, DC: Office of Youth Development.

Polk, K., and W. Schafer (1972). *Schools and Delinquency*. Englewood Cliffs, NJ: Prentice Hall.

Pranis, K., and G. Bazemore (2000). "Engaging the Community in the Response to Youth Crime: A Restorative Justice Approach." Monograph, Washington, DC: U.S. Department of Justice, Office of Juvenile Delinquency Prevention.

Pranis, K, and D. Bussler (1998). "Achieving Social Control: Beyond Paying!" Minneapolis: Minnesota Department of Corrections.

Pranis, K., and M. Umbreit (1992). *Public Opinion Research Challenges Perception of Wide Spread Public Demand for Harsher Punishment*. Minneapolis: Minnesota Citizens Council on Crime and Justice.

Retzinger, S., and T. Scheff (1996). "Strategy for Community Conference: Emotions and Social Bonds." In *Restorative Justice: International Perspectives*, edited by B. Galaway and J. Hudson, 315-336. Monsey, NY: Criminal Justice Press.

Rhine, E., A. Neff, and G. Natalucci-Persichetti (1998). "Restorative Justice, Public Safety, and the Supervision of Juvenile Offenders." *Corrections Management Quarterly* 2:40-48.

Rose, O., and T. Clear (1998). "Incarceration, Social Capital and Crime: Implications for Social Disorganization Theory." *Criminology* 36:471-479.

Rothman, D.J. (1980). *Conscience and Convenience: The Asylum and Its Alternatives in Progressive America*. Boston: Little, Brown.

Rutter, M. (1985). "Resilience in the Face of Adversity: Protective Factors and Resistance to Psychiatric Disorder." *British Journal of Psychiatry* 147:598-611.

Sampson, R., S. Rodenbush, and F. Earls (1997). "Neighborhoods and Violent Crime: A Multi-level Study of Collective Efficacy." *Science* (August):277.

Sampson, R.J. , and J. Wilson (1995). "Toward a Theory of Race."In *Crime and Urban Inequality*, edited by J. Hagan and R.D. Peterson, 37-54. Stanford, CA: Stanford University Press.

Schneider, A. (1985). "Guide to Juvenile Restitution." Washington, DC: U.S. Department of Justice, Office of Juvenile Justice and Delinquency Prevention.

Schneider, B. (1990). *Organizational Climate and Culture*. San Francisco: Jossey-Bass.

Schwartz, I., S. Guo, and J. Kerbs (1992). "Public Attitudes Toward Juvenile Crime and Juvenile Justice: Implications for Public Policy." Ann Arbor, MI: Center for the Study of Youth Policy.

Sherman, L, H. Strang, F. Barnes, J. Braithwaite, N. Inkpen, and M. Teh (1998). "Experiments in Restorative Policing: A Progress Report to the National Police Research Unit on the Canberra Reintegrative Shaming Experiment (RISE)." Canberra: Australian Federal Police, Australian National University.

Shoenwald, S., D. Scherer, and M. Brondino (forthcoming). "Effective Community Based Treatment for Serious Offenders." In *Innovative Models of Mental Health Treatment for "Difficult to Treat" Populations*, edited by S.W. Henggeler and A.B. Santos. Washington, DC: American Psychiatric Press.

Skogan, W. (1990). *Disorder and Decline: Crime and the Spiral of Decay in American Neighborhood*. New York: Free Press.

Stuart, B. (1996). "Circle Sentencing: Turning Swords into Ploughshares." In *Restorative Justice: International Perspectives*, edited by B. Galaway and J. Hudson, 193-206. Monsey, NY: Criminal Justice Press.

Tomkins, S. (1992). *Affect/Imagery/Consciousness*. New York: Springer.

Tonry, M. (1997). *Sentencing Matters*. New York: Oxford University Press.

Umbreit, M.S., R. Coates, and A.W. Roberts (1997). "Cross-National Impact of Restorative Justice through Mediation and Dialogue." ICCA *Journal of Community Corrections* 8(2):46-50.

Umbreit, M., and S.L. Stacey (1996). "Family Group Conferencing Comes to the U.S.: A Comparison with Victim Offender Mediation." *Juvenile and Family Court Journal* 47:29-38.

Van Ness, D., and K. Strong (1997). "Restorative Justice Practice." Monograph. Washington, DC: Justice Fellowship.

Von Hirsch, A. (1997). "Penal Philosophy: How Much to Punish?" In *Oxford Crime and Justice Handbook*, edited by M. Tonry. New York: Oxford University Press.

Walgrave, L. (1999). "Community Service as a Cornerstone within a Systemic Restorative Response to (Juvenile) Crime." In *Restorative Juvenile Justice: Repairing the Harm of Youth Crime*, edited by G. Bazemore and L. Walgrave, 129-154. Monsey, NY: Criminal Justice Press.

Walgrave, L., and G. Bazemore (1999). "Reflections on the Future of Restorative Justice for Juveniles." In *Restoring Juvenile Justice: Repairing the Harm of Youth Crime*, edited by G. Bazemore and L. Walgrave. Monsey, NY: Criminal Justice Press.

Werner, E. (1986). "Resilient Offspring of Alcoholics: a Longitudinal Study from Birth to 18." *Journal of Studies on Alcoholics* 47:34-40.

Wilkinson, R. (1998). "Community Justice in Ohio." *Corrections Today* 59:100-103.

Wilson, J., and G. Kelling (1982). "Broken Windows: The Police and Neighborhood Safety." *The Atlantic Monthly* 249(3):29-38.

Wright, M. (1991). *Justice for Victims and Offenders.* Milton Keynes, England: Open University Press.

Zehr, H. (1990). *Changing Lenses: A New Focus for Crime and Justice.* Scottdale, PA: Herald Press.

Zehr, H., and H. Mika (1998). "Fundamental Concepts of Restorative Justice." *Contemporary Justice Review* 1:47-55.

Zehr, H., and M. Umbreit (1982). "Victim Offender Reconciliation: An Incarceration Substitute?" *Federal Probation* 46:63-68.

6

Community Justice:
Transforming Communities Through Restorative Justice?

ADAM CRAWFORD
TODD R. CLEAR

In this chapter, we discuss the feasibility of underlying assumptions of "community" and "restorative" justice. These justice paradigms, often used interchangeably, are thought to embody a different conception of public safety that: (1) is delivered through a local or neighborhood level operational focus, (2) seeks to involve and empower ordinary citizens, (3) relies upon "private" and "parochial" forms of social control, and (4) operates within a problem-solving approach to social issues. Our discussion of their underlying assumptions leads us to pose a number of critical questions and concerns regarding the role and place of "community" within restorative justice and its potential implications for theory and practice. This leads us to consider the transformative potential and limitations of restorative justice within broader notions of crime prevention, community safety, and social policy. We begin with an attempt to distinguish community and restorative justice concepts.

Community Justice and Restorative Justice in Contrast

In recent usage, these two concepts have become blurred, but there are important distinctions between them. There are good reasons why this is so. Restorative justice advocates and community justice advocates tend to use similar language, begin with a similar critique

127

of the current justice system, and seek similar outcomes of restoration. Nevertheless, a useful distinction may be drawn between restorative and community justice, one that is nuanced and conceptual and (as we shall discuss later) poses distinct issues for reformers interested in either agenda.

At the risk of oversimplifying, restorative justice defines the problem of justice as lying within the processes and outcomes attached to "cases" of crime. In this regard, it is much like a traditional justice model, though it distinguishes itself from established justice processes and outcomes in important ways. Procedurally, restorative justice opens doors to effective participation of those who are normally denied a voice in traditional criminal justice: offenders, victims, their families, and neighbors. It defines successful outcomes in terms of the experiences of these people to whom the doors have been opened. It is radical in the sense that it is suspicious of credentialed professionals, distrustful of formal procedures, and embracing of a creative range of potential in solutions (as opposed to a list of presumptive sanctions). As a reform, though, restorative justice is profoundly traditional in the location of its efforts. It works at the level of particular criminal cases, seeking to alter how they are handled and how they are resolved. When the case is satisfactorily concluded, restorative justice may be seen as having achieved its objectives.

Community justice, by contrast, sets its focus on a different level. It is concerned with, for want of a better phrase, "what it is like for a person to live and work in this place" (see Clear and Karp, 1999). Criminal cases matter, but they matter because of the way crime affects community life in locations that are typically smaller than legal jurisdictions: neighborhoods, rather than cities. Whatever is done about the handling of criminal cases in these locations is justified on the basis of how the strategy in question (as opposed to other alternative strategies) affects what it is like to be in that place. Community justice may be seen as having a more radical reform orientation than restorative justice. It holds its advocates accountable not only for the handling of cases but for the nature of a collective experience. It embraces a much wider array of strategies including crime prevention schemes that fall well outside the restorative justice domain.

The melding of these ideas has been relatively recent. Earlier forms of restorative justice in the northeastern United States came out of a vision on the part of Mennonites and other religious groups of an inclusive, interpersonal, and problem-solving alternative to the traditional adversarial system of justice (Van Ness and Strong, 1997; Zehr, 1990). Outside the United States (and later in the southwestern United States), indigenous traditions served as models for reformers who sought to replace what they saw as sterile—and even bankrupt—formal justice processes with hopeful, participatory, and sympathetic alternatives. Most notable among these have been family group and community conferences, community mediation, and sentencing and "healing" circles (Hudson et al., 1996; Morris and Maxwell, 2000; LaPrairie, 1995; Stuart, 1996). Collectively, these developments involve meetings at which all those with a stake in the resolution of the issues surrounding a crime are brought together in the presence of a facilitator to discuss the harm the offense caused and how it might be repaired.

Outside of the New Zealand experience of family group conferences for young offenders as institutionalized at the heart of youth justice by the Children, Young Persons and Their Families Act 1989, the practice of restorative justice has tended to occupy peripheral positions at the margins of criminal justice. Nevertheless, the ideas that inform restorative justice have had considerable (and increasing) impact upon public policy debates,[1] as well as research-based notions about how we might reconstruct and rethink criminal justice in the future. As such, restorative justice came to constitute "the emerging social movement for criminal justice reform in the 1990s" (Braithwaite, 1998:324).

If restorative justice finds its emotional roots in religious-like exhortations to do good for fellow humans, community justice's emotional roots are located in a faith of civic life, a belief in the importance of "collective efficacy" (Sampson et al., 1997) or "capacity for self-regulation" (Bursik and Grasmick, 1992). While restorative justice is about cases, community justice is about places.

This conceptual distinction shows why the two ideas can be integrated in the minds of so many reformers: restorative justice is often seen as an important way to promote community justice. Likewise, when community justice initiatives aim to improve quality of life for victims, offenders, families, and neighbors who happen to live in a place of high crime, then restorative justice case outcomes may be an important part of the overall approach. However, restorative justice is not the only way to try to bring about the improvement in community life that is sought through community justice. Such disparate ideas as "zero-tolerance policing," community courts, Neighborhood Watch, and police-probation partnerships can be promoted under the community justice banner, because they have as their central justification the improvement of community life *in particular places where crime has damaged community life.*

Finally, this distinction clarifies the questions one would entertain in constructing an evaluation of programs associated with the two different ideas. A restorative justice program "works" when key constituents experience a restorative process and end up feeling restored by it. Community justice programs "work" when the quality of life in a given place improves.

Common Themes in Restorative and Community Justice

While these two visions of justice may be distinguished from one another, they also share certain underlying themes. Practical expressions of both restorative and community justice seek to recognize that crime is more than an offense against the state. They aim to consider the impact on victims and others involved, be they family, kinship, friends, or members of broader networks of interdependencies. They also endeavor to explore how communities can assist in the processes of restoration and conflict resolution. Implicitly, they seek to curtail and limit the role of criminal justice professionals, preferring to empower victims and offenders, as well as other family or kinship members, citizens, and community and voluntary groups or associations as partners in the justice process. These "significant others" are the "stakeholders" of a revised vision of justice, which is about recognizing and bringing into play, through their active involvement, a broader conceptualization of the stakeholders in the process of dispute processing and resolution. In this sense, Braithwaite has described this alternative view of justice as "deliberative justice," in contrast to the "professional justice of lawyers":

> it is about people deliberating over the consequences of crimes, and how to deal with them and prevent their recurrence . . . Thus restorative justice restores the deliberative control of justice by citizens. (1998:329)

In essence, community and restorative justice embody both a critique of existing formal legal procedures and practices (what we might call a "negative attraction") and a quest to revive some notion of community, mutuality, or civic trust (a "positive attraction"). Crime, after all, "is the most emotionally compelling symbol of lost community" (Abel, 1995:118). Consequently, the quest to revitalize the community fabric constitutes a powerful force in the appeal of both community justice and restorative justice, as they envision this as both a means to an end (the prevention of crime) and as an end in itself (community identified as the home of the ideal of genuine human identity, connectedness, and reciprocity).

Both of these negative and positive appeals have different resonances within differing societies, as they are refracted through divergent legal traditions, institutional apparatuses, and cultural context. Moreover, the rise of nontraditional justice expresses itself through, and coincides with, a rearticulation of the relationship between the state and civil society in which the nation-state, and hence the apparatus of criminal justice, appears to be confronting the dual pressures of globalization and localization. As a consequence, the contemporary "monopolistic" and "sovereign" state is increasingly forced to confront its own limitations with regard to its ability to guarantee public order and safety. New challenges now confront the tasks of policing and crime control, the preeminent and central symbols of state sovereignty, while economic pressures from one side collide with claims for greater cultural plurality from another side. Pluralization and fragmentation, in turn, have questioned traditional claims to universal security within a nation's boundaries. Increasingly, modern states find themselves able only to deliver punishment rather than security. In this context, governments have sought to experiment with, and explore, alternative means of crime control that aim to responsibilize individuals, families, groups, and communities as "partners against crime" in a new "corporate" approach (Crawford, 1994). This heralds a fundamental rearticulation of individual and group responsibilities and professional "expertise," as well as traditional notions of state paternalism and monopoly of control—all of which seep into, and affect debates about, community and restorative justice in relation to established modes of state justice.

The community and restorative justice movements have managed to draw support from diverse interests with often conflicting motivations. Particular initiatives have met with enthusiasm from divergent quarters, across the political spectrum, and within professional and community groups. The divergent nature of the interests and groups promoting these reforms in traditional justice has resulted in initiatives often meaning different things to different people. On one level, this has allowed the movement to gain support from diverse sources and to fit into the prevailing political rhetoric at given moments. However, it also means that specific initiatives can be (and have been) pulled in different, and often competing, directions as they attempt to meet multiple aims and objectives and satisfy the divergent demands of the different constituencies. In attempting (or claiming) to "do too much," the danger is that community and restorative justice initiatives can end up falling short on a number of fronts.

Questions Regarding Restorative Justice

The involvement of different stakeholders beyond the individual offender and direct victim is justified by restorative justice commentators on a number of levels. First, some commentators have preferred to extend and expand the notion of "victim" to include those indirectly affected by victimization, such that "it is more fruitful to theorize crime as typically affecting multiple victims in a range of ways" (Young, 2000:227). In this way, "significant others" are seen as having suffered indirectly either through their relationship with the primary victim or because of the disruption caused to communal peace and order by the offense. A common aim, then, is to draw extended family and community members into the process of finding resolutions and redress to crimes. The idea is to assemble actors with the closest relations and social interdependencies to the principal parties in dispute, most notably with a view to bringing together those people with the best chance of persuading the offender of the irresponsibility of a criminal act (Braithwaite and Mugford, 1994:142).

This has led some restorative justice commentators to include the local "community" more broadly as having a stake in the resolution of the conflict and, hence, as a party in restorative responses to offending. The involvement of the parties in the process of disputing through restorative justice is seen by proponents to be an essential element of community membership (Wright, 1991:76-77). For some, the community has a stake as an affected party. For others, the community is seen as a resource for the resolution of disputes and victim/offender reintegration. Still others see dispute resolution as a fundamentally communal activity requiring community input. As such, in some of the restorative justice literature, "the community" is drawn upon to constitute the role of the "third party"—as mediator or facilitator—in place of the state (see, for example, Karp and Walther, this volume).

Finally, restorative justice presupposes that community involvement *per se* in the decision-making process in response to offending assists in the building or reconstruction of community institutions and that, as such, it has the capacity to engender fundamental change in communities. Hence, restorative justice both draws upon, and simultaneously seeks to reinvigorate, a sense of community. Consequently, the response to crime is an activity that is conducted both on behalf of the community and that reflects a community's moral sensibilities. Conflict processing is, therefore, a highly *communal* act. It strengthens and reaffirms communal bonds. It represents not only a "potential for activity, for participation" but also allows the parties "opportunities for norm-clarification" (Christie, 1977:7-8). Hence, it is argued that the process of restorative justice—through party participation in conflict negotiation—is itself socially constructive. Resolving a conflict between parties is instrumental to the construction of shared values and commitment among the local community of residents. Consequently, restorative justice mechanisms are believed to empower the parties and the wider community through a heightened form of communication.

As a consequence, it is argued, community conferences and family group conferences go beyond some of the limitations of traditional victim-offender mediation because of the involvement of participants from the wider community with whom the parties have a "relationship of genuine care." First, it opens up what can otherwise be a private process (Braithwaite and Daly, 1994:206-207). Secondly, in doing so, it can limit the power that mediation accords to professional mediators. Thus, the power of mediators is curbed and the process is open to greater scrutiny. Thirdly, it confirms accountability upon those citizens who have concern for victims and offenders. "In contrast to mediation, conferences are designed to encourage community dialogue" (Braithwaite and Daly, 1994:207). Finally, it addresses the potentially unequal bargaining power of the parties by incorporating extended members.

For some commentators, the strengthening of community bonds that restorative justice mechanisms facilitate is itself crime-preventive. Implicit in this understanding is the idea that strong communities (and, hence, a strong moral order) act to prevent crime. Echoing social disorganization theories of crime, a lack of informal control is associated with criminality; such disputes are seen as arising where "normal" community controls have broken down.

However, restorative justice immediately raises questions about legitimacy, as it reconfigures the notion of the "public interest" through its appeal to a wider notion of stakeholders and to more localized normative orderings that rely upon private and parochial forms of social control. Ideally, the normative order should emerge from the extended parties themselves rather than being imposed from above. However, this tends to presuppose an unproblematic consensus without addressing the question of what the moral community *is*. The restorative justice response tends to assume organic wholeness of a given collectivity, one that accords little space for (or acknowledgment of) intra-community conflict and diversity of value systems. Will victims and offenders always belong to the same moral community? Some restorative justice initiatives explicitly attempt to recognize and accommodate the cultural needs of specific parties or even the cultural differences between victims and offenders. This may extend to the selection criteria of the third party or other parties to the dispute and/or its location and format. However, this recognition of multicultural heterogeneity raises a number of normative, as well as practical, dilemmas. For example, which cultural identities (ascriptions of difference) are sufficiently appropriate or worthy to be acknowledged and accommodated within the process of "representation" or structure of negotiation? How inclusive can such a moral community be before it loses its capacity to induce compliance and encourage conformity?

Perversely perhaps, the expanded notion of "stakeholder" in restorative justice can serve to dilute the centrality of the primary parties: the victim and offender. It can hand power to unrepresentative community members, service providers, and paraprofessionals (potentially with their own interests to serve) that coalesce around restorative justice programs, be they the new "experts" in techniques of reintegrative shaming, conference facilitation, or mediation. Some of the primary lessons from the experiments in "informal justice" in the 1980s were that programs established in the name of community mediation soon became increasingly formalized and professionalized, often under external pressures (Merry and Milner, 1993). The somewhat pessimistic conclusion reached by Yngvesson in relation to the San Francisco Community Boards was that community empowerment may be possible only for a privileged "internal community" of volunteers rather than the external "community of neighbors" (1993:381).

Before rushing to be inclusive by expanding the notion of "stakeholders" to incorporate ever-greater numbers of people, restorative justice needs to problematize, and ask fundamental questions about, the notion of stakeholder. Is a stakeholder in restorative justice someone who either provides, uses, or benefits from a service, or has relevant expert or local knowledge? If so, what does stakeholding entail? Is it merely an appeal to greater inclusiveness and mutual responsibility? Or is it that people "own" disputes such that they should determine outcomes themselves? How far should the involvement of stakeholders be taken in terms of decisionmaking or decision-taking? And finally, what is meant by the *co-production* of stakeholders in restorative justice?

Nevertheless, the identification of different stakeholders raises some important issues with regard to how success (or failure) is to be measured. It forces a reappraisal of the traditional question of "what works?" and introduces new variables into the measurement, posing a tiered series of questions concerning: "what works, for whom, and under which conditions?" As such, restorative justice should cause governments, practitioners, and researchers to rethink the process of evaluation and to broaden notions of success and failure to include the views and experiences of other stakeholders whose voice is all-too-often silenced. Hence, the impact of restorative justice upon victims and the local community may be as important for proponents of restorative justice as its impact upon offenders.

Restoring or Transforming Communities?

For some commentators, the consequences of the community justice and restorative justice movements for communities are more important than the consequences for offenders. This is suggested by Judge Barry Stuart with regard to "healing" circles in North America:

> The principal value of Community Sentencing Circles cannot be measured by what happens to offenders, but rather by what happens to communities. In reinforcing and building a sense of community, Circle Sentencing improves the capacity of communities to heal individuals and families and ultimately to prevent crime. (Stuart, 1994:18-19)

It is argued that the reinvigoration of community through restorative justice mechanisms facilitates strong bonds of social control. Strong communities can speak to us in moral voices. They allow "the policing *by* communities rather than the policing *of* communities" (Strang, 1995:217).

However, by necessity, alternative justice processes presuppose an existing degree of informal control upon which mutuality, reciprocity, and commitment can be reformed. As Braithwaite notes, informal control processes (such as reintegrative shaming), which some community conferences seek to engender, are more conducive to—and more effective when drawing upon—communitarian cultures (Braithwaite, 1989:100). The paradox is that in urban, individualistic, and anonymous cultures, such as those that prevail in most Western towns and cities, informal control mechanisms such as shaming lack potency. The appeal to revive or transform community has arisen at exactly the moment when it appears most absent. In some senses, for some, this paradox provides the basis for the attraction of restorative and community justice.

However, the conception of community extends beyond locality (with its spatial or geographic communities) and embraces a multiplicity of groups and networks to which, it is believed, we all belong (Strang, 1994:16). This conception of community, which is argued to be more in keeping with contemporary social life, does not rely upon a fixed assumption of *where* a community will be found. Rather, it develops upon the notion of "communities of care"—the networks of obligation and respect between the individual and everyone who cares about him or her the most, which are not bounded by geography (Braithwaite and Daly, 1995:195). It marks a significant development in the understanding of contemporary communities. These communities of care are supposed to be more relevant to contemporary modern living in urban societies. They encompass an expanded notion of "community" that, in part, is subjective in that the ascription to community membership or social identity is personal and does not necessarily carry any fixed or external attributes of membership. The fact that communities of care do not carry connotations of coerced or constrained membership is one of the concept's distinctive appeals.

Community, in this sense, begins to look like a set of bilateral relations of trust, rather than a dense, complex social order with rule-making capacities and the means to induce compliance, and which is set in a larger social matrix that can, and often does, affect and invade those internal orders. Insofar as it extends beyond individual feelings of affection and trust, community tends to be seen in symbolic terms as a set of shared or collective attitudes. As such, it lacks what Currie calls "structural awareness" and therefore fails to see community in "much more structural, or institutional terms not just as a set of attitudes we can "implant" or mobilize, but as an interlocking set of long-standing institutions which in turn are deeply affected by larger social and economic forces" (1988:282-283). If community is a product of free-floating social identity, internally ascribed and easily escaped (as Braithwaite and other restorative justice commentators imply), then it does not have the significant characteristics around which to induce compliance. If community is inherently volitional, comprising a collection of similar people who have voluntarily chosen to be together on the basis of some shared commonality, then what is its norm-making and norm-affirming capacity? How much compliance can a community command if individuals are free to move from one community to the next? In order to hold some normative sway over their members, to some degree, communities must be able to exact a measure of compliance, by means of regulation, sanction, and/or coercion.

Hence, for restorative agendas, the present weakness of "community" is often seen simultaneously as the problem (the cause of most contemporary social ills) and as its saving grace, in that people are assumed to be able to move freely between communities if they disagree with their practices or values and/or remain within a community and dissent from the dominant moral voices therein. On the one hand, contemporary "light" communities are held up as examples of how communities can allow sufficient space for individual or minority dissent, innovation, and difference—and yet they are also seen as insufficient with regard to informal control.

This brings us to pose the following question: What is actually meant by the claim to "restore" or "reintegrate" communities, as advanced by proponents of both community and restorative justice (Braithwaite, 1998:325; Clear and Karp, 1999; Van Ness and Strong, 1997:120-122)? The very notion of restoring communities suggests a return to some preexisting state. Is this appeal to community a quest for a retrieval or re-imagining of tradition and authority in some historic sense? Is it born of a nostalgic urge to turn back the clock to a mythical golden age of genuine human identity, connectedness, and reciprocity? Or does community constitute a dynamic force for democratic renewal that challenges existing inequalities of power and the differential distribution of life opportunities and pathways to crime?

In order to consider the genuine potential of restorative and community justice, we need to shed the rose-tinted glasses worn by many advocates and confront the empirical realities of most communities. The ideal of unrestricted entry to, and exit from, communities needs to be reconciled with the existence of relations of dominance, exclusion, and differential power. The reality is that many stable communities tend to resist innovation, creativity, and experimentation, as well as shun diversity. These communities may already be able to come together for informal social control, and the way these processes play out lacks inclusive qualities and offender-sensitive styles. These communities can be, and often are, pockets of intolerance and prejudice. They can be coercive and tolerant of bigotry and discriminatory behavior. Weaker parties within such communities often experience them not as a home of connectedness and mutuality but as a mainspring of inequalities that sustain and reinforce relations of dependence (for example, with regard to gender roles and the tolerance of domestic violence or child abuse). They are often hostile to minorities, dissenters, and outsiders.

Communities are hierarchical formations, structured upon lines of power, dominance, and authority. They are intrinsically exclusive—as social inclusion presupposes processes of exclusion—and may solidify and define themselves around notions of "otherness" that are potentially infused with racialized overtones. Challenging and disrupting established community order, its assumptions and power relations may be a more fundamental aspect of a progressive restorative justice program. *Transforming* communities may be more appropriate than *restoring* communities.

However, the related question begged by this assertion is whether transforming communities is either a feasible or appropriate task of restorative justice.

The Feasibility of Restoration and the Transformation of Communities

Restorative justice holds out the promise that communities can give redress to victims for what has been taken from them and can reintegrate offenders within the community. Yet, not all communities share the same access to resources, nor can they feasibly restore victims or reintegrate offenders in the same ways or to the same extent. Communities are marked by different capacities to mobilize internally on the basis of mutual trust and a willingness to intervene on behalf of the common good—what Sampson and colleagues refer to as "collective efficacy" (1997)—as well as differential relations that connect local institutions to sources of power and resources in the wider civil society in which it is located—what Hope refers to as "vertical power relations" (1995:24). This reminds us that restorative justice, in its appeals to community involvement, must not disconnect a concern for community approval or disapproval from a concern with political and economic inequality.

Neither restorative justice nor community justice should be allowed to become a byword for geographic (in)justice. Rather, they need to be based in an understanding of social justice and a concern for political economy that link notions of restoration with wider social and economic relations. A concern for intra-community attributes must be connected with attention to the context of a community.

The allied questions are: "Who restores what, to whom and why?" and "whose quality of life improves?" These questions raise issues directly concerning obligation and legitimacy. The legitimacy of justice and restoration must rest on the legitimacy of the community itself. Why would someone want to be restored to, or reintegrated within, a moral community that has abused them, marginalized them, or merely not valued them? Many offenders live peripatetic lives on the margins of communities. They may experience community not in its benign form but as one of alienation and sometimes hostility. For them, the community may suffer from significant and important empathy deficits. If we accept the empirical reality that thin and frayed lines exist between offending and victimization, offenders may themselves have been the victims of crimes against which the community has failed to act or respond (particularly given the high levels of nonreporting and nonrecording revealed by victim surveys). This has particular implications for legitimacy in restorative and community justice, which calls out for a mutuality of respect. Similarly, young people who have been the victims of powerful adult abuse may have good reasons not to accept as legitimate the dominant moral voice of a community that neither recognizes their suffering as worthy of attention nor addresses their marginalization. Communities have obligations and responsibilities to offenders and victims if they are to be seen as legitimate moral communities. This raises questions about the feasibility of community integration and, hence, the feasibility of reintegrative shaming.

To what degree is a more or less socialized youth required for reintegrative shaming to be possible? People commonly misunderstand what shame means. Shame is the emotion a person feels when confronted with the fact that one's behavior has been different to what one believes is morally required. Shame is moral self-reproach. Shame is thus personal; it is not produced by the actions of another. A person may humiliate or embarrass someone by a public act of rebuke, but that does not guarantee that such a public act will produce the emotion of shame. The exposure by another will produce shame only when the exposed person holds an aspiration to a different standard than has been exhibited by that past behavior. A community's shaming response may generate a person's humiliation, but humiliation may not lead to reintegration. Rather, it may lead to what Sherman (1997) has described as "counter-deterrence" if the person being humiliated does not feel ashamed. Therefore, we need to differentiate the personal emotion of shame from processes of shaming that may be inscribed into community and restorative justice practices without necessarily producing their desired result. Community and restorative justice should seek to encourage the former—which may be better described as "remorse" (Morris and Maxwell, 2000:215-217)—and avoid the latter. How we inculcate in others a moral self-view that makes productive shame possible is then a major challenge for restorative and community justice enthusiasts.

This raises questions about the feasibility of timescale—the extent to which restorative justice interventions are both *timely* (appropriate in time for parties) and *time enough* (sufficiently durable over time to effect change)—and of community integration. Can a limited intervention (such as that envisaged by family group and community conferences) really turn around people's lives (Levrant et al., 1999)? This is particularly problematic if these interventions are unable to address the structural problems or the causes of their criminality in a long-term and sustained manner. Questions of cost and the availability of adequate resources often hamstring restorative justice practices and community justice initiatives.

From the perspective of the victim, there are also concerns regarding the feasibility of restoration. Victims need recompense for their harm. Although this is a goal to which restorative justice appeals, most young people who have offended will not necessarily be able to make sufficient reparation. In this context, the public interest lies in public restoration to victims of crime (through schemes of compensation, for example). Under the benevolent veil of restorative justice, the state should not be allowed to abandon its responsibility to compensate. Public forms of restoration and redress should not be substituted merely with private restoration.

The Appropriateness of Community Transformation Through Restorative Justice

Making amends and restoring troubled relations in an unequal society may mean restoring unequal relations and, hence, reaffirming inequality. Moreover, restoring the preexisting equilibrium may mean reinstating and reaffirming relations of dominance. As such, Braithwaite is right to note these limitations of restorative justice, which

> cannot resolve deep structural injustices that cause problems . . . Restorative justice does not resolve the age-old questions of what should count as unjust outcomes. It is a more modest philosophy than that. (1998:329)

He goes on to identify two demands for restorative justice in this light. The first is that restorative justice should not make structural injustice worse. The second is that the deliberative processes of restorative justice should require that the outcome be grounded in a dialogue that takes account of underlying injustices (1998:329). All too often, however, in practice, negotiation avoids such dialogue regarding structural conflicts (Crawford, 1997). Consequently, Braithwaite's two demands constitute important bounding mechanisms to which practitioners would do well to accord. Importantly, they place a crucial responsibility for the public interest upon third-party facilitators. There is no reason why the restoration agenda cannot have as an objective the development of socially just improvements in those communities hardest hit by crime.

This also raises the question of the role of the state. The modern welfare state, with its claim to a "solidarity project," has striven to mediate and mitigate such differences in power and relations of dominance. Despite some commentators' arguments that neo-liberal discourses of government have dispensed with the aim of "governing through society," resulting in what Rose (1996) has called the "death of the social," the nation state remains the fundamental "power-container." Nevertheless, appeals to community as embodied in restorative and community justice developments clearly problematize the notion of the social. Not only does community represent the territorialization of political thought and how conduct is collectivized, but the "social" and "community" aspects are no longer necessarily complementary and of the same broad rationality of rule. They constitute different and potentially "competing problematics of government" (O'Malley and Palmer, 1996:140). There is a danger that community justice developments become "club" goods that benefit their members, rather than "public" goods that seek to benefit society at large. How are the particularistic and parochial interests and desires of communities to be accommodated within a wider frame of *social* justice? We need to think about and problematize the nature of the ruptures and disjunctures between social justice and local or parochial justice and determine how these should be regulated and mitigated in the name of the public good.

Moreover, if these new forms of justice seek social control outside of the state, then with what or whom does power-containing rest? The role of community in restorative and community justice raises important questions about the nature, place, and role of third parties in the processes of justice (Walgrave, 2000). If the third party is a representative of the community rather than the state, then the question is: Upon what notion of representativeness does their legitimacy rest? Does it rest on the mere fact that they are not employed by the state? Moreover, there is a further contradiction in that the more attached to the community third parties are, the less likely they are to hold the required "detached stance" that is a central value in establishing facilitator neutrality and legitimacy. The more that facilitators or mediators represent particular interests or value systems, the greater the danger that the interests of one of the principal parties may become sidelined or lost altogether. Ironically, of course, it is exactly this pressure to provide neutral and detached facilitators that increases the likelihood of professionalization of third parties and the formalization of otherwise fluid and open restorative processes.

Much of the community justice and restorative justice literature is infused with an explicit, and sometimes implicit, antistatism. It is no coincidence that the rise of restorative justice and the ascendancy of neo-liberal ideology have unfolded simultaneously. They both proclaim an end to universality and state monopoly and imply a privatization of disputes and justice by prioritizing private and parochial forms of control. Yet, a more plural and party-centered form of justice needs to recognize the crucial role of the state as power-container and norm-enforcer, and must seek to hold in creative tension the ideals of restorative justice and those of state justice. Tensions that are at the heart of attempts to integrate restorative justice into mainstream justice should be acknowledged and used as the source of productive forces as one strives to check the abuses of the other. As Lode Walgrave noted, "It is one of the most delicate challenges in the restorative justice undertaking, to conceive the role of the state (or government) in such a way that it does not impede the real restorative process, while playing its norm-enforcing role" (2000:261).

If this new justice movement is to be an element of a much wider policy concerned with constructing the conditions under which civility and mutuality breed, then it must be recognized that restorative justice (unlike community justice) is limited by its reactive nature. It requires harms to be inflicted before restorative interventions can begin to be put in place. This reactive essence confines restorative justice's potential as a transformative ideology. Restorative justice needs to be connected to a wider program of crime prevention and community safety for it to be anything other than reactive and led by individual case. Moreover, it will need to move beyond a narrow focus upon crime to wider concerns about safety in communities from criminal and noncriminal sources of harms. Wiles and Pease (2000) have termed this a "pan-hazard" approach to community safety. There is much to be gained from a vision that moves beyond reactions to crime to proactive interventions that extend far beyond criminality and disorder. Such an approach would see restorative justice as a limited aspect of broader politics concerned with the promotion of social goods. To some degree, it is this larger picture to which some Republican criminologists, such as Braithwaite (1989; 1995), allude. All too often, however, the restorative justice literature fails to make these broader connections and holds up restorative justice as both an end in itself and the primary transformative logic in the reinvigoration of moral communities.

Social and economic policy (including employment, education, health, and housing) rather than criminal justice policy, regardless of whether it is restorative, must be the primary vehicle for the construction of a just and equal social order. The danger is that restorative justice, by itself, accords a centrality to the reaction to crime that would not have been accorded even by Durkheim (1893). Responses to crime are fundamentally social and cultural events that seek to reaffirm a collective consciousness and social cohesion, but they are not the mainstay out of which the collective consciousness springs. In claiming a centrality in the construction of a just social order, restorative justice proponents give the reaction to crime an overriding position that it may not deserve. A potential consequence is that fundamental public issues may become marginalized, except insofar as they are defined in terms of their criminogenic qualities. The danger is that, as a consequence, we may come to view poor housing, unemployment, racism, failed educational facilities, the lack of youth leisure opportunities, and so on, as no longer important public issues in themselves. Rather, their importance may be seen in terms of the belief that they lead to crime and disorder. The fact that they may do so is no reason not to assert their importance in their own right. The fear is that social deficiencies are being redefined as "crime problems" that need to be controlled and managed rather than addressed in themselves. This would represent the ultimate "criminalization of social policy." Hence, there is an anxiety that a high degree of influence given to restorative justice may result in social policy, as well as its direction and funding, being redefined in terms of its implications for crime alone. This is rendered all the more worrysome given the place of inequality within both neo-liberal ideology and the dominant Durkheimian discourse of "social (dis)integration" that underlies much of liberal thinking (see Levitas, 1996). Inequality, in this context, increasingly is viewed as something that is a problem only because, if extreme enough, it is disruptive of social order—or at least perceived to be potentially disruptive (as in the fear of crime).

Lessons from the past 20 years of research into community crime prevention suggest a certain degree of caution regarding the long-term benefits of restorative and community justice as community empowerment. Almost all studies of local crime-prevention activities identify difficulty in sustaining participants' interest and enthusiasm over time, even in places where initial levels of awareness and participation were high (Palumbo et al., 1997; Rosenbaum, 1988). Communities organized solely or primarily around concerns about crime are often short-lived (Podolefsky and Dubow, 1981). As Skogan notes, "concern about crime simply does not provide a basis for sustained individual participation" (1988:49).

Finally, given crime's capacity to evoke intense emotions and bifurcate through deep-seated fears of "otherness," it may be an inappropriate vehicle around which to construct open and tolerant communities, as opposed to those that solidify around "defensive exclusivity" (Crawford, 1998).

Some Concluding Thoughts

Implicit in restorative justice is a reevaluation of the responsibilities of government, communities, and individuals for responding to victimization and the harms of crime. Where traditional notions of justice treated the public as the recipient of an expert service provided by criminal justice professionals, restorative justice calls upon public participation and active citizenry.[2] Individuals and groups become reconfigured as partners in the process and coproducers of the outcome. The pluralization of responsibility acknowledges the limits of the sovereign state with respect to crime control and security. It begins a recognition that the causes of crime lie far from the traditional reach of the criminal justice system and, as such, it acknowledges the need for social responses to crime that reflect the nature of the phenomenon itself and its multiple etiology, as well as the importance of mechanisms of informal social control in the prevention of crime.

This allows for a more participatory civil society that fractures the state's monopolistic and paternalistic hold. However, it also presents a danger of a conflation of the responsibilities of the state and those of individuals—victims, offenders, and "significant others"—as well as communities and other networks of care. Strategies of responsibilization should seek to clarify the distribution of responsibilities and to ensure the appropriate conditions under which the exercise of those responsibilities can be fulfilled and maximized. Unfortunately, much of the restorative and community justice literature and current policy tends to obfuscate the role of the state and third parties, replacing these with a particularly ambiguous appeal to community ordering and individual choice.

The aim of this chapter has been to raise some critical questions for consideration in a period of significant policy activity and thought regarding the potential of an alternative justice paradigm. The manner of this chapter has been deliberately skeptical. It has sought to connect these developments to wider sociopolitical change and to highlight their possible ambiguous implications. As the modern state appears to be coming to terms with its own inability to guarantee order, albeit in a hesitant and ambivalent manner, we need to ask whether the developments reflect a growing civilianization, humanization, or privatization of criminal justice. The latter option raises the concern that gov-

ernments should not be allowed to use restorative or community justice as a means of unduly shifting the burden of justice onto individuals and communities. These reforms should not result in the state
"washing its hands" through the privatization of disputes. Moreover,
there is a danger of a confusion of aims within restorative justice that
is in part driven and reaffirmed by the diverse support that restorative
justice has received across the political spectrum. Are all the aims of
restorative justice feasible or desirable? Or should proponents priori-
tize realizable objectives for practice? The danger is that restorative justice initiatives can end up falling short on a number of fronts.

There is a need for restorative and community justice advocates not
only to recognize limitations but also to develop an acute understanding of intra- and as inter-community relations. With regard to
intra-community relations, restorative aims need to acknowledge differences within (as well as between) communities and not encourage
the perpetuation of an "ideology of unity" (Crawford, 1997:137-
139), in which a moral order or consensus is taken as given, rather than
constructed through nuanced and complex negotiations. Instead, the
ground rules of communication need to have etched within them
processes that bind the contending parties together while simultaneously rendering the existing differences sharper and more explicit, even
while the parties may arrive at a negotiated outcome. Here, community is not idealized as a cohesive unity but presupposes that differences
are acknowledged within it. Such strong bonds require an engagement,
over time, with intra-communal differences.

We can imagine, however, a notion of restorative justice that may
offer a more fertile soil from which a progressive criminal justice policy can begin to establish itself and flourish, one that turns away
from the "punitive populism" of recent years. Moreover, it affords the
potential to challenge many of the modernist assumptions about professional expertise, specialization, state paternalism, and monopoly,
which have become established aspects of traditional criminal justice.
It would empower victims and offenders and enable them to be treated more humanely and with respect to their interests and needs. Until
the economics of criminal justice become a part of the community and
restorative justice picture, though, there is always the question of
how to resource the initiatives that result in greater justice across
communities.

In essence, the current system in the United States involves a massive, officially managed, economic transaction of the following sort:
residents of affluent communities transfer their wealth in the form of
tax revenues to rural communities (where the prisons are) to pay the
salaries and living expenses of people who "watch" the residents of poor
communities for a couple of years, then send them home. The scope of
the investment is striking. One study (Rose and Clear, 1998) estimat-

ed that about $4.5 million was spent incarcerating a one-year sample of offenders in a 10-by-15 block neighborhood in Tallahassee, Florida. Another study (CASES, 1998) found that $50 million was spent incarcerating the offenders from the Brownsville section of Brooklyn, NY, in 1996—$3 million on residents of a *single* block. These dollar figures reflect the investment of public funds in response to public safety problems in poorer communities from the tax base in wealthy and middle-class neighborhoods to the economies of prison communities. The irony is that almost nothing from this investment goes into the economic infrastructure of the offenders' communities. The justice system investment in these communities is solely "addition by subtraction": removing certain citizens in the hope that it will be easier for those who remain to improve their circumstances. The economics of community justice must come to see these investments as opportunity cost centers. If some portion of the investment in prison community economies can be refocused toward high-crime communities, then the resources for community justice and restorative justice to address structural and other criminogenic problems in communities can be substantial.

A shorthand way of thinking about the economics of restoration goes along the following lines: traditional criminal justice systems route public funds from tax-paying communities to communities providing prison services, leaving crime-affected communities out of the direct economic loop. Community justice (and, to a lesser extent, restorative justice) seeks to capture some of those funds (both human and financial capital) for direct investment in high-crime locations, in the form of improved physical plant, social support, and even contributed offender labor—the kinds of resources that may contribute more broadly to an improved quality of life and, thus, public safety. One of the best examples of this in the United States is the way in which the Deschutes County (Oregon) Department of Community Justice recaptures dollars intended for juvenile training schools and uses them for community crime prevention (Maloney and Bryant, 1998).

Finally, the realization that community justice can be conciliatory and socially constructive, but also punitive and intolerant, requires the construction of more rigorous criteria for the evaluation of both the malignant and benign elements and attributes of community justice. As such, it necessitates standards against which developments and practices can be assessed or, in a different discourse, it requires a basic conception of human rights.

Moreover, a limited notion of restorative justice may offer a fertile soil from which a more progressive criminal justice policy can be established, one that turns away from the "punitive populism" of recent years. Moreover, it affords the potential to challenge many of the modernist assumptions about professional expertise, specialization, state paternalism, and monopoly that have become established aspects of traditional criminal justice. Consequently, restorative justice may empower victims and offenders as well as enable them to be treated more humanely and with due respect to their interests and needs.

It is our contention that neither restorative justice nor community justice can be held out as the primary means through which civil society is to be (re)constructed. Although crime may be a "regressive tax on the poor," it does not follow that reactions to crime should be (or even can be) the appropriate site of redistributive justice. Criminal justice is intrinsically reactive, bound up with state coercion, and limited in its scope. As such, it is not the cradle of a society's civility. It should, however, reflect and express this civility, particularly with regard to the treatment of all those who turn to, or are caught up in, its machinations. In this respect, a qualified understanding of restorative justice that begins to address some of the questions posed in this chapter—while holding in creative tension the notion of the public interest and that of parochial relations—will enable the ideals of restorative justice and those of state justice to act as fundamental social correctives to each other. With an appropriate concern for the real problems affecting life in high-crime communities, restorative justice paradigms can offer some foundation for more just communities.

Discussion Questions

1. What do Crawford and Clear consider to be the main differences between restorative and community justice? What are the common themes? Do you agree with these distinctions? Do you think they are important?

2. Why do these authors think that involving a variety of stakeholders in restorative processes can "dilute the centrality of the primary stakeholders"? Do you agree with this assessment? Why or why not?

3. "Community" is particularly difficult to define for several reasons. What are some obstacles to defining and engaging communities in restorative processes? Are these obstacles insurmountable or can they be overcome? What are some of the implications of how the community is defined and engaged?

4. Crawford and Clear make a distinction between "restoring" and "transforming" communities. What is this distinction and why does it matter? Do you think the goal of the justice system should be either to restore or transform communities, or to achieve some other goal(s)? Do you think restoring or transforming communities is an appropriate role for the criminal justice system?

Endnotes

1   For example, restorative justice ideas inform recent legislative changes to juvenile justice enacted by the Government in England and Wales through the Crime and Disorder Act 1998 and the Youth Justice and Criminal Evidence Act 1999. Together, these pieces of legislation and allied policy initiatives have advanced what policy documents have referred to as, "the 3 R's of restorative justice: Restoration, Reintegration and Responsibility" (Home Office, 1997). This has led at least one British commentator to suggest that these changes should ensure that restorative justice is "no longer a marginal, irregular and highly localised activity" (Dignan, 1999:53).

2   This is explicit in Braithwaite's "republican theory'"which sees restorative justice as a part of wider changes in participatory democracy (1995). See also Pettit (1997).

References

Abel, R. (1995). "Contested Communities." *Journal of Law and Society* 22:113-126.

Braithwaite, J. (1989). *Crime, Shame and Reintegration.* Cambridge, England: Cambridge University Press.

Braithwaite, J. (1995). "Inequality and Republican Criminology." In *Crime and Inequality,* edited by J. Hagan and R.D. Peterson, 277-305. Stanford: Stanford University Press.

Braithwaite, J. (1998). "Restorative Justice." In *Handbook of Crime and Punishment,* edited by M. Tonry, 323-344. New York: Oxford University Press.

Braithwaite, J., and K. Daly (1994). "Masculinities, Violence and Communitarian Control." In *Just Boys Doing Business? Men, Masculinities and Crime,* edited by T. Newburn and E.A. Stanko, 189-213. London: Routledge.

Braithwaite, J., and S. Mugford (1994). "Conditions of Successful Reintegration Ceremonies: Dealing with Juvenile Offenders." *British Journal of Criminology* 34:139-147.

Bursik, R., and H.G. Grasmick (1992). *Neighborhoods and Crime: The Dimensions of Effective Community Control.* New York: Lexington Books.

CASES (1998). "The Community Justice Project." Center for Alternative Sentencing and Employment Services. New York, September.

Christie, N. (1977). "Conflicts as Property." *British Journal of Criminology* 17(1):1-15.

Clear, T.R., and D.R. Karp (1999). *The Community Justice Ideal: Preventing Crime and Achieving Justice.* Boulder, CO: Westview.

Crawford, A. (1994)."The Partnership Approach: Corporatism at the Local Level?" *Social and Legal Studies* 3(4):497-519.

Crawford, A. (1997). *The Local Governance of Crime: Appeals to Community and Partnerships.* Oxford, England: Clarendon Press.

Crawford, A. (1998). *Crime Prevention and Community Safety: Politics, Policies and Practices*. Harlow, England: Longman.

Currie, E. (1988). "Two Visions of Community Crime Prevention." In *Communities and Crime Reduction*, edited by T. Hope and M. Shaw, 280-286. London: Her Majesty's Stationery Office.

Dignan, J. (1999). "The Crime and Disorder Act and the Prospects for Restorative Justice." *Criminal Law Review* 48-60.

Durkheim, E. (1893). *The Division of Labor in Society*. New York: Free Press.

Home Office (1997). *No More Excuses*. White Paper. London: Home Office.

Hope, T. (1995). "Community Crime Prevention." In *Building a Safer Society: Crime and Justice a Review of Research, Volume 19*, edited by M. Tonry and D. Farrington, 21-89. Chicago: University of Chicago Press.

Hudson, J., A. Morris, G. Maxwell, and B. Galaway (eds.) (1996). *Family Group Conferences: Perspectives on Policy and Practice*. Annandale, Australia: Federation Press.

LaPrairie, C. (1995). "Altering Course: New Directions in Criminal Justice. Sentencing Circles and Family Group Conferencing." *Australian and New Zealand Journal of Criminology* 28:78-99.

Levitas, R. (1996). "The Concept of Social Exclusion and the New Durkheimian Hegemony." *Critical Social Policy* 16:5-20.

Levrant, S., F.T. Cullen, B. Fulton, and J.F. Wozniak. (1999). "Reconsidering Restorative Justice: The Corruption of Benevolence Revisited?" *Crime & Delinquency* 45(1):3-27.

Maloney, D., and K. Bryant (1998). *Deschutes County Community Justice*. Bend, OR: Deschutes County Community Justice Department.

Merry, S.E., and N. Milner (eds.) (1993). *The Possibility of Popular Justice: A Case Study of Community Mediation in the United States*. Ann Arbor: University of Michigan Press.

Morris, A., and G. Maxwell (2000). "The Practice of Family Group Conferences in New Zealand: Assessing the Place, Potential and Pitfalls of Restorative Justice." In *Integrating a Victim Perspective Within Criminal Justice*, edited by A. Crawford and J.S. Goodey, 207-225. Aldershot, England: Ashgate.

O'Malley, P., and D. Palmer (1996). "Post-Keynesian Policing." *Economy and Society* 25(2):137-155.

Palumbo, D., J.L. Ferguson and J. Stein (1997). "The Conditions Needed for Successful Community Crime Prevention." In *Crime Prevention at a Crossroads*, edited by S.P. Lab, 79-98. Cincinnati: Anderson.

Pettit, P. (1997). *Republicanism: A Theory of Freedom and Government*. Oxford, England: Clarendon.

Podolefsky, A., and F. Dubow (1981). *Strategies for Community Crime Prevention*. Springfield, IL: Charles C Thomas.

Rose, D.R., and T.R. Clear (1998). "Who Doesn't Know Someone in Prison or Jail? The Impact of Incarceration on Attitudes Toward Formal and Informal Social Control." Presentation to the National Institute of Justice Research in Progress Series, March, Washington, DC.

Rose, N. (1996). "'The Death of the Social?': Refiguring the Territory of Government." *Economy and Society* 25(3):327-356.

Rosenbaum, D.P. (1988) "Community Crime Prevention: A Review and Synthesis of the Literature." *Justice Quarterly* 5(3):323-393.

Sampson, R.J., S.W. Raudenbush, and F. Earls (1997). "Neighborhoods and Violent Crime: A Multi-Level Study of Collective Efficacy." *Science* 277:918-923.

Sherman, L. (1997). "Counter-Deterrence." Presentation to the American Society of Criminology, November, San Diego.

Skogan, W. (1988). "Community Organisations and Crime." In *Crime and Justice: An Annual Review of Research*, edited by N. Morris and M. Tonry, 39-78. Chicago: Chicago University Press.

Strang, H. (1995). "Replacing Courts with Conferences." *Policing* 11(3):212-220.

Stuart, B. (1994). "Sentencing Circles: Purpose and Impact." National Canadian Bar Association, 13.

Stuart, B. (1996). "Circle Sentencing: Turning Swords into Ploughshares." In *Restorative Justice: International Perspectives*, edited by B. Galaway and J. Hudson. Monsey, NY: Criminal Justice Press.

Van Ness, D., and K.H. Strong (1997). *Restoring Justice*. Cincinnati: Anderson.

Walgrave, L. (2000). "Extending the Victim Perspective Towards a Systemic Restorative Justice Alternative." In *Integrating a Victim Perspective Within Criminal Justice*, edited by A. Crawford and J.S. Goodey, 253-284. Aldershot, England: Ashgate.

Wiles, P. and K. Pease (2000). "Crime Prevention and Community Safety: Tweedledum and Tweedledee?" In *Secure Foundations: Key Issues in Crime Prevention, Crime Reduction and Community Safety*, edited by S. Battantyne, K. Pease, and V. McLaren, 21-29. London: Institute for Public Policy Research.

Wright, M. (1991). *Justice for Victims and Offenders*. Milton Keynes, England: Open University Press.

Yngvesson, B. (1993). "Local People, Local Problems, and Neighborhood Justice: The Discourse of "Community" in San Francisco Community Boards." In *The Possibility of Popular Justice*, edited by S.E. Merry and N. Milner, 379-400. Ann Arbor: The University of Michigan Press.

Young, R. (2000). "Integrating a Multi-Victim Perspective into Criminal Justice Through Restorative Justice Conferences." In *Integrating a Victim Perspective Within Criminal Justice*, edited by A. Crawford and J.S. Goodey, 227-251. Aldershot, England: Ashgate.

Zehr, H. (1990). *Changing Lenses: A New Focus for Crime and Justice*. Scottdale, PA: Herald Press.

7

Infancy, Adolescence, and Restorative Justice: Strategies for Promoting Organizational Reform

MARK CAREY

Introduction

Modern-day application of restorative justice in most of the world is now only a few years old. Many correctional and victim rights organizations, criminal justice systems, social service agencies, and community groups have discovered the power of clear language and principles that direct policies, programs, and priorities toward one that seeks, above all else, to correct the harm caused by crime. This attempt at changing traditional justice practices, however, has encountered significant barriers. Examining the experiences of early efforts to move from a retributive model of corrections to one that promotes restorative principles reveals a wide range of success and failure. Even in areas in which major changes have been made, struggles to alter long-standing system and organizational cultures are commonplace. Agencies and systems that have made a more complete transition to a restorative justice policy have at least one thing in common: they have *sustained* the drive for change over several developmental stages and have *modified* policies and procedures based on an evolving developmental state.

It is this author's contention that agencies generally go through three developmental stages that parallel those of human development (i.e., infancy, adolescence, and adulthood). As such, an agency's response to these changing needs must be adapted accordingly. Failure to make these adaptations would likely result in an organizational return to traditional practice, much like a rubber band naturally returning to its original shape. Agencies seeking long-term, cultural changes toward restorative justice principles and practice need to both carefully select an appropriate set of strategies and properly time the techniques to maximize their potential influence.

Restorative Justice Principles and Justice Agency Cultures

Restorative justice is fundamentally different from modern-day American criminal justice interventions (Zehr, 1990). It suggests that crime is a rupture of a social contract. Crime results in harm toward a victim and community (and the offender), which means that the criminal/juvenile justice system must recognize crime as an interpersonal conflict (i.e., a conflict between individuals as opposed to involving a more abstract party such as the state). As with any injury producing conflict, the system is obligated to promote the repair of those relationships, to help "make things right," and to ensure that something good results from intervention.

These principles differ from these guiding criminal justice systems focused almost exclusively on punishment, fairness and proportionality, and due process. One way to understand these differences is by comparing the relative importance attached to several concerns in each approach (see Figure 7.1).

Figure 7.1
Restorative Principles and Concerns

Retributive Justice ◄————————► Restorative Justice	
	Services available for victims
	Victim opportunity for involvement and input
	Offender opportunity and encouragement to take responsibility
Low Importance	Offender involved in repair of harm **High Importance**
	Increase in offender competency
	Community members actively involved in decision making and implementation
	Processes build connections among community members

Restorative justice proponents insist that the criminal/juvenile justice system has three primary stakeholders or "customers" (victim, offender, and community). The call for balance in the response to the needs of each stakeholder then requires a kind of "bottoms-up" systemic change at the agency and staff level (Bazemore, 1997; Bazemore and Walgrave, 1999), based upon:

- New values (e.g., emphasis on repairing harm);
- New skills (e.g., victim or community/offender mediation);
- New roles (e.g., community organizing);
- New expectations (e.g., providing ongoing victim input and communication);
- New training (e.g., victim sensitivity and offender cognitive skill building);
- New set of supports (e.g., training, clinical supervision, community partnership, etc.).

How have the principles and application of restorative justice played out at the level of correctional agencies? Perhaps the most accurate answer is "it depends." In some jurisdictions, the introduction of the principles have wholly revamped services, priorities, use of resources, and thought processes. In others, restorative justice has not dented the shield of current philosophy or practice. In either case, the new philosophy tends to resonate with correctional employees. As Umbreit and Carey (1995) point out:

> Restorative justice has tapped into a stream of energy and excitement within corrections departments nationwide. For many, this energy has remained inert for years under the pressures of changing public expectations, legislative mandates, public safety demands, and escalating probation caseloads. Probation departments are re-discovering the personal and professional motivations for their staffs entering the corrections field. Typically, those motivations are to promote offender change, to assist crime victims toward wholeness, and to make individual communities safer. For too long, the emphasis has been on surveillance and monitoring instead of those tenets brought forth by restorative justice principles such as competency development within the offender, victim participation and services, offender accountability, and community involvement and responsibility. Discovering this energy is a promising beginning for productive changes in corrections but it is not enough.

Philosophical buy-in, therefore, does not guarantee that changes will be made in day-to-day practices. One of the most potent barriers lies within organizational culture. Each organization has a culture that sustains status quo. The failure to understand agency culture usually lies at the heart of failed efforts.

Organizational Culture

Restorative justice emphasizes values, roles, and expectations that are fundamentally different from organizational culture. It is therefore, helpful to examine why organizational culture exists and why it is so hard to change it. Schein (1981) describes culture as:

> The set of basic assumptions which members of a group invent to solve the basic problems of physical survival in the external environment (adaptation) and social survival in the internal environment (internal integration).

The three components that make up organizational culture are:

1. *Artifacts:* Visible creations produced in organizations such as language, art, stratification, and status symbols. There is a high level of awareness of their existence as employees see and/or use them. Examples might include artwork, the display of the agency mission statement, bullet-proof glass, metal detectors, and cleanliness of the office setting.

2. *Values:* Ideals, goals, and means to achieve them. They are typically passed on to successive generations by the "old timers" in an organization. The artifacts are reflections of these values. Examples of values might include statements that the agency is a learning organization, that customers come first, that all offenders can change, that victims are considered primary customers, that respect of human dignity will be upheld, and so on.

3. *Basic Assumptions:* Rules of interaction between members of the agency. They are more difficult to ascertain because they tend to be invisible, taken for granted, and unconsciously held. Examples might include beliefs that one can or cannot voice their opinion without paying a price, that management is hypocritical, that one is empowered or even expected to make changes when needed, and so on.

The combination of artifacts, values, and assumptions helps agency staff avoid or reduce anxiety by reducing cognitive overload through developing and communicating a consistent set of work-related expectations. The employees and agency benefit by passing these assumptions and practices to successive generations rather than reinventing new ones whenever staff are added or replaced. An existing organizational culture creates a sense of predictability that allows employees to feel comfortable, establish meaningful relationships, and understand what it takes to gain career advancements and enjoy work competence. It provides employees with rules for behavior and norms that, in effect, shape the behavior of employees and, therefore, define the organizational culture (Schwartz and Davis, 1981). New values and expectations upset this stability and naturally cause anxiety and consternation. Even under the best of circumstances and processes, one should expect resistance and conflict when new values, roles, and expectations are introduced, as a result of their effect on human relationships and emotions.[1]

"Hard Side" and "Soft Side"

In *The Search of Excellence*, Peters and Waterman (1982) use the McKinsey Seven-S Model to evaluate companies. The model identifies managerial activities used to operate a company. The seven activities (strategy, structure, skills, staff, style, systems, and shared values) can be divided into two groups: those that represent the *hard* side of management, and those that represent the *soft* side. The hard side consists of those activities that are tangible and reflect hierarchy and procedure (such as strategy, structure, and systems). The soft side contains those components that are less tangible but usually more important (e.g., style, staff, skills, and shared values). Pascale and Athos (1981) point out that American companies tend to manipulate the hard side when seeking change, while Japanese companies concentrate on the soft side. It is the soft side that needs to be given prominent attention when attempting to make changes toward restorative justice, as these less tangible components are the primary contributing factors that ultimately shape organizational values and culture.

Developmental Stages Toward Cultural Shift

An organization that attempts to transform its existing practices to achieve consistency with restorative justice is likely to find agency and criminal/juvenile justice system values that are at least partly incongruent with restorative values. Court and correctional systems are derived from legal models that are focused almost exclusively on the rights and punishment of the offender. Early agency attempts at systemic and cultural change confront the collision of different value systems. In doing so, they reveal the evolution of an organization's developmental stages. Such agencies discover a simultaneously exciting and terrifying roller-coaster ride as value systems clash through the change process. Fundamental cultural change in any setting (societal, religious, racial, or organizational) is bound to be wrought with turmoil, confusion, and (hopefully) renewal.

As Figure 7.2 suggests, some characteristics of this difficult process parallel human developmental transformation.

Figure 7.2
Characteristics of Human Developmental Stages

> **Infancy:**
>   Dependency
>   Rapid growth
>   Need for basic nourishment
>   Need for nurturing environment
>   Small muscle and eye-hand coordination
>   High energy level
>
> **Adolescence:**
>   Growth through discovery
>   Rule testing
>   Formulating and testing hypotheses
>   Rebellion
>   Seeking identity
>   Increasing independence
>   Confusion
>   Experimentation
>   Emotional fluctuation
>   Need for clear boundaries
>   Taking of less calculated risks
>   Emergence of independent, critical thinking
>
> **Adulthood:**
>   Settling down
>   Taking on of responsibilities
>   Stability
>   Taking of calculated risks

Correctional agencies can expect to go through similar stages of development, as the existing culture is challenged to become more restorative. Social psychologist Kurt Lewin first developed a change model in 1951 by describing three distinct states: the present state, the transition state, and the desired state. In this model, the transition state parallels the adolescent characteristics of organizational change. Once an organization embarks on a restorative change process, it can expect to encounter specific but unique challenges that follow the three developmental stages (Lewin, 1951).

Stage One: Infancy

Like characteristics found in early stages of human development, an agency seeking to make fundamental value and role shifts can expect major growth spurts by providing basic training and encouragement from the agency's leadership. In areas in which dissatisfaction with current outcomes exists, it is more likely that many employees will quickly embrace restorative principles. It is common, for example, for staff to point out that they entered the correctional field out of a desire to make a difference in people's lives, only to be disenchanted over the years with an emphasis on processes, monitoring activities, and paperwork.

Growth can be exciting and visible as new ideas are enthusiastically expressed and initial outcomes realized. Not all staff, of course, will immediately support the restorative concepts. Many will offer reasons why their support will not be forthcoming. Management needs to encourage those who wish to take those first baby steps. The organization should be gathering information, learning how restorative justice would redefine outcomes and expectations. Support is needed for those who relish the prospect of a better future and the role corrections can play in involving partnerships with others to deal with crime. During this stage, agencies typically devise action plans and anticipate how those plans might transform their work.

Agency leadership must pay attention to both hard-side and soft-side activities (Pascale and Athos, 1981) in order to bring about a cultural change toward restorative justice. However, when and how those activities are employed is paramount to purposeful and guided directed agency evolution. During Stage One (infancy), agency staff need time to absorb the content and context of the new restorative framework and to explore how it might benefit the agency and/or themselves. They need some reassurance that their well-being is also being considered. They need to know what role they would play and how they fit into this newly defined agency mission. In short, the soft-side techniques should dominate management's efforts. Some developmentally appropriate strategies for the infancy stage are listed in Figure 7.3.

Figure 7.3
Primary Agency Strategies in the Infancy Stage

Training
Generating excitement
Media coverage
Staff surveys
Action planning teams
Massive staff input
Brown bag luncheons
Communication vehicles
Vision exercises

Stage Two: Adolescence

The excitement and rapid growth of the infancy stage eventually gives way to conflict when it becomes evident that the proposed changes clash with the existing, dominant culture and with bureaucratic routines. At this point, obstacles begin to frustrate efforts to move forward. In the infancy stage, concepts are often easy to agree to. When these concepts begin to be converted to practice, however, changes that affect employee's long-standing relationships to their jobs and to each other may lead to questioning or even rebellion. Stage One is characterized by discussion, theory, visions of how things could be better, and initial steps of success. The adolescent stage, however, is dominated by clarifying expectations of performance and visible practice changes. Two types of troubling reactions may occur. These include: (1) resistance by those who did not understand the day-to-day changes that would be expected of them, or who did not think the transition would ultimately affect them; and (2) unrealistic expectations of how the agency would institute these changes and the resulting frustrations when attempts to change were too slow or were met with overly daunting obstacles. These reactions may be exacerbated when limited resources (either existing or new) are redirected to nontraditional customers (i.e., victims and the community) in order to achieve balance between the three stakeholders. To both administrators and line staff, it can feel like the unsettled shifting of sand underneath their feet. It may be marked by discomfort, anxiety, or anger.

It is helpful, on the other hand, to remember that adolescence, marked by a predictable period of unrest, discomfort, and conflict, is a normal process of development and should be expected. Rather than being angered by the natural course of events, leadership should attempt to steer the agency through these difficult times in a persistent but nonjudgmental way. On the other hand, this is the period in which most failures occur. The pressure from both sides (those who embrace the change and are frustrated by the obstacles, and those resistive to the change and who *create* some of the obstacles) can be extreme. Those with management responsibility often succumb to the pressure to buckle under or overcompromise in order to restore peace and comfort. Yet, this is the time when persistence is most needed. The length of the adolescence period varies tremendously on a number of factors, including but not limited to the degree to which preexisting organizational values conflict with restorative values, the flexibility of management and staff to think and act differently, the type and style of leadership, key position turnover, and how well an agency can maneuver the transition out of adolescence without reverting to traditional values and practice. Small but visible victories are extremely helpful at this time. It will embolden those taking the risks and help tone down the noise of the resistance, which can cause discouragement to those on the front line of the change process.

It would be a mistake to operate solely on the basis of soft-side strategies throughout Stage 2 (adolescence). Given the assumption that some people in the agency will find the changes threatening to their comfort or self-interest, the agency can become stalled in its change efforts. If agency structure, incentive systems, and strategies must line up with the expected practice changes, then inconsistent messages, reward mechanisms that continue to support practices incompatible with restoration, (Bazemore and Washington, 1995), and other incongruencies will create organizational ambivalence, apathy, confusion, or chaos. Even when focused on the hard side, however, the *process* of applying these strategies (such as those listed in Figure 7.4) still needs to be balanced by activities that address soft-side issues such as relationships, staff roles, skill development, and so on. In other words, implementing hard-side strategies requires an employee-sensitive approach that involves staff in decisionmaking and seeks to accommodate concerns over their ability to be competent in new roles (Umbreit and Carey, 1995).

Figure 7.4
Primary Agency Strategies in the Adolescent Stage

Change of mission statement
New staff orientation and training sessions
Change of employee civil service exams
Use of different interview questions
New promotional criteria and other reward mechanisms
Different outcome measures
Change in job performance measures
Organizational structure change
Shift in how resources are allocated
Use of restorative-justice-guided case plans and reports

The need for discussion, negotiation, support, and reassurance does not evaporate during this period; it actually increases. However, the agency needs to balance its reform activities. Figure 7.5 illustrates how the agency needs to emphasize the corresponding activities at the appropriate developmental stage, with greater attention given to soft-side processes in the beginning, and an increase in hard-side applications as the agency evolves into a new common vision and purpose.

Figure 7.5
Timing of Hard-Side and Soft-Side Activities

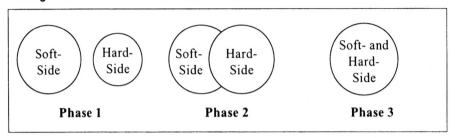

Timing is critical to the long-term success of restorative justice reforms. Implementing the hard-side changes before opportunities are provided for staff input, buy-in, support, and the like will probably create problems around staff morale, trust, and ownership. Failure to emphasize the hard side in the adolescent stage can result in mixed messages, frustrations, confusion, and failed outcomes, as the agency structure and resource decisions fail to line up with the messages about vision and staff expectations. Moreover, neglect of the soft side during the process is almost always counterproductive in acquiring desired results because staff participation and ownership almost always increases long-term success.

Stage Three: Adulthood

After the period of adolescence, the organization finally begins to settle into its new practice. Procedures that may have taken tremendous effort to initiate now begin to become routine. Having accepted the new course of action as normal and comfortable, staff and managers begin to abandon routines associated with prior practice. At this time, a new set of concerns may arise around the danger of settling into a form of complacency. Correctional practice can take on a new form of rigidity, however, and may eventually need another renewal period. Management can take action to prevent this from happening. Because few, if any, agencies have reached this stage of development in restorative justice, rigidity around new practices and processes does not appear to be a matter of immediate concern. Agencies are expected to cycle through stages and must be prepared to respond accordingly, depending on the needs at the moment.

Moving Past Adolescence

As noted earlier, agencies generally tend to seek changes in structural and system activities too early or fail to apply soft-side techniques to the change process. A cultural shift in values that can bring about long-lasting change takes time to accomplish. Leadership needs to provide a supportive environment to allow the shift to happen. However, the failure to apply structural and system changes when the timing is appropriate can lead to disastrous results. When agency staff have had sufficient time to understand what the cultural shift is and how it might apply to them, when the staff have had sufficient input, and when the agency has made adjustments based on that input and has decided to move ahead, the time is ripe for making these hard-side changes. Failure to act decisively at this point causes frustration to those whose own values have been supported by restorative justice. Having made the philosophical shift, they are ready to be supported by the rest of the agency. It is therefore crucial that the agency's structural components begin to "line up" in a consistent manner so that the cultural shift is fully supported and new expectations are understood by all. Mission statement, policy manuals, organizational structure, hiring practices, training activities, performance measures, and so on must all be changed to communicate a consistent message about agency objectives and staff expectations (e.g., Lipsky, 1980).

It is often difficult to determine the most appropriate strategies to integrate restorative justice practice into an existing correctional culture that is not completely restorative. Most correctional agencies are providing traditional services (as defined by stated objectives such as monitoring of probation conditions, conducting assessments for the bench, and application of sanctions for use by the sentencing courts) (Bazemore, 1997a). However, all agencies include some restorative programs and features, including, for example, restitution assessment and collection, victim impact panels, competency development programs, community work service, and so on. Yet, even the more restorative practices often are missing major components that would make them more fully restorative. Managers should ask, for example, whether community work service projects provide meaningful work for offenders that provides value to the community and increases the bond between offenders and law-abiding citizens and neighborhood groups. Do restitution policies allow for victim input and communicate information to victims on a regular basis? Do offenders have the opportunity to participate in the development of their reparative and competency development and plans? Is the community fully informed and engaged to perform crime prevention and intervention activities?

At first blush, many corrections professionals perceive that restorative justice policies and programs are being practiced in their jurisdiction and may suggest that little would need to change. Upon closer examination, however, it is usually evident that the agency does not balance the needs and interests of the three customers (victim, offender, and community) and that few specific components of the services provided are directed at the overarching goal of repairing harm and restoring relationships. As illustrated in Figure 7.6, it is more common for correctional agencies to emphasize offender needs over community and victim needs.

Figure 7.6
Customer Emphasis (Current Practice)

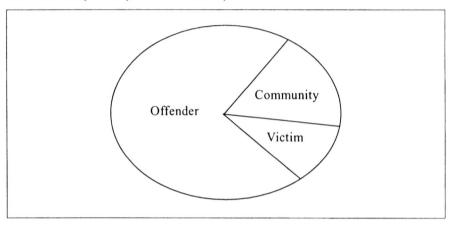

The question then is not whether an agency is "restorative," but to what degree their policies, practices, values, programs, and directions support restorative objectives (Bazemore and Washington, 1995). Restorative justice is not a yes-or-no issue, but a matter of degree. It is the extent to which an agency's practices and values are congruent with restorative justice that determines how extensive the strategies for change need to be. Once an agency has determined its action plan (and is about to enter the second stage of development), it is imperative that it examine how likely it is that those strategies will or will not be accepted and carried out by correctional staff. Schwartz and Davis (1981) suggest that an agency compare its selected strategies with the level at which the existing organizational culture is compatible with the proposed change (see Figure 7.7).

Given the level of compatibility, an agency has four alternatives. They include:

1. *Ignore the culture.* In most cases, this is not advised. When significant differences exist between the strategy and existing culture, it is most likely that ignoring the culture will result in little or no change and lead to devastating results.

2. *Manage around the culture.* When major obstacles toward implementing the strategy exist, an agency may want to bypass or work around the culture by changing the plan. The changed plan under this alternative does not, how-

Figure 7.7
Compatability with Current Culture

Importance to Strategy		High	Medium	Low	Cultural Risk Assessment
	High	2	3	3	
	Medium	1	2	3	
	Low	1	1	2	

3	Unacceptable Risk
2	Manageable Risk
1	Negligible Risk

Source: Schwartz and Davis, 1981.

ever, change the intent or focus. It recognizes the strength of the existing culture and determines that the strategies will come into sharp contrast with that culture and will likely be met with too much resistance (Schwartz and Davis, 1981).

3. *Attempt to change the culture.* This is the most difficult alternative of the four and takes the longest to accomplish. It can, however, result in the greatest likelihood of long-term success. As Schwartz and Davis (1981) observe:

> When a cultural change is explicitly intended, it should be coordinated with all the necessary internal changes in management systems and organizational structure to seek a mutual and positive reinforcement of overall strategic management infrastructure.

4. *Change the strategy to fit the culture.* This approach does not attempt to change the culture in the long or short term. Management accepts the existing culture as it is and tries to align the proposed strategic changes for compatibility. When there are no significant differences

between the proposed change and the existing culture, this can be an appropriate strategy. In other cases, it represents a compromise of the principles of restorative justice and has the effect of "watering down" the richness of the potential change and reducing expectations for outcomes.

Managers, Leaders, and Restorative Justice Reform

Much has been written about management and leadership, and the differences between them (Conner, 1993; Oakly and Krug, 1993). While certain characteristics are prevalent in both qualities, some characteristics that differentiate between managers and leaders include:

Manager	Leader
Focuses on policies	Leads by inspiring
Focuses on procedures	Interested in vision
Concerned with measurements	Seeks flexibility
Relies on guidelines	Values the ability to change
Sets up rules	Committed
Seeks consistency and predictability	Concerned with attitude
Concerned with structure	Values creativity and synergy
Focuses on tools needed	Seeks to overcome resistance
Process-oriented	Self-leader
Directs staff	Empowers staff
Seeks short-term outcomes	Draws broader conclusion
Seeks to minimize risks	Takes risks
Seeks agency stability	Pushes others beyond their comfort zone

Leadership can come from inside or outside an agency—from the line staff or the agency head. Some of the most vibrant organizations are ones in which leadership is situational and in which any employee is encouraged to take on a leadership role when the situation dictates (Peters and Waterman, 1982; Schein, 1981). The spreading of broad-based cultural change is more potent when non-management staff members take the initiative, but this often does not happen, because of hierarchical organizations, staff workload, or other factors. However, the role of the designated, titular leader should not be diminished. These individuals are key to freeing up the resources, making the decisions, and setting the priorities that determine whether a reform initiative has the chance to succeed.

Organizational change is more likely to be long-lasting and comprehensive when agency leadership is promoting it, expecting it, and supporting it. As noted earlier, leadership can greatly accelerate an agency's movement from Stage 2 to Stage 3 by ensuring that all of the organizational components (both the hard and the soft sides) line up with restorative goals. Frequently, however, change strategies are applied to the organization in a fragmented way, particularly when the management team fails to adapt its leadership style to the needs of the organization. One of the most important characteristics of a leader is that of flexibility—the ability to provide whatever the organization needs at any particular time. The agency needs different things from its management staff at different stages in its restorative development. For example, when administrators act like managers at a time when *leadership* is needed, even the best-laid plans can lose their effectiveness. At such times, administrators exercising leadership should be communicating on a daily basis what is expected of all agency staff, both verbally and through modeling, and doing so in an inspiring way.

Employees are hired by organizations based on what is needed at a particular time. As agencies change, what is needed from the staff changes. Although the staff must be flexible as the agency changes, it is equally imperative that administrators be able to adopt different styles of management and leadership as the needs of the organization dictate. Figure 7.8 depicts two corrections organizations along a continuum of relative need for management and leadership.

Figure 7.8
Continuum of Leadership

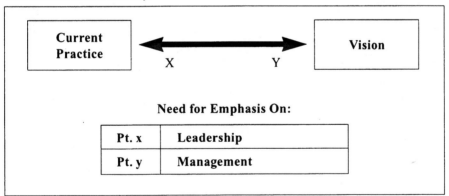

On the far left of Figure 7.8 is common correctional practice representing those activities and objectives traditionally provided and supported by the correctional agency. On the far right is the vision of where the organization would like to go. If it is a restorative vision, practices and values (and therefore the culture) will be different from traditional practice. Agency X on the continuum is far from the restorative vision, and Agency Y is closer to it. In reviewing the characteristics of a manager and leader, it is evident that each agency requires different things from its administrative staff. Agency X needs strong leaders because the culture is not going to change without leadership characteristics being employed. As the agency gets closer to the vision (such as Agency Y), the needs of the agency change. It is then less important to demonstrate leadership skills and more important to manage those practices already put in place to sustain a restorative agency.

The need for strong leadership by managers at the appropriate time is a key factor in helping move an organization out of the adolescent stage and into Stage 3, adulthood. Managers/leaders can complete the following inventory to determine what course of action is needed in order to move ahead to fuller implementation of restorative justice:

1. Describe your agency's artifacts, values, and basic assumptions. What does that tell you about your agency's culture?

2. Review your restorative justice action plan and strategies. How well do your strategies match your current culture?

3. Review your leadership style. Do you tend to manage or lead? Given how closely your organizational values and activities match up with restorative justice, what changes do you need to make? Taking into account your leadership skills and style, what is the best action choice(s) given your agency's level of incongruency of strategy and culture?

4. Define your next steps within your selected strategic plan and action choices.

The Role of Joy

A revolution for change in society must be a joyful revolution. No whipping and grim looks. It must be a party so others will want to join in.

Anonymous

We all perform better, and are more likely to adapt to changes, when we:

• Have a sense of purpose at work;

• Are appreciated for our contributions; and

• Have fun doing it.

Restorative justice can result in fundamental changes in what is required of the individual corrections worker. Such changes demand that the worker concentrate on three customers, rather than one; be concerned with healing rather than simply surveillance or treatment; become a community organizer of sorts; and facilitate face-to-face meetings between offenders, victims, and the community (often in an emotionally charged situation). Why would anyone sign up for such a job? Because the expected outcomes are better. In other words, restorative justice touches the deep, abiding sense of purpose that brings many well-meaning individuals to a corrections career in the first place.

Equally important, and closely related, is the role of joy. When people experience a sense of accomplishment, it meets a deeper sense of purpose, and a type of euphoria sets in. The mind is freed up, quicker to respond, and more open to creativity and the support of new ideas. Joy through purpose produces motivation, excitement, creativity, and optimism. Corporate America's understanding of this is evidenced by the frequent celebration about new visions, goals, and positive outcomes.

Conclusion

The transformation in organizational culture that must occur when agencies move toward restorative justice is both exciting and frustrating. Stages of development should be expected and managed. The timing of reform strategies and leadership styles is a key consideration to making the kind of cultural shift necessary for becoming a restorative correctional agency. The potential for improved outcomes is as great as the obstacles facing correctional agencies enmeshed in a traditional justice system. Despite these challenges, major advancements are being made. Agencies will improve their chances for success in meeting the restorative outcomes when their managers and leaders pay close attention to organizational culture, stages of development, and leadership needs.

Discussion Questions

1. What are the three components that make up organizational culture? Can you apply these to organizations you have either worked in or experienced in some other way (e.g., you might look at your academic institution, church, or community group)? How do these artifacts contribute to organizational culture and how do they contribute to understanding how an organization works?

2. What are the three levels of development that organizations may go through? What are some of the key characteristics that indicate these different stages? Can you apply these to organizations in which you have worked, volunteered, or have otherwise experienced?

3. Does Carey suggest that agencies can be characterized as restorative? Why or why not? Does he suggest that most restorative agencies are at a particular stage of development?

4. Which is more important in implementing restorative justice: leadership or management? Explain.

Endnote

[1]   In addition, an organization has a climate. Schwartz and Davis (1981) describe "climate" as a measure of employee's expectations about what work should be like and the degree to which these expectations are being met:

> What climate really measures is the fit between the prevailing culture and the individual values of the employees. If the employees have adopted the values of the prevailing culture, the climate is "good." If they have not, the climate is "poor," and motivation and presumably performance suffer. While climate is often transitory, tactical, and can be managed over the relatively short term, culture is usually long-term and strategic. It is very difficult to change. Culture is rooted in deeply held beliefs and values in which individuals hold a substantial investment as the result of some processing or analysis of data about organizational life.

References

Bazemore, G. (1997). "What's New About the Balanced Approach?" *Juvenile and Family Court Journal* 48(1):1-23.

Bazemore, G., and L. Walgrave (1999). *Restorative Juvenile Justice: Repairing the Harm of Youth Crime.* Monsey, NY: Criminal Justice Press.

Bazemore, G., and C. Washington (1995). "Charting the Future of the Juvenile Justice System: Reinventing Mission and Management." *Spectrum: the Journal of State Government* 68 (2): 51-66

Braithwaite, J. (1989). *Crime, Shame and Reintegration.* Cambridge, England: Cambridge University Press.

Conner, D.R. (1993). *Managing at the Speed of Change.* New York: Villard Books.

Depree, M. (1992). *Leadership Jazz.* New York: Doubleday.

Hax, A.C., and N.S. Majluf (1984). *Strategic Management, An Integrative Perspective.* Englewood Cliffs, NJ: Prentice Hall.

Kotter, J.P. (1996). *Leading Change.* Boston: Harvard Business School Press.

Kriegel, R.J., and L. Patler (1991). *If It Ain't Broke. . . . Break It!* New York: Warner Books.

Lewin, K. (1951). *Field Theory in Social Science: Selected Theoretical Papers.* New York: Harper.

Lipsky, M. (1980). *Street-Level Bureaucracy: Dilemmas of the Individual in Public Services.* New York: Russell Sage Foundation.

Maloney, D., D. Romig, and T. Armstrong (1988). "Juvenile Probation: The Balanced Approach." *Juvenile and Family Court Journal* 39 (3).

Oakley, E., and D. Krug (1993). *Enlightened Leadership.* New York: Simon and Schuster.

Pascale, R.T., and A.G. Athos (1981). *The Art of Japanese Management: Applications for American Executives.* New York: Simon and Schuster.

Peters, T.J., and R.H. Waterman, Jr. (1982). *In Search of Excellence.* New York: Harper & Row.

Pritchett, P., and R. Pound (1993). *High Velocity Culture Change: A Handbook for Managers.* Dallas: Pritchett & Associates.

Schein, E.S. (1981). "Does Japanese Management Style Have a Message for American Managers?" *Sloan Management Review* 23(1), Fall 1981.

Schwarz, H., and S.M. Davis (1981) "Matching Corporate Culture and Business Strategy." *Organizational Dynamics*, 10.

Umbreit, M.S., and M. Carey (1995). "Restorative Justice: Implications for Organizational Change." *Federal Probation* 59(March):1.

Zehr, H. (1990). *Changing Lenses: A New Focus for Crime and Justice.* Scottdale, PA: Herald Press.

Part IV
The Content: Practice and Intervention in Restorative Community Justice

8

Restorative Conferencing

ALLISON MORRIS
GABRIELLE MAXWELL

Introduction

There are now a number of examples of conferencing in operation in different jurisdictions.[1] Not all operate in the same way.[2] Moreover, not all have the same theoretical underpinnings. Some systems of conferencing, like those in New Zealand, South Australia, and New South Wales, are based on principles of restorative justice (though not necessarily explicitly or to the exclusion of other, even contradictory, objectives).[3] Other systems are explicitly based on Braithwaite's (1989) notion of "reintegrative shaming."[4] Examples of the latter are the system of conferencing first introduced in Wagga Wagga in New South Wales (Moore, 1995), and subsequently developed in the Reintegrative Shaming Experiment (RISE) in Canberra in the Australian Capital Territory (ACT) (Sherman et al., 1998; Strang et al., 1999) and copied in some areas of the United States through the Real Justice organization (McCold and Wachtel, 1998).

This chapter identifies what we view as necessary characteristics for successful *restorative conferencing* and reviews some of the different examples of conferencing against these characteristics. In this way, the strengths and weaknesses of specific examples can be identified irrespective of how they have been implemented in any particular jurisdiction. That is to say, the essence of restorative conferencing is not the adoption of one model of conferencing; rather it is any model of conferencing that reflects restorative values and that aims to achieve restorative processes, outcomes, and objectives. We would suggest, therefore, that there is no "right way" to deliver restorative conferencing. The key question is not "Does the New Zealand model of conferencing work better than the Wagga Wagga model, RISE, or whatever?" but rather "Are the values underpinning the model and the processes, outcomes, and objectives achieved restorative?"

The primary focus of this chapter, then, is restorative conferencing of all types. Some commentators view victim-offender mediation programs as also a type of restorative conferencing (Bazemore and Umbreit, 1999; Schiff, 1998). Victim-offender mediation programs, however, emerged very much from within the victim's movement, whereas conferencing more commonly emerged as a response for dealing with offenders. This means that, at least until recently, there were a number of differences between the two in both practice and emphasis.[5] For example, victim-offender mediation programs tended to deal primarily (though not exclusively) with minor offending;[6] they tended to give a more limited role to "communities of care;"[7] and they tended to give primacy to victims' interests rather than emphasizing putting things right for both victims and offenders, which is a key part of restorative conferencing.[8] Thus, the central focus of victim-offender mediation programs was on repairing the harm rather than reintegrating the offender into the community. However, victim-offender mediation programs clearly share some of the characteristics of restorative conferencing—for example, giving victims a voice and making restitution or amends to victims[9]—and current practices in some victim-offender mediation programs seem to have blurred the boundaries between conferencing and victim-offender mediation (Roberts, 1999). For this reason, we include some discussion of victim-offender mediation programs in this chapter. As with examples of conferencing generally, the extent to which particular programs can be described as examples of restorative conferencing will depend on the extent to which they endorse restorative values, result in restorative processes and outcomes, and achieve restorative objectives.

The Values, Processes, Outcomes, and Objectives of Restorative Conferencing

There is no single agreed definition of restorative conferencing. In preparing this chapter, we examined a few of those commonly referred to in the literature but decided that, given emerging models and practices, a specific definition would constrain rather than aid this review. We have chosen, therefore, to set out what we see as the critical values, processes, outcomes, and objectives of restorative conferencing.

The values underlying restorative conferencing give primacy to the interests of those most affected by offending—victims, offenders, and their communities of care.[10] Accordingly, the state no longer has a monopoly over decisions about how to respond to the offending; rather, the principal decisionmakers are the affected parties themselves. Restorative conferencing, then, gives the state a diminished role and locates crime—and responses to it—within these "communities of care." In addition, restorative values endorse a collective ethos and collective responsibility. Thus, restorative conferencing emphasizes the existence of shared values that can be used to address the offending and its consequences (for victims, offenders, and communities) and to reintegrate victims and offenders at the local community level. It is premised on the belief that the reasons behind the offending, and hence the solutions to it, lie in the community. Restorative values also emphasize human rights and the need to recognize the impact of social or substantive injustice. Restorative conferencing stresses addressing such injustices in small ways rather than simply providing offenders with legal or formal justice and victims with no justice at all. Finally, restorative conferencing encourages cultural relativity and sensitivity rather than cultural dominance. Processes and outcomes can be shaped by the parties themselves to take account of cultural differences. In essence, the social values underlying restorative justice rely on connections—between offenders, victims, and communities—rather than on exclusion.

Thus, restorative processes involve, ideally, a meeting between all those involved in the offense (victims, offenders, and their communities of care), their participation in a search for ways to resolve the harm that has been done, acknowledgment by those responsible for the harm of their role in causing that harm, and some understanding among those harmed of the reasons underlying the harm. All of this should take place in a context that is culturally relevant and that respects all participants. Restorative goals include the acknowledgment of responsibility for the harm caused through making amends for it and acceptance by all participants of the appropriateness of the outcome. The ultimate objective of restorative conferencing is increasing the chances of the reintegration of victims and offenders into the community by restoring connectedness, reducing reoffending, and healing the victims' hurts. Above all else, the aim of restorative conferencing is to change the hearts and minds of both those responsible for the offenses as well as those who have suffered because of them and, as far as possible, to make amends for the harm done to offenders and victims. These critical values, processes, outcomes, and objectives are summarized in Figure 8.1.[11]

Figure 8.1
Critical Characteristics of Restorative Conferencing

Critical Values
Primacy of victims, offenders, and communities of care

Collective responsibility

Social justice

Cultural flexibility

Critical Processes
Inclusion—participation of victims, offenders, and communities of care in processes and decisions

Increased understanding on the part of victims, offenders, and communities of care

Respect—the avoidance of stigmatic shaming

Cultural relevance

Critical Outcomes
Acknowledgment of responsibility through making amends—apologizing to victims, repairing the harm, and completing tasks

Acceptance of outcomes as appropriate by offenders, victims, and communities of care

Critical Objectives
Restoring connectedness and reintegration: feeling good about process, outcome, self, and life prospects

Reducing reoffending

Healing victims' hurt

We will use Figure 8.1 to measure the extent to which different examples of conferencing reflect restorative values and achieve restorative processes, outcomes, and objectives. When possible, we will refer to research findings.[12]

Reflecting Critical Values

Primacy of Victims, Offenders, and Communities of Care

The key participants at restorative conferences are the offender, the victim(s), and their communities of care. In addition, in most jurisdictions, a representative of the police is usually present and a specific individual acts as the facilitator of the process. In some jurisdictions, the police also act as the facilitator. There is considerable debate about the appropriateness of this. On the one hand, it can be argued that the skills of the facilitator and his or her understanding of and commitment to the values of restorative conferencing are the key issues, as opposed to his or her professional background (Moore, 1995). On the other hand, it can be argued that it is difficult for many offenders, especially aboriginal or indigenous offenders, to view the police as neutral facilitators or police stations as neutral venues for conferences (Blagg, 1998).[13] There is, as yet, no empirical data on the impact of these contextual elements.

In our view, the key issue for restorative conferencing is not who is the facilitator but who are the *decisionmakers* and the extent to which the state (through its representatives) exercises a veto over the decision reached. We elaborate on this later in the section on restorative processes but would suggest at this stage that some curtailment of the power of criminal justice or social welfare professionals is essential for conferences to be restorative. Thus, in New Zealand, the police cannot prosecute a young offender unless he or she has first been referred to a conference and the conference recommends a prosecution.[14] In practice, most conferences reach an agreement that avoids prosecution. Similarly, judges in New Zealand cannot sentence a young offender without referring him or her to a conference and taking into account its recommendation. In practice, most judges accept the recommendations of the conference. No other example of conferencing goes this far in empowering victims, offenders, and their communities of care. Indeed, Blagg (1998) suggests that, somewhat paradoxically, the Australian versions of conferencing have the potential to increase state power (see also Polk, 1994; White, 1994).

Collective Responsibility

For responsibility to be collective requires an acceptance that we, as members of a particular community of care, have played a role in the genesis of the particular crime and have, therefore, some responsibility both to prevent its recurrence (through, for example, ameliorating those conditions that give rise to it in the first place) and to address its consequences (through, for example, providing services to the victims of crime or developing programs aimed at reintegrating offenders). However, it requires more: the skills and resources in communities of care to achieve this. Few systems of conferencing have gone beyond rhetoric in this respect.[15] Some systems of conferencing have stressed parental responsibility in determining and even resourcing conferencing outcomes (Levine et al., 1997). This may be preferable to parental exclusion, but in our view, collective responsibility does not mean that the state should abdicate its responsibilities. Rather, it demands the development of partnerships between the state and communities of care and, in particular, the resourcing of communities of care by the state in order that they might assume these responsibilities.

Social Justice

Much of what was said above about collective responsibility is relevant with regard to social justice. The majority of the children and young people who come into the youth justice system (though not necessarily the majority of those who offend) are characterized by poverty and disadvantage. Longitudinal studies have provided a rich source of data on this (see, for example, Fergusson et al., 1997; Farrington, 1997). These researchers have identified a number of background factors that have negative consequences for children. These include, in particular, adverse family circumstances (such as being abused; poor relationships between the child and their parents; a lack of parental supervision; and parental problems with money, crime, alcohol, and other drugs), the lack of educational opportunities, and frequent changes of schools. The need to redress these inequities, to respond to unmet needs, and to assist children and young people in developing their full potential constitutes part of the restorative agenda. Achieving this, however, requires action and the allocation of resources by the state.[16]

Cultural Flexibility

Restorative justice closely parallels some systems of indigenous justice (see, for example, New Zealand Maori Council and Durie Hall, 1999). Consequently, restorative conferencing can be viewed as offering the potential for indigenous cultures to transform conventional processes and to reshape these to better fit indigenous values. In New Zealand, colonization had meant that the customs and values of Maori were marginalized and that Maori processes and institutions were largely displaced (at least formally) by processes and institutions of European origin (Jackson, 1998). The Children, Young Persons and Their Families Act 1989, therefore specifically advocates the use of processes and the provision of services that are culturally appropriate—partly as a result of a resurgence of Maori culture and values in the 1980s and partly in recognition of the cultural diversity of New Zealand. In this respect, New Zealand has gone further than most jurisdictions in at least acknowledging the importance of cultural flexibility. None of Australian states in which conferencing is practiced can be said to have done this with respect to Aboriginal communities

(Blagg, 1998). Sentencing circles, discussed in a separate chapter in this book, provide a further example of the links between the values of restorative and indigenous justice.

Successful Restorative Processes

Inclusion in Processes and Decisions

In restorative conferencing, as noted previously, offenders and victims can meet face to face and, in some examples, the meeting will not proceed unless both are present. Arguably, it is not essential (however desirable) for victims to attend conferences in order for them to be potentially restorative. Though such meetings can lose some of their emotive power (and, hence, some of their potential) without victims being present, victims' views and feelings can be communicated by their friends and family members.[17] The key issue is not simply presence at a meeting, but inclusion in that meeting. After all, offenders are present at court, but can hardly be said to play a significant role in the proceedings. Inclusion means that offenders are expected to participate directly in the process, to speak about their offending and matters associated with it, to interact with the victim, to express their remorse about what has occurred, to apologize for what they have done, and to contribute to decisions about eventual outcomes. From all this, offenders are expected to have a better understanding of their offending and its consequences and to become accountable for it. The contribution made by offenders in all of this should be acknowledged and valued.[18]

Young offenders attending conferences and courts in New Zealand were asked whether their views were sought and listened to (Maxwell and Morris, 1993). It was fairly clear that most felt more involved and more listened to in conferences than in courts. Findings from RISE (Sherman and Strang, 1997) point in this direction as well: more than three-quarters of the young offenders who had experienced conferences said that they were able to express their views compared with a little more than one-half of those who went to court.[19]

Victims are arguably the parties most affected by offending and are the parties most in need of healing for the damage caused by it, yet they have had little direct voice in the juvenile (or criminal) justice system and have received little from it to aid their healing. In contrast, as noted above, victims can be involved in conferences by being present at the conference. Though the research on New Zealand conferences (Maxwell and Morris, 1993) indicated that victims attended only around one-half of the family group conferences,[20] the reasons for this were related primarily to poor practice.[21] There will always be a minority of victims who choose not to participate in conferencing, but the New Zealand research found that only 6 percent of victims, when asked, said that they did not wish to meet the offender. This is a clear indicator that most victims are willing (and indeed desire) to be involved in such processes. Wundersitz and Hetzel (1996) reported that 75 to 80 percent of conferences in South Australia involving offenses with victims had at least one victim present[22] and victims were present at 86 percent of RISE conferences compared with only 3 percent at court cases (Strang and Sherman, 1997).

On the other hand, according to Young (1998), the "primary" victim is not commonly present at restorative conferences in Thames Valley. This is perhaps indicative of the relatively low level of offending dealt with by conferences there and also the fact that most "conferences" there are, strictly speaking, "restorative cautions" at which there is no victim present.[23] Victims attended only about one-half of the conferences in a small pilot program in Hampshire (Jackson, 1998); the reason for this seem to be that many of the victims were retail companies.

Overall, then, there seems to be considerable variation in the extent to which victims attend conferences. Perhaps the clearest example of this is the comparison by McCold and Wachtel (1998) of one form of conferencing (police-based) with six victim-offender mediation programs with regard to the level of participation (that is, the proportion of cases referred for mediation or conferencing that actually proceeded with both victims and offenders present). The figures varied significantly, from 42 percent (in the police-based conference) to only 6 percent and 8 percent (in two English programs in which negotiations where the mediator met separately with victims and offenders were sometimes used).

Increased Understanding on the Part of Victims, Offenders, and Communities of Care

Palk et al. (1998) found that only a few offenders (9%) and victims (6%) felt discomfort at meeting each other.[24] This was also found in Maxwell and Morris's (1993) research. Overall, their research showed that, when victims were involved in conferencing, many found this a positive process. About 60 percent of the victims interviewed described the conference they attended as helpful and rewarding. Generally, they said that they were effectively involved in the process and felt better as a result of participating. The conference had provided them with a voice in determining appropriate outcomes and with the opportunity to meet the offender and the offender's family face-to-face so that they could assess their attitude, understand more why the offense had occurred, and assess the likelihood of it recurring.[25]

Data from RISE also show that conferences can make victims feel safer (Strang and Sherman, 1997). Only 6 percent of victims involved in conferences feared revictimization, compared with 19 percent of victims whose cases went to court. Overall, compared with those victims whose offenders appeared in court, victims who participated in conferences had more information, were more likely to attend the hearing, were more likely to feel some sympathy toward the offender, and were less likely after the conference to feel angry.[26] Umbreit (1994) found that, after meeting the offender, victims were significantly less fearful of being revictimized. Palk et al. (1998) reported that 84 percent of victims were able to put the offense behind them after the conference. Almost all (ranging from 92% to 94%) of the victims in McCold and Wachtel's (1998) research said that the meeting had been helpful, that they would choose to do the same again, and that they would recommend participation to others.

Palk et al. (1998) found that all the offenders interviewed for their research felt that the conference had helped them understand the impact of the offense; 73 percent of victims felt this was also true for "their" offender. According to Jackson (1998), hearing from the victim and realizing the effect of the offense on their family were the two most powerful aspects of conferencing for the small sample of young people in her study who had attended conferences. Also, two-thirds of participants believed that meeting the victim had increased the young person's sense of responsibility for the offense. Finally, 90 percent of the victims in Fercello and Umbreit's (1998) survey (quoted in Friday, 1999) felt that the offender was adequately held accountable.

Acknowledging responsibility for the harm done is an integral part of restorative conferencing, and most offenders involved in conferencing accept this. Maxwell and Morris (1999) report asking young offenders about six years after participating in a conference how they felt about the offense and the victim's feelings. Three-quarters said that what they had done was wrong, almost two-thirds said they understood how the victim felt, and almost one-half said that they had felt sorry for the offense at the time of the conference and had showed the victim that they were truly sorry. Strang et al. (1999) also report that offenders often report feeling that the offense was wrong, based on interviews conducted approximately two years after they entered the RISE experiment. However, the differences between the court sample and conference sample on this question were not significant.

Respect—The Avoidance of Stigmatic Shaming

In Braithwaite's analysis, shame is a necessary part of the process of reintegration. This is said (Makkai and Braithwaite, 1994, cited in Harris and Burton, 1997) to be achieved through certain steps: disapproval of the offense while sustaining a relationship of respect for the offender and without labeling the offender as "bad" or "evil"; ceremonies to certify the deviance followed by ceremonies to decertify it; and not allowing deviance to become a master status trait.[27] Setting aside for now the extent to which these steps can be achieved in practice,[28] it is our view that there is not yet evidence that shame is a necessary precursor to reintegration.

Data from RISE help support this (Sherman and Strang, 1997). They indicate that offenders who had experienced conferences were more likely than offenders who had experienced courts to say that they felt ashamed of the offenses they had committed (79 percent of conference participants, compared with 66 percent of those whose cases went to court). The offenders who had experienced conferences were also more likely to say that they felt that they had repaid their debt to society (77%, compared with 42% of those whose case went to court) and to the victim (77%, compared with 40% of those whose cases went to court). Overall, those who had experienced conferences felt that the conference had enabled them to make up for what they had done.

It seems important to distinguish the two components—"shaming" and "making amends." There is certainly no evidence from the research that "feeling ashamed" was the key ingredient in offenders feeling that they had made amends. Moreover, the researchers' observations that conferences were more likely than courts to produce the "right" kind of shame (courts were likely to produce either "no shame" or the "wrong" type of shame) do not help us make that connection. It requires the offenders themselves to make this linkage. It seems unlikely that young offenders see shaming by the police (the facilitators in the RISE conferences) or by members of a community to which they may have no connection as reintegrative and hence as restorative. It also seems unlikely that the potential power of meetings between offenders and victims is realized when the primary role of the victim is scripted as "shamer." Overall, although results from RISE (Sherman et al., 1998) have demonstrated that there is more reintegrative shaming in conferences than in courts and that there is more stigmatic shaming in courts than in conferences, there were few significant differences between the court and conference samples on the 12 items used to measure reintegrative shaming[29] or on the six items used to measure stigmatic shaming (Strang et al., 1999).[30] There is also no information yet from the RISE project on the impact of these shaming processes on reoffending or on reintegration.

On the other hand, Maxwell and Morris's (1999) research on young people who were reconvicted six years after their conference shows that they and their parents were both more likely to report leaving the conference "feeling bad about themselves" compared to those who were not reconvicted. This may be measuring what Braithwaite

(1988) called *disintegrative shaming*.[31] Maxwell and Morris (1999), however, also found that those young people who were significantly less likely to be reconvicted six years after the conference said they felt remorse. "Remorse" was, as we will see later in this chapter, a composite construct that included, among other variables, "feeling sorry about the offending and showing it." It is possible that this construct is measuring what Braithwaite (1989) referred to as *reintegrative shaming*. However, again, we would wish to distinguish "feeling shame or ashamed" and "feeling sorry." We are not convinced that they are the same.

Cultural Relevance

We noted above that no jurisdiction had gone as far as New Zealand in trying to introduce cultural flexibility. However, some 10 years on, this potential has still not yet been fully realized. Although Maxwell and Morris (1993) provide case studies of conferences that met this ideal—for example, a large number of *whanau* (extended family) present and meetings held on a *marae* (meeting place), facilitated by *kaumatua* (elders), and following the *kawa* (protocol) of the marae—these were the exceptions rather than the norm. The potential of restorative conferencing to transform conventional processes and to make them more culturally appropriate still remains, however (compare Tauri, 1998). It is important not to demand or expect too much. LaPrairie (1998) draws attention to certain negative findings with respect to circle sentencing: for example, only slightly more than two-fifths of all participants found the process a positive experience and one-third described it negatively; specifically, only 28 percent of victims found sentencing circles to be a positive experience and less than one-half of them felt that offenders had been dealt with appropriately. This reinforces that communities and the state must work in partnership. LaPrairie identifies a number of principles that she believes have to be met by the state to assist indigenous communities to better meet victims,' offenders,' and their own needs.

Successful Restorative Outcomes

Acknowledgment of Responsibility Through Making Amends

Most young offenders in Maxwell and Morris's (1993) research were held accountable for their offenses and made amends to their victims: they apologized for their offense and made reparation or performed community work or services for the victim. In general, the tasks agreed to were completed. This was also true in Wundersitz and Hetzel's (1996) review of conferencing in South Australia: 86 percent of offenders complied with the agreement reached. Umbreit (1994) found that meeting the victim made a difference in whether offenders completed their obligations: 81 percent of offenders who had met their victim completed their obligations compared with only 58 percent of those who had not met with their victim. Sherman et al. (1998) compared outcomes from conferencing and courts. They found that victims who participated in conferences were more likely to receive an apology than those whose offenders appeared in court (74% compared with 14%); and they were more likely to receive restitution (83% compared with 8%). As noted earlier, they also found that offenders who had experienced conferences were more likely to say that they felt that they had repaid their debt to society and to the victim. Maxwell and Morris (1999) also report asking young people (some six years after they first attended a family group conference) whether they had been able to make good the damage they had done. More than one-half said that they felt that they had. All of the young people interviewed by Palk et al. (1998) felt that the conference had helped them "make up" for the offense (although only 73 percent of victims felt this).

Acceptance of Outcomes as Appropriate by Offenders, Victims, and Communities of Care

Most conferences and victim-offender mediations result in an agreed outcome (Maxwell and Morris, 1993; Umbreit, 1994). As noted previously, these outcomes usually take the form of apologies to victims and community work (either for the victim or for an organization nominated by the victim) rather than direct reparation to victims (because of the limited resources of most offenders). Research also shows that most offenders appear satisfied with the outcomes to which they have agreed. McCold and Wachtel (1998), for example, compared one form of conferencing (police-based) with six victim-offender mediation programs on offenders' satisfaction. Their findings for offenders' satisfaction ranged from 97 percent for the police-based conference to 62 percent for one of the English victim-offender mediation programs. In Umbreit et al.'s (1997) comparison of victim-offender mediation in Canada, England, and the United States, the figures for offenders' satisfaction ranged from 91 percent to 100 percent. What this actually means, however, is difficult to say because uniform measures were not used and "satisfaction" could simply indicate relief that nothing worse happened.

A significant percentage of victims also tend to be satisfied with the agreements or outcomes reached at conferences and victim-offender mediations. For example, Umbreit (1994) found that more than three-quarters of the victims who met their offender were satisfied with the way in which their offenses had been responded to; this was so for only 57 percent of victims who went through court processes. Furthermore, in Umbreit et al.'s (1997) comparison of victim-offender mediation programs, the figures for victim satisfaction ranged from 84 to 90 percent. McCold and Wachtel's (1998) findings for victims' satisfaction ranged from 57 percent for one of the American victim-offender mediation programs to 96 percent for the police-based conference. It is not easy to interpret these diverse findings on victims' satisfaction. Certainly, victims appear to be more satisfied when they are involved in a process with offenders in contrast to conventional court processes. However, it is more difficult to draw clear conclusions about conferencing in comparison with victim-offender mediation in their impact on victims and it seems likely that something more complicated is going on rather than simply that the process was mediation or conferencing.

Before concluding this section, it is worth reflecting briefly on Tyler's (1990) suggestion that citizens treated with respect and listened to were likely to see the law as fair; conversely, when they were treated without respect and were not listened to, they saw the law as unfair. He thus distinguished between "process control" and "outcome control" and concluded that "having a say" was more important than determining the outcome of the decision. Daly et al. (1998) infer from this that young people (and, presumably, they would extend this point to include victims) might regard outcomes as fair if they have "had a say," irrespective of whether they actually decided the outcome. Data on the high level of satisfaction of young people with outcomes compared with their stated lower level of involvement in conferencing processes and outcomes would certainly seem to support this. However, when we queried what the responses on satisfaction actually mean, it was clear that some victims were dissatisfied because they viewed the outcomes as inappropriate despite having had a say. Having a say is undoubtedly better than not having a say, but there is some evidence from victims that having a say that is subsequently ignored causes them concern (Morris et al., 1993). It is important to note that Tyler's research was based in a context in which decisions were made by third parties (judges). To this extent, his conclusions may not be relevant for restorative conferencing, which is premised on *consensual* decisionmaking. Feeling good about outcomes might be a key precursor for restoring connectedness.

Achieving Ultimate Objectives

Restoring Connectedness and Reintegration

Restoring connectedness is a difficult objective to measure. Maxwell and Morris (1993) describe handshakes and hugs between offenders and victims, victims extending invitations to offenders to share a meal with them, and victims attending court with offenders to provide them with support. There are also examples of victims arranging for "their" offender to live with one of their family for a while. While all of these seem to be good examples of connectedness being restored, they are measures that rely on the researcher's assessment that these actions mean that connectedness has been restored. We need to try and find a way of measuring this from the offender's and victim's perspectives. Perhaps "seeking, receiving, and accepting an apology" is one such measure and "seeking and receiving forgiveness" is another. "Feeling better about the whole experience" might be yet another. During the re-interviews with their conference sample, Maxwell and Morris (1999) asked the young people: "Do you think the victim accepted your apology?" Only one-half of the young people who made an apology felt that the victim had accepted it. Significantly, however, this did not distinguish between those who were not reconvicted and those who were persistently reconvicted.

Reintegration is also a difficult objective to measure. Maxwell and Morris (1999) attempted to explore this for offenders through a composite variable based on two separate questions that they called "feeling good about oneself and one's life." The particular events identified as indicative of reintegration into the community were: (1) gaining educational qualifications and vocational skills, (2) developing close and positive relationships with family, friends, and partners, and (3) settling into a stable lifestyle. These were all found much more commonly among those not reconvicted six years after a family group conference than among those who were persistently reconvicted.

Reducing Reoffending

Arguably, restorative conferencing could be described as successful if victims and offenders felt involved in the process and in the decision, if victims felt better as a result of the process, and if offenders made amends to victims. However, preventing reoffending is also a critical objective. Moore (1995) presents some data (from Wagga Wagga) indicative of the reduction of reoffending as a result of conferencing, but the methodology used does not allow firm conclusions to be drawn. Similarly, McCold and Wachtel (1998) suggest that those who opted for conferencing had a lower reoffending rate than those who elected to go to court. However, as they acknowledge, this finding is confounded by the fact that the two groups may have been different in the first instance through processes of self selection. Umbreit (1998), using a matched sample, found that young people involved in a victim-offender mediation program were significantly less likely to reoffend than those involved in conventional processes, and their reoffending was less serious. However, this was based on the follow-up period of only one year.

To date, the most extensive examination of the potential of restorative conferencing to reduce reoffending has been carried out by Maxwell and Morris (1999). They found that more than two-fifths of those who were in involved in a family group conference in 1990/91 were not reconvicted or were convicted once only about six years later; not much more than one-quarter were persistently reconvicted within that time period.[32] They then carried out a series of statistical analyses to identify those factors that distinguished the nonreconvicted from the persistently reconvicted. An important finding for the purposes of this chapter is that aspects of conferencing *processes* contributed to lessening the chance of reoffending even when key factors identified by the literature on reoffending (such as adverse early experiences and previous offense history) were taken into account.

The following conference-related variables, based on data from parents, were predictors (at the level of $p < .10$ or more) of not being reconvicted: remorse (feeling that your son/daughter was sorry); not feeling shamed (not being made to feel a bad parent); participation (the parents felt they had actively participated in the conference); and acceptance (the parents agreed with and perceived as fair the family group conference outcome). Similar factors, based on data from the young people themselves, were also predictors (at the level of $p < .10$ or more) of not being reconvicted: meeting (the presence of a victim at the conference and the young person apologizing to him or her); acceptance (the young person agreed with the family group conference outcome); remorse (the young person remembered the conference, completed the tasks agreed to, felt sorry for the offending, showed it to the victim, and felt he or she had repaired the damage); not shamed (the young person was not made to feel a bad person); and participation (the young person felt involved in the family group conference decisionmaking). Thus, Maxwell and Morris (1999) provide evidence that family group conferences, *when they are effectively restorative,* can have an impact on future offending. Conferencing per se, however, does not necessarily achieve this.

Healing Victims' Hurts

We have already alluded to the fact that many victims feel better as a result of participating in conferences, that fewer fear revictimization, and that many would recommend conferencing to others. There are no data, however, on the extent to which victims feel reintegrated after conferencing or on the longer-term effects of conferencing on victims. We know from victim surveys and from in-depth qualitative interviews with victims that for many victims the effects of crime are long-lasting. We need, therefore, to know from longer-term follow-ups with victims whether the positive short-term effects of conferencing remain over time.

Conclusions

Conferencing is a mechanism for making decisions about how best to deal with a young person's criminal behavior. To the extent that the young person, the victim, and their respective communities of care are involved in this decision, are treated with respect, and are not made to feel bad about themselves, then conferencing processes can be described as restorative. Outcomes from conferencing may (and often do) include putting things right for victims and offenders. For example, the young person or his or her family may make reparation to the victim or the young person may perform some work either for the victim or for an organization or person nominated by the victim. The young person, as a result, may feel that he or she has made amends not only to the victim but to society. In addition, the young person may agree to participate in a drug or alcohol program or employment training. To this extent, conferencing outcomes may also be described as restorative for both victims and offenders. In combination, restorative processes and outcomes may result in meeting restorative objectives: that is, to change the hearts and minds of offenders through reducing the probability of reoffending, of victims through healing their hurt, and of both by reintegration within their communities. This review of research on conferencing signifies the potential of conferencing to impact in significant and positive ways. Restorative conferencing offers a new way forward from the failures of the past.

Discussion Questions

1. Do Morris and Maxwell believe that there is one single model of conferencing that should always be followed? What do they think is most important to building successful restorative conferencing models?

2. What are the critical values of restorative conferencing and why are these important?

3. There are several key outcomes from restorative conferencing that Morris and Maxwell (and others) have found to be most important for conference participants. Name at least three key outcomes that have been measured by research and how these have been perceived by conference participants.

4. Reduction of subsequent offending has, historically, been an important outcome indicator of the effectiveness of criminal justice interventions. How important is this in restorative conferencing? Do you think recidivism is the most important indicator of success for a restorative conference? Do you think there are other important indicators for assessing the effectiveness of a restorative conference? What are they?

Endnotes

[1]   A variety of names have been used—family group conferences, family conferences, effective cautioning conferences, community accountability conferences, diversionary conferencing, and community youth conferencing. See Alder and Wundersitz (1994), Bargen (1995), Palk et al. (1998), Hayes and Prenzler (1998), Sherman et al. (1998) and Daly and Kitchner (1999) for a discussion of various Australasian models; LaPrairie (1995) for a discussion of the contrasts between Australasian models and sentencing circles in Canada; Hardin (1996) and Immarigeon (1996) for a discussion of the relevance of conferencing for the United States; McCold and Wachtel (1998) for an evaluation of an American example; Jackson (1998), Young (2000), and Pollard (2000) for descriptions of English examples; Branken and Batley (1998) for an evaluation of a South African example; Maxwell and Morris (1993; 1999) for analysis of the New Zealand system of conferencing; and Hudson et al. (1996) for an examination of examples of conferencing in a number of other jurisdictions.

[2]   For example, in some jurisdictions, conferencing is managed by the police [Australian Capital Territory (ACT)]; in some, by the courts (South Australia); in some, by social welfare (New Zealand); and in some, by other organizations relying on community facilitators (New South Wales). In some jurisdictions, conferencing has a statutory basis (New Zealand and all Australian states except the ACT); in others, it does not. In some jurisdictions, conferencing deals with minor to medium serious offenses and/or first offenders (as in all the Australian examples); in

others, it deals with the most serious offenses and repeat offenders (as in New
Zealand). In some jurisdictions, conferencing is central to the operation of the
youth justice system (as in New Zealand); in others, it is part of police diversion
(as in the ACT).

³   The Young Offenders Act 1993 in South Australia, for example, specifies deter-
    rence, community protection, accountability, and restitution among its objectives.

⁴   Stigmatic shaming is a recognized part of the criminal justice system; many of its
    rituals serve to signify the separation and segregation of defendants. In "reinte-
    grative shaming," at least in theory, the offense rather than the offender is con-
    demned and the offender is reintegrated with, rather than rejected by, society.

⁵   Dignan and Cavadino (1996) distinguish restorative conferencing (an example,
    in their terms, of a communitarian model of justice) from mediation (an exam-
    ple, in their terms, of a reparation model of justice) on the basis of four charac-
    teristics: (1) the delegation of powers from the state to members of the commu-
    nity; (2) the convening of a meeting to which supporters of victims and offenders
    are invited as a mechanism for arriving at a negotiated community response;
    (3) the empowerment of the offender and his or her family through formulating
    a plan that is acceptable to the other participants; and (4) monitoring of those
    plans. It does not seem to us to be as clear-cut as this. Not all of these charac-
    teristics, for example, apply to all examples of conferencing and some apply to
    examples of mediation.

⁶   Umbreit and Greenwood's (1998) survey of victim-offender mediation programs
    specifies vandalism, minor assaults, and theft as the most frequently dealt with
    offenses.

⁷   Thus, in some victim-offender mediation programs, even the parents of the
    young offender are discouraged from participating.

⁸   Umbreit and Greenwood (1997), for example, in their guidelines refer to reassuring
    the victim that the program is not "offender-focused," to giving priority to the vic-
    tim's schedule in arranging the timing of the mediation, to allowing the victim to
    determine the venue, and, commonly, to allowing the victim to speak first.

⁹   See also Umbreit and Stacey (1996) for a discussion of the similarities and dif-
    ferences between victim-offender mediation and the Wagga Wagga model of
    conferencing.

¹⁰ It is quite common to refer to the community in a criminal justice context: "com-
    munity policing," "community crime prevention," "community corrections,"
    "community accountability panels," and so on. In each of these, what or who is
    actually meant by community is not always obvious and is quite likely to differ.
    Within the context of restorative conferencing, we question the use of elected,
    appointed, or self-appointed community representatives as conference participants
    (as in RISE and the "community conferences" organized by the Thames Valley
    police, though significantly the Thames Valley police also organize "restorative
    conferences" in which community representatives do not take part). What we mean
    by "community of care" is much narrower. It is the collection of people with shared
    concerns about the offender, the victim, the offense, and its consequences, and with
    the ability to contribute toward a solution to the problem that the crime presents
    or represents. These people can support and negotiate with victims and offend-
    ers about appropriate outcomes through restorative processes and are arguably
    in a better place than judges and other professionals to identify what might pre-
    vent future crime.

11   In sharp contrast, courts involve a public ritual. Judges, defense lawyers, and prosecutors are the principal players in that ritual. Lawyers are responsible for most (if not all) of the dialogue, and judges make the decisions. Even the structural and spatial arrangements of the courtroom, and the positioning of the parties involved in the proceedings, indicate who has the power and who the "real" participants are. When offenders plead "guilty" in court, the effects of their offenses on victims are communicated to the court, if at all, by the prosecutor. Even when victims attend court, they are merely witnesses for the prosecution or observers; they are not allowed to participate meaningfully. Consequently, victims, particularly of serious offenses, frequently feel alienated from and by the court process. Offenders rarely participate directly in court processes; they are generally expected to communicate with the court through their lawyer, and they are discouraged from any direct dialogue with the victim. They thus can feel alienated from the process and frequently have only a vague idea of what has happened to them. Overall, they remain fundamentally untouched by both processes and outcomes.

12   Not all examples of conferencing have yet been evaluated. This means that we inevitably draw on some examples more frequently than others. The most systematic evaluations published to date have been Maxwell and Morris's (1993) research on New Zealand, Sherman et al.'s (1998) evaluation of RISE, Hayes and Prenzler's (1998) evaluation of pilot conferencing projects in Queensland, and McCold and Wachtel's (1998) analysis of the Bethlehem restorative policing experiment. See also the various writings of Umbreit (for example, 1994 and 1998) on victim-offender mediation.

13   As a result, the police are now specifically excluded from this role in New South Wales although the first examples of conferencing there began with the police in Wagga Wagga.

14   The only exception to this is when he or she has been arrested by the police (there are statutory restrictions on this and only a small minority of juvenile offenders are arrested).

15   The Children, Young Persons and Their Families Act 1989 in New Zealand, for example, specifically states [in Section 4(f)(ii)] that young offenders should be dealt with in a way that "acknowledges their needs" and that gives them the opportunity to develop in "responsible, beneficial and socially acceptable ways." It also states in section 208(g) that in determining outcomes, due regard should be paid to the interests of victims. However, few resources have been provided to achieve either of these.

16   These are all responsibilities placed on signatories to the United Nations Convention of the Rights of the Child. The United States stands virtually alone in not having ratified this convention.

17   We doubt, however, that the presentation of views by victim representatives (for example, from the community at large of from pressure groups) or by delegated professionals such as the police has the same value. This issue could be empirically tested. The effectiveness of the presence of victims' supporters as opposed to victims themselves could also be empirically tested.

18   It is our understanding that, in the script followed by Thames Valley police, everyone at the conference is thanked for attending except the offender (Young, 2000). This seems to us to indicate a departure from restorative values and processes.

[19] Sherman and Strang (1997) also found that almost all of the young offenders who had experienced conferences said that they had understood what was going on in the process but so too did 80 percent of those who went to court. The proportion of the young offenders who said that they felt they had been treated with respect was also not dissimilar for those attending conferences and courts: 75 percent compared with 62 percent. These high proportions of young people reporting positive experiences at courts are somewhat puzzling and stand out from previous research on courts. McCold and Wachtel (1998:109) also comment on the very high level of satisfaction (96%) expressed by offenders about the handling of their cases in courts. Because the same offenders rarely have experience with both courts and conferences with respect to the same offending (New Zealand would be the exception here with respect to at least some of the offenders who experience conferencing), these findings might be highlighting the methodological problem of asking offenders about one process and then comparing these findings against the views of offenders who experienced another process. The participants themselves have no basis for comparison.

[20] The proportion attending family group conferences is certainly now greater in some areas, but a small unpublished study in one region suggests that there, at least, there has been little change over the past 10 years in the proportion of victims attending conferences (Underhill, 1998).

[21] They were not invited to the conference, the time arranged for the conference was unsuitable for them, or they were given inadequate notice of the conference.

[22] This figure is not, however, supported by the Annual Statistical Report of the Office of Crime Statistics (1998). It is stated there that only 47 percent of conferences in 1997 had at least one victim present

[23] See Pollard (2000) for a description of the three types of conferencing offered in Thames Valley: (1) community conferencing, (2) restorative conferencing, and (3) restorative cautions. Pollard states that, by September 1998, Thames Valley police had conducted 1,300 "conferences/cautions"; only 274 (21%) were "full" community or restorative conferences.

[24] In Queensland, victims must agree to the conference taking place though they need not actually attend, and in New Zealand, Western Australia, Queensland, and New South Wales, victims who are present at the conference have a veto over the proposed plan.

[25] On the other hand, about one-quarter of the victims in Maxwell and Morris's (1993) sample said that they felt worse as a result of attending the family group conference. There were a variety of reasons for this. The most frequent and perhaps most important reason was that the victim did not feel that the young person and/or his or her family were truly sorry. Other, less common reasons included the inability of the family and young person to make reparation, victims' inability to express themselves adequately, their difficulty in communicating cross-culturally, the lack of support offered to them, the perceived failure of the offender to show remorse to the victim for the offending, feeling that their concerns had not been adequately listened to, and feeling that people were disinterested in or unsympathetic to them. Most victim concerns, therefore, were primarily rooted in poor practice and were not fundamental objections to conferencing per se.

26   In addition, the conference itself seemed to alleviate victims' anger. Thus, 60 percent of victims who attended conferences said they felt "quite" or "very" angry at the beginning of the conference, but only 30 percent said so afterwards.

27   Braithwaite and Mugford (1994) elaborate 14 conditions for successful reintegrative shaming. These include "uncoupling" the offense and the offender so that the offense but not the offender can be viewed as "bad" (and denounced); facilitators who identify with all participants as well as the public interest; the empowerment of victims, offenders, and families through control of the process; the encouragement of empathy and generosity; rituals of inclusion and reintegration, avoidance of power imbalances; completion of agreed outcomes; and further "ceremonies" if reintegration fails.

28   Generally, Harris's (1999) findings show that for shaming to be effective, it needs to be applied by those close to the offender, and this is not always the approach adopted in some examples of conferencing.

29   The only exception was the item "people said I could put the offense behind me."

30   The exceptions were: for the juvenile personal property sample, "treated as though I was a bad person"; for the juvenile property (security) sample "treated as though I was a criminal"; and, for the youth violence sample, "people will not let me forget what I did."

31   Psychological studies (for example, Tangney et al., 1996) have also shown that shame can have negative consequences for self-esteem.

32   These reconviction rates cannot be directly compared with data from other jurisdictions, but they are certainly no worse and may be better in some respects than the closest comparisons available to us (see, for example, Lovell and Norris, 1990; Coumarelos, 1994; and Coumarelos and Weatherburn, 1995). It is also important to stress that what is being measured here is the effects of restorative *processes* on reoffending. Most research has measured the effects of outcomes on reoffending.

References

Alder, C., and J. Wundersitz (eds.) (1994). *Family Conferencing and Juvenile Justice.* Canberra: Australian Institute of Criminology.

Bargen, J. (1995). "A Critical View of Conferencing." *The Australian and New Zealand Journal of Criminology*, Special Supplementary Issue, 100-103.

Bazemore, G., and M. Umbreit (1999). *Conferences, Circles, Boards and Mediations: Restorative Justice and Citizen Involvement in the Response to Youth Crime.* Washington, DC: Office of Juvenile Justice and Delinquency Prevention.

Blagg, H. (1998). "Restorative Visions and Restorative Justice Practices: Conferencing, Ceremony and Reconciliation in Australia." *Current Issues in Criminal Justice* 10(1):5-14.

Braithwaite, J. (1989). *Crime, Shame and Reintegration.* Cambridge, England: Cambridge University Press.

Braithwaite, J., and S. Mugford (1994). "Conditions of Successful Reintegration Ceremonies: Dealing with Juvenile Offenders." *British Journal of Criminology* 34:139-171.

Branken, N., and M. Batley (1998). *Family Group Conferences: Putting the Wrong Right.* Report of the Family Group Conference Pilot Project of the Inter-Ministerial Committee on Young People At Risk.

Coumarelos, C. (1994). *Juvenile Offending: Predicting Persistence and Determining the Cost-Effectiveness of Intervention.* Sydney: New South Wales Bureau of Crime Statistics and Research.

Coumarelos, C., and D. Weatherburn (1995). "Targetting Intervention Strategies to Reduce Juvenile Recidivism." *The Australian and New Zealand Journal of Criminology* 28(1):54-72.

Dignan, J., and M. Cavadino (1996). "Towards a Framework for Conceptualising and Evaluating Models of Criminal Justice from a Victim's Perspective." *International Review of Victimology* 4:153-82.

Daly, K., and J. Kitchner (1999). "The (R)evolution of Restorative Justice through Research-Practitioner Partnerships." In *Youth Justice in Focus: Conference Proceedings*, edited by A. Morris and G. Maxwell. Wellington, New Zealand: Institute of Criminology, Victoria University of Wellington.

Daly, K., M. Venables, M. McKenna, L. Mumford, and J. Christie-Johnston (1998). *South Australia Juvenile Justice (SAJJ) Research on Conferencing, Technical Report, No.1: Research Instruments and Background Notes.* School of Criminology and Criminal Justice, Griffith University: Queensland. Available at *http://www.aic.gov.au/rjustice/sajj/index.html.*

Farrington, D. (1997). "Human Development and Criminal Careers." In *Oxford Handbook of Criminology*, edited by M. Maguire, R. Morgan, and R. Reiner, 361-408. Oxford, England: Clarendon Press.

Fergusson, D., L. Horwood, and M. Lynskey (1997). "Family Change, Parental Discord and Early Offending." *Journal of Child Psychology and Psychiatry* 33:1059-75.

Friday, P. (1999). *An Overview of Restorative Justice Programmes and Issues.* Paper presented to International Scientific and Professional Advisory Council of the United Nations Crime Prevention and Criminal Justice Programme. Unpublished paper.

LaPrairie, C. (1995). "Altering Course: New Directions in Criminal Justice Sentencing Circles and Family Group Conferences." *The Australian and New Zealand Journal of Criminology*, Special Supplementary Issue, 78-99.

Hardin, M. (1996). *Family Group Conferences in Child Abuse and Neglect: Learning from the Experience of New Zealand.* Washington, DC: American Bar Association Center on Children and the Law.

Harris, N. (1999). "Can State or Civil Institutions Shame?" Unpublished paper presented at a conference on Restorative Justice and Civil Society, Australian National University.

Harris, N., and J. Burton (1997). *The Reliability of Observed Reintegrative Shaming, Shame, Defiance and Other Key Concepts in Diversionary Conferences.* RISE Working Paper No. 5. Canberra: Australian National University.

Hayes, H., and T. Prenzler (1998). *Making Amends: Final Evaluation of the Queensland Community Conferencing Pilot*. Brisbane: Centre for Crime Policy and Public Safety, Griffith University.

Hudson, J., A. Morris, G. Maxwell, and B. Galaway (eds.) (1996). *Family Group Conferences: Perspectives on Policy and Practice*. Annandale, Australia: Federation Press.

Immarigeon, R. (1996). "Family Group Conferences in Canada and the United States: An Overview." In *Family Group Conferences: Perspectives on Policy and Practice*, edited by J. Hudson, A. Morris, G. Maxwell, and B. Galaway. Annandale, Australia: Federation Press.

Jackson, S. (1998). *Family Justice? An Evaluation of the Hampshire Youth Justice Family Group Conference Project*. Southampton, UK: University of Southampton.

LaPrairie, C. (1995). "Altering Course: New Directions in Criminal Justice Sentencing Circles and Family Group Conferences." *The Australian and New Zealand Journal of Criminology*, Special Supplementary Issue, 78-99.

LaPrairie, C. (1998). "The 'New' Justice: Some Implications for Aboriginal Communities." *Canadian Journal of Criminology* 40(1):61-79.

Levine, M, A. Eagle, S. Tuiavii, and C. Roseveare (1997). *Creative Youth Justice Practice*. Wellington, New Zealand: Social Policy Agency.

Lovell, R., and M. Norris (1990). *One in Four: Offending from Age 10 to 24 in a Cohort of New Zealand Males*. Research report No. 8, Wellington, New Zealand: Department of Social Welfare.

Maxwell, G.M., and A. Morris (1993). *Families, Victims and Culture: Youth Justice in New Zealand*. Wellington, New Zealand: Social Policy Agency and Institute of Criminology, Victoria University of Wellington.

Maxwell, G.M., and A. Morris (1999). *Understanding Reoffending*. Wellington, New Zealand: Institute of Criminology, Victoria University of Wellington.

McCold, P., and B. Wachtel (1998). *Restorative Policing Experiment*. Pipersville, PA: Real Justice Community Service Foundation.

Moore, D. (1995). *A New Approach to Juvenile Justice: An Evaluation of Family Conferencing in Wagga Wagga*. Wagga Wagga, Australia: Centre for Rural Social Research, Charles Sturt University.

Morris, A., G.M. Maxwell, and J.R. Robertson (1993). "Giving Victims a Voice: A New Zealand Experiment." *The Howard Journal* 32(4):304-21.

New Zealand Maori Council and D. Durie Hall (1999). "Restorative Justice: a Maori Perspective." In *Restorative Justice: Contemporary Themes and Practice*, edited by H. Bowen and J. Consedine. Lyttelton, New Zealand: Ploughshares Publications.

Office of Crime Statistics (1998). *Crime and Justice in South Australia, 1997: Juvenile Justice: A Statistical Report*. Office of Crime Statistics, Attorney General's Department, Adelaide, Australia.

Palk, G., Pollard, G., and L. Johnson (1998). "Community Conferencing in Queensland." Unpublished paper presented at the Australian and New Zealand Society of Criminology Annual Conference, Gold Coast.

Polk, K. (1994). "Family Conferencing: Theoretical and Evaluative Questions." In *Family Group Conferencing and Juvenile Justice*, edited by C. Alder and J. Wundersitz. Canberra: Australian Institute of Criminology.

Pollard, C. (2000). "If Your Only Tool is a Hammer, All Your Problems Will Look Like Nails." In *Restorative Justice and Civil Society*, edited by H. Strang and J. Braithwaite. Cambridge, England: Cambridge University Press.

Roberts, A.W. (1999). Personal communication.

Schiff, M. (1998). "Restorative Justice Interventions for Juvenile Offenders: A Research Agenda for the Next Decade." *Western Criminology Review* 1(1).

Sherman, L., and H. Strang (1997). *The Right Kind of Shame for Crime Prevention.* Canberra, Australia. Unpublished paper.

Sherman, L., H. Strang, G. Barnes, J. Braithwaite, N. Inkpen, and M. Teh (1998). *Experiments in Restorative Policing: A Progress Report to the National Police Research Unit on the Canberra Reintegrative Shaming Experiment.* Canberra: Australian National University.

Strang, H., G. Barnes, J. Braithwaite, and L. Sherman (1999). *Experiments in Restorative Policing: A progress report on the Canberra, Reintegrative Shaming Experiment (RISE).* See: *www.aic.gov.au/rjustice/rise/progress/1999.html*

Strang, H., and L. Sherman (1997). *The Victim's Perspective.* Paper 2, RISE Working Paper. Canberra: Australian National University.

Tangney, J., P. Wagner, D. Hill-Barlow, D. Marshall, and R. Gramzow (1996). "Relation of Shame and Guilt to Constructive Versus Destructive Responses to Anger Across the Lifespan." *Journal of Personality and Social Psychology* 70(4):797-809.

Tauri, J. (1998). "The Indigenisation of New Zealand's Justice System." *Criminology Aotearoa/New Zealand.* Institute of Criminology, Victoria University of Wellington, No. 9:2-3.

Tyler, T. (1990). *Why People Obey the Law.* New Haven, CT: Yale University Press.

Umbreit, M. (1994). *Victim Meets Offender: The Impact of Restorative Justice and Mediation.* Monsey, NY: Criminal Justice Press.

Umbreit, M. (1998). "Restorative Justice through Victim-Offender Mediation: A Multi-Site Assessment." *Western Criminology Review* 1(1).

Umbreit, M., R. Coates, and A.W. Roberts (1997). *Impact of Victim-Offender Mediation in Canada, England and the United States.* Kingston, NJ: The Crime Victims Report, Civic Research Institute.

Umbreit, M., and J. Greenwood (1997). *Criteria for Victim-Sensitive Mediation and Dialogue with Offenders.* St. Paul, MN: Center for Restorative Justice and Mediation.

Umbreit, M., and J. Greenwood (1998). *National Survey of Victim-Offender Mediation Programs in the U.S.* St. Paul, MN: Center for Restorative Justice and Mediation.

Umbreit, M., and S. Stacey (1996). "Family Group Conferencing Comes to the US: A Comparison with Victim-Offender Mediation." *Juvenile and Family Court Journal* 47(2):29-38.

Underhill, L. (1998). *Victims and the Family Group Conference: Restorative Justice in Practice.* Wellington, New Zealand: Institute of Criminology. Unpublished paper.

White, R. (1994). "Shaming and Reintegrative Strategies: Individuals, State Power and Social Interests." In *Family Group Conferencing and Juvenile Justice*, edited by C. Alder and J. Wundersitz. Canberra: Australian Institute of Criminology.

Wundersitz, J., and S. Hetzel (1996). "Family Conferencing for Young Offenders: The South Australian Experience." In *Family Group Conferences: Perspectives on Policy and Practice*, edited by J. Hudson, A. Morris, G. Maxwell, and B. Galaway. Annandale, Australia: Federation Press.

Young, R. (2000). "Intergrating a Multi-Victim Perspective into Police Cautioning: Some Data from the Thames Valley." In *Integrating a Victim Perspective within Criminal Justice*, edited by A. Crawford and J. Goodey. Aldershot, England: Ashgate.

9

Community Reparative Boards in Vermont: Theory and Practice

DAVID R. KARP
LYNNE WALTHER

Community boards are one of several nonadversarial decision-making innovations inspired by restorative and community justice philosophies. Others include victim-offender mediation, family group conferencing, and circle sentencing (Bazemore, 1998). The overarching goals of all of these program models are: (1) to better include community members in the justice process, (2) to identify and rectify harm caused by criminal offenses, and/or (3) to successfully reintegrate offenders into community life. Community boards are exemplified by the Vermont model, in which citizen volunteers serve on local boards that negotiate reparative agreements with offenders. In 1999, the Vermont Department of Corrections (VDOC) received the prestigious Ford Foundation Innovations in Government Award for its development of the reparative boards. As of August 1999, there were 46 boards operating in 24 townships, with a pool of 315 board members. These boards have processed more than 4,000 cases since their inception in November 1995.

The mission of the community board model is to enhance social control at the local level by involving citizens in the justice process. Community members, with their high stake in the quality of their neighborhoods, work with local offenders to resolve problems caused by the offenses. Cases are sent to community boards by judges. Thus, it is not the task of the boards to determine guilt. Rather, it is to negotiate a course of action that will rectify the harm caused by the offense.

199

Under the current sentencing guidelines available to Vermont judges, community boards are an option for offenders convicted of minor offenses who would have otherwise received more traditional probation or short-term jail sentences. Offenders who appear before the boards negotiate a "reparative contract" that might include such tasks as letters of apology, community service, or alcohol screenings. Offenders have 90 days to complete the contract.

This chapter describes the Vermont Reparative Probation Program, locates it within the framework of a community justice model, and presents some preliminary evaluation data that examine the program's effectiveness. These data are drawn from two sources. First, qualitative data are based on Karp's ongoing research project that involves content analysis of videotaped board meetings. Second, quantitative data are drawn from Walther's in-house outcome report of the reparative program for Fiscal Year 1998 (July 1997–June 1998). Other descriptions of the Vermont reparative program may be found in Dooley (1996), Karp (2000; forthcoming), Perry and Gorczyk (1997), and Walther and Perry (1997). Vermont serves as a case study for the examination of the board process, primarily because it is a well-known program and represents, currently, the only statewide institutionalization of restorative justice in the United States.

Vermont Reparative Board Process

In this section, we provide a systematic description of how the boards function. The process begins with a judge who sentences an offender to "reparative probation." Immediately after sentencing, a corrections staff person working in the probation unit conducts an intake meeting with the offender, explaining the board process and gathering background information. This information, along with the police report, is provided to board members for review before a case is seen. Before a meeting is scheduled, the staff board coordinator or volunteer victim coordinator will contact the victim, encouraging him or her to attend. Any information from the victim is also provided to the board members before the case is seen.

Board meetings are open to the public and it is not uncommon, given the program's publicity, for one or two observers to be present in addition to the board members. Boards vary in size, but typically three to seven board members are present for a given meeting.

Board meetings begin with personal introductions and a review of the mission of the program and goals for the meeting. Specifically, the boards work with the offender so that he or she can:

(1) learn about the impact of the crime on victim(s) and the community;

(2) restore and make whole the victim(s) of the crime;

(3) make amends to the community; and

(4) learn ways to avoid reoffending in the future.

The sequence proceeds from a discussion of the offense and its impact on victims and the community to a discussion of strategies for reparation and reintegration, and finally to the creation of a contract that is signed by the offender and the board. This is important, as it stresses to the offender that he or she is making a compact with community members, with victim input. Often, the discussion begins with a recounting of the circumstances of the offense by the offender (and the victim, if present). In this open-ended discussion, board members often ascertain: (1) whether the offender takes full responsibility for the harm done, (2) the extent of the harm, (3) problems in the offender's life that may lead to future offending, and (4) the willingness of the offender to make reparations and commit to law-abiding behavior. With this knowledge, the group proceeds to identify strategies for reparation and offender reintegration. Reparative strategies typically include letters of apology and community service, while reintegrative strategies often involve written statements or short papers by the offender that describe the impact of the crime, appearances before victim-impact panels, or participation in some form of competency development such as GED classes or driver safety courses. Boards often require a drug and alcohol screening in which the offender is assessed by a professional.

After the initial meeting, most boards will require offenders to reappear after 45 days (half of the probationary period) in order to review their progress. Boards also ask offenders to appear for a closure meeting to offer congratulations for their successful completion of the contract. Victims and other affected parties are invited to all subsequent meetings.

Offenders who violate the terms of reparative contracts are returned to court. Sometimes they may go back to the board to renegotiate their contract. Several boards have review processes that help prevent violations by providing advice and encouragement to offenders that are getting off schedule. Offenders may always choose traditional sentencing in lieu of reparative probation. Sometimes they will choose monetary burdens, such as a fine, from a judge rather than face the challenge of appearing before community peers who make extensive use of "reintegrative shaming" (Braithwaite, 1989).

Although it varies from one board to the next, most boards meet once a week for two hours. In this time, they will often hear two new cases, and conduct two or three reviews and/or closure meetings. The latter are generally brief (perhaps five to 15 minutes), while new cases generally range from 20 to 60 minutes.

Board Structure, Training and Recruitment

The VDOC employs specially trained probation staff to manage reparative caseloads and work closely with community volunteers in the various court jurisdictions, primarily as board liaisons. When the program was new, a "reparative coordinator" position was created. Now that the number of cases has increased, a generic but restorative probation officer role exists. Training standards for this position have been developed with a focus on victim needs, alternative dispute resolution, and working with community members. In many sites, this staff handles both reparative and traditional cases.

Other staff members belong to the reparative team. The supervisor of the Court and Reparative Services Unit (CRSU) manages the personnel, marketing to the court, caseload distribution, and general operations of both reparative probation and traditional probation. Four regional "community resource coordinators" devote their time to recruiting and training board members and support volunteers, developing community capacity, and running victim-impact programs.

When reparative probation is assigned to a case from a district court, it is forwarded to the local CRSU. The reparative team (which also includes community volunteers, in roles such as victim liaison and community service opportunities developer) is responsible for managing the reparative caseload of the local boards. Responsibilities include: (1) conducting an intake interview with offenders that orients them to the program, (2) processing paperwork and acting as liaison to the court, attorneys, other interested parties, and community justice centers, (3) scheduling the offender to appear before the board, (4) identifying and contacting victims or other parties who may wish to attend the reparative board meeting, (5) recruiting and coordinating training of volunteers for board membership and other volunteer roles associated with the program, (6) developing reparative resources, such as community service opportunities, family group conferencing, victim-impact panels, and other activities relevant to reparative contracts, and (7) monitoring offender compliance with the reparative agreement.

All Vermont residents who live within the particular jurisdiction of a community board are eligible to serve on it (except current offenders and youths under age 18). Board bylaws define terms locally, but a volunteer is expected to serve at least one year. Many board members have served continuously since the program's inception in 1995. No mechanism is in place that ensures broad representation in the community (except a corrections directive), so it appears that board members are disproportionately middle-class and well-educated. Boards are almost equally represented by men and women. Some internal discussion has taken place regarding the board composition, and several board members and VDOC staff members have encouraged the recruitment of people who share characteristics with many of the offenders who appear before the board. In Vermont, this primarily means recruiting younger, working-class board members. Some offenders who have successfully completed reparative probation have been recruited to serve on the boards. Another discussion pertains to members of the criminal justice community, such as state troopers or local police, and whether (as residents of the community) they are eligible to serve. Several are board members now, and, upon occasion, appear in uniform.

Community resource coordinators, other reparative staff, and board members recruit new board members by word of mouth and through a departmental volunteer recruitment plan. Initially, however, a leader nomination process was used. For example, in Brattleboro, VDOC staff identified 50 community leaders and sent letters to each explaining the program and asking them to nominate other members of the community (or themselves) who they believed would participate in the program. Thirty residents were nominated, and 15 were recruited for participation.

Prospective board members are expected to observe some board meetings before completing their three-to-four hour pre-service orientation. When they do become board members, they must participate in several more hours of training within the first year. This training includes an introduction to restorative justice principles and various restorative models such as victim-offender mediation, circle sentencing, and family group conferencing. Board members participate in role-playing exercises and other activities designed to develop good communication skills in their interactions with offenders, victims, and other board members. In addition, ongoing board members are encouraged to participate in seven hours of in-service trainings each year. These include conferences, local workshops, corrections staff training, and other development opportunities.

The role of the boards complements, rather than conflicts with, that of the judge. Boards do not retry a case, nor can they overturn a judge's determination of guilt. Sometimes, however, board members reach a different conclusion about a case than is indicated by the verdict or the police affidavit. That is inevitable given the different mechanisms used by these parties to gather information as well as the idiosyncrasies of the legal process (such as plea bargaining) that may cause an offender to be convicted of one offense when he or she has, in fact, committed another. For example, in one case, board members were convinced by the offender that he was justly provoked in a case of simple assault. Personally, they felt that the conviction was not war-ranted. Their task, however, was not to determine guilt or innocence; instead, it was to recommend a sanction. They proceeded to do so, but in this case, they emphasized reintegrative activities rather than repar-ative ones.

What are Boards Trying to Accomplish?

Board authority is not arbitrary. They cannot, for example, create a contract that continues beyond the 90-day probationary period (although they can negotiate an extension if need be). They cannot stip-ulate any formal terms of supervision or incarceration. Each jurisdic-tion has established specific parameters for boards, primarily limiting the total number of community service hours and the number of dif-ferent types of activities that can be assigned. In addition, only the court can establish the terms of restitution (and it is required of the court that it assess the offender's ability to pay). Thus, the boards typically pro-vide oversight for the court's terms of restitution (such as when the court neglects to include such terms or if they are insufficient) and for assessing other aspects of the harm to victims and community. Despite these parameters, they do have substantial latitude in negotiating a con-tract that is tailored to the specifics of the case and offender. Because of this, similar offenses may yield dissimilar reparative contracts. One offender might get a writing assignment, another might be asked to take an adult education course, and a third might be assigned com-munity service. They do try to fit activities to the actual crime, espe-cially when victim input is available. For instance, the department mea-sures how much of community work service hours are done in the town where the crime is committed.

Community Justice and Community Boards

Community boards are organized under a community justice model (Clear and Karp, 1999). Most generally, the goals of community jus-tice are to improve a community's capacity to resolve local problems and to realize common goals, thus leading to greater satisfaction in the quality of community life. Toward these ends, the model prescribes par-allel processes of community building through problem identifica-tion/resolution and social participation/integration. As Clear and Karp (1998:13-14) define it,

> Community justice refers to all variants of crime prevention
> and justice activities that explicitly include the community in
> their processes and set the enhancement of community qual-

ity of life as an explicit goal. Community justice is rooted in the actions that citizens, community organizations, and the criminal justice system can take to control crime and social disorder. Its central focus is community-level outcomes, shifting the emphasis from individual incidents to systemic patterns, from individual conscience to social mores, and from individual goods to the common good.

One of the central components of the community justice model is the development of a community's capacity to address local problems. With capacity must come autonomy, and with autonomy must come variation. VDOC has purposefully (and rather uncharacteristically for a state power) relinquished some of its authority to the boards. As such, all boards must conform to the same mandate but can fulfill it in a variety of ways. For example, some boards ask offenders to leave for a period of deliberation during the meeting, while other boards keep the offender involved in all discussions of the contract. It is clear, too, that some boards place a greater emphasis on reparation while others emphasize reintegration. Some boards are quite formal in how the meeting proceeds, carefully following a predetermined script. Others are informal, focusing more on spontaneity and interpersonal connection. Some boards are more lenient. Some are more philosophical. Some are more argumentative. This variation can be heightened when the actual board for a given case has different volunteers from one time to another, due to scheduling difficulties, the addition of new board members, and so on. It is the responsibility of VDOC staff, however, to ensure that no board or board member contradicts the restorative justice mission of the program.

Community boards seek several goals in keeping with restorative and community justice ideals. Boards seek to realize these ideals in terms of concrete outcomes but also by embodying principles of practice that distinguish board meetings from traditional criminal justice encounters with offenders, which are primarily adversarial, impersonal, disempowering, and stigmatizing. In particular, boards seek the active participation of victims and other parties in the decision-making process. This serves not only to gather useful information about the harmfulness of the crime and how it might be repaired but also to engage victims in a process that will be healing and empowering. Boards also seek the active engagement of offenders so they might articulate and demonstrate remorse, become more committed to making amends, and enact positive social behaviors, such as through community service or acquiring a GED, that will relegitimize their membership in the community. Finally, boards seek to fulfill a "communitarian" conception of community in which citizens are actively engaged in resolving local problems and that enhances social institutions that provide for the quality of community life.

In the community justice model, four characteristics distinguish community justice programs: (1) citizen accessibility to the justice process, (2) citizen participation in justice decisionmaking, (3) restorative justice activities, and (4) social reintegration of victims and offenders (Karp and Clear, in press). Such program, or process, characteristics are designed to accomplish restorative and reintegrative goals, which, in turn, lead to a greater quality of community life—enhanced community capacity to resolve local problems and greater satisfaction of residents with community life (see Figure 9.1).

Figure 9.1
Community Justice Logic Model

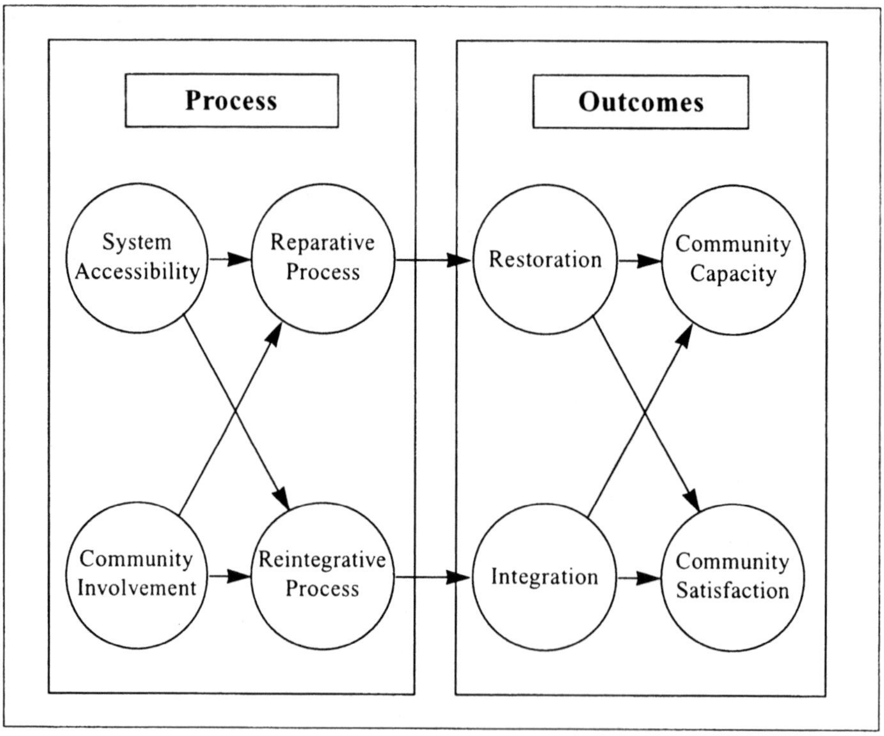

Accessibility

The first characteristic, *accessibility*, refers to the decentralization of justice activities so that local communities can play a greater role in the process. This would include the creation of community courts, neighborhood police and probation offices, and community justice centers that offer victim services, conflict mediation, and space for justice-related community organizing. Accessibility also refers to a program's flexibility in meeting local needs and an informality in social interactions that reduces the social distance between justice professionals, citizen volunteers, and affected parties (e.g., victims, offenders, onlookers). In Vermont, accessibility is realized by the creation of local boards. As the program has grown, boards serving relatively large geographic areas or population sizes have divided to serve smaller areas.[1] Thus, new boards form wherever there are enough cases to process and sufficient staff capacity and local volunteers willing to serve. While each board has a clear mandate, it is also free to craft reparative agreements to suit local concerns and the specific context of the case. Because board members are volunteers, they meet with offenders in informal settings (often a conference room in the local library, town hall, or probation office) and sit in a circle around a small table symbolizing the democratic and egalitarian nature of the process.

Accessibility is demonstrated not only in the decentralization of formal justice processes but also in the dynamic interplay between formal and informal social control. This is made possible by the interaction between board members and offenders (victims or affected parties, when possible) who share membership in the local community. Consider, for example, the following conversation between one board member and an offender.[2] The conversation not only reflects the overlapping social ties between these people but also the potential for ongoing informal social control as a complement to the formal justice process.

Board Member:	How do you get to work?
Offender:	My friend, we both work up at Middlebury.
Board Member:	Who are you working for up in Middlebury?
Offender:	[Name of contractor.] They're out of Boston.
Board Member:	Yeah, what are you doing up there?
Offender:	Slate roofing.
Board Member:	Which building do you work on now?
Offender:	On the college. It's a huge building.
Board Member:	Yeah, I'm working on the same building.
Offender:	You are?!?
Board Member:	Yeah. The science building.
Offender:	Yup! That's where it is.
Board Member:	I thought I'd seen you before.

Reparative boards see a wide variety of cases, but not all offenders can gain "access" to this justice model. Boards do not work with violent or domestic cases or with sex offenders. Occasionally, however, simple assault cases are heard. Boards can elect not to see cases referred by a judge if it does not fall into the targeted list of offenses. Cases typically referred include drunk driving, possession of minor drugs, furnishing alcohol to minors, theft, vandalism, and fraud, among others.

Determination of the target offender population is based on a risk management protocol, described by VDOC as "the 42-box model."

This refers to a 6 x 7 table that sorts offenders by the severity of the offense and the risk for reoffense. Severe offenses, even if first-time offenses, do not qualify for reparative probation. In general, low-severity, nonviolent offenses are targeted for reparative probation. Sometimes judges will send to the boards cases that fall outside the target population but, in general, the boards handle relatively minor cases. In Fiscal Year 1998, 1,234 of the 1,320 cases (93%) consisted of offenders who met the eligibility criteria for the program, and 86 cases were referred to the board even though the offenders were identified as in need of greater supervision than the program provides.

While most cases that are referred to reparative probation qualify for the program, it is not yet the case that all cases that do qualify get referred. Although many cases fall within the eligibility target, it is assumed that judges will exercise discretion with regard to supervision needs, sentencing offenders with a standard probation order (with higher supervision requirements) rather than to reparative probation. Thus, the program's goal is to achieve a 60 percent referral rate of all eligible cases. In July 1998, for example, 39 percent of all qualified cases were referred to the program. Other eligible cases received traditional probation. This figure, however, represents a steady increase in referrals since the program's inception, and a 288 percent increase in referrals from Fiscal Year 1997.

It is also likely that many cases are not referred to reparative probation for reasons other than concern about supervision needs. It may be that the program, being new, is not sufficiently known or trusted by the court community. It may also be that some judges, prosecutors, and public defenders dislike the program and try to avoid placing offenders in the program. Some do not believe community volunteers should play a role in the decision-making process. Others (particularly public defenders, for example) are uncomfortable with the program because they do not know what the boards will require of the offender. All of these problems speak to the difficulties of accessibility—creating partnerships between criminal justice professionals and local communities.

Citizen Participation

The second feature of the community justice model is *citizen participation*. This refers specifically to the participation of key stakeholders—not only community volunteers but also victims, offenders, and other members of the community affected by the crime, such as parents, spouses, employers, or friends. Citizen participation in the justice process is defined by extensiveness—the variety of parties brought to the table, and intensiveness—the degree to which each participates and has a voice in the decision-making process. Community boards illustrate this idea by their large numbers of citizen volunteers and their authority to negotiate reparative contracts independently of judges, prosecutors, and correctional officials. Offenders, too, have an unusual opportunity to share in the decision-making process. Victims are always invited to attend, and their attendance is strictly voluntary. When victims and other relevant parties, such as a parent or friend, attend board meetings, they are encouraged to participate freely in the discussion. When victims do not attend, which is common, they will sometimes provide a statement to be read at the meeting.

Citizens are elemental to the community justice model because their participation represents a dramatic institutional change in the locus of responsibility for resolving local problems from the state to the community—from formal to informal social control. They represent the "social capital" that undergirds healthy and organized communities (Sampson et al., 1997). Research commissioned by the Vermont Department of Corrections demonstrates the intensity with which citizens in Vermont desire participation in the criminal sanctioning process (John Doble Research Associates and J. Greene, 1999; Perry and Gorzcyk, 1997). In the Doble survey, 91 percent of the respondents supported the use of reparative boards while only 8 percent were opposed. Eighty-seven percent reported that they would attend the board meeting if they were a crime victim. In general, the public is highly critical of traditional criminal justice practice and supportive of alternatives that provide higher levels of engagement by victims, offenders, and community members.

Board members often try to make it clear to offenders that the boards are an unusual entity in the justice system, and that their role as volunteers should highlight for the offender that they are sincere in their concern for the offender's and the community's welfare. In one case, for example, a board member begins the meeting with the following statement:

> We usually start with having you give us an overview of why you are here, what happened, what led up to the events bringing you here. As you know this isn't a trial; you've already been through that process. We are only volunteers, we don't represent anything but people in the community. We are here to try and help you, so why don't you help yourself by giving us a little bit of the background.

Such a statement by a board member frames the meeting as one *of* the community and *for* the community rather than as one of the state against an individual. This framing may reduce the formality and power differentials of the process (though it certainly does not eliminate them) while also implying that there is something unique and important about the voluntary participation of the local citizen.

Board Volunteering The Vermont Reparative Probation Program depends upon local citizens to volunteer. These citizen volunteers work closely with correctional staff but otherwise manage a number of important responsibilities. They must commit to initial and ongoing training; they are expected to serve for at least one year; and many often see cases on a weekly basis, often commuting some distance in rural areas. In addition, new roles for volunteers have been created such as victim liaison, community work service development, and board assistant, which are indispensable to the operation of the program. The VDOC estimates that the 75 volunteers serving in these auxiliary roles alone donated 7,281 hours statewide during Fiscal Year 1998. To staff the reparative program, a pool of 334 volunteers (259 board members plus 75 auxiliaries) served in that year.

In October 1998, a loosely knit group of board members from around the state formed a "reparative board association." These individuals felt the need to compare notes, share information about process and cases, provide feedback to the VDOC, and develop some autonomy as community members. Distinct from corrections, this group is growing, and provides support to volunteers in the state. Recently, they have begun inviting VDOC program staff to portions of their meetings and worked with them to develop new board member training standards.

A more profound consequence of the Reparative Probation Program has been the development of Community Justice Centers (CJCs), which the State Agency of Human Services has seeded with start up funds. Aimed at "encouraging and supporting justice services for victims and communities, providing methods for citizens to resolve disputes at a community level, and working with justice agencies to address crime in their communities" (Spinelli and Perry, 1997), the first Justice Center opened in October 1998 in Burlington—Vermont's largest municipality (pop. 40,000).[3] The CJCs host a variety of justice-related activities such as educational forums, community mediation, family group conferencing, victim services, and faith community initiatives. To receive seed money, the centers must handle local reparative probation cases using the reparative board model. Burlington's CJC has chosen the name "restorative justice panels" for their boards, because they also handle youth cases and noncriminal quality-of-life disputes. Another mandate of the state grants is that the majority of services are provided by volunteer community members. This partnership represents further accessibility for community members and offers a unique opportunity for both crime prevention and ownership of community conflict resolution.

Victim Participation Victims are actively encouraged to participate in the board process. The VDOC has a required volunteer role of victim liaison for each board site, and if that is not filled, staff perform that role. When victims do attend, they are encouraged to participate in reconstructing the circumstances of the offense, how the offense impacted them, and what reparative terms they would prefer. Nonetheless, victim participation has been infrequent and inconsistent.

For Fiscal Year 1998, 424 victims were identified for contact in the 702 reparative cases that terminated that year. Therefore, 60 percent of cases heard by the boards involve offenses with direct victims. Often, however, they will hear "victimless" offenses such as drunk driving or underage drinking. Commercial establishments are included among those identified as victims; for example, a store owner or manager may be contacted in the case of retail theft. Program personnel contacted 378 (89%) of the victims either by letter or by telephone. Despite this high rate of victim contact, victim participation in reparative meetings was quite low; only 62 (15%) victims attended a board meeting.

Several reasons may account for this low participation level. Because of the novelty of the approach, victims may not understand the potential benefits of participation. Alternatively, for many of these minor offenses, victims would rather put the event behind them than "belabor" it. Also, often in minor cases, victims are primarily concerned with receiving restitution (in Vermont, restitution is court-ordered and boards primarily provide oversight). Thus, victim needs might be sufficiently addressed before the board meeting is convened. Another reason might be that board staff and volunteers are not sufficiently attendant to victims' emotional needs, and victims are "put off" rather than welcomed by the process. Currently, VDOC is attempting to increase victim participation.

Restorative Justice Decisionmaking In community justice, a third feature of the model is *restorative justice decisionmaking*. In this justice philosophy, the goal of the sanctioning process is not punishment. Instead, offender accountability is defined as the obligation to make amends to the victim and the community for any damage caused by the offense. Perhaps the centerpiece of the discussion during a board meeting is the identification of harms wrought by the offense and the delineation of strategies to rectify them. The restorative focus provides a stark contrast to the punitive model that characterizes the traditional justice system. In addition, it can be distinguished from rehabilitative models that fail to consider the offender's obligations to the victim and the community.[4]

For Fiscal Year 1998, 592 (52%) offenders successfully completed the terms of the probation, which includes all reparative tasks to victims and the community. Of the 592 offenders, 374 (63%) were assigned community service work. This group contributed 11,886 hours of service to Vermont communities.

In one case, an offender, while taking an Aikido class, stole a wallet from another student at the studio. He subsequently used the victim's credit card to make fraudulent purchases. Present for the meeting were board members, the offender, the offender's parents, the victim, the Aikido instructor, and a representative of the bank that issued the credit card. In their discussion, the theft was identified as harm to the victim and the consequences of the theft were enumerated. These ranged from the tangible (e.g., the victim lost a discount card for travel in Europe that he was unable to replace before his trip) to the intangible (e.g., the theft compromised the atmosphere of trust and respect at the Aikido studio).

Aikido Instructor:	Apparently what happened is that [the offender] came over to do a make-up, saw a coat hanging in the hallway, and took a wallet. And it was his wallet (pointing to victim) . . . The breach of trust was where I was hurt.
Board Member:	Can you tell us a little more about that, about how it affects you?
Aikido Instructor:	At our Dojo, we are learning cooperative spirit and to have one apple turn it around is kind of bad and it affects everybody.

The challenge of the boards is to elicit the various impacts of the offense and devise specifically tailored strategies to remedy them. The burden for reparation, of course, falls to offenders, but a part of community capacity building includes the creation of reparative opportunities and providing assistance to offenders to facilitate their completion of tasks.

Reintegrative Decisionmaking A final feature of the community justice model is *reintegration*. Offending and victimization are considered to be experiences that shred the fabric of community life. Offenders and victims are marginalized by the event in different ways, and a central goal of community justice is to foster both parties' reintegration back into conventional life. This may include services to victims that provide help in ways that do not involve the offender (e.g., legal or mental health services). For offenders, several steps are necessary. First, terms must be specified for offender supervision in order to ensure public safety. Second, because the offender has violated basic normative standards, a process is needed that clarifies expectations for behavior and elicits commitments from the offender to abide by them. Third, strategies for enhancing conventional social ties must be explored. Fourth, competency development may be necessary to ensure that the offender is capable of successfully pursuing conventional opportunities.

In Vermont, all cases are screened for appropriate referral to the boards. Only those cases that judges and correctional officials believe do not require strict supervision qualify. Therefore, boards do not concern themselves with questions of risk assessment and management. They do, however, explicitly discuss local normative standards and offenders' social ties to the community, and typically negotiate terms for competency development, such as a driver safety course for a reckless driver.

The norm affirmation process is illuminated in the following example. The offender had been arrested for driving without a license. The license had been suspended because the driver had failed to pay his registration fees.

Board Member:	Do you understand why—this on the surface seems like a pretty innocuous or minor type of an offense—I mean we're taking your time and our time and the Department of Corrections' time to deal with this thing, which is something you could have taken care of two or three years ago by paying simply what you owed and making right what you'd done. Do you understand why we're making such an issue out of this?
Offender:	Probably because it's been a repetitive sort of thing. I can understand where I ignored my fines—I did. I'm more than happy to pay them now.
Board Member:	I mean you wouldn't come into my house and steal something and break the law doing that would you?
Offender:	No.
Board Member:	Yet you're willfully breaking the laws here. I mean a law applies to me and you whether you like it or not and whether I like it or not and I think that's the point we need to get across with you today. You can't just selectively say, "Oh, the heck with it, I'm not gonna pay the fine, or I don't have time, or I didn't think about it." You gotta pay attention to this stuff cause you're a member of the community and that's your responsibility.
Offender:	Yup, I understand that—now. Now that I'm older and I've got a daughter and everything.

First, the board member establishes that the offender shares the same moral universe by inquiring about his willingness to engage in more significant criminal activity ("you wouldn't come into my house and steal something?"). Clearly, this is a rhetorical question, but he did wait for the offender to reply in order to gain that reassurance. Second, he reminds the offender of his responsibilities as a member of the community—responsibilities that are equally shared by all members. To underscore this point, as part of the contract with the offender, he was asked to write a three-page essay on "why I should obey the laws of my community." It is through such conversational tactics that offenders and boards negotiate a place for the offender in the community.

The standard criterion for evaluating offender reintegration is the recidivism rate. At present, the VDOC has completed only one recidivism study of reparative offenders (a second is currently underway). These data are based on a sample of 157 offenders who completed reparative probation in 1996. The study found the recidivism rate (conviction for any new crime in the six-month period following probationary termination) to be 8.2 percent compared with an 11.6 percent rate for comparable probationers who were not referred to the reparative program. Because this population represents low-risk offenders, recidivism rates are likely to be low under any circumstances. More importantly, recidivism is a poor indicator of reintegration. Under a community justice model, integration is evidenced by prosocial community behavior, such as continued community service beyond those hours required by the reparative contract, in addition to the absence of antisocial behavior.

Conclusion

Community reparative boards are part of a new justice decision-making model that seeks to fulfill both the restorative and reintegrative goals of community justice. Boards operate at the local level, addressing problems within their own communities by including victims, offenders, and neighbors in a decision-making process that repairs harm and promotes greater social integration and community capacity.

Reparative probation has become fully institutionalized in the state of Vermont, and represents the largest-scale restorative justice initiative in the United States. While boards have been enthusiastically received among practitioners and community members in Vermont, external observers have been critical of several features of the model. For example, critics have argued that boards have an imbalance of power between older, middle-class, well-educated board members and more youthful, working-class, less-educated offenders. As a result, they are concerned about whether offenders are truly empowered by this process and if their contributions to the decision-making process are meaningful. Board members may not be sufficiently trained to follow restorative principles and treat offenders disrespectfully or violate their individual rights. The fact that victims do not often appear at board meetings undermines the possibility of reconciliation and a clear articulation of harm and identification of appropriate strategies of repair. Other restorative initiatives, such as victim-offender mediation and family group conferencing, differ from boards in that they are moderated by a professionally trained mediator. In contrast, community volunteers involved in the boards often appear amateurish, undiplomatic, and less knowledgeable about restorative principles than trained mediators.

These criticisms, voiced from within the restorative justice movement, represent an important dilemma as restorative justice initiatives move from experimental pilots to full-scale projects. Should projects be small but very closely approximate an ideal, or should they be large but often flawed in delivery? Both victim-offender mediation and conferencing are difficult to implement on a large scale because organizing each session is time-consuming and difficult. In part, this may be because of the greater level of emotional intensity associated with these processes and the correspondent level of care necessary to ensure that the process is helpful and not harmful. In contrast, boards are able to manage higher caseloads. In addition, a large number of board cases have no direct victims, thereby making this process applicable to cases that cannot be handled by the other models.

A community justice initiative can be only as good as the community that sponsors it. Critique of the boards is wise, as is tolerance of an evolving experiment. The right questions to ask are: What goals do community board participants embrace and to what degree to they succeed in achieving them? The Vermont boards need careful evaluation that assesses their effectiveness in contrast to traditional court procedures and in light of other restorative models that highlight variation in how a progressive justice idea can be realized in practice.

Discussion Questions

1. What are the goals of community reparative boards? At what point in the system are they invoked? How do they interact with the judge? Are boards free to determine any contract they choose or are there limits? Are these limits appropriate?

2. To what degree does the Vermont Department of Corrections relinquish power to the boards and what are some examples of this? Is this typical: Why or why not?

3. What are the four characteristics that distinguish community justice programs and how do reparative boards exemplify these (or not)? Give some examples.

Endnotes

[1]   Formally, boards subdivide into other "boards" when geographic territory is differentiated and into "panels" whey they continue to serve the same area but that area has more cases than one group can handle.

[2]   Quotations are drawn from video transcriptions of 53 reparative case hearings, which are part of Karp's ongoing research on the Vermont reparative boards. A description of this project is found in Karp (2000).

[3]   Two others have opened since, one in St. Johnsbury, another in Bennington. Each has developed a unique mission and programming objectives. Bennington's CJC has a website at *www.justicevermont.org/Pageone.htm*. Burlington's website is *www.communityjusticeburlvt.org*

[4]   Community and restorative justice are not antithetical to rehabilitation, but they emphasize that the purpose of rehabilitation is reintegration (a community-level outcome rather than an individual outcome).

References

Bazemore, G. (1998). "The 'Community' in Community Justice: Issues, Themes, and Questions for the New Neighborhood Sanctioning Models." In *Community Justice: An Emerging Field*, edited by D.R. Karp, 327-372. Lanham, MD: Rowman and Littlefield.

Braithwaite, J. (1989). *Crime, Shame and Reintegration*. Cambridge, England: Cambridge University Press.

Clear, T.R., and D.R. Karp (1998). "The Community Justice Movement." In *Community Justice: An Emerging Field*, edited by D.R. Karp, 3-30. Lanham, MD: Rowman and Littlefield.

Clear, T.R., and D.R. Karp (1999). *The Community Justice Ideal*. Boulder, CO: Westview.

Dooley, M. (1996). "Restorative Justice in Vermont: A Work in Progress." In *Community Justice: Striving for Safe, Secure, and Just Communities*, 31-36. Washington, DC: National Institute of Corrections.

John Doble Research Associates and J. Greene (1999). "Attitudes Towards Crime and Punishment in Vermont: An Experiment with Restorative Justice." Waterbury, VT: Vermont Department of Corrections.

Karp, D.R. (forthcoming). "The Vermont Reparative Boards." In *Frontiers of Probation: Case Studies of Community Justice*, edited by T.R. Clear and D.R. Karp. Boston: Pine Forge Press.

Karp, D.R. (2000). "Harm and Repair: Observing Restorative Justice in Vermont." Unpublished manuscript. Department of Sociology, Skidmore College, New York.

Karp, D.R., and T.R. Clear (2000). "Community Justice: A Conceptual Framework." In *Criminal Justice 2000: Boundary Changes in Criminal Justice Organizations*, 323-368. Volume 2 in *Criminal Justice 2000*. Washington, DC: National Institute of Justice.

Perry, J.G., and J.F. Gorczyk (1997). "Restructuring Corrections: Using Market Research in Vermont." *Corrections Management Quarterly* 1:26-35.

Sampson, R.J., S.W. Raudenbush, and F. Earls (1997). "Neighborhoods and Violent Crime: A Multilevel Study of Collective Efficacy." *Science* 277:918-924.

Spinelli, J., and J.G. Perry (1997). "Vermont Community Restorative Justice Centers: A Concept Paper." Waterbury, VT: Vermont Department of Corrections.

Walther, L., and J. Perry. 1997. "The Vermont Reparative Probation Program." *ICCA Journal on Community Corrections* 8:26-34.

10
Guiding Principles for Peacemaking Circles

BARRY STUART

"Not possible to solve a problem with the same consciousness that created it."

—Albert Einstein

Based on experiences in different communities, this chapter proposes guiding principles for designing and using peacemaking circles. These guiding principles are not limited to circles but can be readily adapted for designing and introducing most consensus processes.

We begin with an overview of peacemaking circles. Then we offer an example of a peacemaking circle that will be used to illustrate the guiding principles. Finally, some of the challenges to designing and using the circle process are discussed.

What are Peacemaking Circles?

Peacemaking circles are used in many different circumstances to resolve differences, prevent conflict, or simply to build better relationships (Bazemore and Umbreit, 1998; Stuart, 1996). In the past several years, circles have been used in nonindigenous communities and for a wide variety of conflicts other than crimes. In the United States, Minnesota has led the movement to integrate circles into the American justice process and in other settings (Pranis, 1997).

Circles are not appropriate for all conflicts and will not always achieve inclusive, enduring results (LaPrairie, 1996). However, if properly designed and used, peacemaking circles have the capacity to address underlying causes of conflict, to build meaningful connections within and to a community, and to develop innovative and long-lasting solutions.

Peacemaking circles create open dialogues that can foster supportive relationships between people who would otherwise be adversaries. A focus on building relationships differentiates circles from most dispute processes by generating direct participation and interaction between previously silenced or ignored stakeholders (Bazemore, 1997). In generating new relationships, circles aspire to change individual and group behavior.

Mary Parker Follett may not have been the first to see opportunities in conflict, but she was the first to exhort us to use conflict as a constructive opportunity:

> As conflict . . . is here in the world, we cannot avoid it, we should I think use it. Instead of condemning it, we should use it, set it to work for us.

If properly processed, conflict presents an opportunity to integrate disparate and contending influences (Simmel, 1955). Similarly, conflict can be either disintegrative for individual and community relationships or it can be an opportunity to build integrative and supportive relationships among previously fragmented individuals and community members (Bazemore, 2000; Braithwaite, 1989). Circles endeavor to exploit the integrative potential of conflict by extracting and building on shared values in order to change individual and group behavior.

Peacemaking circles involve a four-stage process: (1) deciding to use a circle, (2) preparing for a circle, (3) the circle itself, and (4) follow-up. Each stage should be locally designed to fit the unique circumstances of a community. Experience suggests that when all stages are designed in accord with the guiding principles, the capacity of peacemaking circles for transformative changes is fully engaged.

The following story illustrates the potential of a peacemaking circle in sentencing for a serious crime to provide opportunities for transformative changes in individuals and communities.

A Sentencing Peacemaking Circle

Louis found his common-law spouse, Anna, with another man. In a rage, he pulled out a knife. The other man escaped without injuries, but Anna was stabbed in the stomach when she tried to leave. Based on the violent nature of the offense, the police and prosecutor opposed a restorative justice process. Based on the nature of the offender and the underlying causes of the crime, the community believed a circle was necessary. They were both right.

The prosecutor was right because most community-based restorative justice processes do not have adequate community resources to handle serious crimes. The community was right in believing they had to be directly involved because the offender needed to be reconnected to family and community to ensure that his substance abuse, anger, and other issues did not perpetuate his violent behavior. Further, and perhaps most important, the community knew much more about the story than what was revealed in how the incident was written up in police reports or related in court.

During the *first stage* of the circle, in deciding whether the circle process was appropriate, the committee justice community began working through the immediate concerns of the police. Bail conditions were established to respond to any safety concerns of the victim or community. Most police reluctance about using a circle was surmounted when it was understood that if a consensus that included them was not reached, a judge would impose a sentence.

During the first stage, time must be taken to ensure that the practice and principles of circles are understood, especially if any participants are unfamiliar with circles. Written materials describing the process help, but investing time in answering specific questions ensures that informed decisions are made. In this case, the time two "keepers" from the community spent with the victim and her support group, with Louis and his support group, and with the police and prosecutor was instrumental in developing all parties' understanding of—and comfort with—the circle process. Beginning in such a way is critical to a successful process.

During the next stage, the *preparation stage,* healing circles were held privately for the victim. Anna had been pregnant with Louis's child at the time of the offense. In the healing circle for Anna, her needs were clarified and the necessary support garnered from her family, friends, community, and state agencies. The offender participated in another healing circle with his family and support system. In these preparatory circles, issues, concerns, needs and feelings were shared and plans to address his needs began to evolve. In his healing circle, Louis made clear his willingness to accept responsibility for his actions and to participate in the circle process with the understanding that he would be held accountable for his behavior.

One keeper was assigned by the justice committee to work with the victim's healing circle and another keeper was assigned to work with the offender's healing circle. The two keepers collaborated in deciding when a larger circle could be held, who should participate, and what resources needed to be made available at the full circle.

Anna and her support group were kept informed of what was happening with Louis. During the preparation stage, after Louis had began to "walk the talk," Anna decided to participate in his sentencing circle. Before the large peacemaking circle was held, representatives from the justice system, the community, the victim and her family, the offender, and other interested participants and supporters were asked by the keepers to suggest guidelines to create a safe place for an open dialogue in the circle. These suggestions were discussed by the keepers with key participants before the circle and were finalized in the circle.

The *large circle* was held in the community center. The keepers welcomed everyone at the door. Refreshments were available. The opening ceremony of the circle, prepared by keepers, included an elder and others from the community. Before the crime was discussed, the circle went through two rounds of the *talking piece*.[1] People introduced themselves and shared their expectations and feelings. Key information arising from the healing circles and other preparations for the circle were shared. During the circle, Louis heard clearly how inappropriate his conduct had been. The unmistakable condemnation of his actions by his community was balanced by a genuine appreciation of his past good deeds and of his enormous potential to contribute to his family and community. The community was clear: Louis did a bad thing, but he was not a bad person. There were other parts in his life worth developing.

> . . . make no mistake about it. I will not ever see what you did was a good thing, and I will never forget that, but nor do I want my anger about what you did shut down or make me forget the good things about you and what you can be. (Circle participant, 1994)

The circle provided everyone involved with an opportunity to communicate his or her fears, concerns, anger, and hopes in determining what to do. The circle dialogue brought people closer together. While a courtroom often fosters exchanges that exacerbate differences and polarize a community, the circle, in working toward a creative solution that everyone can support, repairs and strengthens connections within a community. By finding and building common ground between those in the circle who demanded accountability and a deterrent punishment and those who sought to heal broken relationships, the circle engaged the crime as an opportunity to share responsibility for dealing with the past and for preventing similar crimes in the future.

The circle agreed that Louis should be placed under strict house arrest for a long time. While under house arrest, he was to continue caring for Robert, Anna's brother. Robert, who was dying from cancer, had been depending increasingly on Louis, his long-standing friend, for help. No one else in Robert's family could dedicate the time or had the ability to meet Robert's needs. An alcohol counselor agreed to meet with Louis at Robert's house. Part of the anger management treatment for

Louis would begin immediately in Robert's home. The only time Louis could leave the home was to take Robert to the doctor or to the hospital. Several people promised to help Louis and to visit regularly while he was under house arrest.

The plan also imposed numerous conditions that encompassed the need for additional punishment, healing, restitution, and reconciliation with the victim and her family, and for connecting Louis to his family and community. The plan also asked Louis to work with others in the circle to develop a men's talking circle to explore ways to prevent and respond to the violence and substance abuse in the circle. Anna and her support group participated in developing this plan for Louis. Much of the circle dialogue focused on Anna and on ensuring that her needs were met.

The circle ended with a final round to give everyone an opportunity to share their feelings and express their hopes or concerns about what would happen next. The keepers had arranged for others in the circle to lead a closing ceremony. Refreshments were again available when the circle was closed. The first circle did not reach a consensus, except to meet again after Louis had "walked more of his talk." Two months later, after further work by the keepers with key participants, and after parts of the proposed plan had been tested, a few more refinements were made and a consensus was reached in the second sentencing circle.

In the fourth phase of the circle process, the *follow-up*, review circles were held every two months to monitor commitments made in the circle. Both support groups remained active and included representatives from the community justice committee. Anna's plan was modified to respond to changes in her life. Louis, with the help of his support group, lived up to all of his commitments to the circle. Robert, who died several months later, was lovingly cared for throughout his last months by Louis. All of Robert's family and many people in the community expressed their appreciation for the love and care that Robert received from Louis during the last year of his life. Anna and Louis eventually reconnected as a family.

Five years have passed since the circle. There have been no further offenses. Both Anna's and Louis's families believe that the long history of crime and substance abuse that plagued Louis's life are now relegated to being a sad part of his past.

Louis still has issues to address. However, he is now more connected to his family and community and knows his past bad deeds no longer deny him access to their support. As he faces his issues each day, these connections will be important in preventing low self-esteem from combining with other difficulties in his life to lead to violence and crime as readily as they had in the past.

> You know it makes me feel good to know we made a differ-
> ence not just in his life, but in his family too. . . . I'm real proud
> of what he did—he honored our circle—that makes me proud
> of us—it's hard work but worth it for sure. . . . (Circle par-
> ticipant, 1999)

Guiding Principles

This circle and many other circles for other purposes in different
kinds of communities have demonstrated the importance of the following guiding principles for designing and using a circle process. These
principles should not be seen as definitive but rather as a work in
progress that has, and continues to be, shaped by many hands.

Personal Values

Circles are based on *values*. Circles must be grounded in the personal values used to guide a person's conduct in dealing with difficult
issues. The most important contributions to the design and use of circles emanates from participants who are conscious of and act on their
personal values. Before leaping to the challenge of designing or using
circles, participants need to clarify their values. From the sharing of personal values, community connections begin to form and shared values
begin to emerge as the basis for designing circles. Learning circles, as
part of the community's preparation to use peacemaking circles, provide a time and place for people to identify, clarify, and recognize the
importance of their values in working through conflict. In dealing with
conflict, most people act on values that are very different than those
we believe define who we are or who we aspire to be. Most dispute
processes do not encourage us to rely on the values we espouse but
instead call upon values that protect us from our fears of harm by trying to defeat others, or at least not revealing ourselves in any manner
that renders us vulnerable. For instance, when asked how they might
act in resolving differences with others, many say they are honest,
respectful, and seek to be fair. In the midst of conflict, though, respect,
honesty, and fairness are readily sacrificed to "winning." If properly
used, circles encourage and support interactions based upon the values we want to define how we behave with others. These values call
upon us to respect others and ourselves.

Throughout the use of circles, time must be continually devoted to
identifying and clarifying personal and shared values. The work on values never ends. Peacemaking circles depend upon respect for personal and shared values. It is not that other (e.g., adversarial) processes

are not value-based. However, peacemaking circles are more dependent than most other processes on participant actions being grounded in personal values. For instance, in court, respect for opposing counsel or the judge reflects good manners and professional courtesy. The respect required in court need not be genuine or profoundly felt. Specifically, it helps the process run "smoothly" and lends a "professional civility" to handling volatile issues. In a circle, on the other hand, respect for others cannot be superficial. It must be genuine and emerge from an understanding of the different values, perspectives, and experiences of others. In court, respect for others and the process assists participants in reaching decisions by avoiding the expression of strong emotions. In circles, respect for others enables parties to work through strong emotions in reaching a better understanding of each other. Respect in court *assists* the process; in the circle, it is an *essential part* of the process.

In Louis's circle, the circle dialogue enabled the police and members of the community to discover that they shared several personal values. Many differences in the outcomes they initially sought were resolved when the circle provided an opportunity to act on their personal values.

Respect

Respect enhances our ability to see, hear, and value the perspectives of others. All stages in the design and implementation of a circle process encourage and demonstrate respect for participants and for the circle. Respect for others does not require adopting their values or perspectives; it requires understanding and giving credence to their values and perspectives. Respect for oneself, for others, and for the circle is fostered by the open dialogues within circles and by the circle being grounded in all of the guiding principles.

In Louis's circle, the justice committee was disappointed and initially angered by the prosecutor's opposition to the circle for Louis. The first stage of the circle process is designed to use a talking circle to assess the suitability of a circle process. In the talking circle, positions are broken down into interests. Respectful listening and speaking enables everyone to understand and respect "where they were coming from." As one participant noted, ". . . it sure helped me see what they were so concerned about. . . ."

Understanding and respecting the concerns of others provides the foundation for exploring how everyone's concerns can be addressed. Working out differences is not easy, but without circles to provide respectful exchanges, most serious crimes would not proceed to circle with the support or participation of the prosecutor, police, or victims.

In the talking circle that was held to assess the suitability of a circle for Louis, procedures were put in place to ensure the safety of the victim and to meet the concerns of the prosecutor. Most immediate concerns were included in demanding bail conditions. The rest of the concerns were alleviated by a better understanding of the circle process and by all participants acquiring a much better understanding of (and respect for) each other. Many prosecutors leave talking circles, surprised to discover:

> You know, there's not as much difference between what I want
> to see happen and what they want—much less, for sure, than
> I first thought. (Prosecutor, Haines Junction, 1996)

Early talking circles provide the forum for the work required to move beyond assumptions and positions and to develop respect for different views and concerns. Talking circles do not always reach a consensus about using a circle, but most reach a consensus about how to proceed to the next stage. Proceeding to the next stage puts to the test concerns about what might go wrong and hopes for what can go right. A consensus at the first stage is usually only about going to the next stage. A circle process depends on building a consensus at *each* stage. The actions of each party in carrying out the consensus agreement to go to the next stage can significantly deepen mutual respect. Acting on reciprocal commitments builds confidence in the process and in each other.

Inclusiveness

Everyone affected by a circle has a moral right and a responsibility to participate in designing the circle process. The greater the degree of participation, the greater the potential to develop innovative, community-appropriate, community-supported, and enduring processes. Every effort should be made to encourage involvement and provide readily accessible information to promote informed decisions about whether to become involved. By reaching out to involve the community, many key contributions to forge a consensus plan for Louis and Anna were made by people who would not otherwise have had a voice.

Enormous pressure arises in designing circles to exclude people who are (or are assumed to be) opposed to circles. Inclusivity is tested when a key player in the community impedes the design of a circle. Even if the process will take longer, be more contentious, or surface underlying issues that have long been avoided, diligent efforts must be made to include those opposed to circles before moving past them. Strategic assessments that recommend excluding known opponents of circles must be ignored until all reasonable efforts have been made to include them. Guiding principles are more than a set of "good strategies" for introducing circles; they are critical to the effectiveness and longevity of the process.

In Louis's circle, there was an early suggestion that the prosecutor should be excluded because of his opposition to the idea. Someone suggested a private circle called by the community justice committee to work out a sentencing recommendation so the court could avoid including either the police or the prosecutor. This proposal was challenged by one of the founders of the community circle process:

> They are a part of our community. . . . if we don't respect them
> by excluding them how can we expect them to ever understand
> or respect what we do. . . .(Keeper, Haines Junction, 1996)

Circles change how power is shared and exercised, both between the government and the community as well as among community members. Ultimately, such changes can affect the allocation of resources (see Carey, this volume). Those whose existing resources or jobs may be threatened may (and often do) oppose circles to protect their interests. While circle processes rarely threaten personal or institutional interests to any significant extent, the anticipated changes can provoke significant fear among like professionals.

> If circles get going, what will my job be? Can't see in circles
> any room for me. (Probation officer, Minneapolis, 1997)

It is important to respect the concerns of anyone affected by changes imposed by a circle process.

The values behind the principle of inclusivity require ensuring that circles are sensitive to the interests of anyone adversely impacted by the introduction of a circle process. How a circle is introduced has everything to do with how it will be used and how it will be respected. It is both impossible and impractical to design a process based on one set of values and then to operate it based on a conflicting set of values. Efforts must be made to include everyone impacted by changes incurred by introducing circles. Otherwise, the underlying values of a circle process will be violated. Open circle dialogues are the best place to discover how to maximize the use of resources and minimize any adverse impacts on employment.

Equal Opportunity While involvement may vary according to interest and need, it should never vary according to ability or means. People are more likely to believe the process will be fair if they are given a fair opportunity to participate in designing and using a circle process. It is essential to provide opportunities for everyone to participate in a manner that draws on their skills and resources. Broadly based, meaningful participation enhances: (1) commitment to implementing the circle process, (2) capacity for creative problem-solving, (3) sensitivity of the process to all community interests, and (4) actual and perceived fairness of the process. Sometimes simply knowing that a fair opportunity to participate was available will engender a belief that the process is fair. While it is impossible to ensure completely equal opportunities to participate, belief in the circle process depends on diligent efforts to remove inequalities in the opportunities to participants.

The following parts of the circle process for Louis provide examples of what can be done to promote equal opportunities for everyone to participate.

1. The circle was held in the evening to maximize the opportunity for people working during the days to participate.

2. Information about Louis and the crime was readily available to everyone before the circle.

3. The talking piece creates equal opportunity for everyone to have a voice in the circle.

4. Honoring the requirement for a consensus promotes equal power over outcomes.

Voluntariness

Voluntary participation is the hallmark of a circle process. Much of the power of the circle process flows from its voluntary nature. Giving choices is giving power. Efforts to create spaces and means for voluntary participation must be vigilantly monitored to ensure freedom from dominating and inappropriate pressures as well as respect for the civil liberties and human rights of all participants.

Circles depend on volunteers to manage the process and to participate in support groups and throughout the circle process. It is the presence of volunteers that constitutes the basis for both the peacemaking and community-building capacity of the circle process. It is the input of third parties (those without a direct interest) that often provides the pieces necessary for a consensus.

In Louis's process, at the talking circle, at the healing circle, and again at the full circle, it was the third-party input that enabled a consensus to emerge. For instance, it was the volunteers participating in determining whether a circle could be used for Louis who provided the conditions for the prosecutor to join in a consensus to move to the next stage. When volunteers who did not have any attachment to the offender or victim spoke in support of trying a circle and offered to monitor progress and provide help with the plan for a house arrest, the police and prosecutor were willing to go along "to see what happens." Community input in talking circles can help prosecutors feel that ". . . we are working not just for the community, but with the community" (Prosecutor, Haines Junction, 1996).

Louis had to volunteer to participate, as did everyone else. During the first stage of a circle process, victims do not usually wish to participate in the offender's circle. Some victims, like Anna, send someone to represent their interests. When communities give unqualified support to victims, many victims (like Anna) feel sufficiently supported and respected to participate during the latter stages of the process.

Direct Participation

Speaking through others often detracts from the vitality and sensitivity of being fully engaged. The capacity to take responsibility for past and future conduct depends on the capacity to participate directly in decisions about such conduct. Direct participation generates new connections to others and to shared visions; it also fosters the skills necessary to participate effectively. A stumbling, inarticulate, personal attempt to reach out secures a deeper, stronger connection to others than does an eloquent representation made on someone else's behalf. Personal stories can be very powerful in shaping personal and public decisions and in building relationships. These stories are the primary currency of trading information, ideas, and feelings within circles. Owning and committing to agreements is a function of participating directly in designing the process and in shaping the outcome. The direct participation of Louis, Anna, and their families was instrumental in developing a consensus.

Shared Vision

A genuinely shared vision is built by and belongs to everyone; it strengthens both commitment and connection. Such shared visions are woven from the common threads of personal visions and values. A shared vision constantly evolves through community experiences within the circle process. By giving direction and coherence to collective decisions and actions, a shared vision enables participants who have a history with the process and newcomers to work together.

Only after the first circle did a shared vision emerge among the participants in the sentencing circle for Louis, one focused on healing, accountability, and prevention. Once this shared vision emerged, the capacity of the circle to reach a consensus in the second circle became easier.

A community justice committee that has participated together in a learning circle and has developed a shared vision (about the *process* of the circle as well as its *purpose*) strengthens their capacity to retain commitments to each other and to the process when confronted with the challenges of using the circle in controversial cases.

In the circle process for Louis, many members of the justice committee had not been through a learning circle, and the justice committee had not worked through a process that produced a shared vision. Consequently, the circle process for Louis raised difficult challenges around the appropriateness of circles in violent crimes.

Local Design

Each circle process must be "home grown" and emerge from the particular needs of each community. The viability and sustainability of circles depends on participants sharing the pride of development and ownership—of building, maintaining, and running it locally within the community. Those who use the circle *must* help design the circle. The capacity of the circle to engage participants depends on the extent to which the values, needs, visions, and circumstances of the community are incorporated into the design and use of the circle process.

During the first two stages of the sentencing circle process for Louis, all new participants, the prosecutor, police, victim, and offenders as well as support groups all participated in shaping the process. Their concerns were partly addressed in the talking circle that was employed to decide whether the circle process was appropriate. During the next stage, in preparing to use the circle, other concerns were incorporated regarding when and how the circle process would take place and who would be involved.

At the sentencing circle, suggestions from various participants regarding what would make the circle a safe place for their participation were incorporated into the guidelines. Finally, everyone had a hand in designing how the circle consensus would be implemented and monitored.

Flexibility

Not only should the overall circle process be locally designed, but each use of the circle should be sufficiently flexible to adjust to the particular circumstances of each conflict.

Conflicts are dynamic. They change every day. Every injection of new information produces change, and assumptions can change as readily as circumstances. A chance or planned interaction among the parties can change the importance and primary focus of a conflict. It is particularly important that the process used for resolving a conflict is sensitive to changes in the conflict itself. Processes that are inflexible, that march parties along predetermined routes that cannot accommodate the dynamic changes in a conflict, may miss opportunities to forge agreements. They will certainly overlook many of the constructive opportunities that conflict generates (Hocker and Wilmot, 1995).

To take full advantage of the opportunities that flow from dealing with conflict, the process must be flexible. The flexibility to make changes in the process must be governed by underlying principles; otherwise, the changes may introduce very different values. For instance, altering the process solely in order to reach a compromise may violate the principle of inclusivity. In so doing, the opportunity for building better relationships and mutual respect will be sacrificed. In Louis's case, the prosecutor and defense counsel were privately working toward a sentencing deal during the preparation for a circle. Had they reached an agreement without the direct participation of the families and community, as well as the victim and offender, many of the new connections generated by the circle dialogue—and certainly the creative solutions shaped by all voices in the circle—would have been lost. The counsels' bargaining exchanges about the sentence were precipitated by changes in the conflict, but this back-room private bargaining violated many of the guiding principles and could have inadvertently sacrificed many of the vital changes the circle dialogue eventually contributed.

Hard rules defeat the purpose of circles. Guiding principles, not hard rules, govern each stage of circles. The circle process must be sufficiently malleable to accommodate the specific needs of participants and affected communities. This degree of flexibility is not as scary, chaotic, or difficult as it may seem, as long as the adaptations for each circle are guided by core principles.

Accessibility

Complex processes hinder accessibility. Simplicity in the procedures for circles promotes easy access and permits everyone to be meaningfully involved. When all sectors of a community know they can easily be involved in designing or using a circle, general acceptance of circles in the community is readily promoted. Participation in designing and implementing circles must not depend upon having skills or resources that are (or are perceived to be) beyond the reach of anyone in the community.

The first two stages in the circle process remove many of the imagined and real barriers to using the circle. While the circle process in Louis's community was locally designed, few of the participants involved in Louis's circle previously had much to do with the circle. Participation in both the first and second stages of the circle process for Louis was important in removing concerns about—and in generating comfort with—the circle.

Holism

To develop a holistic approach, the design or use of a circle process should strive to ensure that:

1. all affected parties are invited to participate;

2. all relevant issues are taken into consideration in reaching a consensus;

3. the connection and interdependence of all things is explored; and

4. participants are given ample opportunity to recognize their responsibility for what has happened and for what can happen.

The more time that is taken to share and probe personal stories, the more effort is made to create a safe environment for personal stories to be shared. The greater the number of people who participate in an open dialogue, the greater the prospects for a holistic approach. In taking a holistic approach, peacemaking circles create the possibility of unearthing and dealing with the underlying causes of conflict.

Conflicts are shaped by social environments and by history. They become an inextricable part of the forces that shape relationships. Conflicts live in relationships; they do not live in the abstract. Guiding principles recognize the importance of taking a holistic view of conflict that encompasses the history and social environment that has fed and sustained conflict. Circle processes enable participants to recognize that they cannot resolve the larger, complex problems surrounding any conflict with the same perceptions and decision-making systems that produced the conflict. In promoting new ways to see the world, a circle promotes the sharing of responsibility for current difficulties as well as responsibility for deciding how to shape the future. The guiding principles create the capacity to see old conflicts in a fundamentally different light.

The time invested in the preparatory stages of Louis's circle enabled the victim and her family to understand what happened and to assess what they could do and wanted to do. The exchange of information from the preparatory circles for Louis and for Anna served all parties' ability to understand the underlying causes of Louis's behavior and develop what was needed to move beyond the crime.

Spirituality

The presence and encouragement of a spiritual experience sets a circle process apart from other decision-making processes. Different aspects of the circle may engender the emergence of spirituality for each participant. The opening ceremony, the profound risks a participant may take in sharing their personal story or their pain, the feeling of connectedness to others in the circle, or the humanity and courage revealed by many in the circle—any of these or other aspects of the circle may promote a spiritual experience.

Everyone experiences conflict in four dimensions: mentally, physically, emotionally, and spiritually. Most processes focus only on the mental and physical aspects of conflict. While some engage the emotions surrounding conflicts, most discourage or exclude emotions. A court adjourns to allow a witness to gain his or her composure or to settle down the emotions of spectators. Although courtrooms are full of deeply felt emotions, the court process ignores and suppresses these emotions. Circles, on the other hand, encourage emotions to be expressed. Working through, sharing, and respecting emotions can open the circle to spiritual experiences.

Very few processes recognize the importance of the spiritual dimension in conflict. Conflicts can penetrate deeply into all aspects of one's life. A connection to spirituality in working through conflict can deepen the mutual will to resolve differences and strengthen commitments to solutions.

> It surprised me—I didn't know what it was at first. . . but then as others reached out with courage to share themselves—I did too—and the connection made, well—it had a spirituality—it really did. . . from that moment for me—I knew—really knew—I wasn't going to quit until we got—all of us got to a better place—like it was real—I know that. . . It was a spiritual feeling in the midst of that circle. (Participant, Sentencing Circle for Juvenile, Minneapolis, 1997)

Creating space for spirituality in the conflict process is as essential as creating space for the physical, mental, and emotional aspects of conflict. The aboriginal medicine wheel recognizes that the physical, emotional, spiritual, and mental dimensions must all be equally addressed in order to acquire and maintain balance within individuals and communities. Making space for—and embracing—all these dimensions calls for using the guiding principles for designing all stages of a circle process.In developing a sentence plan for Louis, the courage of both families to work through difficult issues and to share the responsibility for moving all parties to a better place induced a spiritual experience for many people.

Consensus

A consensus approach flows from and reinforces all other practices and principles of peacemaking circles. Consensus is critical in designing and introducing circles. However, consensus does not mean unanimity. If the process earnestly strives to embrace the interests of its members and fails, those who disagree with the direction of the circle are usually willing to "live with the outcome." Consensus depends on the full opportunity to speak, to be heard with respect, and to experience sincere efforts to attend to interests of all participants. A consensus in the circle requires being able to accept the decision of a circle, even if one disagrees with it.

Talk alone is rarely sufficient to develop a consensus. In the circle process for Louis, many participants (especially the police) could not support a house arrest plan for Louis until he proved, by his actions during the preparation stage, that he was a good prospect to successfully complete treatment programs for substance abuse and anger management. Positive progress reports from treatment professionals helped bring many participants around to joining the consensus. When the talk in circles is translated into action, the ability to reach a consensus is vastly improved.

Important gains can be realized in a circle process without reaching a consensus. For instance, the purpose of a sentencing circle is not only to produce a sentence; it is also to challenge assumptions about the offender, the role of community, the needs of victims, and many other matters surrounding perceptions of crime and the role of the community. Sentencing circles challenge traditional notions about the justice process, and particularly about who has responsibility for preventing and processing crime. The average citizen's perspective that crime falls exclusively within the reach of professionals, as well as the belief by many justice agency representatives that they alone are competent to deal with crime (especially serious crime), are both challenged in a circle. Both perspectives can be changed *without* reaching a consensus about a specific sentence. When a sentencing circle does not reach consensus and must revert to the judge for sentencing, many participants can gain a great deal from the *process*.

> I had to decide in the end because we didn't quite reach a consensus. However, don't be fooled to think that made the circle a failure—far from it—there were so many good things happening for so many people just by participating in the circle. (Judge H. Lilles, Whitehorse, 1999)

The specific sentence produced by a peacemaking circle is less important than *how* each circle builds individual, family, and community capacity to assume responsibility and become self-reliant.

Achieving a "fair" sentence that works is important, but changing perspectives about what communities can do and forging new, cooperative working relationships can do much to change the underlying conditions of crime (Clear and Karp, 1998). This same notion can be applied to institutions as well: settling differences within institutions is important, but if the circle fails to reach a consensus yet succeeds in fostering cooperative working relationships, the institution is ultimately healthier and the same conflicts are less likely to recur. If a circle fails to reach a consensus, but improves relationships, the parties, in time, may resolve their differences on their own.

Accountability

There are many levels of accountability within a circle process. Those who participate in designing a circle process need to act in accord with the guiding principles of the circle. For instance, some communities struggle to design and use a process because their organizing and planning meetings are not held in a circle and Robert's Rules of Order prevail.

Participants in a circle are accountable to each other and to the agreements they reach. Nothing helps more to build confidence in and connection to the process than follow-up on commitments. Nothing damages credibility in the circle process more than failing to follow up on such commitments. A circle process significantly depends on follow-up to make adjustments and celebrate successes. Follow-up reinforces and gives reality to being held accountable for shared responsibilities.

Many unforeseen events can challenge a consensus plan. To accommodate these unforeseen events and maintain accountability to the spirit of the consensus (even if not to the details) a follow-up process that allows for adjustments is critical. When Robert died, much of the sentencing plan for Louis had to be changed. By returning to the underlying shared vision of the plan, participants found the basis to agree on changes to the original plan.

Overview of Guiding Principles

These principles are *guides,* not rules. Guiding principles must be respected, rather than mindlessly applied. Respect for these principles includes questioning and identifying how best to employ them in each situation. While innovative adaptation is encouraged, minimizing any principle is discouraged. These principles must be recognized as standing together; ignoring one undermines all. Practices that respect any one principle serve to reinforce others. The *relative* importance of each principle may depend upon the immediate circumstances but in no circumstances can any principle be ignored without imperiling the potential of the circle process.

A "community" using a circle process might be located in a small rural setting or in the center of a large urban area. It might be a community of nations or a community of local agricultural producers. It might be in a plant, or among business partners, or within a private or public institution. Any group of people who share common issues, experiences, patterns of interactions, and objectives can be regarded as a community.

All communities are different. Differences between the circumstances of a community within an organization, as opposed to a geographic community, are particularly striking. The rigid power structures, particular organizing purpose, and nature of control over individuals arising from employment contracts might suggest that all principles do not apply in companies or bureaucracies. They do though. These principles are not just derived from or useful only for neighborhood empowerment; they are relevant to any form of community that seeks to incorporate a circle process to share responsibility and leadership and to pursue a common vision.

Key Characteristics of a Circle Process Promoted by Guiding Principles

Reducing Dependence Upon Power

Power can settle differences. Yet, "effective conflict resolution can be derailed by the exercise of power . . . and power by itself is rarely enough to resolve conflict." (Tidwell, 1998:168). A predominant reliance on power in addressing differences can produce a solution without changing the underlying causes of a conflict or troubled relationship. The persistence of underlying causes can often provoke future conflicts.

The guiding principles redress power imbalances and substantially reduce the ability of anyone to rely on his or her power to force an outcome that shuts down other interests or ignores the chronic causes of conflict. Circles generate a sharing of power and a collective will to call on the resources everyone contributes to implement the outcome.

Open Dialogues

Communication has the power to bring people together or drive them further apart. Exchanges that are adversarial and manipulative rarely bring people closer. In circle dialogues, participants begin to question their own interests, assumptions, and beliefs. In revealing their questions and doubts about themselves, they invite others to do the same. The resulting exchanges are imperative for working through the history of their differences, digging down to the causes of conflict, establishing new understandings, and making connections that bring people closer to each other.

> I had no idea I would open myself up like that—and no idea I would get so much out of doing so. (Circle Participant, Haines Junction, 1996)

In the preparation circles for Louis, when members of his family and his friends told their stories, shared their fears, and questioned their beliefs, they created the foundation for Louis to do the same.

Transforming Relationships

The guiding principles are critical to creating conditions that can transform relationships. Circles can be faulted for being less interested in achieving a specific settlement than in building connections to and within a community. For instance, the actual sentence imposed on Louis may be less important than the process used to produce the sentence. In the process, many relationships were transformed. The police and prosecutor gained new relationships with several people in the community. The prosecutor became known in the circle as a person first, prosecutor second. As a result, his story was heard and his voice respected. In turn, he gained a new insight into and respect for others in the circle. Through his participation, Louis set in place the beginning of new relationships with Anna, her family, and his own family and community. By carrying out his sentence, Louis entrenched the new relationships that began in the circle, but the basis for this new relationship began in circle dialogues.

There are many cases in which an offender will fail to carry out the sentence yet retain the support arising from new relationships formed in the circle.

> No he is not doing very well. He is now back in jail. We visit him and all of us in that circle would welcome him back to the circle. . . . We respect he tried and we respect how difficult changing his life will be. We will not give up on him—and

> he needs to know that. . . . Yes we are very disappointed—but
> we are not into giving up—we now know him and he knows
> us. (Circle Keeper, Minneapolis, 1998)

A process designed on the basis of all guiding principles promotes the changes in relationships that are needed to generate and sustain the collective will to address underlying causes of conflict.

Challenges to Designing and Using a Circle Process

Changing Beliefs and Perspectives

Introducing a circle to completely *replace* an existing conflict resolution system provokes significantly different challenges than introducing a circle to *supplement* existing systems. Replacing existing processes does not simply change where disputes go for resolution but profoundly alters the values and culture of that community. For example, when a community is accustomed to sending serious criminal cases to court, and is then asked to consider sending these cases to a circle, considerable resistance may be encountered. The use of circles for serious cases calls for a significant change in public perceptions about the utility of punishment and the relative importance of invoking immediate vengeance as opposed to investing in the prospects of long-term rehabilitation.

Time Consumption

The circle process is time-consuming. Community members may not initially be inclined to put in the time and effort necessary to develop a viable and reliable circle process. Adherence to principles is particularly important in this initial growth and development stage. It is difficult to resist the temptation to take shortcuts, to ignore or rush past probing and developing shared values, in order to "get on with it." Circles take more time to design and more time to use because they deal with much more. The ideal outcomes of other processes are much narrower. If, for instance, the outcome sought is no more than, a declaration of a legal right, circles are not the best process to use. If the ideal outcome includes forging better relationships, changing the underlying causes of conflict, developing innovative and enduring solutions, and creating a commitment to sustain the collective will to advance mutual best interests, then circles are more appropriate and the investment of more time is worth the return.

Partners from Very Different Worlds

This following comment by a volunteer reflects the feelings of many community volunteers striving to develop partnerships with justice professionals to introduce and operate sentencing circles.

> Don't get me wrong—just because I think this justice system don't work, don't mean it can't work. Look, I mean no disrespect to you. I understand what you do, why you do it. I'd just like you to understand a little about what I do—and why I do it. (Circle Participant, Haines Junction, 1996)

Volunteers tend to believe that justice professionals do not respect (or understand) their input or way of "doing business." Many volunteers bring to the partnership natural skills in peacemaking, mediation, conciliation, and facilitation practices. Professionals, who are imbued with highly developed analytical skills, are experienced survivors of hierarchical power structures in which power relationships are played out within adversarial processes. This difference in approach and experience can cause divisive tensions when trying to forge and sustain the partnerships necessary to develop guiding principles for designing and operating peacemaking circles.

Creating the basis for new partnerships among people with very diverse backgrounds and skills requires time, patience, tolerance, and a will to "find a way." The introduction and the sustainability of circles has been adversely impacted by moving too quickly to "do things." Moving too rapidly overlooks those people whose lives are affected by introducing circles. When sufficient time is taken and circles are used to explore how people are affected, many perceived barriers to working together disappear.

> At first, this was very threatening to me. I'd been a probation officer for many years, and it seems I was now being cast aside. The community didn't seem to want me and didn't see anything of value I could add to the circle. Now, I see, and so do they, I believe—see what I can add. (Probation Officer, Minneapolis, 1998)

Conclusion

Without developing and using guiding principles for designing the use of peacemaking circles, the potential of peacemaking circles to produce fundamental changes may be lost. Circles are not just about settling a dispute but are directed at fostering self-reliance and self-governance (Bazemore, 1999).

This chapter's focus on circles should not suggest that other methods of conflict resolution are not important. On the contrary, the court process has made important contributions to healthy democratic systems. For many societal purposes and many types of conflict (especially those conflicts that communities recognize they cannot or do not wish to handle), existing adversarial processes may be better suited than peacemaking circles. In other circumstances, other alternative dispute resolution processes are more appropriate.

The most important work for the future lies in developing new dispute resolution processes that include the best practices from a variety of models. Developing approaches to conflict in all types of communities will rarely call for replacing one dominant process by another. In most communities, the best means of handling conflict will call for a variety of options, whereby a particular type of conflict can be matched to the process that best suits it. The guiding principles for circle processes envision within communities that there will be a *spectrum of conflict options* for responding to conflict.

All those engaged in developing new consensus processes must learn to see their different experiences and perceptions as the inspiration for dialogue rather than as the basis for attacking or defending favored processes. No magical process is capable of engaging all participants, in all circumstances or to resolve all conflicts in a manner that produces universally acceptable solutions. Open and constructive dialogue about the appropriateness of each process improves our understanding of which processes are most suited to which conflicts and provides invaluable insights into how conflict can best be used as an opportunity for transformative change.

Discussion Questions

1. Why are guiding principles fundamental to the design and application of peacemaking circles? Must all circle projects employ all guiding principles? Do the same principles apply to all circles?

2. What is the difference between guiding principles and general guidelines when designing and implementing circles? Name and describe at least three guiding principles and three general guidelines and why they are important.

3. What does Stuart mean when he says circles must emerge from a local design and that they must be flexibile? Why is flexibility so important in designing and implementing circles?

4. What are some of the challenges to designing and implementing circles and to what degree do these impede developing effective circle processes? Are these challenges the same as or different from traditional justice procedures?

Endnote

[1] Used to signify who speaks in the circle, a talking piece can be anything. Communities have used feathers, stones, sticks, and pieces of sculpture. It is important that a talking piece has a connection to, and meaning for, the community.

References

Bazemore, G. (1997). "The Community in Community Justice: Issues, Themes and Questions for the New Neighborhood Sanctioning Models." *The Justice System Journal* 19(2):193-228.

Bazemore, G. (2000). "Community Justice and a Vision of Collective Efficacy: The Case of Restorative Conferencing." In *Criminal Justice 2000*, edited by National Institute of Justice. Washington, DC.

Bazemore, G., and M. Umbreit (1999). *Conferences, Circles, Boards and Mediations: Restorative Justice and Citizen Involvement in the Response to Youth Crime*. Washington, DC: Office of Juvenile Justice and Delinquency Prevention.

Braithwaite, J. (1989). *Crime, Shame and Reintegration*. Cambridge, England: Cambridge University Press.

Clear, T., and D. Karp (1998). "The Community Justice Movement." In *Community Justice: An Emerging Field*, edited by D. Karp, 3-28. Lanham, MD: Rowman and Littlefield.

Follett, M.P. (1925).

Hocker, J.L., and W. Wilmot (1995). *Interpersonal Conflict*, 4th ed. Madison, WI: Brown & Benchmark.

Karp, D. (1999). *Community Justice: An Emerging Field*. Lanham, MD: Rowman and Littlefield.

LaPrairie, C. (1996). *Examining Aboriginal Corrections in Canada*. Ottawa: Aboriginal Corrections, Ministry of the Solicitor General.

Pranis, K. (1997). "Peacemaking Circles." *Corrections Today* 59(7):72-76, 122

Simmel, G. (1955). *Conflict and the Web of Group Affiliations*. New York: The Free Press.

Stuart, B. (1996). "Circle Sentencing in the Yukon Territory, Canada: A Partnership of the Community and the Criminal Justice System." *International Journal of Comparative and Applied Criminal Justice* 20:291-309

Tidwell, A. (1998). *Conflict Resolved? A Critical Assessment of Conflict Resolution*. London: Printer.

Part V
Critical Perspectives on the
Restorative Community Justice Ideal

11

Restorative Justice, Indigenous Justice, and Human Rights

EVELYN ZELLERER
CHRIS CUNNEEN

Restorative justice calls for a new relationship between community and government, and nowhere are issues surrounding community-government relations more central and more contentious than with respect to indigenous peoples.[1] This chapter raises issues surrounding the creation and implementation of restorative programs in indigenous communities. We argue that at the foundation of dialogue and justice initiatives must be a recognition of the inherent rights of indigenous peoples to self-determination and self-government. All justice reform, whether in the dominant justice system or through new restorative initiatives, must be contextualized within the broader recognition of the special political and legal rights of indigenous peoples. Once recognition is given to the inherent right to self-determination, then it follows that recognition must also be given to one of the most important components of that right—jurisdiction over justice where this is desired. A number of dangerous assumptions are outlined when a restorative model is simply presumed to be applicable to indigenous individuals and communities. We discuss restorative justice and self-determination within the context of specific issues relating to aboriginal youth and women—using examples from Australia and Canada to illustrate our arguments.

Indigenous Rights

A fundamental principle of restorative justice is reconciliation: reconciliation between the offender and victim, and between offender and community. We argue that respect for human rights must underpin processes of reconciliation. Human rights involve both individual and collective rights, and we draw attention to the collective human rights of indigenous people as distinct peoples. It is also important to acknowledge Blagg's (1998) point that restorative justice must not be narrowly defined to simple notions of individual crime. Among the greatest crimes committed in the last 200 years have been various acts of genocide by governments against indigenous peoples, yet we see little application of the principles of restorative justice in cases in which the victims are indigenous people and the offenders are the state. The principles of restorative justice must also be applied in cases in which gross violations of human rights have been perpetrated by colonial states.

The specific rights of indigenous peoples are being increasingly recognized in international law as well as within nation states (Anaya, 1996; McNamara, 1995, Nettheim, 1995). Indigenous peoples have legal rights that derive from their status as first peoples in areas that have been colonized primarily, but not exclusively, by European expansion from the fifteenth century. Although it is beyond the scope of this chapter to discuss the processes of colonization, it is vital to highlight the fact that *every* part of traditional aboriginal society was attacked. Government policies and practices have attempted to assimilate, "civilize," and Christianize aboriginal peoples who were viewed as pagan, childlike, and primitive. This was done through legislation, the establishment of reservations, forced removal of children, forced education in residential schools, the banning of cultural and spiritual practices, and the imposition of the criminal justice system. The devastation to families and communities caused by government policies is only beginning to be confronted.

It is important to avoid thinking of these issues as merely historical facts or that they are relegated to past practices. The justice system continues to have a particularly devastating impact on indigenous peoples. Findings from Royal Commissions, inquiries, and independent research continue to reveal the prevalence of problems such as racism and the overrepresentation of aboriginal peoples in prisons. The evidence calls into question the practices and, more importantly, the legitimacy of mainstream justice for aboriginal peoples. For example, in Australia, the National Inquiry into the Separation of Aboriginal and Torres Strait Islander Children from their Families (1997) found that the previous policies of forced removal of children constituted genocide under international law. The inquiry also found that the *contemporary* removal of children and young people through high levels of criminalization and subsequent incarceration effectively amounted to a new practice of forced separation. The recommendations of the inquiry were to implement a framework for self-determination in relation to decisions affecting children and young people. To date, no Australian governments have responded adequately to these recommendations.

The best place to begin to understand the emerging human rights norms that reflect the aspirations of indigenous people is in the United Nations Draft *Declaration on the Rights of Indigenous Peoples*. This declaration contains a number of basic principles, including self-determination, that directly impact on how restorative justice programs that are respectful of indigenous rights might develop.

The draft declaration affirms "the right of Indigenous people to control matters affecting them." Article 3 describes the right of self-determination as involving the free choice of political status and the freedom to pursue economic, social, and cultural development (it is established in the same terms as Article 1 of the ICCPR). Article 4 provides that "Indigenous peoples have the right to maintain and strengthen their distinct political, economic, social and cultural characteristics, *as well as their legal systems*" [emphasis added]. Article 31 sets out the extent of governing powers of indigenous peoples, which include the right to autonomy or self-government in matters relating to their internal and local affairs. Taken together, it is clear that the declaration provides the basis for indigenous people to maintain cultural integrity and exercise jurisdiction over various justice matters. At the same time, the provisions provide for the right of indigenous people to participate fully, if they choose, in the political, economic, social, and cultural life of the state (Burger and Hunt, 1994; Coulter, 1995).

The draft declaration also protects indigenous peoples from genocide through prohibiting the separation of children from their families "under any pretext" (Article 6). This prohibition is of clear relevance to the contemporary removal of children and young people through both child welfare and juvenile justice mechanisms. Article 7(d) prohibits "any form of assimilation or integration by other cultures or ways of life imposed on them by legislative, administrative or other measures." Such a provision also has implications for juvenile justice laws and restorative justice programs that may seek (either directly or indirectly) to impose the standards and sociocultural mores of the dominant group on indigenous children, youth, and families.

While the draft declaration is clearly of great importance, it remains to be seen how the principles will translate from this symbolic realm into concrete practice in specific jurisdictions. Aboriginal peoples continue their struggle with governments, with varying degrees of success, for recognition of their inherent rights. The specific parameters of self-government have yet to be clearly defined. However, domestic recognition of indigenous rights has occurred through a number of mechanisms, including, for example, various land claims settlements and forms of self-government (such as the new Nunavut Territory in Canada) and special political representation (such as the Aboriginal and Torres Strait Islander Commission in Australia, the Sami Parliament in Norway, and reserved parliamentary seats in New Zealand). From the early nineteenth century, the U.S. Supreme Court recognized that Native American nations continued to exercise jurisdiction through a form of residual sovereignty that survived colonization. Australia, New Zealand, Canada, and the United States have also given some recognition to the indigenous relationship to the land through the development of common-law native title.[2]

Of particular relevance is the collective right of indigenous peoples to maintain and develop their distinct identities and characteristics. The protection of indigenous culture and modes of governance has direct implications for the assessment of any restorative justice program. The introduction and implementation of restorative justice in indigenous communities cannot ignore the fundamental issue of the protection of indigenous cultures.

Restorative and Indigenous Justice

Having identified numerous limitations of the dominant justice system, indigenous peoples and advocates of restorative justice, began parallel movements.[3] Indigenous peoples drew attention to the plight of aboriginal individuals within the justice system and focused on reclaiming and developing their own traditional methods of social control. Restorative justice advocates developed an alternative paradigm to the dominant system. There are clearly differences between restorative justice and the dominant justice system as well as between indigenous approaches to justice and the dominant justice system. However, one question rarely asked is whether the vision of justice for restorative advocates and indigenous peoples is the same. There is rarely any discussion of the similarities and differences between restorative and indigenous justice. There is often either an explicit or implicit assumption that they are one and the same, falling under the umbrella concept of restorative justice. It is interesting that a brief reference is often made to the fact that some restorative initiatives, such as family group conferencing in New Zealand and circle sentencing in Canada, were derived from indigenous practices of resolving conflict. Little critical discussion, however, typically follows such observations (Tauri, 1998).

There is no doubt that there are certain similarities between the newly created restorative justice initiatives and some indigenous approaches to conflict. It is ironic that the dominant system, after ignoring and more often trying to destroy indigenous legal systems, is now exploring restorative approaches that have certain commonalities with indigenous justice. Potential similarities, such as being nonadversarial and holistic, should be explored. However, differences must also be acknowledged and the cultural assumptions that are embedded within justice models need to be examined.[4]

Indigenous peoples draw upon their own cultural and spiritual practices that have developed since time immemorial. Restorative justice is a new alternative to the dominant system. For indigenous peoples, indigenous justice is the ongoing re-creation and development of existing practices; it is the dominant system that is the foreign alternative. In discussing alternative dispute resolution, Monture-Okanee (1994) argues that aboriginal justice does not embrace the same philosophy and agenda as this movement. Aboriginal justice is different and much broader. The emphasis of restorative justice is on individual accountability and responsibility, while for aboriginal justice it is on collective responsibility (Jackson, 1992). In aboriginal justice, the process of restoration and healing takes place within a larger circle of relationships—often an extensive clan system. Indeed the fundamental terms taken for granted in Western criminal justice systems, such as "justice" and "guilt," do not have any comparative terms in many indigenous languages.

It is difficult to go beyond certain tentative, general statements of indigenous justice. One runs the risk of overgeneralization and stereotyping. The discussion of similarities and differences must proceed at a local rather than universal level. There are a diversity of indigenous definitions of "crime," as well as methods and forums for responding to crime. Therefore, there is another added layer to the exploration of similarities and differences—those that exist between indigenous justice approaches of differing nations. We must be careful not to simplify indigenous mechanisms for resolving conflicts nor assume that all indigenous cultures are the same. To ignore the historical circumstances and complexity and to assume the sameness and simplicity of indigenous cultures is insulting, or worse, racist.

Any restorative justice project, therefore, must consider its relationship with aboriginal modes of governance and dispute resolution in the particular jurisdiction of question. It is up to aboriginal peoples to interpret and explain their cultural ways. It is the responsibility of all outsiders, especially those involved in justice, to listen to and understand indigenous approaches within the context of their societies.

Avoiding Assumptions

There are a number of dangerous assumptions made when a restorative model is simply presumed to be applicable to indigenous individuals and communities. First, there is an assumption that indigenous cultures utilize the same processes in resolving conflicts as the restorative model. This may or may not be true. For example, unlike aboriginal methods of dispute resolution, those often used by nonaboriginals demand an impartial, neutral mediator who does not know the parties involved (Astor, 1991). Many restorative approaches focus on bringing the parties together to confront and resolve the problem. There are a variety of sanctions used by indigenous peoples, including temporary exile, withdrawal, and restitution. Many of the sanctions are based on avoidance rather than confrontation between offender and victim. While there are processes and sanctions that a restorative model uses that may be deemed culturally inappropriate by indigenous peoples, conversely, there may be aspects of indigenous justice that are not adopted by restorative justice. There is a tendency to romanticize the harmonious and peaceful existence of pre-colonial indigenous communities so that certain traditional sanctions, such as whipping or scarring, are not acknowledged.

A second and related assumption is that indigenous peoples will experience the restorative process in a manner similar to nonindigenous peoples. There is evidence of difficulties and disadvantages that indigenous people face in the formal legal process that primarily derive from cultural and communicative (verbal and nonverbal) differences. For example, an aboriginal individual may avoid eye contact out of respect, which might be negatively misinterpreted by the dominant culture. The difficulties faced in the formal legal system may also be experienced in restorative programs. How indigenous individuals will experience a restorative approach must be considered, and recognition must be given to their potential disadvantage when they experience an imposed, albeit restorative, model.

A third assumption is that of a healthy or stable relationship between indigenous communities and the state. The relationship has traditionally been anything but healthy, for the state has invariably been the colonizer of indigenous peoples, leaving a legacy of destruction (see, for example, Dussault et al., 1996; Johnston, 1991). That is, if a restorative program is initiated and endorsed by the state, it may be viewed with suspicion rather than embraced. It is important to understand whether the restorative program and the law from which it gains legitimacy is seen as oppressive or silencing by indigenous peoples. The goals of restoration and reintegration will remain elusive if indigenous peoples are silenced either at the individual or societal level due to the undermining of existing indigenous modes of governance. The net result of political silencing is to further marginalize indigenous people from the legal process.

These assumptions all point to the issues of ownership, control, and rights. A restorative program cannot be designed and then imposed on an indigenous community. It is also not enough to simply "indigenize" or add on aboriginal persons to restorative projects. While the restorative justice movement has provided recognition and legitimization of indigenous dispute resolution, there are dangers of co-optation. Indigenous peoples have had to struggle to gain "permission" to create, implement, and run their own justice practices. Pressures continue to be placed on indigenous initiatives to conform to criteria of the dominant system. There is also the risk that restorative justice will place demands on indigenous justice. Nielsen (1996), for example, points out that Navajo Peacemaker Courts are different from alternative dispute resolution (ADR) techniques but that their superficial similarity may lead to pressures on the Navajo Nation to conform to ADR structures and standards.

In acknowledging the uniqueness of aboriginal societies and the differences of these from the dominant society, one scholar concludes that the current movement toward restorative principles within the dominant justice system "while necessary to permit greater accommodation between our system and aboriginal systems . . . cannot be seen as a sufficient legal pathway to justice for aboriginal peoples. That pathway must be found in their initiatives" (Jackson, 1992:195). At a very minimum, negotiation and consultation with indigenous communities and organizations must occur throughout all phases of the development of judicial approaches. Ultimately, it is up to indigenous communities and nations to determine what "justice" means and how best to respond to conflict.

Case Example: Conferencing in Australia

Restorative justice for juveniles in Australia has been largely incorporated into and equated with community or family group conferencing. The introduction of conferencing in Australia has had a particular impact on indigenous communities. Conferencing serves as an example of the issues and concerns discussed above (see also Blagg, 1998, 1997; Cunneen, 1997; Tauri, 1998). Three issues are raised—human rights, police powers, and the bifurcation of the justice system along racialized lines. The analysis does not refer to any one particular state or territory in Australia—each has its own particular idiosyncrasies in how conferencing has been introduced. However, the following problems exist in all jurisdictions to some extent.

In line with recommendations from a number of national inquiries and royal commissions, Australian governments nominally commit themselves to recognizing the collective right to self-determination for indigenous people. However, conferencing provides a clear example of how this right is routinely ignored by government. There has been a failure to negotiate and consult adequately with aboriginal communities and organizations. Where consultation has occurred, there has been insufficient regard paid to indigenous views. As a result, the model of conferencing (which legally compels a particular form to the interaction between offender and victim) has been imposed on indigenous communities without consideration of indigenous cultural values and without consideration of how communities might wish to develop their own indigenous approaches to the issue (Blagg, 1997; Cunneen, 1997; National Inquiry into the Separation of Aboriginal and Torres Strait Islander Children from their Families, 1997).

There is no statutory obligation to require indigenous participation in the process of conferencing. There are no legal provisions for indigenous organizations and communities to make decisions about whether their children would be best served by attending a conference or any other form of justice intervention. In other words, the right of indigenous self-determination is ignored in what is seen to be a primary mechanism not just for diverting young people from the juvenile justice system but reintegrating them back into the community.

The second issue is police powers. The police have a significant role and great discretionary powers over access to conferencing, the operation of the process, and the final agreement that is reached. This leads to procedural concerns about the extension of police powers at various stages of the decision-making process. The reinforced and extended role of state police is not accompanied by any greater accountability or control over police decisionmaking. Aboriginal individuals and organizations are skeptical that police can be viewed as independent arbiters in the process. When police utilize discretionary powers, there is the potential danger that indigenous youths will receive adverse or more punitive decisions. Although there is limited research, the available evidence shows that indigenous young people are less likely to be referred by police to the conferences and more likely to be referred to court (National Inquiry into the Separation of Aboriginal and Torres Strait Islander Children from their Families, 1997).

The role of police in the conferencing process also raises a number of theoretical issues about their role in restorative processes more generally in cases concerning indigenous people. The effectiveness of the police role in restorative justice programs is tied to respect for the authority of police. As different relations have developed between the police and communities in different jurisdictions, it is possible that the police, in partnership with an aboriginal community, could assist in the development and implementation of an effective restorative justice initiative. However, a sense of legitimacy and respect for police often may be missing in aboriginal-police relations. For indigenous young people, the symbolic role of police may be one of racism and harassment. The role of police in any restorative justice program must be viewed in the context of their particular relationship with aboriginal communities—a relationship that has been structured through the colonial process. At the very least, there must be recognition that police have played an important role during the nineteenth and twentieth centuries in implementing colonial policies, including the forced removal of aboriginal children from their families and communities—a policy now recognized as genocide (Cunneen, 2000).

The third and related issue is that conferencing models have been introduced in the context of a greater *bifurcation* in juvenile justice systems within Australia. Juvenile justice systems are increasingly responding to two categories of offenders: those defined as "minor" and those who are seen as serious and/or repeat offenders. Minor offenders are channeled into various diversionary programs such as conferencing schemes. Serious and repeat offenders, on the other hand, become ineligible for diversionary programs and are dealt with more punitively through sentencing regimes that are more akin to adult models. There is substantial evidence in Australia that indigenous young people are discriminated against by police in their decisions to utilize diversionary options (Luke and Cunneen, 1995). This discrimination is an important factor in the accumulation of prior criminal records, which in itself leads to harsher sentencing outcomes. In several Australian jurisdictions, conferences are available only for first offenders—a policy that effectively excludes many indigenous youths because of their prior offending records. There is also the further issue of whether a prior record *should* be taken into account in the use of restorative justice programs (Braithwaite and Mugford, 1994).

The end result is the increased bifurcation of the justice system along "racialized" boundaries, with indigenous youths receiving more punitive outcomes. The custodial situation for indigenous youths has steadily worsened during the 1990s. Thus, at the very time when jurisdictions throughout Australia have been introducing various conferencing mechanisms, the actual level of incarceration of aboriginal young people has been increasing. At a time when nationwide levels of incarceration of nonaboriginal juveniles have remained stable, the number of indigenous youths incarcerated increased by 55 percent between 1993 and 1997 (Cunneen, 1997). The deepening of indigenous overrepresentation in detention should cause concern when restorative justice programs are presumed to have beneficial impact on indigenous young people. It is erroneous to accept at face value that restorative justice programs will improve the position of those entrenched within current juvenile justice systems.

There is an important theoretical issue in how we conceptualize restorative justice within the complex of approaches being used to deal with young people. Much of the juvenile justice legislation in Australia basically relies on a "just deserts" rhetoric of individualized rationality and responsibility. Punishment for wrongdoing should be proportional to the seriousness of the offense in order to protect the community and ensure specific and general deterrence. State-run restorative justice programs need to be seen against the totality of policing and criminal justice strategies. Those strategies have increasingly moved to treating young people more in line with adult offenders. The application of mandatory minimum sentencing regimes and "three strikes" legislation to both adults and juveniles are examples of this trend.

Therefore, we need to confront the contradictory relationship between conferencing and indigenous people. Aboriginal people have been denied the right to develop their own restorative justice mechanisms for dealing with young people and have been legally compelled to operate within an imposed model of conferencing. At the same time, conferencing programs have been developed without negotiation with aboriginal communities with regard to the disadvantages indigenous youths are likely to experience within its operations. As a result, indigenous young people have been increasingly pushed into the more punitive reaches of the juvenile justice system. Indigenous communities have been denied the chance to develop their own restorative justice procedures as well as an opportunity for effective participation in the existing system of juvenile conferencing.

The Role of Government

Justice initiatives involve forging a partnership between aboriginal communities and government that respects the inherent rights of indigenous peoples This partnership and recognition of human rights does not mean that government can then wash its hands of any responsibility or role in aboriginal communities. Government has a number of obligations and responsibilities, a few of which are briefly outlined below.

One of the first and foremost state obligations to indigenous nations is to develop a genuine and trustworthy government-to-government relationship. In this relationship, there must be a transference of power and ownership from the state to indigenous peoples. The respectful and peaceful coexistence of aboriginal and nonaboriginal justice approaches can then be explored. There will not be one model appropriate for all communities but rather a range of aboriginal justice initiatives. Government policies must be designed to support rather than construct such initiatives. Melton (nd:7) explains that indigenous rights include the capacity to enact and apply oral and written laws through their own mechanisms; the role of nonaboriginals is to "assist and support the tribes in strengthening their justice systems and to suppress the urge to take over or replace them."

Recognizing indigenous rights does not mean ignoring the complex realities of contemporary aboriginal communities. Although indigenous peoples maintain their unique cultural and spiritual traditions, we need to be careful not to romantice or idealize these communities. A number of factors, primarily colonization and industrialization, have dramatically altered aboriginal communities. Many communities suffer extraordinarily high rates of crime, violence, substance abuse, suicide, and unemployment.

Communities are embarking on a long road of healing and revitalization. Government has an obligation to assist community revitalization and development efforts. As Hazelhurst (1995:ix) argues, "the beginning of wisdom lies less in government initiatives than in the regeneration of communities. Re-empowered peoples can do for themselves what no outsiders, however well-meaning, can do for them." This requires political will and investment. Government must be prepared to provide the necessary resources and support for community development.

The rebalancing of power, revitalization of communities, and implementation of aboriginal justice is a complex process. The Gitksan and Wet'suwet'en, two indigenous nations in northern British Columbia, Canada, submitted an extensive proposal for implementing an alternative justice model based on the dispute resolution laws and methods of their people. They place their proposal within the long-term goals of self-government yet also acknowledge contemporary problems:

> It is recognized that in many areas there cannot be a simple switch from the imposed state system to Indigenous self-government. The acute social crisis in which the people find themselves together with external circumstances much changed since they last exercised complete jurisdiction, demand a careful thinking through of how social repair and control of anti-social behavior is to be accomplished . . . The usual bureaucracy of judges, police and social workers, even if nominally under the control of the tribal group, would be a seductive ineffective alternative to real community responsibility. But professionals will be needed. The process of social repair will require the skills of health, social workers and others.[5]

Government must provide both financial and human resources—for the support of aboriginal justice initiatives. In terms of financial obligations, there are a number of issues. The nature of aboriginal societies and approaches often defies government-imposed criteria. In their resubmission to government, the Gitksan and Wet'suwet'en (1990:3) correctly anticipated that their proposal would not fit government guidelines for funding: "Government institutions find it difficult to comprehend and interact with decentralized societies." A task force on indigenous peoples and criminal justice in Alberta, Canada, similarly points out that the holistic approach of a particular community program, while being a reason for its effectiveness, caused funding problems. "Because the activity could not be fitted into social services, recreation, crime prevention, or cultural program, obtaining funding was difficult at best . . . Government departments must look for reasons to say yes to Aboriginal projects and programs instead of finding reasons to say no" (Cawsey, 1991:27).

Government must develop a more flexible and creative approach to funding indigenous initiatives. This will entail coordination between government departments. Money alone will never solve problems or lead to a viable justice initiative. Human resources are also required, from both outside of and within communities. Resources include such things as education, training, professional expertise, and committed individuals willing to take on the responsibility of an initiative.

It is unrealistic to assume that all communities have the interest, willingness, and capability to confront crimes, especially violence. The Chair of the Inuit Justice Task Force in Nunavik, Canada, for example, stated that "the region we come from is bare of infrastructure and resources to deal with these kinds of issues. A community is swamped dealing with the magnitude of problems" (Buller et al., 1994:46). It is unfair and unrealistic to expect communities to be able to confront offenders and support victims by simply giving them the responsibility to do so. As LaPrairie (1998; 1995) argues, rather than simplistic thinking, we need to *critically* and *realistically* examine aboriginal communities as well as justice initiatives.

Aboriginal Women and Justice

The concerns of power, control, and participation that have been outlined in this chapter—and their relationship to restorative justice—are brought to the fore in complex layers by issues surrounding aboriginal women. There are not only power imbalances *between* aboriginal communities and government, but also within communities. Aboriginal women have been politically disempowered. Gender inequality, particularly within aboriginal political leadership, can cause aboriginal women to be grossly underrepresented in aboriginal government and organizations.

As discussed earlier, restorative initiatives cannot be imposed from the outside; initiatives must be developed within the context of the specific culture and by those in the community. However, power dynamics and inequalities within communities cannot be allowed to perpetuate harm against individuals. If a justice initiative transfers power to a handful of already-powerful individuals within the community, then there is great potential for corruption or tyranny of the less powerful. This is particularly problematic for women.

Aboriginal women have had to work hard to have their voices and concerns heard, finding themselves at a greater disadvantage due to their race *and* gender. Monture-Okanee (1992:250) argues: "The goal we set for ourselves should be to eliminate the disadvantage that Aboriginal women face because it is more startling than the experience of either race or gender alone . . . in some circumstances it is no longer the descendants of the European settlers that oppress us, but it is Aboriginal men in our communities who now fulfil this role."

Aboriginal women not only have inherent indigenous rights but also have fundamental human rights as women that include the right to live without discrimination and violence. That is, an aboriginal woman experiences the world as both an aboriginal *and* as a woman. Perhaps the greatest challenge for restorative and indigenous justice initiatives is to effectively confront both racism and sexism. As aboriginal women are particularly vulnerable to discrimination during the development and implementation of justice initiatives, conscious effort and care must be taken to ensure that they are participants during all phases of an initiative and that their concerns are addressed. For example, in many communities, there are extraordinary levels of violence perpetrated against women, as well as high levels of tolerance for such violence. Much discussion, education, and planning is required to ensure that their interests are served and safety guaranteed (see Zellerer, 1996; 1999).

The South Vancouver Island Justice Education Project, which involved eight aboriginal communities in British Columbia, Canada, serves as an example and valuable learning experience. This community justice initiative was able to gain government support. Their story is long and complex: it will only be noted here that ultimately it had to be discontinued and a full review ensued (Sheila Clark & Associates et al., 1994). Although there were clear strengths, many weaknesses led to the initiative's demise, including insufficient initial community consultation, politics within communities, and failure to meet the needs (including safety) of victims. Family and political connections meant that victims were pressured and certain offenders were able to evade responsibility for their behavior, often sexual offenses against women. Aboriginal women bore the brunt of most of the problems.

Another informative example is the introduction of circle sentencing in an Inuit community in Nunavik, Canada (Crnkovich, 1993). A judge decided to hold a circle in a case involving a man who pleaded guilty to assaulting his wife. There was little prior organization or preparation and the parties involved did not know why the judge was holding a circle, the history and purpose of sentencing circles, or how circles relate to Inuit traditions. During the actual circle, the focus remained on the offender. The victim was unprepared, nervous, afraid, and spoke very little. The harm done to the offender's wife and family was basically not discussed. Tellingly, it appears that subsequent to the circle, she had been beaten again.

Highlighting such case examples is not done to imply that indigenous communities are incapable of handling their own justice issues. Nor is it done to say that restorative and indigenous justice initiatives inevitably lead to such end results. Instead, the message is that living up to the visions of indigenous and restorative justice is not an easy or quick matter. We must examine the development and implementation of initiatives to understand a project's challenges and learn from mistakes. Valuable lessons are embodied in their stories.

There must be space and respect created to hear and understand aboriginal women's perspectives and experiences. It is imperative to remember that aboriginal women do not form a homogenous group, so there cannot be one singular, representative voice. To help ensure the full participation of aboriginal women, recognition and funding must be provided to aboriginal women's groups at the local, regional, and national levels. Aboriginal women, in addition to communities, must be empowered to make informed choices.

Conclusion

Throughout this chapter, it has been argued that the foundation for justice reform and progress begins with the recognition of indigenous rights, particularly within the broader political framework of self-determination and self-government. We outlined a number of dangerous assumptions and implications, using conferencing in Australia as an example, in which justice initiatives have been simply imposed on indigenous communities.

While power and control must be returned to indigenous communities, the responsibility for the multitude of problems facing contemporary communities cannot rest solely on indigenous shoulders. Government also has obligations and responsibilities. Relationships need to be forged based on mutual understanding and respect.

Restorative justice advocates must also develop such relations with indigenous peoples. As we examine the justice system and develop alternative models, we are presented with yet another opportunity for cross-cultural sharing and learning. Time and time again, government representatives and others of the dominant society have simply ignored indigenous values and approaches to conflict resolution. They have often assumed that their institutions and ways are superior and that they knew what was best. They displaced indigenous ways by imposing their own systems. Although it may seem obvious that indigenous justice must be developed and implemented by and within the community, it is surprising how often this is ignored, even by well-meaning professionals.

The road to reform is long and complex. There are many challenges, including the specific discrimination faced by aboriginal women. Initiatives must be community-specific, yet the power dynamics and resources within communities must be realistically assessed. Violence against women is a particularly horrific issue that requires careful attention. Aboriginal women must be given a place at the table of all negotiations and discussions, and their perspectives and experiences must be honored and respected.

Indigenous peoples and advocates of restorative justice can share insights and support each other on the journey of healing, empowerment, and discovery. Both can potentially impact and inspire positive changes in the dominant legal system. The lessons learned along the way have wide-reaching implications for all communities.

In conclusion, it is important to think about the principles that might underlie a restorative justice approach in indigenous communities. They include:

- open negotiation with indigenous communities and their organizations, including aboriginal women's groups;

- respect for indigenous peoples and their cultures;

- respect for indigenous people's rights, including the right to self-determination;

- relinquishment by government and their departments of their assumed right to make decisions for indigenous peoples;

- ongoing practical support for communities to remedy the problems of social, economic, and gender inequality—an approach that relies on community building.

Developing community-based and restorative justice programs within a context of self-determination is a practical task. Although there are successful examples, there are no simple blueprints. The lesson from successful indigenous community justice responses is that efficient, practical, and ongoing support from governments is required to facilitate communities in the difficult process of finding acceptable solutions to the problems facing indigenous people.

Discussion Questions

1. Why do Zellerer and Cunneen believe that indigenous rights are especially important to protect from governmental human rights abuses?

2. Many restorative practices are derived from indigenous cultures; however, they are not always implemented in ways that are consistent with indigenous values or practices. Moreover, there is some evidence that such practices may even discriminate against native peoples when applied in non-native settings. What are some of Zellerer and Cunneen's concerns about the application of non-indigenous practices in indigenous settings? Do you agree with these concerns and feel they are a threat to the implementation of restorative justice?

3. Why do these authors feel that restorative conferencing in Australia has been unfairly implemented? What evidence is offered to support this contention and what have been some of the results of this biased implementation?

4. What do Zellerer and Cunneen think should be the role of government with respect to interacting with indigenous populations? Do you agree? What do you think would be an appropriate way to structure the relationship between government and native communities?

5. What are some of the particular problems faced by indigenous women in the justice process?

Endnotes

[1]   There are a number of terms used to refer to the original inhabitants of a country, including indigenous, aboriginal, Native, and First Nations. We use indigenous and aboriginal interchangeably.

[2]   For an overview of the way various countries have recognized particular indigenous rights, see ATSIC [the Aboriginal and Torres Strait Islander Commission] (1995).

[3]   For discussion of the limitations of the criminal justice system in dealing with indigenous issues, see, for example, Dodson (1997; 1993) and the National Inquiry into the Separation of Aboriginal and Torres Strait Islander Children from Their Families (1997), as well as the various reports of the Australian Royal Commission into Aboriginal Deaths in Custody (Johnston, 1991) and the Canadian Royal Commission on Aboriginal Peoples (Dussault et al., 1996).

[4]   For further discussion of these issues in the Australian context, see Blagg (1998; 1997) and Cunneen (1997); for the New Zealand context, see Tauri (1998) and Jackson (1995).

5   Their proposal is titled *Unlocking Aboriginal Justice: Alternative Dispute Resolution for the Gitksan and Wet'suwet'en People*. Submitted to the B.C. Ministry of the Attorney General. For extensive discussion, see Jackson, 1992.

References

Anaya, J. (1996). *Indigenous Peoples in International Law*. New York: Oxford University Press.

Astor, H. (1991). *Mediation and Violence Against Women*. Canberra: National Committee on Violence Against Women.

ATSIC (1995). *Recognition, Rights and Reform*. Canberra: Aboriginal and Torres Strait Islander Commission.

Blagg, H. (1997). "A Just Measure of Shame?: Aboriginal Youth and Conferencing in Australia." *British Journal of Criminology* 37(4).

Blagg, H. (1998). "Restorative Visions and Restorative Justice Practices: Conferencing, Ceremony and Reconciliation in Australia." *Current Issues in Criminal Justice* 10(1):5-14.

Braithwaite, J., and S. Mugford (1994). "The Conditions of Successful Reintegration Ceremonies." *British Journal of Criminology* 34(2):139-171.

Buller, E., J. Ekstedt, B. Henderson, K. Koe, Z. Nungak, and R. Ross (1994). "Making it Work." In *Justice and Northern Families in Crisis . . . In Healing . . . In Control*, edited by M. Nicholson, 27-47. Burnaby, BC: The Northern Justice Society, Simon Fraser University.

Burger, J., and P. Hunt (1994). "Towards the International Protection of Indigenous Peoples' Rights." *Netherlands Quarterly of Human Rights* 12(4):405-423.

Cawsey, R.A. (1991). *Justice on Trial. Report of the Task Force on the Criminal Justice System and Its Impact on the Indian and Metis People of Alberta*. Edmonton, Alberta: Attorney General and Solicitor General of Alberta.

Crnkovich, M. (1993). *Report on the Sentencing Circle in Kangiqsujuaq*. Prepared for Pauktuutit and Department of Justice Canada.

Cunneen, C. (1997). "Community Conferencing and the Fiction of Indigenous Control." *Australia and New Zealand Journal of Criminology* 30(3):292-311.

Cunneen, C. (2000). *Policing Indigenous Communities*. Sydney: Allen and Unwin.

Coulter, R. (1995). "The Draft UN Declaration on the Rights of Indigenous Peoples: What is it? What Does it Mean?" *Netherlands Quarterly of Human Rights* 13(2):123-137.

Dodson, M. (1993). *Aboriginal and Torres Strait Islander Social Justice Commissioner First Annual Report*. Sydney: Human Rights and Equal Opportunity Commission.

Dodson, M. (1997). *Aboriginal and Torres Strait Islander Social Justice Commissioner Fourth Annual Report*. Sydney: Human Rights and Equal Opportunity Commission.

Dussault, R., G. Erasmus, P. Chartrand, J. Meekison, V. Robinson, M. Sillett, and B. Wilson (1996). *Report of the Royal Commission on Aboriginal Peoples*, Five Volumes. Ottawa: Canada Communications Group.

Gitksan and Wet'suwet'en (1990). *Unlocking Aboriginal Justice.* Resubmission to the BC Ministry of the Attorney General.

Hazlehurst, K. (1995). "Introduction: Post-Colonial Governance: The Maturing Contract." In *Perceptions of Justice,* edited by K. Hazlehurst. Hants, England: Avebury.

Jackson, M. (1992). "In Search of the Pathways to Justice: Alternative Dispute Resolution in Aboriginal Communities." *UBC Law Review* (Special Edition):147-238.

Jackson, M. (1995). "Justice and Political Power: Reasserting Maori Legal Processes." In *Legal Pluralism and the Colonial Legacy: Indigenous Experiences of Justice in Canada, Australia, and New Zealand,* edited by K. Hazlehurst. London: Avebury.

Johnston, E (1991). *National Report, 5 Volumes, Royal Commission into Aboriginal Deaths in Custody.* Canberra: Australian Government Printing Service.

LaPrairie, C. (1995). "Community Justice or Just Communities? Aboriginal Communities in Search of Justice." *Canadian Journal of Criminology* 37(4):521-545.

LaPrairie, C. (1998). "The 'New' Justice: Some Implications for Aboriginal Communities." *Canadian Journal of Criminology* 40(1):61-79.

Luke, G., and C. Cunneen (1995). *Aboriginal Over-Representation and Discretionary Decisions in the NSW Juvenile Justice System,* Report to the Criminology Research Council, Canberra. Published by the Juvenile Justice Advisory Council.

McNamara, L. (1995). "Aboriginal Justice Reform in Canada: Alternatives to State Control." In *Perceptions of Justice,* edited by K. Hazlehurst. Hants, England: Avebury.

Melton, A.P. (nd). *Indigenous Justice Systems and Tribal Society,* Restorative Justice On-Line Notebook, National Institute of Justice. See *http://www.ojp.usdoj.gov/nij/rest-just/*

Monture-Okanee, P. (1992). "The Roles and Responsibilities of Aboriginal Women: Reclaiming Justice." *Saskatchewan Law Review* 56:237-266.

Monture-Okanee, P. (1994). "Alternative Dispute Resolution: A Bridge to Aboriginal Experience?" In *Qualifications for Dispute Resolution: Perspectives on the Debate,* edited by C. Morris and A. Pirie, 131-140. Victoria, BC: UVIC Institute for Dispute Resolution.

National Inquiry into the Separation of Aboriginal and Torres Strait Islander Children from their Families (1997). *Bringing Them Home.* Canberra: Australian Government Printing Service.

Nettheim, G. (1995). "Mabo and Legal Pluralism: The Australian Aboriginal Justice Experience." In *Legal Pluralism and the Colonial Legacy: Indigenous Experiences of Justice in Canada, Australia, and New Zealand,* edited by K. Hazlehurst. London: Avebury

Nielsen, M. (1996). "A Comparison of Developmental Ideologies: Navajo Nation Peacemaker Courts and Canadian Native Justice Committees." In *Restorative Justice: International Perspectives,* edited by B. Galaway and J. Hudson. Monsey, NY: Criminal Justice Press.

Sheila Clark & Associates, Valerie Lannon & Associates, Inc., and A.M. Research Services (1994). *Building the Bridge: A Review of the South Vancouver Island Justice Education Project.* Victoria, BC: Ministry of the Attorney General, Department of Justice Canada, and Solicitor General of Canada.

Tauri, J. (1998). "Family Group Conferencing: A Case Study of the Indigenisation of New Zealand's Justice System." *Current Issues in Criminal Justice* 10(2):168-182.

Zellerer, E. (1996). "Community-Based Justice and Violence Against Women: Issues of Gender and Race." *International Journal of Comparative and Applied Criminal Justice* 20:233-244.

Zellerer, E. (1999). "Restorative Justice in Indigenous Communities: Critical Issues in Confronting Violence Against Women." *International Review of Victimology* 6:345-358.

12

Positive Youth Development, Restorative Justice, and the Crisis of Abandoned Youth

KENNETH POLK

Introduction

This chapter addresses the implications for restorative justice presented by the widespread collapse of work and schooling opportunities for a large proportion of the youthful population. Using the Australian experience as a case study, we begin with an analysis of the various economic factors that have resulted in the collapse of the full-time work market for those young people who attempt to leave school in the middle to late teenage years without qualifications, skills, or work experience. Whereas in an earlier time there was a great demand for the labor of such young people, the transformation of the economy has resulted in this group being increasingly abandoned in terms of work, schooling, or training alternatives. As a result, these individuals become prime targets for control by the juvenile and adult justice systems.

What are the implications of attempts to control the behavior of these young people that do not address the economic and social sources of abandonment? As a component of the justice system's control mechanism, is restorative justice to be narrowly conceived of as only involving attention to immediate problems of misbehavior, or should it be seen in a wider context of an expansion of social justice? This chapter will argue that the danger of the former approach is that narrow strategies

265

implemented under the banner of restorative justice may become little more than another aspect of the abandonment experienced by marginal young people. On the other hand, there are many precedents in youth policy, both in recent decades and in current writings, for a view that places restorative justice in a broader framework of positive youth development and social justice within communities.

The Collapse of the Youth Labor Market

The current social context for youth is one characterized by high levels of unemployment, increasing poverty, reductions in state welfare and educational services and benefits, and a public culture of competitive individualism (Wyn and White, 1997). These general trends have had a particularly negative impact on large sections of the youth population (Boss, Edwards, and Pitman, 1995). Indeed, it has been argued that the present era is significantly different from previous decades: whereas for most of this century the state has played a major supporting and interventionist role in assisting young people in the areas of education, welfare, and rehabilitative juvenile justice, particularly when youth unemployment was stagnant, the same is not the case today. Rather, we are seeing a simultaneous reduction in youth employment prospects and in state support programs for young people—leading to what can be described as the phenomenon of "abandoned youth" (Polk, 1997).

It is our view that one of the important general conditions shaping the current situation of adversity for young people is the collapse in the availability of full-time work for the young. Whereas barely 25 years ago, two-thirds of all young people between the ages of 16 and 19 in Australia were employed full-time, by the 1990s this had dropped to below 20 percent. Moreover, some economists are predicting that some time early in this century, there will be no full-time jobs for teenagers in Australia (Spiering, 1995). While the onset of this trend may have been more rapid in Australia, the same general facts hold for all of the developed countries. There are, simply, very few full-time opportunities for teenagers who want to work but who lack qualifications, skills, and experience. This shift has come about as a result of a number of structural features of the Australian economy, polity, and labor market.

The Decline of Manufacturing Employment

One of the elements observed early in the evolution of this crisis was the reduction in the demand for labor within the manufacturing sector. While specific figures vary across the developed countries, depending in part on when the growth in the industrial sector occurred, the common pattern has been that the robust development of the post-World War II period began to soften in the late 1960s, then suffered a profound shock with the oil crisis in the early 1970s. From that point on, there has been a rapid decline in the number and proportion of persons working in the manufacturing sector. Because manufacturing is concerned with the production of various machines and gadgets, and because the demand for such gadgets has actually increased in the developed world, real questions exist as to why these countries are experiencing such a profound loss of manufacturing activity. Two general kinds of explanations have been offered: technology and trade (Kapstein, 1996).

The Impact of Technology and the Flight of Capital It is obvious that technological changes continue to offer one important explanation for not only the loss of work in manufacturing but also a restriction of the range of jobs that traditionally have been available to those with lower levels of skill, experience, or qualifications. Factory work has been undergoing improvements in productivity since its inception, and a persistent goal of the manufacturer is to increase the productivity of workers through the more efficient mechanization of factory work. While the assembly line was the creation of the 1920s that majorly revamped factory work, in contemporary times, various forms of robots and computerized machines continue the process of increasing worker efficiency at the potential cost of eliminating jobs, especially those jobs that require little skill.

What is often less well understood is how deeply such technological changes drive throughout the work structure, because the elimination of jobs occurs in the white-collar sector as well. Because of modern innovations such as the word processor and computerized communications processes, we have seen the disappearance of such jobs as copy typists, file clerks, telephone operators, and clerks in such fields as banking, insurance, and government. Thus, for one example, what were major sources of full-time career work entry for teenagers in Australia barely a generation ago (banking and government agencies) today hire hardly any teenage workers, especially on a full-time level (Polk, 1988).

Clearly, though, it is more than technology that accounts for the kinds of job loss that developed countries have experienced. One additional factor is what has been called the "flight of capital." Simply put, many large manufacturing conglomerates now shop around the world for pools of cheap labor. One of the better known examples of this is the story of the Nike Company in the United States (Ballinger, 1992). The Nike Company did not even exist in the early 1960s; it emerged as a small company in Oregon making specialist running shoes, only to become a major corporate player by the 1990s. While its headquarters are still based in Oregon, Nike closed its last factory in the United States in the 1980s because it could make shoes much cheaper in countries where labor in the rubber-shoe industry averaged $6.94 an hour. In places such as Indonesia, workers earn as little as 14 cents an hour and, furthermore, the government strongly discourages union activity, which might attempt to provide some protection for workers. Thus, shoes that sell for $80 or more in the United States are produced for a labor cost of approximately 12 cents. Work done overseas is not work done at home; it results, in the apt phrase of Bluestone and Harrison (1982), "in plant closings, community abandonment and the dismantling of basic industry."

Nonreciprocal Tariff Reductions Capital flight is not a simple process. In part, it has depended upon politicians who create nonreciprocal, asymmetric changes in tariffs that place domestic workers at risk with no particular gain for the developed country making such changes. For example, Australia has fallen under the spell of the "economic rationalists" and has systematically reduced its previously high tariffs on motor cars. As might be expected, this has resulted in the loss of roughly one in four (23%) jobs in the motor car industry between 1988 and 1994 (Fell, 1996). Because the argument for such changes tends to be an economic one that domestic consumers will benefit from the process, what is less well understood is that on average, and taking into account inflation, car prices have doubled in the past two decades in Australia. Despite repeated claims, there is no gain to consumers. Similarly, there are enormous direct and indirect economic costs that result from increased dependence upon imported cars, as well as welfare costs that rise as the numbers of persons on unemployment benefits grow. Australian consumers have not gained; nor have unemployed workers and Australian taxpayers who must cover many of the direct and indirect costs of the new tariff policy (such as shifting employed workers from the category of tax payers to the category of the unemployed, at which point they become dependent upon government support).

The nonreciprocal character of such changes can be seen by examining industries such as plastics. Countries such as Australia and the United States, influenced by economic rationalism, have been aggressive in pursuing policies of lowering tariffs so that duty on polyethylene imports into both Australia and the United States is set at 5 percent. It is probably less well known that the European countries set their levels at slightly more than twice that (11%) and in Japan the duty is more than 20 percent. More critically, in the countries that are benefiting from capital flight, polyethylene tariffs are even higher—the level is set at 30 percent in Malaysia, India, and Thailand, and even higher in Indonesia (40%) and Pakistan (50%) (Wood, 1997). These figures came to light when one of the major multinational players in Australian plastics made a decision to leave Australia because of the tariffs. When companies leave, jobs go with them.

New Patterns of Retail Sales:
The "McJobbing" of the Labor Force

A different but related factor is the creation of new patterns of retail activity—patterns that depend in part on a new shape to the retail labor force. This can be seen most easily by comparing the traditional department store with the new, high-volume discount outlets (seen in their most advanced form in the United States). The department store itself emerged with the onset of the twentieth century as an innovation, replacing the previous widely dispersed specialized shops with a central shopping location offering a wide range of goods. Examples include such giants as Macy's, Filene's, or Sears in the United States, Marks & Spencer in the United Kingdom, and Meyer in Australia. In such stores, the workers would typically enter into employment in the stock room or as a sales assistant in a department; then, after working under close supervision, they would gradually move upward within a full-time career structure, first in sales within the department, then perhaps in the higher management levels of the store. Workers, in short, started at the bottom and gradually moved outward and upward as they gained knowledge and skill, in most cases with the reasonable expectation of full-time and life employment (assuming satisfactory performance).

In contrast, new organizations such as Kmart or Price Club have a remarkably different structure. While there may be a thin layer of full-time, career-oriented management staff, the bulk of the sales staff will be paid on a minimum-wage level, earning few or no benefits (holiday pay, retirement loadings, or, in the United States, medical benefits) with part-time and casual employment that expands or contracts with the needs of the sales organization. Such workers are not expected to know much about stock except the price, and they certainly cannot reasonably expect the work to constitute a career. These "McJobs" are hardly the stuff of long-term, life planning. As the retail business shifts to these high-volume, discount forms of sales, and this "dual labor market" pattern spreads, the entry-level positions to careers in retail sales that used to exist in a previous time become progressively restricted.

The "Leaning and Meaning" of
the Private Sector and Government

A further component of the economic mix that has contributed to this crisis is the "leaning" (and "meaning") that is taking place in the private sector. Workers at all levels of the larger corporate giants are confronting the specter of "downsizing." To use an Australian example, from 1990 to 1995, Holden (one of the largest Australian car manufacturers) increased its sales by 28 percent (from $2.42 billion to $3 billion), increased is profits by 72 percent (from $150.9 million to $260 million), and increased its return on sales by 39 percent (from 6.2% to 8.6%). Yet, these increases were accompanied by a loss of 13 percent in terms of persons employed (from 6,447 to 5,625) (Fell, 1997). Organizations engaged in employment losses at this level are hardly in the position to take on new employees, especially young employees without qualifications, skills, or experience.

A similar trend has taken place in governmental sectors. Partly under pressure from such financial institutions as the International Monetary Fund, the World Bank, and the Organization for Economic Cooperation and Development, but also in response to the ideologies of economic rationalists and conservatives at the national political level, there is worldwide pressure to reduce government spending. In the United States, several individual states have faced taxpayer revolts that have restricted the power of states to tax, while Congress and the presidential administration have been consumed with the task of "balancing the budget" (i.e., reducing spending, especially in such areas as health, education, welfare, and housing). Similarly, in Australia, after the present conservative government came into power in 1996, a "black hole" in the budget was invented or discovered that has resulted in a round of massive cuts in governmental expenditures, with promises of larger cuts to follow in the coming years. In Europe, the cutting of public expenditures is one of the main criteria established for governments as part of the Maastrict Treaty on European Union (Kapstein, 1996). Cutting governmental expenditures has immediate effects on unemployment, both directly in terms of persons thrown out of government jobs and indirectly in terms of cuts that must be undertaken in other agencies as their governmental support is withdrawn. Furthermore, a government in the throes of downsizing is hardly in a position to consider vibrant, challenging yet expensive new options in terms of education and training, and certainly there will be few opportunities within constricting work forces for new jobs for young people attempting to enter work careers without qualifications, skills, or experience.

The Structural Consequences for Young People

The weaving together of these economic and political forces sets the structural frame for the present situation of economic adversity for the young. The rapid decline of teenage employment in Australia, and comparable trends observed in other developed countries noted above, are noncyclical phenomena. Instead, they reflect a deep, directional structural change within developed economies. There have been a number of consequent alterations, which have a direct impact on the life choices available to young people. Four major consequences are relevant to the present discussion. These include: (1) the rise in youth unemployment, (2) the increase in school retention, (3) the increase in casual employment, and (4) the limiting of income opportunities.

Youth Unemployment, School Retention, Casual Employment, and Income Opportunities

First and foremost, there has been the persistent problem of high levels of youthful unemployment throughout the developed world, which (averaging around two to three times the level of adult unemployment) ranges anywhere from 15 percent upward, depending upon the country, the specific group of young people being examined, and the way unemployment is defined (for example, a common ploy to reduce the official figures is to remove "discouraged" workers from the figures because such individuals are "no longer in the labor force"— they may not have jobs, but they are not officially unemployed), and the minor cycles of upward and downward movement of unemployment. In Canada, for example, youth unemployment rates since 1976 have tended to average between 15 and 20 percent for the 15- to 19-year-olds, with the rate in 1993 being 19.7 percent (Glenday, 1996:159). In Australia, the figures are similar, with peaks and troughs across the years since the world-wide jump in unemployment in the mid-1970s— the low point being in the 12 percent range in 1982, the highest peak at more than 25 percent in 1991, but with the long-term underlying trend being distinctly upward. In the words of Wooden, the rate is "ratchetting upwards" during each recession peak ". . . and never quite returning to pre-recession levels" (Wooden, 1996:151).

Rising Retention Secondly, and related to these developments, there has been a dramatic and steep increase in school retention. In Victoria, for example, in the years between 1983 and 1992, the percentage of students undertaking studies at the Year 12 level (the last year of high school) more than doubled, moving up from 36 percent to 78 percent (Dwyer, 1996). Unfortunately, neither in Australia nor in other developed countries can it be said that the school curriculum has been modified to meet the needs imposed by this new group of students. Thus, for those students who wish to flow into the traditional university entry curriculum (the old "college track" in American terms, see Polk and Schafer, 1972), the ploy of educational retention may have some payoff. For those without this interest, however, the curriculum is a virtual wasteland. Students find themselves stranded in an educational holding pattern without purpose or direction. It is hardly surprising, then, that a common finding in Australia is that retention rates are actually now reversing direction, as discouraged students choose the streets over the situation they face in schools. Since the 1992 high point in Victoria, the levels of Year 12 have steadily declined to a level of 71 percent in 1995 (Dwyer, 1996).

The Increase in Part-Time Work Third, insecure part-time and casual positions have increased dramatically, with the numbers of 14- to 20-year-old part-time workers more than doubling between 1980 and 1996 (Spoehr, 1997:2). Systematic study of labor market trends indicates the dramatic nature of the shifts in youth participation from full-time to part-time work, from paid work to educational participation, and from educational and work participation to unemployment. A substantial proportion of Australian young people are locked into marginal activities, precarious forms of work, and withdrawal from the labor market (see Dusseldorp Skills Forum, 1998). This part-time work tends to be casual, with minimum pay and conditions, and limited prospects for either training or further advancement. While technically keeping young people off the rolls of the unemployed, most such work will not provide avenues into full-time, long-term, career-oriented jobs.

The Closing Off of Earning Opportunities Fourth, it is important to acknowledge how each of these developments has impacted upon the income opportunities of young people. The income of young people has been severely affected by broader economic restructuring, both directly in terms of potential paid work by the young person and indirectly through the financial pressures placed on families to support their children. Many young people have no income at all and are dependent upon their parents. That paid work which is available for teenagers tends to be reserved for students and is located primarily in the retail and services sectors (White et al., 1997). It is comprised of low-skilled work in both the formal and informal (i.e., cash-in-hand) waged economic spheres, and wages for youths continue to be pegged at a level below that of other workers, regardless of their productivity (White, 1997). Recent figures show that real earnings from full-time work among 15- to 19-year-olds fell by 6 percent between the early 1980s and the mid-1990s, and earnings from part-time work fell by 29 percent (Sweet, 1998:9). More generally, for those receiving outside income from a variety of sources, the average income of 15- to 19-year-olds has fallen significantly in real terms since 1982. This includes incomes for full-time workers, part-time workers, and those receiving government benefits (Landt and Scott, 1998). The struggle to make ends meet is, then, a major problem for young people and their parents.

Teenagers and Economic Adversity

For the present group of adolescents who leave school early, these trends give precise meaning to the concept of economic adversity. We argue that there is a particular form of denial of opportunity for full-time employment with the collapse of the full-time youth labor market in Australia, which is reflected in trends that have emerged in recent years, such as high levels of youth unemployment. These trends pose a fundamental problem in terms of what was the previous expected pattern of development in the movement from adolescence into adulthood. The absence of qualifications, skills, and experience results in the "early school leavers" being unable to make the transition from school into waged, full-time work. The inability to make this critical transition means that, in turn, other important life decisions have to be deferred or altered, including the movement into an independent life in terms of housing, marriage, and the start of their own families.

The social location of the problem of blocked transition needs to be underscored. For those who stay on in school through the tertiary years and obtain higher-level qualifications, the transition into work is still relatively smooth, the periods of unemployment tend to be short, and rates of unemployment low. It is those who attempt an early departure from the educational system who are vulnerable to the new forms of economic adversity. In the United States, among high school dropouts, in 1988-1989, just under one-half (47%) were employed, with 18 percent unemployed looking for work, and just over one-third (35%) unemployed but not looking for work (Dwyer, 1996:64). Analysis of the post-school experience of a group of young people who left school before the end of Year 12 in Australia found that upon leaving school only 38 percent had either a job or an apprenticeship, and in fact

> . . . 70% lacked any reliable source of income, many of them being dependent on occasional handouts or pocket money from family or friends, and perhaps an occasional loan or even illegal means of some kind. (Dwyer, 1995:268)

Furthermore, there is an important way in which this pattern of adversity poses a new kind of problem for those still in school who (as has been true for large numbers of students in recent generations) do not see themselves as going into the tertiary education system. In the past, there was a clear relationship between the "track" or "stream" in which a student belonged and the probability that the person would engage in delinquency, that is, "trouble" tended to be concentrated in the "nonuniversity" streams of secondary schools (Polk and Schafer, 1972). In the contemporary context, it can be presumed that in addition to the problems of denigration and humiliation observed in the nonuniversity secondary school tracks, there is an emerging problem that such students are becoming increasingly aware of the economic wasteland that looms before them. An anticipated future of limited economic opportunity becomes a part of the pains of being caught in the lower streams of the contemporary secondary school.

Alienation, Trouble, and Youth Crime

How and where young people spend their spare time has also been fundamentally affected by the developments described above. For example, the post-war period saw big changes in the nature of consumption in society. During the long boom of economic development up to the late 1960s and early 1970s, paid work for young people was readily available and a disposable income there to be spent. One consequence of the shifts in spending ability and market weight given to young people was a significant change in leisure activity, time, and space (Stratton, 1992). In a nutshell, leisure increasingly became a commodity—in order to play, people need money.

The cultural importance of consumption changed as well. Fads and fashions, youth-oriented and otherwise, began to dominate public life. In essence, it seems that who you are is partly a reflection of what you wear and where you shop. The processes of cultural formation today are such that youth "identity" is forged through how young people consume what is provided in the mass commercial market, and how they consciously produce their own self-generated cultural forms (Wyn and White, 1997). The reshaping of youth employment and educational opportunities has also contributed to a major alteration in the basis for identity formation. This can be conceived as a shift away from what a person does (i.e., the sphere of production) to how persons present themselves in the public domain (e.g., the sphere of consumption).

A recent British study on youth consumption points out that "it was the symbolic qualities of consumer goods, as opposed to their intrinsic qualities, that appeared to provide the cultural capital with which social peer groups could interact" (Miles, Cliff, and Burr, 1998:89). The study concluded that young people consume material things as a means to facilitate social participation and thereby to construct a recognizable identity. A crucial issue arising from the findings is the experience of those young people who do not have the basic resources they need to become participants in this sort of consumer culture. It also raises questions about the social status of young people who, from the point of view of commercial consumption, are unable or unwilling to purchase the goods and services that are offered in "consumer" spaces.

One manifestation of this is the so-called "mall problem." New retail strategies, in combination with patterns of automobile usage, have resulted in the creation of large shopping centers with easy access for consumers. For young people without a job to occupy their time, and with little money, these centers provide an obvious locus for low-cost entertainment and recreation. The use of this space by low-income, marginal groups of young people, however, brings them into potential conflict with other users of this space, including both shop owners and potential customers. With this conflict comes the invoking of police powers to either move the young people on to another location or create grounds for an arrest. These are young people who have "no space of their own" (White, 1990). Yet, the response of the state police and private security firms has largely been to exclude young people (particularly marginalized young people) from such places. Thus, the use of space itself is increasingly constructed around the notion of space as a commodity—those with the resources have access; those without money are in essence being purged from the public domain.

This problem of space and conflict spills over into other problems as well. That this is a worldwide issue can be seen in the following description of a "hot spot" found in a discussion of crime prevention in a city center:

> One hot spot was a small cross street where the entrance to a restaurant, often frequented by pupils of upper secondary school, and a high-class dance restaurant, frequented by somewhat older people, were located on one side of the street, while a hamburger bar was located on the other side. The latter was a place where many of the rockers (often working class) of the city spent time in the late evenings. The "hot spot" was peaceful during the day and most of the evening. It was only in the evenings, especially on the weekends, that it was a "hot spot" for stranger-to-stranger assault. (Wikstrom, 1995:441-442)

While the above narrative happens to be located in Stockholm, the basic dynamics are such that the potential for conflict is recognizable in comparable areas in most developed countries. The potent mixture of aggressive and youthful machismo, alcohol use, the movement of small collectives in public space, and the presence of onlookers, which may aggravate challenges to honor, results in social friction that in turn can lead to violence in the form of assault or even homicide (Polk, 1994).

For some people in adolescence, there is experimentation with the expected forms of "trouble" that bring them into potential conflict with adults, which then can be followed by movement into more solidified "careers" of delinquency. The critical feature of the present youth crisis, however, is that the important structural features of maturational reform, which provide exits from such criminal careers (e.g., establishing a job, marriage, and family) are not occurring, and as a result some young people are not desisting from crime, but are in fact continuing their criminal activities into their twenties. This is a potentially ominous pattern because it creates the possibility of a much larger collective of individuals who see themselves as having little option but to continue to pursue life careers in criminality. In the United States, these trends are particularly notable in the African-American population (Duster, 1995). Recent data suggest that that in a typical day in the United States, one in every four African-American males between the ages of 20 and 29 are in jail, prison, or on probation. In cities such as Washington, DC, or Baltimore, more than 40 percent of the 18- to 35-year-old males were in jail, prison, on probation or parole, out on bond, or being sought on an arrest warrant (Miller, 1996:7-8).

Sustained and increasingly technologically sophisticated intrusion into the homes and lives of urban African-American families by law enforcement agents for mostly minor reasons has left the inner cities with a classical situation of iatrogenic conduct—a "treatment" that maims those it touches and exacerbates the very pathologies that lie at the root of the problem (in this case, crime). It suggests that the criminal justice system itself has become a major contributor to the breakdown of the inner cities (Miller, 1996:9).

Policy Options: The Interplay of Developmental and Control Strategies

There is nothing new about the idea of youth unrest in general. Since the beginning of time, older generations have complained about the behavior of younger generations, and will continue to do so. Some of these complaints find their way into print, reflecting such matters as the lack of manners or morals of the young. Therefore, it is important to note if an attempt is being made to assert that there is a distinctive period of youth crisis. Of course, this is precisely what is being asserted here. It is our argument that at the turn of this twenty-first century we face turmoil among youth (and about youth policy) that is comparable in many ways to similar turmoil that took place at the end of the previous century. At that time, a distinctive set of economic trends, having to do with increasing industrialization and the consequent formation of large cities with what were seen as their attendant social pathologies, set in motion a wide-ranging debate on the status of the young.

As a result of those discussions, there were two separate strands of social policy that evolved with the dawning of the twentieth century. On the one hand, there was a fundamental transformation and expansion of such developmental institutions as schools and training organizations. This was a time of tremendous expansion of educational and vocational training agencies, the purposes of which were the positive development of the social capacities of young people (although, to be sure, it can be argued that there were strong themes of discipline and control contained within these, especially around questions of the futures of working-class youth).

On the other hand, a response to the heightened perception of social problems concerning "youth in the street" resulted in the formation of new forms of children's and juvenile courts and, with these, training schools and correctional programs aimed specifically at the rehabilitation of young offenders. Thus, new forms of control institutions were put into place that were premised in alterations of the criminal law that would enable the criminal justice system to accommodate the particular demands of dealing with young offenders.

What is distinctive about comparing the general two-pronged strategy of a century ago with the present crisis of abandoned youth is the virtual absence of any systematic attempts to address in a positive way the development needs of the abandoned youth. Unlike with the previous crisis, there are no major new educational initiatives being put in place, nor are there new vocational or work preparation programs being proposed and implemented. Instead, the public policy debate has been increasingly dominated by a focus on social control solutions to "youth problems." It is this context that must be considered as a major frame for the debate on restorative justice for young people.

Do we need a two-pronged strategy that is analogous to what happened a century ago? There are new problems among young people that are crying out for new patterns of education and training. Huge populations of young people throughout the developed world are leaving school at an early age, and because of rapid and devastating changes that have taken place in the workplace, they find themselves abandoned by their communities, without the skills, experience, or qualifications necessary for a secure entrance into career work. Wholesale restructuring is called for if this crisis is to be addressed in a positive and developmental sense.

We need not fear that there is any chance of an absence of control strategies. We may not be able to find jobs, new forms of schooling, or new patterns of training for the abandoned young, but we are able to consistently elaborate on and expand our juvenile justice systems, creating new forms of correctional institutions. We continue to create devices such as boot camps, electronic monitoring, and the like, and— at the soft end of the system—restorative justice programs.

There is much to be commended in the rapid evolution of restorative justice. Independent of the particular time and place, restorative justice gives an emphasis to victims and the reconciliation of victims and offenders that has long been neglected in legal systems derived from the English Common Law. As an idea recognizing time and place, in environments such as the United States that have become distinctly punitive and deterrence-based in their philosophies, restorative justice can be seen as providing essential leadership both to expand the softer options of the justice system and to call attention to the needs of victims and young offenders and the obligations of communities to both of these groups (including the developmental needs of young offenders). Thus, as envisioned especially in the works of writers such as Bazemore, within the harsh policy climate of many American states, restorative justice is one of the few institutional sources of advocacy for the needs of young people and for the responsibilities of communities with respect to these needs.

From a theoretical point of view, however, it is important to step back and to recognize where we are and what is needed. The virtual collapse of employment and educational opportunities for young people attempting to leave schooling at an early age is fundamentally a developmental problem. While their abandonment may result in a wide-ranging set of conflict problems that eventually enter into the arena of juvenile justice, it is nothing short of tragic that our public policies seem to be exclusively based in control and coercion, even if some of that coercion is at the soft end as represented by restorative justice.

There can be no doubt that restorative justice is fundamentally about control and coercion. One can speak about "shame" and "reintegration," but these procedures are built upon social control institutions that derive their power from the coercion inherent in the criminal law, and from the stigma that is an institutional consequence of the operations of these institutions. One might argue, perhaps with reason in some instances, that restorative justice programs are less coercive and less stigmatizing than traditional methods, but as alternatives that derive from the justice system, their coercive and stigmatizing effects are manifest to those who undergo them.

In an ideal world, there would be a place for both expanded development options, such as new forms of training, and for new forms of restorative justice designed to address more effective forms of approaching offenders and victims. However, we live in times that are far from ideal, and it is the resulting conditions that must frame our analysis of the place of restorative justice within a framework of youth policy.

There are few advocates for abandoned youth. One of the strongest sources of advocacy resides precisely within the very system that poses a significant threat in terms of its potential for exceptional coercion. When it is argued that there is a large segment of youth that are abandoned, the reference point for the abandonment is the set of development institutions. These abandoned young people will not be abandoned by the justice system. Quite the opposite, the nature of the lifestyles of the young people, and the demands of the conventional society, will dictate the development of what can easily become a spiraling fabric of surveillance and control.

It will be agents within the justice system who see most clearly the nature of this problem and who then have much to gain by advocating more effective control strategies as well as movement within the developmental arena. Examine, for a moment, the language of one stream of theory of restorative justice concerned with reintegrative shaming.

Within this language, there is a major flaw given the present circumstance of abandoned youth. Simply put, how can you "reintegrate" individuals who have never had a chance to be "integrated" in the first place? If the process is to work, there ultimately must be a range of mechanisms put in place that assures that there is a caring context with a clear commitment to young people and their place in the community. Within this view, integration of young people is seen as a fundamental obligation of the total community.

Within at least some conceptions of restorative justice, there is a recognition of precisely this problem. When Bazemore elaborates a triangular scheme that discusses the reciprocal expectations and obligations between offenders, victims, and the community, one goal is to call attention to the important obligations that the community has— not only to provide a context for restoration in which the offender makes some form of amends to both victim and community but also to provide supports and opportunities so that the young offender can be assured of a place within the community as the restorative process moves to its successful conclusion (Bazemore, 1997).

In one way, it is not anomalous that the justice system, as part of restoration, takes on a wider task of participation in positive social change within developmental institutions. For many years, those working close to or within the justice system have been aware of the unfortunate readiness of many teachers and administrators within schools to treat some young people who are seen as "difficult students" as "throwaway" children, stating that they are unwilling to alter school process for the small percentage of troublesome young people when they feel they have scarce resources and time to address the needs of what they see as a great majority of "motivated" students. Many professionals, such as outreach workers and probation officers, have long understood that it is a personal disaster for those youngsters who are abandoned by the school system. Thus, they struggle both to advocate for some "negotiation room" for individual clients as well as for institutional alternatives that allow wider learning opportunities for those seen as troublesome (given they have the time and resources). Because restorative justice presumes that there will be a place to which the young person will return within the community, it is natural that restorative work will focus on assuring that there are ways to negotiate the re-entry of offenders back into institutions (such as school).

There are two theoretical problems that arise in this process. First, it is clear that as important as such negotiations are for the process of restoration, a worker located within the juvenile justice system has little in the way of power to negotiate with what are often closed bureaucratic systems (such as the schools), and in these times is not likely to be able to offer much in the way of resources as an inducement. Second, there is always the danger that the location of the restorative process within the coercive system of justice may mean that when collaborative work with other agencies (such as schools or youth service agencies) does occur, it may extend coercive control mechanisms into these developmental settings rather than expanding developmental choices.

Discussion

There is little doubt that there is worldwide interest in the topic of restorative justice, and that one of the major focal points of that interest is juvenile offending. Young people in the developed economies are thus going to be prime targets for restorative justice programs. In an ideal world there might be aggressive public policy directives aimed at changes in both developmental and legal/control institutions in responding to the youth problems that have emerged as a result of major economic trends. In fact, however, we are seeing a common problem that contemporary policy is focused on social control solutions.

Developmental and Social Control Strategies

What are the major social policy directives that might be advanced to deal with this problem of abandoned youth? Specifically, where do policies of restorative justice fit within such policies? The view taken here is that this new crisis is similar in many of its outline elements to the crisis that confronted developed nations as they moved into a mature phase of industrialization. The shift from extractive activity to factory-based employment changed in fundamental ways the shape of economic and social organization, impacting upon such diverse phenomena as land use patterns (the emergence of cities) and family life (with the new separation of work place and living place). That created a particular problem among the children of the new working-class communities, a problem of "idleness" (note the similarity here) that was solved by action on two fronts. On the social development side, new forms of educational and vocational training were put in place. This was the period that saw the emergence of broadly based public education, especially at the secondary level. On the "control" side (criminal justice agencies), this was the time of the emergence of new forms of courts for children, and the subsequent rapid spread of juvenile or children's courts throughout the English-speaking world.

What is distinctive about the present period is that the major approaches being taken throughout the developed world have progressively withdrawn from attempts to address needed changes in the development institutions involving schools and training, and instead are increasingly concentrating upon control solutions that are based on the manipulation of coercion. Put simply, youth policy increasingly concentrates on the juvenile justice system, rather than on schools, training, or jobs.

The argument offered in this chapter is that a coherent response to the problem of abandoned youth must (as was true a century ago) address both the developmental and the control aspects of the problem. This sets the backdrop for a discussion of restorative justice. In this author's view, there is no question about the importance of restorative justice. First, it can be argued that there is a need for a range of educational, training, and employment programs available to provide a diverse set of pathways (that do not now exist) that would provide the progressive mix of training, skill development, experience, and qualifications to make them eligible for jobs in a technologically developed economy. Second, the program should provide alternatives for re-entry routes into these structures for individuals who have "fallen out" of the institutional pathways. The creation of these is the responsibility of professionals within the developmental sector who work with public policymakers to establish new patterns for social development.

If there were a range of developmental options available, then the challenge of redrafting the procedures of social control within the boundaries of restorative justice might take forms remarkably close to what is described in Braithwaite's (1989) classic *Crime, Shame and Reintegration*. Clearly, "reintegration" as a concept presumes the possibility of "integration." Where adolescents have many opportunities for participation and integration into mainstream activities of the community and school, then when there are violations of norms it makes good sense to speak of a process that makes clear (for instance, through an exercise such as shaming) that such violations are not to be taken lightly. Then the youngster's demonstrated commitment to being a part of the community is reinforced through a reintegrative process.

The abandoned youth of today, however, are far from being integrated. They are at the margins of our schools and neighborhoods (if, indeed, they are in schools at all). They do not see themselves as participants in the community. They read their abandonment as a statement of the low value placed on their existence by the wider community. Further, they see the juvenile justice system as one of the major instruments reinforcing the message of abandonment.

The past decade has only served to further this oppositional view of juvenile justice. Throughout the developed world, we have seen the political furor over crime, and then the implementation of such ideas and programs as "three strikes and you're out," "zero tolerance," "electronic surveillance," "Scared Straight," and "boot camps," to mention but a few. As popular as these might be to the conservative leaders of the community, they speak a powerful message of rejection to the highly marginalized young.

Restorative Justice in Context

All of this comprises the context within which we encounter restorative justice. It is a set of strategies that have their origins in the justice system. In its actual manifestations, it will have as key actors persons connected to justice agencies. It carries with it the coercive sanctions of the criminal courts, and these are an important part of the "choices" that young people encounter as they confront restorative justice. However we soften the labels, there will be institutional consequences in terms of the inherently stigmatizing labels that are attached to experiences within the justice system. In short, restorative justice is a justice process, and as such, it shares with other parts of the justice system a basis in the coercion of the criminal law.

In my view, we are at a crossroads with restorative justice. One path (what may be the most popular) is to conceive of restorative justice narrowly, focusing on its capacity to expand (at times in interesting and innovative ways) its control capacity by creating new processes that involve agents of the justice system, offenders and their representatives, and victims and their representatives in some form of conflict negotiation. As important as these efforts may be, there is a grave danger that such programs for abandoned youth are merely one more layer of social control, one that widens the reach and capacity of the justice system to engage in coercive control over the troublesome and law-violating behavior of the new class of abandoned youth.

The other path is to conceptualize restorative justice in a wider framework of social justice, linking restorative procedures aimed at deviant young people to patterns of institutional change that widen the developmental opportunities for young people generally. There is both tradition and guidance behind such an approach to restorative justice. In the 1960s, such community change efforts as "Mobilization for Youth" were explicitly aimed at expanding opportunity structures for working-class adolescents as part of community programs of delinquency prevention and control. In the years when diversion was popular, some attempted to provide a national strategy that emphasized the importance of providing all young people with opportunities to engage in responsible and meaningful social roles in the community. Some who write about restorative justice, such as Bazemore, attempt to focus part of that discussion on the reciprocal responsibilities of communities to the needs of both victims and offenders in the conceptualization of the restorative process.

These are not good times. Few governments seem able or willing to address successfully the deepening crisis of youth abandonment. Instead, justice systems, are moving in the direction of increasing punitiveness, as indicated by persistently increasing sizes of prison populations. Whether we like it or not, these facts serve as boundaries for what we do under the banner of restorative justice. This chapter has tried to underscore the danger that restorative justice, narrowly conceived, may easily become simply one more of the ever-expanding social control mechanisms that governments reach for in the absence of positive solutions for the plight of abandoned young people. The alternative is to insist that restorative justice be conceptualized as part of a wider social justice agenda, and that some emphasis of restoration be given to positive community change in such developmental arenas as schools, employment training, and recreation. Those who work closely with disenfranchised young people know well the pattern of dejection, hopelessness, and despair that is so common among them. These are not young people who are in any sense "integrated." They are often homeless, have no connection or hope of a connection with schooling, and are even ignored by most training institutions. To speak of their "reintegration" is nonsense. In this author's view, the issue is clear. Where social justice is absent, the imposition of any form of criminal justice process, including restorative justice, is no less than the imposition of coercion by the powerful on the powerless. We believe we can do better than that.

Discussion Questions

1. What problems in the social position of young people make restorative justice an incomplete strategy from a social justice perspective? Do you agree that lack of integration of young people makes restorative community justice strategies for integration impractical?

2. In Polk's view, why are restorative justice responses, or any criminal justice responses, limited in scope?

3. What macro or socioeconomic forces have produced youth abandonment? What is needed to address these problems? Can restorative justice help? Should it?

References

Ballinger, J. (1992). "The New Free Trade Heel: Nike's Profits Jump on the Backs of Asian Workers." *Harper's Magazine* (August):46-47.

Bazemore, G. (1997). "What's New About the Balanced Approach?" *The Juvenile and Family Court Journal* 48:1-23.

Bazemore, G., and M. Umbreit (1995). "Rethinking the Sanctioning Function in Juvenile Court: Retributive or Restorative Responses to Youth Crime." *Crime & Delinquency* 41:296-316.

Boss, P., S. Edwards, and S. Pitman (1995). *Profile of Young Australians: Facts, Figures and Issues.* Melbourne: Churchill Livingstone.

Braithwaite, J. (1989). *Crime, Shame and Reintegration.* Cambridge, England: Cambridge University Press.

Bluestone, B., and B. Harrison (1982). *The Deindustrialization of America: Plant Closings, Community Abandonment, and the Dismantling of Basic Industry.* New York: Basic Books.

Centre for Labour Studies (1997). *Regional Youth Unemployment Profile—1988-96,* (1). Adelaide: Centre for Labour Studies, University of Adelaide.

Cunneen, C., and R. White (1995). *Juvenile Justice: An Australian Perspective.* Melbourne: Oxford University Press.

Dusseldorp Skills Forum (1998). *Australia's Youth: Reality and Risk.* Sydney: Dusseldorp Skills Forum and Others.

Duster, T. (1995). "Post-Industrialism and Youth Unemployment." In *Poverty, Inequality and the Future of Social Policy: Western States in the New World Order,* edited by K. McFate, R. Lawson, and W.J. Wilson, 461-486. New York: Russell Sage.

Dwyer, P. (1995). "Disjunction Between Pathways Policy and Student Outcomes: Experience of Early School Leavers." *Australian Journal of Education* 39:265-278.

Dwyer, P. (1996). *Opting Out: Early School Leavers and the Degeneration of Youth Policy.* Hobart, Australia: National Clearinghouse for Youth Studies.

Empey, L.T. (1982). *American Delinquency: Its Meaning and Construction.* Belmont, CA: Wadsworth.

Fell, M. (1996). "Why Car Policy is Up the Wrong Street." *The Age* (19 December, 1996):C-1.

Fell, M. (1997). "Holden's Hamel Years." *The Age* (27 January, 1997):B-1.

Freeman, K. (1996). "Young People and Crime." *Crime and Justice Bulletin* 32. Sydney: NSW Bureau of Crime Statistics and Research.

Glenday, D. (1996). "Mean Streets and Hard Time: Youth Unemployment and Crime." In *Not a Kid Anymore: Canadian Youth, Crime and Subcultures,* edited by G.M. O'Bireck, 147-174. Toronto: Nelson Canada.

Graycar, A., and A. Jamrozik (1989). *How Australians Live: Social Policy in Theory and Practice.* Melbourne: Macmillan.

Gregory, R., and B. Hunter (1995). *The Macro Economy and the Growth of Ghettos and Urban Poverty in Australia.* Canberra: Discussion Paper No. 325, Centre for Economic Policy Research, Australian National University.

Johnston, E. (1991). *National Report, Royal Commission into Aboriginal Deaths in Custody,* Vols. 1-5. Canberra: Australian Government Publishing Service.

Kapstein, E. (1996). "Workers and the World Economy." *Foreign Affairs* (May/June):15-37.

Landt, J., and P. Scott (1998). "Youth Incomes." In *Australia's Youth: Reality and Risk.* Sydney: Dusseldorp Skills Forum and Others.

Miles, S., D. Cliff, and V. Burr (1998). "'Fitting In and Sticking Out': Consumption, Consumer Meanings and the Construction of Young People's Identities." *Journal of Youth Studies* 1(1):81-96.

Miller, J.G. (1996). *Search and Destroy: African-American Males in the Criminal Justice System.* New York: Cambridge University Press.

Moss, I. (1993). *State of the Nation: A Report on People of Non-English Speaking Background.* Canberra: Australian Government Publishing Service.

Moynihan, J., and C. Coleman (1996). "Unemployment and Crime." *New Law Journal* (27 September):1382-1384.

Pearl, A., D. Grant, and E. Wenk (1978). *The Value of Youth: A Call for A National Youth Policy.* Davis, CA: Responsibility Action Press.

Platt, A. (1969). *The Child Savers.* Chicago: University of Chicago Press.

Polk, K. (1987). "When Less Means More: An Analysis of Destructuring in Criminal Justice." *Crime & Delinquency* 33:358-378.

Polk, K. (1988). "Education, Youth Unemployment and Student Resistance." In *Discipline and Schools: A Curriculum Perspective,* edited by R. Slee, 109-131. Melbourne: Macmillan Australia.

Polk, K. (1994). *When Men Kill: Scenarios of Masculine Violence.* Melbourne: Cambridge University Press.

Polk, K. (1997). "The Crisis of Youth Abandoned." In *Juvenile Delinquency in Australia,* edited by A. Borowski and I. O'Connor, 489-501. Sydney: Methuen (1997).

Polk, K., and W. Schafer (1972). *Schools and Delinquency.* Englewood Cliffs, NJ: Prentice Hall.

Reiss, A. (1986). "Why Are Communities Important in Understanding Crime?" In *Communities and Crime,* edited by A. Reiss and M. Tonry. Chicago: University of Chicago Press.

Schur, E.M. (1973). *Radical Nonintervention: Rethinking the Delinquency Problem.* Englewood Cliffs, NJ: Prentice Hall.

Spiering, J. (1995). *Young Australians in the Working Nation: A Review of Youth Employment Policies for the 1990s.* Adelaide: Social Justice Research Foundation.

Spoehr, J. (1997). "Alternatives to Despair—Reflections on the Youth Employment Policy Debate." *Australian Options,* No. 9:2-6.

Stratton, J. (1992). *The Young Ones: Working-Class Culture, Consumption and the Category of Youth.* Perth: Black Swan Press.

Sweet, R. (1998). "Youth: The Rhetoric and the Reality of the 1990s." In *Australia's Youth: Reality and Risk.* Sydney: Dusseldorp Skills Forum and Others.

Vinson, T., M. Abela, and R. Hutka (1997). *Making Ends Meet: A Study of Unemployed Young People Living in Sydney.* Uniya Research Report No.1. Sydney: Uniya Jesuit Social Justice Centre.

Watts, R. (1996)." Unemployment, The Underclass and Crime in Australia: A Critique." *Australian and New Zealand Journal of Criminology* 29:1-19.

Weatherburn, D. (1992). *Economic Adversity and Crime.* Trends and Issues in Crime and Criminal Justice No.40. Canberra: Australian Institute of Criminology.

White, R. (1990). *No Space of Their Own: Young People and Social Control in Australia.* Melbourne: Cambridge University Press.

White, R. (1997). "Young People, Waged Work and Exploitation." *Journal of Australian Political Economy* 40:61-79.

White, R., with M. Aumair, A. Harris, and L. McDonnell (1997). *Any Which Way You Can: Youth Livelihoods, Community Resources and Crime.* Sydney: Australian Youth Foundation.

Wikstrom, P.H. (1995). "Preventing City-Centre Street Crimes." In *Building a Safer Society: Strategic Approaches to Crime Prevention,* edited by M. Tonry and D.P. Farrington, 429-468. Chicago: University of Chicago Press.

Wood, L. (1997). "Hoechst to Quit Plastics Industry." *The Age* (30 January 1997):B-1.

Wooden, M. (1996). "The Youth Labour Market: Characteristics and Trends. *The Australian Bulletin of Labour* 22:137-160.

Wyn, J., and R. White (1997). *Rethinking Youth.* Sydney: Allen & Unwin.

13

Restorative Justice, Social Justice, and the Empowerment of Marginalized Populations

KAY PRANIS

Introduction

Serious and important challenges have been raised to the restorative justice movement concerning its capacity to impact structural inequalities that are seen as causal factors in the incidence of crime. Because factors such as racism and poverty are outside the control of individual offenders, holding offenders accountable for individual harm, without accountability for the harms of social inequalities, risks reinforcing an unjust social order.

This author believes that restorative justice has the potential to advance social justice concerns. However, effectiveness in addressing social inequities will depend upon clear ties between values and practice and upon open lines of communication for continual feedback from those who do not have equal access to resources and power.

The critique that restorative justice has not addressed these issues has frequently referred to the lack of literature on the subject as evidence of failure (Arrigo and Schehr, 1998; Immarigeon, 1999). However, academics have not been primary leaders in the development of restorative justice philosophy, and restorative justice literature generally lags two years behind the 'healing edge' (Zehr, 1998) of restorative practice and the current state of dialog in the field. At the level of practice, there is an ongoing exploration of the challenges and possibilities of impacting structural inequities.

It is very clear to practitioners that restorative justice efforts alone cannot resolve social inequities, but that many community-based initiatives have the potential to shift power to allow for more inclusive decisionmaking and more meaningful and just relationships. Over time the cumulative effect of those shifts at the micro level can make a significant contribution to social justice. Paradoxically, crime is generating opportunities to understand and practice democracy in the community in ways that build community and increase grassroots power. It has become clear that creating safe communities requires active citizen involvement. Such involvement means re-engaging all citizens in the process of determining shared norms, holding one another accountable to those norms, and determining how best to resolve breaches of the norms in a way that does not increase risk in the community.

Principles of Restorative Justice and the Relationship to Social Justice Issues

Social justice seeks equal consideration for the well-being and wholeness of all community members—socially, emotionally, economically, physically, and spiritually. Well-being requires being able to meet one's needs without harm to others and being able to exercise control in one's life. Personal power and a sense of personal efficacy, exercised with respect for the needs of others, play an important role in individual well-being, and likewise in realizing advances toward social justice.

The fundamental values of the restorative justice framework have much in common with social justice values. Restorative justice affirms the worth of every individual and insists that no human being is a "throw-away." Restorative justice asserts that one of the functions of a community is to promote the well-being of all its members, and recognizes that a community is responsible for all its members.

A core restorative justice principle is direct participation by key stakeholders in decisions affecting them. Van Ness's second principle of restorative justice calls for active involvement of victims, offenders, and communities in the justice process as early and as fully as possible (Van Ness and Strong, 1997). Direct participation and the exercise of power in decisions affecting one's life are essential elements of a just social order and are at the center of restorative justice.

Restorative justice emphasizes the importance of both individual accountability and collective accountability. Individuals are responsible for choices they make resulting in harm to others, but collectives at the neighborhood, city, county, state, or national level are responsible for social conditions that increase the likelihood of crime. "Mutual responsibility is the loom on which the fabric of community is woven. Crime represents a failure of responsibility—often on many levels, individual, family, and community. Our response to crime must strengthen or build relationships and emphasize and reestablish mutual responsibility on all levels . . . based on a pattern of answering to and for one another" (Pranis, 2000).

Restorative justice practice seems to be encouraging a concept of community based on voluntary commitments beyond the self that honor both individual and group needs and that allow those most impacted by crime and injustice to determine the content of commitments (Pranis, 2000). This is neither the rampant individualism of modern Western culture nor the mindless obedience of highly controlled cultures. Such communities can provide fertile ground to raise and address social justice concerns.

A restorative community is a community that embraces those who have been harmed and those who have caused harm. A restorative community is one that uses the event of a crime as an opportunity to strengthen the community, to deepen understanding of one another, and to build caring relationships. A restorative community is a learning community, a community that learns about itself from those who have been hurt and those who have caused hurt, and uses that learning to improve community life for all.

Inclusiveness, equality, community responsibility, fair treatment, and all stakeholders having a voice in decisionmaking are values that are common to both restorative justice and social justice. Restorative justice practices that are genuinely based on those values will naturally support social justice.

Restorative Processes: Grassroots Democracy at Work

> "Practicing social democracy—that's what I contend circles are."
>
> Darrol Bussler, former victim and founder of the
> South St. Paul Restorative Justice Council

Those in the United States are educated to think of themselves as practicing the ultimate form of democracy. It is assumed that Americans have already arrived at and understand the full implications of the concept of democracy—and that democracy is defined as majority rule with protection of individual rights. Americans have been taught that their democratic process is superior to all others. That belief is embedded so early and so deeply that it is rarely questioned.

Limitations of Majority Rule

However, a closer examination of majority-rule democracy reveals several problems. When democracy is defined as majority rule, the interests of minority groups may not be addressed at all. Their rights may be protected, but their interests may be completely ignored. Majority rule allows those in the majority to be cavalier about minority interests. Power becomes a numbers game. If you want your interests met, you must bring more people to the decision-making process. If your position has the larger numbers, there is little incentive to seek common ground or ways that the interests of all might be served. In fact, if you can outvote the other position, you do not need to understand that position.

Majority-rule decisionmaking often leaves a significant number of groups and individuals feeling left out, alienated, and resentful because no attempt was made to understand their needs or to meet those needs, even though the group may represent a substantial part of the citizenry. Majority-rule decisionmaking also encourages parties to exaggerate their differences and to belittle or denigrate other positions in order to recruit more supporters. That process increases the barriers between different perspectives and undermines the likelihood of a united effort toward policy implementation after a decision is made. It does not build a sense of mutual commitment to the welfare of all community members.

Under majority rule, voting is typically viewed as the primary way of exercising democratic responsibility and power. Yet, voting power is very limited in its ability to reflect the complexity of public interests and needs, and it places little responsibility on citizens for the quality of day-to-day life. Restorative justice invites a broader view of democracy by involving citizens in decision-making processes that allow interaction and reflection, thus capturing nuanced understandings of the issues at hand and engaging citizens in concrete responsibility for some aspect of community life.

In order to have strong, cohesive communities, it is important for all legitimate interests to be understood and addressed—and for them to be addressed in a voluntary, collaborative process, not through an adversarial, rights-driven process. To gain commitment for the hard work of devising and implementing solutions to difficult problems, everyone must feel included, respected, and served by the process and the solution. It stands to reason that someone whose interests were not addressed in the solution will feel no obligation to make the solution work.

Deference to professional expertise has contributed over the past three decades to a redistribution of power from neighborhoods to government and private social services (Bazemore, 1999; McKnight, 1995). Restorative processes—which give equal weight to the wisdom and contributions of the immediate parties, their family members, and citizens—seek to reverse this trend and return decision-making power to families and neighborhoods.

Strengths of Consensus Processes

As consensus-based processes, most restorative justice decision-making models require respectful interactions and relationships and *necessitate* gaining an understanding of the needs and interests of all parties. Consensus decisions involve the endorsement of the decision by all parties. Endorsement does not necessarily imply enthusiastic support, but it does mean a willingness to accept the decision because it addresses one's needs at some level, or because sincere attempts were made to understand and meet those needs. Consequently, consensus decisions are more likely to incorporate multiple perspectives and meet multiple needs. Consensus processes, which involve listening carefully to all positions in order to find the common ground and devise solutions serving many interests, are fundamentally more democratic because the decisions are representative of more people.

In addition to producing decisions meeting more interests, consensus processes also encourage greater participation by all parties in making decisions and in subsequent action. On the one hand, if you believe your interests will be ignored or treated disrespectfully, there is little reason to participate. Lack of participation not only leaves out voices of the community but also reduces the potential resources the community may draw on to solve difficult problems. On the other hand, decisions or plans that address the interests of all participants have a far greater likelihood of success because every participant has something to gain by successful completion of the agreement; that is, every participant has a stake in success. In processes based on majority rule, the minority group often has a stake in the failure of a decision in which they feel they had no voice.

Consensus decisionmaking is not an easy fix to the problems of majority rule. Consensus decisionmaking takes more time up front, depends upon clear communication, may create undue pressure on dissenters, and is easily misunderstood as a right to hold out for your position rather than an obligation to understand others' needs and contribute to a positive alternative. Though it is not an easy process and the skills required are not yet well developed in our communities, it promises possibilities of more complete representation of interests.

Consensus, Indigenous Justice, and Circles Several processes emerging from tribal and ancient cultures, and embraced by the restorative justice movement, use consensus decisionmaking that allows all interested parties to have a voice in decisions. The two characteristics—(1) inclusion of all parties who claim a stake in the outcome, and (2) consensus-based decisionmaking—push our concept of democracy to a new frontier. Consensus-based processes give power to all participants because participation is open to all affected individuals. Achieving consensus requires that the group pay attention to the interests of those who are normally powerless. In order for consensus to be achieved, decisions must ultimately represent everyone involved. The use of consensus processes for resolving crimes means that the victim, the offender, their families, and the affected community will all have a voice in making decisions.

Family group conferencing, based on a Maori tradition for resolving conflict, and the peacemaking circle process, based on the talking circle tradition of North American native peoples, both use consensus decisionmaking and allow participation by affected parties. Both processes have been adapted for use in resolving crime in a variety of ethnic and geographic communities in Western countries.

The peacemaking circle process, developed in Yukon, Canada (Stuart, 1996), and adopted with local variations in several Minnesota communities, provides a clear example of the potential of a new vision of democracy for community problem-solving. The peacemaking circle process is used to support victims, to encourage offenders to make amends and change behavior, and to determine how to best address the underlying problems (of the individual and the community) associated with the crime. Circles are open to all interested parties. Those who attend are encouraged to speak and are expected to participate in decisionmaking. The opportunity to be heard and the responsibility to contribute to a good solution go hand in hand. Because decisions in the circle process are based on consensus, everyone in the process has an equal voice—including the judge, the offender, the victim, the prosecutor, the defense attorney, family members of key participants, and any community member who attends. Decisions must be acceptable to everyone; therefore they must address the interests of everyone to some degree.

Equal Voice and Equal Responsibility In addition to the use of consensus, several aspects of the circle process reinforce the democratic ideal of equal voice and equal responsibility. Structurally, sitting in a circle conveys a message of equality to participants. Titles are not used in the circle process, thus minimizing institutional authority as a relevant element of decisionmaking. A talking piece, rather than a mediator, chairperson, or facilitator, is used to structure the dialogue. Participants may only speak when holding the talking piece, which is passed clockwise around the circle in order to provide an opportunity for every participant to speak. The talking piece creates space for the ideas of participants who would otherwise find it difficult to insert themselves into the usual dialog process. In the circle process it is assumed that everyone present has something to contribute to the resolution of the problem. The use of the talking piece reduces the responsibility of the facilitator and increases the responsibility of every participant to guide the dialog toward a good end. Every participant in the circle is encouraged to draw on his or her life experience in order to add to the understanding of the problem and to generate possible solutions. Every life story has relevance to finding a resolution that facilitates healing for all those affected by the crime.

Redistribution of Power and Accountability

Victims and offenders and their supporters frequently are part of the most disenfranchised groups in society. They typically lack access to power over social or economic resources and often feel powerless over major forces shaping their lives. Restorative consensus processes can give voice and respect (and, therefore, personal power) to these individuals. The use of a consensus process that can bring together some of the most disempowered citizens and neighborhoods in encounters with the most powerful players of the criminal justice system is slowly creating a redistribution of power at a grassroots level.

In a reversal of the usual power dynamics, as part of a peacemaking circle project in North Minneapolis working with African-American adolescents, several judges now defer to community members who are active in the project concerning processes and dispositions used with the juveniles involved in the circle. When a probation officer was asked what he was doing with a particular juvenile, he responded, "I'm waiting for the circle to tell me what it wants me to do." In a circle project in a diverse neighborhood of St. Paul, community members of the circle respectfully, but firmly, confronted a judge when they felt he had made decisions without consulting them. Participants feel genuine ownership and power to hold professional systems accountable. Because this happened in the presence of the offender, it sent a powerful message about accountability at all levels—regardless of status.

The energy generated by concern about crime can be channeled into processes that increase democratic participation in a process focused ultimately on creating strong communities that are capable of taking responsibility for the welfare of all members, including victims and offenders. This development of grassroots democratic processes is a significant contribution of restorative justice to advancing social justice. These restorative processes constitute grassroots democracy in a form that does not pit groups against one another but instead, through consensus, builds a sense of shared commitment and collaboration. Consensus-building encourages cooperation with all other interests and the pursuit of balanced interests for oneself and the larger community, and it ensures that no one leaves the table with their interest ignored (Pranis, 2000).

"Personal Problems" as Collective Issues: Creating Spaces for Community Dialogue and Problem-Solving

> "We need to take on those people's problems as if they are our own."
>
> Probation officer participating in a circle sentence

Nurturing Community Dialog

The fundamental principles and values of restorative justice are being applied to create new avenues for community dialog. Respectful treatment of all views, deep listening to understand the perspective of others, acceptance of emotions as valid—all of these characteristics of restorative dialog produce interactions that do not degenerate immediately into hard ideological positions. People are more likely to alter their opinion if they have first felt heard and respected. Restorative dialog avoids the polarization common in so much of the discussion about social justice issues, a polarization that has not served social justice advocates well.

Processes that allow community members to discuss and reflect upon possible connections between the crime and social conditions raise awareness and may begin the formation of strategies to address the problem. Peacemaking circle discussions about individual crimes often become discussions about general problems, as the process organically links individual criminal incidents with larger social issues of the community, the state, or the nation. Circles provide a forum for problem-solving to prevent crimes in the future—a forum that operates on core principles of democracy, inclusion, equality, and respect.

Citizens are more likely to become engaged by a concrete problem perceived to have an immediate impact on their lives than around a generalized concern about community health or social problems. Restorative justice creates opportunities to link specific problems, especially crimes, to larger issues by dealing with those incidents in a contextual way, by providing those most affected with meaningful roles in resolving the problems, and by conducting the dialog in a different way.

When community members become involved in resolving crimes, they rarely view each event as isolated and related only to those individuals directly involved. Unless confined by the process to a narrow response, community members typically draw connections to other problems in the community or patterns of community life. Community members are interested in the whole picture and often wish to address broader problems that they see as related to the criminal event.

Making the Links to Larger Community Responsibility

Participation in a conferencing project in downtown Minneapolis raised awareness among white community members of the struggles of Somali immigrants in their neighborhood and resulted in outreach efforts by the neighborhood organization to the Somali community. Working with an offender who was caught in a cycle of inability to pay fines in several counties, arrest warrants and then additional fines as sanction for nonpayment, members of a rural community raised questions with the judge about the appropriateness of the fines. In the process of working with 12 juveniles in a vandalism case, a suburban community became aware of the need for youth to have a place to hang out and subsequently developed more structured activities for adolescents in the community. A circle project in a rural community piloted a peace camp for adolescents to respond to concerns about racism toward Native Americans in the schools.

In a sentencing circle for a domestic abuse case in Yukon, Canada, five women in the circle talked about their own experience with abuse, which was not related to the particular offender being handled. The circle raised the question of what was wrong with the community that so many women have experienced abuse. The process facilitated exploration of broader underlying causes of the problem beyond that individual offender.

In an upper-middle-class suburb of St. Paul, an adolescent girl was charged with marijuana possession. Initially, the mother could not believe her daughter could be involved with drugs. In the family group conferencing process, which this city uses for all diversion cases, the mother was confronted with the reality of her daughter's use of drugs. The mother became concerned about the role of the broader community context in her daughter's behavior. She suggested to the police department that there was a need for a community-wide dialog on shared values and community standards to communicate clear boundaries to the young people of the community. The police department worked with her to organize a process called "Focus on Community United by Shared Values," which aims to establish a committed relationship between the youth and adults of the city and to focus on developing the character and capabilities of both young and old people to be responsible members of the community.

Increasing the Sense of Community Capacity

In spite of difficulties with the offender, participants in one peace-making circle project in a diverse inner-city community expressed confidence that through this process the community will be strengthened. In the words of one community member, "What's most important here is the community coming together. The details of how we do it are not as important as the community doing something." Use of the circle process as a response to crime has increased participants' sense of their ability to address difficult community problems.

In a suburban community, a large group of neighbors used the family group conferencing process to resolve a case of juvenile delinquency without professional help. Previous experience by one resident in the process inspired the confidence to do it on their own. Their resolution included responsibilities not just for the delinquent youth but also other juveniles and adults in the neighborhood.

The lack of spaces for reflective conversations about individual struggles and community life has hampered development of comprehensive solutions to larger social problems. The use of restorative processes is filling a void in community life by encouraging expression of new and often unexpected perspectives reflecting collective responsibility. For example, a police officer talking about the circle process said, "We are all on trial in that circle." A probation officer stated, "We need to hear. We need to take on those people's problems as if they are our own." Restorative processes are creating both the opportunities to bring people together and the formats that encourage respectful and reflective dialog about community issues, leading to a broader recognition of underlying causes of crime, a sense of responsibility about those causes, and a sense of potential to change those conditions.

Social Distance: The Enemy of Social Justice

Social distance is a key factor in public support for punitive responses to such issues as welfare mothers, increasing use of incarceration, hostility to affirmative action, and other public policies inimical to social justice concerns. Most people never expect such policies to affect their own lives; therefore, they do not reflect deeply on what they would want or need for themselves and their families in similar circumstances. When they are touched closely in their personal lives, their beliefs about public policy are often profoundly changed.

Social distance is the degree to which people do not identify with other community members or do not feel connected by common interests or a sense of common fate. Social distance is when we cannot imagine ourselves in the other person's shoes, cannot feel the other person's pain, or cannot experience another person as a full human being. The more separated people feel from each other, the easier it is to harm the other or to turn away from the other's pain. Because it is sustained by barriers—physical, social, emotional, or spiritual—between human beings, social distance crumbles in the presence of authentic ways of connecting.

Citizens whose lives include no personal contact with people of color, poor people, or those struggling at the margins of society are vulnerable to images shaped by talk shows, news broadcasts, and television dramas. Questions of the impact of social policy on those lives are abstract questions; they have no real human context. The greater the social distance between individuals or groups, the less investment people have in one another's well-being. Increasing numbers of people live and work in economically homogeneous suburbs. Young people growing up in suburbs may never experience a personal encounter with peers who are poor or in very different circumstances. An Irish-American law professor at the University of Wisconsin in Madison tells of students who look at him as though he is from Mars when he tells them he grew up in the Bronx. It seems beyond their comprehension that folks who live in the Bronx could be so much like them.

The processes of restorative justice, particularly face-to-face processes, involve the telling of personal stories in an intimate setting. Stereotypes and broad generalizations about groups of people are difficult to sustain in the face of direct contact with an individual in a respectful setting. Restorative processes assume value in every human being and thus present individuals to one another in a way that draws out human dignity in everyone. Victim-offender dialog, family group conferencing, community panels, and peacemaking circles all involve face-to-face opportunities for telling personal narratives that humanize all participants. These processes not only help resolve the particular incident, they also reframe the relationships of all parties because of a shared commitment to positive outcomes and mutual responsibility. Restorative processes break down social distance between participants—victims, offenders, their families, community members, and criminal justice system professionals.

In addition to the use of face-to-face decision-making processes, restorative justice also reduces social distance by encouraging side-by-side community service work involving offenders and community members. Working with others to, in the words of Dennis Maloney, "ease the suffering of others" creates common interests, connections, and relationships that dismantle community members' stereotypes about offenders and offenders' stereotypes about other community members. Social distance is reduced. Understanding of other perspectives on life is increased; tolerance of differences is increased. It is more difficult to support policies or decisions that are harmful to another when you are looking that person in the eye in a setting that allows you to experience that person as a human being. Personal narratives are a powerful way to reduce social distance, to recast the "other" as one of "us" and, in so doing, see our fates intertwined. As Andre Codrescu has observed: "face to face one tries to find one's better nature because one can see the soul."

Commitment to the Common Good: The Ally of Social Justice

Social justice concerns are generally advanced when there is an increased commitment by individual citizens to the common good. Restorative justice values encourage awareness of connections and interdependence among all members of society. Restorative justice mechanisms provide opportunities for individuals to take action based on that awareness.

For two decades, the climate of public discourse has often been one of intimidation and ridicule of those speaking for compassion or for collective responsibility for the welfare of all. The airwaves often have been so dominated by the voices of hate, intolerance, and selfish interests that it has appeared that there is scant interest in becoming involved in the problems of others in a helpful way. Contrary to that perception, the experience of developing restorative processes in communities indicates the existence of a deep untapped reservoir of concern and willingness to help others for the good of all.

The peacemaking circle process is demonstrating not only that a more democratic form of decisionmaking is possible but that a more caring form of decisionmaking is also possible. Many citizens are willing to devote time and provide support and caring to victims and offenders who need help. In six communities in Minnesota, the circle process has been introduced as a possible option for dealing with certain criminal offenses. The typical approach is to hold a series of open community meetings to explain the process and answer questions. At these meetings, those attending are asked why they are present. The responses to that question have been very moving. Many people express a desire to help others and to build a healthy community and a willingness to give time and resources to achieve that. Those experiences suggest that the circle process is providing a safe place for citizens to express values of compassion and caring for marginalized people. Restorative processes are breaking down some of the barriers that have for the past 20 years disempowered individuals who wished to act for the common good but did not know how to offer their gifts to the larger whole. Drawn by a sense of mutual responsibility and shared fate, citizens are committing themselves to helping others in large and small ways.

Shifting Power from Professionals to Citizens

The concentration of power and influence in the hands of professionals to identify and determine solutions to problems of individuals and communities has not served social justice interests because it undermines democracy and encourages dependency. Dependency erodes the sense of personal power and personal efficacy necessary for social justice. As John McKnight observes:

> A preliminary hypothesis is that services that are heavily focused on deficiency tend to be pathways out of community and into the exclusion of serviced life. We need a rigorous examination of public investments so that we can distinguish between services that lead people out of community and into dependency and those that support people in community life. (1995:20)

In both philosophy and practice, restorative justice emphasizes the capacity of ordinary folks to identify and solve their own problems. The role of government systems and agencies is to provide structure, support, and resources. Restorative justice calls for a transformation in the relationship between communities and professional systems, returning authority and legitimacy to communities as long as communities honor values of fairness, equity, and due process.

Restorative justice processes are built on the belief that individuals and communities need to own their own conflicts and struggles and that the dominance of professional responses in criminal justice has deprived communities of important opportunities to gain skills and create healthier communities.

Approaching Social Justice from a Restorative Paradigm: Strategic Differences

Because restorative justice efforts are based on accountability in a context of caring, both at an individual and societal level, the challenge to the current social order may appear "soft," but restorative justice holds that "power with" is more effective than "power over" for long-term change in behavior.

Traditional social justice activism often involves confrontational approaches to advancing social justice issues. That approach is sometimes adversarial, involves emphasizing the distance or "otherness" of those who hold different views, is often framed around abstract intellectual questions of rights, and may seek to achieve its agenda through power over opposing forces. Restorative justice includes concerns about social justice issues but relates to those issues in a different way. Restorative justice holds a vision of mutual responsibility for the welfare of everyone and uses personal narratives in a nonconfrontational exchange to build from individual experiences to an understanding of broader social needs or harms.

Social justice issues are frequently pursued in terms of rights, but if rights do not translate into increased well-being on an individual level, then social justice is not achieved. Pursuit of rights relies on a legal framework to achieve the desired outcome. That is a strategy, not an end in itself. Often, however, the establishment of rights is treated as the end and the ultimate well-being of individuals is lost in the process. Moral commitments are a better foundation for ensuring the well-being of others than legal requirements. Terry O'Connell, a pioneer in developing family group conferencing in Australia, asserts, "A legal threat undermines a moral commitment." Moral commitments are internally driven and self-regulating, while legal requirements are externally driven and require some kind of enforcement. Legal remedies must, by their nature, be created to deliver the minimum acceptable behavior, while approaches engaging on a moral level can strive to deliver the maximum behavior.

The establishment of rights is symbolically crucial as a legal formulation of a moral imperative. Coercive rights enforcement remains an important last-recourse strategy when appeals based on respectful, nonconfrontational dialog have failed repeatedly. While we are still reliant on coercive interventions to ensure adherence to certain standards, restorative justice affirms a preference for noncoercive relationships. Both legal and moral influences on behavior are important in promoting social justice outcomes, but we have depended much more heavily on legal forces to achieve social justice. Restorative justice is attempting to engage the moral authority of communities toward similar goals in ways that are inclusive of every point of view.

The core values of restorative justice call for respectful treatment of all, including those we might deem responsible for social injustice. Restorative justice presumes that harm to one is harm to all, and so we cannot create change in a way that demonizes those with whom we disagree. Instead, it calls for proceeding with compassion. Restorative justice seeks the common ground among different perspectives and views respectful relationships in a context of truth-telling as the foundation for a just society.

A Vision of Radical Change

Restorative justice calls for us to apply these values in all aspects of our lives and in all our relationships—with family, coworkers, neighbors, clients, and adversaries. Acting on the basis of "power with" requires that we have respectful relationships with our adversaries—that we hear from the heart even when we vehemently disagree. One of the paradoxes of restorative justice, therefore, is that it is a vision of radical change but one that asks us to change in a gentle way. Restorative justice asks us to create major transformation without relying on the techniques of threat and control. Attempting to decide for others, to control them, violates the values of restorative justice.

The restorative justice movement cannot by itself correct the structural inequities in our society, but it can do two things. On a micro level, it can bridge social distance, affirm values of mutual responsibility, and reallocate power in individual cases of crime. On a macro level, it can provide a model for transforming relationships and power across multiple systems and structures. Think globally, act locally. Restorative justice combines a larger vision, a social justice vision, with concrete actions available to every individual to work toward that vision.

Social Justice and Spirituality

Major social justice efforts have been inspired by people following a spiritual path (for example, Ghandi, Martin Luther King, Dorothy Day). Although they and many of their followers consciously drew on their understanding of spiritual forces to enhance their work, spirituality was a largely private matter. Political discourse and public business have generally been conducted devoid of a clearly articulated spiritual dimension, mostly because of the history of groups of people who used religion as a justification for harm to others. Attempts to correct that injustice have resulted in public discourse that often does not address the spiritual dimension of human existence. However, trying to weave a vision of social justice without connecting to spiritual inclinations drastically diminishes the power of the vision to move people to new behaviors. Engaging moral forces toward greater social justice naturally engages a sense of spirituality for most people.

Because invoking spirituality in public processes carries risks, it must be approached with great care. A formulation of spirituality separate from religion, developed by the Dalai Lama in his book, *Ethics for the New Millennium*, may provide an answer to this dilemma. The formulation of his ideas closely parallels central tenets of restorative justice. He defines spirituality as, "concerned with those qualities of the human spirit—such as love and compassion, patience, tolerance, for-

giveness, contentment, a sense of responsibility, a sense of harmony—
which bring happiness to both self and others." He goes on to say, "There
is thus no reason why the individual should not develop them even to
a high degree, without recourse to any religious or metaphysical belief
system." Spirituality, based not on a set of religious beliefs but on
those core values, could be introduced into public processes without the
risks associated with religions. The Dalai Lama suggests that, "spiritual
practice according to this description involves, on the one hand, acting
out of concern for others' well being. On the other, it entails transforming
ourselves so that we become more readily disposed to do so."

Actions taken out of concern for others' well-being are social justice actions. Appealing to this vision of spirituality promotes social justice. Restorative justice appeals to this vision by promoting awareness
of and actions toward the well-being of all parties affected by crime and
transformation of ourselves so that we carry that vision to all aspects
of our lives.

The Dalai Lama goes on to discuss the importance of empathy in
determining whether our actions enhance the well-being of others. He
writes, "if we are not able to connect with others to some extent, if we
cannot at least imagine the potential impact of our actions on others,
then we have no means to discriminate between right and wrong,
between what is appropriate and what is not, between harming and non-
harming." He also notes that if we enhance our capacity to feel the suffering of others, then our tolerance for other people's pain will be
reduced. He also contends that, "we can indeed enhance our capacity
for empathy." Restorative justice places a similar emphasis on the
importance of empathy and on strategies to increase empathy for the pain
of victims, for community harms, and for the struggles of offenders.

The values the Dalai Lama ascribes to spirituality and the feeling
of empathy can be developed and promoted without reference to spirituality and often are. However, linking them to spirituality dramatically increases the moral suasion of those ideas. In public-sector work,
restorative justice has most often been advocated and practiced without reference to spiritual links. Peacemaking circles, however, consciously engage the spiritual dimension of human experience in theory and in practice. They define spirituality in the same terms as the Dalai
Lama and are inclusive in forms of spiritual expression.

Empathy, or reducing tolerance for other people's pain, is a powerful force for social justice. Defining spirituality in terms of empathy
and enhancing the well-being of others has enormous potential to
increase individual commitments to social justice. Restorative justice
provides opportunities to take spiritual practice, understood as "acting out of concern for others' well-being" from the confines of religious
buildings (churches, synagogues, mosques, etc.) into the realities of community living and community decisionmaking.

Some Precautions

Although restorative justice carries values of social justice at its core, restorative justice advocates are attracted to the framework for a wide variety of reasons. Not all are related to social justice concerns. In that multifaceted appeal lies both a risk and an opportunity. The risk is that restorative justice may be understood and implemented in a limited way that meets the needs of certain administrators or community leaders but does not impact power structures. In this case, techniques will be used without attention to underlying values and intent. On the other hand, the interest in restorative justice from so many different perspectives creates an opportunity to bridge what have been thought to be irreconcilable differences. Across the political spectrum, from the religious right to radical feminists, restorative justice offers islands of common ground on which previously polarized interests can learn to listen to and respect one another.

Holding that common ground will not be easy. There are very powerful forces operating against the use of an approach that calls for taking time to hear one another, reflecting on core values, giving voice to all perspectives, allowing a spiritual dimension in public process, and prioritizing relationships over power. Our cultural addiction to linear plans and processes, applied universally with little discretion, makes it extremely difficult to shift to a flexible, relational problem-solving approach that creates responses and structures as it goes along and requires decisions for individuation. Western culture is accustomed to figuring it all out—drawing blueprints or procedural manuals and then strictly following the directions. The process of creating restorative responses to crime is necessarily holistic and circular, shaped by those closest to the problem, responsive to the specifics of the environment, and messy.

If narrowly conceived, restorative justice will not contribute significantly to social justice. Certain aspects of a restorative approach are critical from a social justice perspective. Social justice benchmarks for restorative justice include:

- Restorative justice is implemented in ways that emphasize values more than technique.

- There are measurable shifts in decision-making power from professionals to those individuals most impacted by the decision.

- Collective responsibility is acknowledged.

- All kinds of victimization are recognized and given voice.

- Space is created for reflection and for drawing links between individual struggles and larger social conditions.

- Personal narratives are a primary process for gaining information.

- Decisions are not made in the abstract but in a process of direct encounter.

Restorative justice is about caring *and* accountability. If only accountability is emphasized and caring neglected, then restorative justice will not produce improvements in social justice.

Conclusion

Social justice cannot be delivered from the top down. Good social justice policy is necessary but not sufficient. In addition to good policy, social justice requires individual commitment to a just social order: a moral commitment. Social justice is the result of hundreds of small actions and decisions made by individuals daily, but to have a positive effect on the larger social fabric, individual actions need to be guided by a shared vision. Restorative justice engages people in a discussion of shared values and vision and then provides ways for individual community members to experience the human dimension of those through direct participation in the lives of others. Direct participation moves commitment from the head to the heart and fuels the engine of social change on a much deeper level than policy alone.

A sense of connection, of shared fate, and of oneness with others, including those who are oppressed, fuels interest in and commitment to a social justice agenda. Concern about social justice follows naturally from a recognition of interdependence. If the well-being of another will impact directly on my well-being, then I have a vested interest in ensuring the well-being of that person. Restorative justice is making much more explicit in our lives our fundamental interdependence at all levels. Our survival depends upon our ability to become more loving, more accepting, and more accountable to one another.

> In a real sense all life is inter-related. All men are caught in an inescapable network of mutuality, tied in a single garment of destiny. Whatever affects one directly affects all indirectly. I can never be what I ought to be until you are what you ought to be, and you can never be what you ought to be until I am what I ought to be. This is the inter-related structure of reality.
>
> (Martin Luther King, Jr.)

Once we are clear about healing as a goal and we begin to share our stories of healing with one another, there is no limit to the creative possibilities for advancing individual and collective well-being through the justice process. The stories of healing (reaching past our pain to touch one another as human beings), whether in South Africa or Texas or Northern Ireland, are the substance of a new vision of our capacity as human beings to move beyond retaliation and violence as responses to our pain. This vision entails a capacity to see ourselves in the "other" and to connect in the weave of our inseparable lives. In the new global village, there is no escaping the truth that harm to one is harm to all. When we hurt another, we wound ourselves. When we give to another, we enrich ourselves. When we love another, we deepen ourselves. Restorative justice is giving many people a way to take that profound truth into public life, thereby creating a resonance between public behavior and personal values. In that lies the passion and power of the restorative justice movement and its potential to transform our social structures.

Discussion Questions

1. What is the relationship between restorative justice and social justice?

2. What limitation does Pranis see in the Western concept of democracy? Do you think response to crime, and the justice system in general, is an appropriate place to address social justice issues?

3. How can restorative justice begin to address social justice issues?

4. Can restorative justice decisionmaking "democratize" social control? Should it?

References

Arrigo, B., and R. Schehr. (1998). "Restoring Justice for Juveniles: A Critical Analysis of Victim-Offender Mediation." *Justice Quarterly* 14:629-666.

Bazemore, G. (1999). "The Fork in the Road to Juvenile Court Reform." *The Annals of the American Academy of Political and Social Science* 564:81-108.

Immarigeon, R. (1999). "Implementing the Balanced and Restorative Justice Model: A Critical Appraisal." *Community Corrections Report* (March/April):35-47.

McKnight, J. (1995). *The Careless Society: Community and Its Counterfeits.* New York: BasicBooks.

Pranis, K. (2000). "Conferencing and the Community." In *Family Group Conferencing: New Directions in Community-Centered Child and Family Practice*, edited by G. Burford and J. Hudson, 40-48. New York: Aldine de Gruyter.

Stuart, B. (1996). "Circle Sentencing: Turning Swords into Ploughshares." In *Restorative Justice: International Perspectives*, edited by B. Galaway and J. Hudson, 193-206. Monsey, NY: Criminal Justice Press.

Van Ness, D. and K.H. Strong (1997). *Restoring Justice*. Cincinnati: Anderson.

Zehr, H. (1998). "Principles and Practice in Restorative Justice." Paper presented the Second International Conference on Restorative Justice for Juveniles, Ft. Lauderdale FL, November.

Part VI
The Future of Restorative Community Justice

14

Dangers and Opportunities of Restorative Community Justice: A Response to Critics

MARA SCHIFF
GORDON BAZEMORE

Introduction

Cogent criticism of an idea or practice, such as that provided by several of the contributors to this text, can provide either an occasion for defensiveness or an opportunity to refine an evolving model. In this chapter, we respond to some of the important concerns voiced by these authors and also attempt to identify strategies that have been suggested to address these issues. Properly implemented, such strategies may enable restorative community justice to develop fully as a viable model for the future.

Many restorative and community justice practices and initiatives are, at best, fledgling efforts to experiment with new ways of preventing and responding to crime. Indeed, relatively speaking, modern experimentation with restorative justice has a very short history. In this context, critics should be cautious about concluding at this stage that restorative community justice policies have "failed." For example, it is one thing to point out that after 10 years of full implementation, restorative justice has failed to resolve pervasive justice system problems of insensitivity to minority cultures, legal coercion, or inadequate attention to due process. It is quite another to *blame* such long-standing problems on restorative and community justice. Yet today, restorative and community justice interventions are being criticized by some for justice system dysfunctions such as net-widening, coercion, violations of due process, failure to provide true alternatives to incarceration, and other problems that most would agree were institutionalized long before even minimal experimentation with these practices. Other reforms, such as just deserts policies, case management in community corrections, or the "what works" or "effective correctional treatment" movements have, quite frankly, had considerably more time and resources with which to cause the harm implicitly attributed to restorative justice—or, alternatively, to make things better.

However, in clarifying the context within which to view such concerns and criticisms, this response would miss the mark if it were premised on defensiveness and blame-laying. Some very real concerns have been articulated here about the extent to which restorative community justice is truly a viable justice strategy for the future. While the magnitude of these concerns may vary by country, type of community, type and age of restorative process, and a variety of other concerns, the fact that they have been raised at all makes them worthy of recognition and response.

We have three main objectives in this chapter. First, we want to acknowledge and briefly respond to some of the critical concerns about restorative community justice that have been made in this volume. Second, we want to clarify the context in which these concerns have been voiced and thus interpret them accordingly. Specifically, we will consider the criticisms expressed here in relation to: (1) comparison with the current justice system, and (2) available research that either supports or rejects the efficacy of restorative policies and practices. Third, we want to place such concerns within a framework that reflects both the dangers and opportunities that these critiques offer for the future of the restorative community justice approach as well as its relation to broader social justice issues.

Four Criticisms

Four primary criticisms of restorative community justice appear in this volume. Although it is impossible in this brief response to do justice to the complexity of some of the concerns raised by authors, we have grouped these criticisms into the following general categories :

1. The "myth of community," as suggested in particular by Crawford and Clear (Chapter 6).

2. The extent to which restorative community justice is exclusive and perpetuates inequalities of culture, gender, and status, as suggested by Zellerer and Cunneen (Chapter 11), and Achilles and Zehr (Chapter 4).

3. The flexibility and responsiveness of the models in their practical contexts, as suggested by Stuart (Chapter 10), Zehr and Achilles (Chapter 4), and Zellerer and Cunneen (Chapter 11).

4. The impact of structural inequalities on stakeholder participation, offender reintegration, and community involvement, and the degree to which restorative community justice should also be responsible for social justice on a broad scale, as suggested by Polk (Chapter 12), Zellerer and Cunneen (Chapter 11), and Pranis (Chapter 13).

The Myth of Community

In most Western societies today, "community" is difficult if not impossible to define, demarcate, and demystify. Any social movement grounded in notions of community participation and responsibility therefore confronts significant challenges. Crawford and Clear raise a number of important general points about the ambiguity of the term "community." They point out that in most discussions about community, a common definition is presumed. Such discussions are premised on a belief that communities have some "organic wholeness" wherein their boundaries and characteristics are clear and defined. To address the difficulties presented by simple geographic distinctions, restorative justice advocates have offered the term "communities of care." However, "communities of care" are fluid and flexible entities that arise in response to a particular need (e.g., a crime), and thus members may enter and exit at will. If entry and exit is self-determined, then members may choose to leave whenever the "rules" of membership displease them. From this perspective, there are no essential characteristics that define and characterize such communities.

A corresponding concern is that if communities are self-defined, what are their norm-generating and norm-affirming capacities? Crawford and Clear suggest that this lack of essential characteristics may result in limited compliance with norms and may minimize the extent to which members share norms. In order for a community to have substance, there must be some consensus around rules of behavior and some means by which to exact compliance with those norms through regulation, sanction, or coercion. If membership is determined solely by individual preference, then the fabric that binds the community together may fall apart at the seams.

Questions of resources, cohesion, power relationships, and equality within the community are important in identifying the definition and boundaries of community. It is important to understand that current community structures, with their inherent inequities, took many years to erect; they may take just as long to deconstruct. The fact that restorative community justice has been unable to resolve adequately the issue of what constitutes "community" relative to criminal justice concerns in a decade (more or less) is predictable; what is surprising is the extent to which dialogue about community and how to engage it is occurring within the justice system context at all. Moreover, the degree to which governments and community groups and members are participating in the conversation may be unprecedented. There are increasing examples of inclusive and participatory community-based structures beginning to take hold in previously fragmented neighborhoods (Pranis, 1998). In other words, the question is not so much whether community does or does not exist, but rather *"at what stage of development* is the community and how much direction and assistance does it need?"

Another concern addresses the implications of including an unlimited number of "stakeholders" in community-based restorative processes (e.g., conferencing, circles, other policy decision-making bodies). It follows that if community is not solidly defined, it may be difficult to identify who to include as its "stakeholders." One concern expressed by Crawford and Clear is the fear that restorative justice interventions may inadvertently dilute the primacy of the victim and the offender by involving and giving power to unrepresentative community members (see also Bazemore and Griffiths, 1997). To the extent that these members identify themselves as "experts," the problem is exacerbated as "in-groups" of volunteers may come to dominate what are supposed to be inclusive processes. This might then make it difficult for others to feel valued and welcomed, further weakening the possibility of "community" as representative and inclusive. As such, Crawford and Clear suggest, restorative (and community) justice must consider precisely what is meant by "stakeholder" and how such participants should be determined.

We agree that understanding and defining the notion of a "stakeholder" in a criminal justice event is a complex issue. However, it is predominantly *because* of restorative justice that this critical issue is being addressed at all. Moreover, it is important to clarify that this is not simply a problem with restorative community justice, but rather with justice systems in general, which have either completely ignored or simply silenced "troublesome" participants (such as victims). Restorative justice has opened the door to include nontraditional players in the justice dialogue; what is now called for, as Crawford and Clear rightly point out, is to distinguish more precisely who should constitute such players, why, and how to recognize them. Again, this is part of the evolutionary process to which such critiques as these contribute. The fact is that restorative justice has not restricted such discussions, but rather has, in many ways, enabled them to be held at all.

Crawford and Clear also examine the concept of "reintegrating" an offender back into the community. If there is no preexisting state of community into which to return, "reintegration" becomes little more than a fanciful abstraction that mostly allows people to feel better about their own lofty and visionary goals. The fact is that many stable communities are indifferent, if not actually opposed, to change and innovation, and are certainly not paragons of inclusiveness. Rather, they often breed intolerance and prejudice and may consider the concept of taking responsibility for *each and every* community member inconceivable, if not actually a bit repulsive.

To us, this is all the more reason to engage communities now, rather than live with the belief (and concomitant resignation) that communities cannot change, will not change, and, hence, there is little point in trying. To suggest that we should leave communities alone because they are exclusive and inequitable is a bit like saying that because victims are angry and bitter, we should just leave them out, or that because offenders are unremorseful and manipulative, we should exclude them from restorative processes. Indeed, this tendency to preserve the status quo and then justify the reasons for so doing is exactly what restorative community justice is attempting to redress. While there may be significant obstacles to engaging communities, including those comprised of "haves" who would prefer not to rock the boat and "have nots" who are tired of listening to unfulfilled promises, this sounds to us more like a challenge than a deterrent.

Crawford and Clear suggest that government efforts to devolve justice to the community level may have some negative implications. They are concerned about the extent to which government can or should turn what have traditionally been its responsibilities over to communities that may be uninterested, underempowered, and unqualified. To what extent do "community involvement" and "community responsibility" imply government absolution from accountability (Crawford, 1997)? Such devolution must at *minimum* include attention to the availability and distribution of resources (Crawford, 1997). Where exactly should the line between governmental accountability and community empowerment be drawn? In the worst case scenario, restorative and community justice may minimize the value of certain social policy issues (such as poor housing, inadequate schooling, and poverty) as critical concerns in their own right, and overemphasize their relevance as conditions that may lead to crime and thus threaten the security of the majority (this is discussed further later in this chapter). Crawford and Clear suggest that criminal justice may not be equipped, and perhaps should not be held responsible, for rectifying social inequity, and that restorative justice, because of its reactive rather than preventive nature, may be especially inappropriate for such a task.

It is, of course, extremely important to maintain the distinction between certain social policy initiatives and criminal justice ones. For example, young people in need of services and assistance should not have to commit crimes to receive these, nor should a homeless person's needs be considered important simply because of that individual's potential to commit crime. Meeting such needs is important because we choose to be a just and caring society responsible for the well-being of *each and every* member. Poverty, illiteracy, or mental health issues are important not because of their relationship to crime or because individuals so afflicted may ultimately engage in criminal acts. We must not lose sight of the values inherent in the type of society we consider (or wish) ourselves to be. Strong communities are fundamental to preserving these values, and the extent to which we are able to strengthen and support such communities will determine the extent to which we live in safe and peaceful environments.

Adhering to the values underlying the restorative model would hopefully limit precisely the kind of overarching criminal justice expansion and system dominance of which these authors forewarn, in part because it can be invoked only after a crime has been committed. Moreover, restorative community justice principles necessarily demand placing clear limits on the government role in the response to crime and require a rethinking of the system role in order to empower and strengthen the community (Christie, 1977; Van Ness and Strong, 1997).

Most major policy changes occur following some triggering event that inspires resultant action. Crime, especially serious crime, is such an occurrence. A broad, preventive community justice approach is an important component of a holistic justice strategy; however, it is often the "up-close and personal" emotion triggered by an intimate event that ultimately inspires people to take action. We believe there are aspects of a holistic restorative community justice approach best addressed by a preventive community focus, and others that may be better served by a responsive, criminal-event-driven strategy. We believe these two approaches complement rather than divide one another (see Chapter 1 for a more complete discussion of restorative community justice).

Crawford and Clear's concern that some critical characteristics of "community" are, at present, rather ill-defined has implications for clarifying certain cornerstones of restorative community justice. The concept of community in a postmodern world is emergent and transient; this is both a challenge and an opportunity for restorative community justice. The mere fact that this discussion is occurring in the context of the criminal justice system, and that it is about something other than how professionals should "protect" or "treat" the public (who, in fact, live and function in the context of community), is noteworthy in itself.

Inequality of Culture, Gender, and Status

Concern about cultural, gender, and status inequalities is an important issue discussed in this volume by Zellerer and Cunneen and by Achilles and Zehr. These authors are worried that, without attention to these important issues, restorative community justice may perpetuate and exacerbate injustices inflicted upon indigenous peoples, women, and victims of crime.

There have been some egregious historical and current violations perpetrated on indigenous and other low-status populations. Zellerer and Cunneen are concerned that current and past justice approaches have tended to impose practices and structures on indigenous peoples that deny the latter's basic human rights to self-determination and self-government. They maintain that colonizers have no right to impose their own notions and structures of criminal justice on indigenous populations and that such populations should neither be obligated nor expected to submit. Restorative justice, they argue, is replicating some of these abuses. The right of the indigenous to choose and implement their own justice strategies should not only be respected, it should be required, and government should take special pains to ensure this end.

Zellerer and Cunneen suggest that by imposing Western justice strategies, child welfare regulations, and delinquency statutes on Australian (and other) aboriginals, institutional representatives of Western culture have in fact committed, or are in the process of committing, acts tantamount to genocide. By taking indigenous children out of the homes of their families, or by devising juvenile justice laws that, intentionally or unintentionally, discriminate against indigenous peoples, governments systematically perpetuate reprehensible violations of basic human rights.

There is no question that the criminal justice system has perpetuated some extremely racist and insensitive policies that exacerbate injustices inflicted on indigenous communities and their members. The real question here is not whether this has occurred but rather the degree to which restorative community justice bears responsibility for these abuses. More specifically, the issue is whether restorative community justice is likely to perpetuate such abuses, remain oblivious or indifferent to them, or become a remedy to the tradition of bias within the criminal justice system (e.g., Pranis, this volume). When implemented according to principle, we believe restorative community justice offers the best option for halting the pattern of abuse inflicted on minorities and other underempowered stakeholders in criminal justice policy and practice.

Achilles and Zehr are concerned about the special needs of crime victims in the justice process. They recognize that historical violations have been visited upon victims by traditional systems, and argue that restorative justice must be especially careful not to replicate these injustices. In particular, they contend that the traditional justice system has not only ignored the special needs of victims to be heard, respected, and repaired (when possible), but that in many cases victims have been "revictimized" by the justice process. Restorative justice, they argue, has the potential to remedy some of these concerns, but must be wary of critical pitfalls along the way.

Although the initiation of such abuses began long before the implementation of restorative justice, without care, restorative initiatives may simply reinforce old patterns of insensitivity and abuse. For example, by making family group conferences in Australia available only for first-time youthful offenders, for example, policymakers exclude a majority of indigenous youth with prior records. Zellerer and Cunneen argue that these acts are not only morally wrong but that they violate the United Nations Declaration on the Rights of Indigenous Peoples and are hence violations of international convention.

Zellerer and Cunneen also argue that such oversights are further aggravated when perpetuated against indigenous women. Being both indigenous and female exacerbates powerlessness, and government has an obligation to protect such persons. The ability of an indigenous woman to speak out about and/or receive reparation for abuse or other injustices is often challenged by issues of power, inequality, and safety that are insufficiently protected either in Western or traditional indigenous justice practices. Devolving justice to small oppressive community groups or clans may threaten what minimal protections women enjoy from the most insidious forms of abuse.

According to Zellerer and Cunneen, another mistake has been in assuming that because some restorative and community justice practices arise out of native traditions (e.g., family group conferencing, circle sentencing), a single basic restorative model should not be expected to fit the needs of multifarious indigenous communities. This is exacerbated by the presumption of a healthy and stable relationship between indigenous and governing majority cultures, which is erroneous in itself and also wrongly assumes that interventions prescribed by the state will be readily accepted by the indigenous population.

Zellerer and Cunneen suggest that while restorative justice and indigenous justice are often incorrectly assumed to be synonymous, certain important differences must be acknowledged and respected. For example, the use of a neutral mediator/facilitator may be appropriate in a restorative community justice process but anathema in an indigenous one. Another example would be the tendency to avoid, rather than confront, other societal members; for instance, behaviors such as looking one another in the eye may be expected in a Western culture while they are considered rude and offensive in an aboriginal one. There is, in addition, substantial anecdotal evidence that restorative justice practices (like traditional practices) have been misapplied to non-indigenous communities. This may suggest either evidence of discrimination or simply an inappropriately applied "one size fits all" approach that must be corrected (this is discussed in later sections).

Restorative justice, according to Achilles and Zehr, provides both opportunities and challenges for redressing some of the ills historically visited upon victims. While these authors specifically reference individual crime victims in their approach, their suggestions are easily applicable to other disadvantaged groups. Important cornerstones are restorative justice's value-based principles of encouraging victim participation, considering victims as equal stakeholders in the process, and designing processes that are responsive to the needs of victims rather than the state. There are, however, several omnipresent dangers when considering the potential of restorative community justice to address the needs of victims (or other disadvantaged groups) in the justice process. These potential pitfalls include:

- viewing restorative justice as a set of programs rather than as a methodology with important underlying values and principles that must drive all processes;

- tending toward uniformity when developing and managing policy rather than maintaining a flexible and responsive emphasis on meeting stakeholder needs;

- failing to include victim voices in the design and implementation of restorative community justice practices;

- failing to incorporate rigorous victim-sensitive process and outcome evaluations into the development of restorative community justice programs (Achilles and Zehr, this volume).

The absence of unyielding devotion to principle as the guiding force behind restorative justice policy and practice may result in justice processes that are no better than those that currently dominate the system. In fact, paying lip service to restorative community justice while continuing with "business as usual" could disguise abuses and could potentially be more damaging to victims and other disadvantaged populations than current approaches. For example, if restorative justice in a given jurisdiction means funding several victim-offender mediation programs or other conferencing approaches when little or no funding is provided to compensate and support victims of violent crimes, victims can justly conclude that restorative justice has not served their interests. Under such circumstances, restorative justice practitioners seeking strong victim support for their initiatives will surely be disappointed.

While we do not dispute that there are instances in which restorative processes are perhaps less sensitive than optimal, it is also important to note contradictions in the positions taken by some of its critics. For example, Zellerer and Cunneen argue that family group conferences (FGCs) are discriminatory because they are limited to first offenders and hence indigenous offenders are typically excluded on the basis of past records. On the other hand, they argue that FGCs are, in any case, *not good* for indigenous offenders because they are insensitive to unique cultural concerns of indigenous peoples and therefore are inappropriate justice system interventions. The problem here is one of trying to have it both ways. If the programs are insensitive to the unique needs and interests of aboriginals and thereby harmful, they should not be imposed; if they are practical and helpful justice system alternatives to which aboriginals should have access, then the issue is the validity of the qualifying criteria, not the process itself. These are mutually exclusive categories of criticism that should not be invoked differentially when convenient to the argument.

It is important to recognize that restorative justice is an evolving process. The critical question, as echoed throughout this chapter, is the degree to which such actual and potential abuses perpetuated by restorative justice compare with those currently and historically perpetuated by the current system. While restorative justice has clearly not eradicated discrimination against victims or minority cultures in the justice process, at a minimum it can be credited with building opportunities to do so into the restorative process. In intent at least, principle-based restorative justice processes seek to specifically include the voices of previously unheard stakeholders, and in so doing provide opportunities to redress macro-level as well as micro-level harms perpetuated by the criminal justice system (for example see Pranis, this volume). It is particularly important to recognize that attention is paid by restorative justice not only to the outcome of such processes but also to *how* such concerns are addressed. In restorative justice, because *process* is of paramount concern, opportunities for flexible responses are provided through forums designed to reflect diverse interests. The question here is not so much "have we resolved all inequity" but rather "what are we doing about it" and how will we measure and evaluate our efforts.

Zellerer and Cunneen are right in suggesting that there are some important differences between and among indigenous and majority communities that must not be overlooked. However, it is also true that, perhaps for the first time in postmodern criminal justice reform history, restorative and community justice approaches are *trying* to integrate native practices into Western strategies (Griffiths and Hamilton, 1996; Stuart, 1996; this volume). Zellerer and Cunneen suggest that several principles should underlie a restorative approach in indigenous communities, including open negotiation with indigenous groups; respect for indigenous populations and their culture; respect for indigenous rights; government relinquishment of the right to make decisions for indigenous peoples; and ongoing support in communities to address social, economic, and other inequities. These ideals should, of course, permeate any justice approach that affects indigenous populations and should guide relationships between indigenous and dominant cultures. Restorative community justice that is driven by principles rather than programs should be especially suited to addressing these ideals and for providing opportunities for inclusiveness and responsiveness.

What is needed is to develop a means by which to cultivate working partnerships between dominant and minority interests; no one culture should be dominated by another simply on the basis of might and majority. Because of its dedication to value and principle as tantamount to the restorative vision, restorative community justice, while obviously imperfect at this stage of its development, has the potential to better achieve this ideal than do most of its justice or social welfare predecessors.

With respect to crime victims, Achilles and Zehr offer a variety of guidelines that can minimize the prospects of counterproductive and insensitive efforts to implement restorative justice, such as having victims and/or their representatives on criminal justice governing and planning bodies; ensuring that victims clearly understand their roles and are provided with information, confidentiality, and opportunities for involvement; and advocating for victims' services even in the absence of an apprehended offender. Such policies may not ensure the full representation and participation of victims, but they will go a long way toward righting some of the wrongs that persist in the current system and will provide meaningful opportunities to create a more responsive justice system in the future.

Flexibility of Process/Responsiveness to Stakeholder Needs

In Chapter 10, Judge Barry Stuart is perhaps most adamant about the need for "flexibility in process governed by underlying principles." Such processes must address multiple components of a conflict/crime, as well as physical, emotional, spiritual, and mental dimensions of stakeholder needs. The reality, however, is that even in some well-intended restorative community justice efforts, the "one size fits all" response that we have mentioned before continues to ask stakeholders to adapt their needs to those of a program model rather than vice versa. As suggested above, for example, Achilles and Zehr make it clear that part of the anger and frustration victims experience with the criminal justice system is the rigidity and lack of choice provided by its limited options.

This lack of flexibility is a dilemma for proponents of restorative community justice because practitioners must often weigh the risks of operating a "pure," though marginalized, restorative justice program against those of becoming more accessible and widely available but also institutionalized as a part of an overly bureaucratic justice system. Vermont's reparative boards, for example, are perhaps among the most widely implemented restorative justice initiative in a U.S. state. They offer a systemic response that has brought some 300 volunteers into a highly efficient, community-based, informal decision-making process that at least minimally offers community input into a sanction/obligation focused on repair. Yet, as Karp and Walther (this volume) suggest, this approach is currently the object of a great deal of criticism from some restorative justice practitioners for its alleged inflexibility and inattention to the individual needs of victim and offender.

Several core ideas in restorative community justice flow from the general idea that the response to crime and conflict must be dynamic. First, the idea of repair itself as a primary goal mitigates against the idea of a "one size fits all" solution (Bazemore and Dooley, this volume), and it demands an individualized response to the needs of victim, offender, and community. Second, Christie's (1977) idea of crime and conflict as opportunities for transformative change is not only an interesting and optimistic way of examining crime, it is also one that requires an openness to complexity and a tolerance for nonlinear responses. As further developed in Stuart's chapter on the peacemaking circle process, this outlook clearly flies in the face of mandated, uniform policies and practices. Indeed, Christie's argument that crime is essentially "stolen conflict" is also a reaction against third-party, "fast food" responses to crime that are stripped of any real connection to stakeholder needs.

The trend toward what Umbreit (1999) has called the "McDonaldization" of victim-offender mediation (VOM) raises concerns that even as highly principled restorative practices become more mainstream, in order to appear efficient they may begin to look more like the adversarial processes they are designed to displace. Notwithstanding its relatively limited scope of community involvement relative to other restorative conferencing models, New Zealand family group conferencing (FGC) appears to have maintained much of its integrity as a restorative process despite its status as the most widely institutionalized restorative decision-making process in the world (Maxwell and Morris, 1996; this volume). Consistent with our arguments about allowing time for effective implementation, New Zealand conferencing appears to have made continuous improvements in process after early troubles in garnering victim participation and achieving victim satisfaction.

In contrast to the limited community participation that is thus far apparent in VOM and New Zealand's FGC, and to the apparent inflexibility of some reparative boards, the circle process described by Stuart seems theoretically most intensive and capable of meeting the multiple needs of diverse stakeholders. However, the process is highly labor-intensive relative to other models, which thereby limits its potential for broad system impact. Nonetheless, Stuart's more generic concern with adaptability of restorative processes to dynamic stakeholder needs must be addressed in order to achieve true adherence to restorative principles of repair and community involvement. Stuart's critique of current restorative community justice programs might lead ultimately to a more seamless "menu of options" for victims, offenders, and citizens affected by crime rather than a single-program focus.

Structural Inequalities

Polk's concern with formal institutions of socialization—especially work and school—and the vital connection of these to social justice focuses on a missing component in most restorative community justice dialogue. First, his critique suggests that in addition to public, private, and parochial forms of social control (Hunter, 1985), a fourth domain of *public informal control* in the form of public socializing institutions has been neglected.

At the turn of the twentieth century, the transition from adolescence to adulthood was marked by a smooth movement away from the controls of extended family and a much more restricted school experience to the controls of the workplace. For modern young people who have virtually no access to work, the connection to community and the source of legitimate identity is through the school and by the prospects of a future career and access to higher education (Hirschi, 1969; Polk and Schaefer, 1972). For those not doing well educationally, Polk argues that because career ladders are now virtually nonexistent for large populations of young people, the bond to school is weak at best. Schools in the United States, for example, have become especially proficient at relinquishing responsibility to the justice system for disruptive children. Indeed, so-called "zero tolerance" policies often amount to a complete release of any informal control that schools might otherwise exercise over young people.

In general, schools are the breeding ground for trouble and youth crime, more often than neighborhoods or even family. They are also the primary pipeline for referrals to police and court—and thus also to restorative community justice interventions. Viewed as the core of "community" for young people, school should also be the primary context for enhancing both support and social control for young people by providing a smooth transition to work and family life. Yet, according to Polk's data, the connection between school and work has grown much weaker and is virtually nonexistent for huge segments of the youth population in countries such as Australia. Moreover, the exclusive policies of some schools in countries such as the United States greatly limit (through outright suspension or in effect through in-school segregation) the possibilities of developing a bond to the community that might have a preventive impact.

According to Polk, there is clearly a power imbalance between young people and adults, and between those accused of crime and those making these accusations. More importantly, Polk emphasizes that there is a larger crisis of socialization driven by international changes in the political economy that have rendered many Western societies incapable of providing avenues for integrating young people into the world of work and productive citizenship. In his view, even the most humane and effective criminal justice reforms will be unlikely to reintegrate young offenders unless coupled with more macro, structural reforms.

Polk's critique can be taken at face value to simply proclaim the irrelevance of restorative community justice, or it can be used as a springboard to integrate restorative principles and processes into schools, the workplace, and other contexts of socialization and social control. At a practical level, experimentation with restorative conferencing—especially circles—as a means of addressing trouble and conflict in some United States schools has provided an effective problem-solving alternative to conflict and disciplinary infractions as well as to potentially destructive zero-tolerance policies of suspension and expulsion. Such experimentation has also slowly begun to impact power dynamics by giving students a voice in decisionmaking about disciplinary policies (Riestenberg, 1998; Ticiu, 2000). From a restorative community justice perspective, schools as communities may also become targets for capacity-building preventive interventions. Such interventions might not only address school safety concerns but also incorporate positive youth development and alternative learning strategies that engage both marginal and well-integrated young people (Pearl, Grant, and Wenk, 1978; Pittman and Fleming, 1991).

It is probably at the mid-range level of harms and community-based responses that restorative community justice may contribute directly or indirectly to community building and "collective efficacy" (Sampson, Roedenbush, and Earls, 1997). This may occur, for example, through "initiatives to foster community organization in schools, neighborhoods, ethnic communities, and churches, and through professions and other non-governmental organizations that can deploy restorative justice in their self-regulatory practices" (Braithwaite, 1998:331). Included at this level are any other activities that mobilize informal social controls, "social support" mechanisms (Cullen, 1994;

Rose and Clear, 1998), and vehicles that serve as educational tools through which community learning can occur (Hudson et al., 1996; Stuart 1996). At a macro level, some restorative and community justice advocates have argued that there is ultimately a need to:

> Design institutions of deliberative democracy so that concern about issues like unemployment and the effectiveness of labor market programs have a channel through which they can flow from discussions about local injustices up into national economic policy-making debate. (Braithwaite 1998:333)

Though there are clearly macro and structural connections to be made that lie beyond the scope of this book, Pranis's contribution to this volume suggests that restorative community justice not only has relevance for social justice but is already breaking new ground in what she and others have described as a "democratization of social control." Although criminal justice is not the primary vehicle for addressing social justice concerns, it has an important role to play. Indeed, some have argued that far from being a neutral player, criminal justice actually exacerbates problems facing inner-city African-American communities by offering a response that breaks up families and reduces the pool of adult males able to participate in community and family life and local economies (Rose and Clear, 1998).

Because state intervention is clearly capable of doing more harm than good, when criminal justice decisionmakers cede discretion to local neighborhoods, as in the examples Pranis provides, a significant shift in power has occurred. Based on this shift, it may be possible to move from a singular debate about issues of crime and criminal justice to a meaningful discussion of problems of social justice and their relationship to crime. Such dialogue may also be a vehicle for breaking down barriers between young and old as well as between "haves" and "have nots," and ultimately may become a core feature of the broader school and work reform initiatives desired by Polk and others. The challenge here, as suggested by Zellerer and Cunneen, is to be sure that the process does in fact shift power, rather than simply replicate persistent inequalities of race, gender, or status.

A critical step in moving toward such a larger vision is to begin a dialogue about crime and justice that encompasses these issues. True democratization of social control involves a kind of "bubbling up" from local responses to crime, which are increasingly aired in community justice forums linked intentionally to what Braithwaite has described as a "vibrant social movement politics" (Braithwaite, 1994; Braithwaite and Parker, 1999). As Pranis suggests in her discussion of the possibilities inherent in circle sentencing and other conferencing approaches for addressing such issues:

The problem of crime is generating opportunities to understand and practice democracy in the community in new ways.
It has become clear that creating safe communities requires
active citizen involvement. This calls for a reengagement of
all citizens in the process of determining shared norms, holding one another accountable to those norms and determining
how best to resolve breaches of these norms in a way that does
not increase risk in the community. (1998:3)

Setting the Context

In this section, we will assess the context in which concerns about
the viability of restorative community justice have been voiced and
respond to them accordingly. The contextual issues we believe most
important to consider are: (1) the relative inadequacy of restorative
community justice in comparison to its alternatives, and (2) the
research, if any, on which such criticism is based.

Comparison to What?

The first context for critical analysis is the yardstick against which
the practice in question is being measured. There are two possible standards of comparison against which the restorative community model,
and its critiques, can be considered: one is in reference to a utopian ideal
of what a justice model "should" do; the other is in reference to the current system. It often seems that the former is the implicit yardstick
against which the restorative community model is measured, and yet
the effect of so doing is not only to divert attention from the shortcomings of existing approaches but also to approach the potential of
the restorative community model myopically.

Critical analysis of the restorative justice *vision* is especially important at this early stage, as is honest examination and acknowledgement
of system and agency "failure" to implement restorative justice according to its principles. What is unhelpful, and potentially destructive, is
to present alleged shortcomings of the restorative vision as failures of
practices when those practices have not been adequately implemented nor realistically compared to existing models in terms of either positive outcomes or negative unintended consequences. Like so-called evaluation that claims "success" for programs based on the fact that very
few program clients reappear in court for new offenses, claims of
"failure" that lack a comparison group may likewise fail to allow for
valid inferences about effectiveness.

When considering concerns such as the feasibility of community
involvement, discrimination against indigenous and other popula-

tions, flexibility of process or structural inequities, and the ability (or lack thereof) of restorative community justice mechanisms to address them, the first question must be "in comparison to what?" It is important to identify, for example, exactly *where* such discrimination is occurring, under what conditions, to whom and by whom, then determine whether this is better than, worse than, or equivalent to the discrimination (or other weakness) being perpetuated by current strategies? Criticism is valuable when it is used as a vehicle for refining policy and practice rather than being a diatribe about what is not working. In virtually all cases, the response must be "in comparison to current practice." This important distinction should not be overlooked or minimized.

Research on restorative community justice programs and policies must examine the extent to which these strategies produce outcomes that are better, worse than, or the same as current approaches. It is no secret that the restorative community justice model is fallible in such areas as preserving individual rights, assuring due process, avoiding coersion of defendants (and often victims), and other issues. However, despite these imperfections, there is little evidence that such issues are any better addressed by the current system. For example, in the face of criticism that conferences may fail to adequately protect the rights of youthful offenders (Feld, 1999), it can hardly be said that current criminal or juvenile justice practices in most countries do a significantly better job. In the United States, despite efforts to preserve juvenile rights (e.g., *In re Gault*, 1967, *Kent v. United States*, 1966), youths are still routinely held pending adjudication, provided with inadequate or nonexistent counsel, or subjected to discriminatory transfer practices. Furthermore, it should be noted that current safeguards were not put in place until the juvenile justice system had been operating for close to 75 years.

While restorative community justice is far from having achieved perfection at working with and inviting the full and equal participation of indigenous and other populations or protecting the rights of such groups, it would be hard to defend traditional criminal and juvenile justice practices on the same basis. Research has yet to offer conclusive evidence that restorative community justice models are intrinsically any worse at considering the needs of their participants than are current juvenile justice strategies

State of Research

It seems appropriate (and correct) to observe that in some jurisdictions, to quote Gertrude Stein, "there is no *there* there," when it comes to principle-based and theory-driven restorative and community justice practice. It also seems appropriate to challenge the "vision" behind this practice as inconsistent or incomplete, and there are certainly *different* visions that need to be considered. If presented as one person's hope for what restorative justice should seek to accomplish (and avoid) in the *future*, or as an assessment of what is missing in some restorative justice policies and practices, abstract criticisms may be helpful. However, to declare something a failure that has for the most part not really been tried is misleading at best and disingenuous at worst. Moreover, it is quite possible that the most effective restorative community justice practices are yet to be developed. There is already evidence of a hybridization of these processes and an even greater potential for mixing the best elements of different approaches (Bazemore and Griffiths, 1997).

As evaluators, we must insist that restorative community justice should rise or fall based on rigorous assessment of empirically demonstrated effectiveness. Most researchers would probably agree that the kind of piloting and self-correction that can lead to policies and practices truly consistent with restorative community justice principles and theory has not sufficiently occurred. If we can agree that research on the *implementation* of restorative community justice that reflects restorative principles is in its infancy, we must also agree that *research* on restorative interventions is also immature.

The potency of criticism about a policy or program must depend on the extent of our knowledge about it. In this context, the concerns articulated by authors in this volume should be seen not only as issues for careful thought and reflection but also as calls for further research on the outcomes and processes that characterize the restorative community justice movement. This, in turn, leads to some fundamental questions about how "success" and "failure" of restorative community justice programs should be measured. The real question to be considered here is not so much "what works?" but rather "what works, for whom, when, and how should it be measured?" (Bazemore, 1999a; Schiff, 1998; Van Ness and Schiff, this volume). Many of the concerns presented here are more aptly considered appeals for research than final or authoritative assessments of what works or does not work with respect to restorative community justice.

There is a critical need to ask and address questions such as:

- Where is this happening?
- To whom?
- Why in one jurisdiction and not another?
- What circumstances lead to the formation of exclusive community cliques and how might they be managed?

- What is the best structure for different processes and how should that be managed?

- How can communities be recognized, engaged, and preserved?

The challenge is not only in identifying the questions but, more importantly, in determining what to do about them and how to measure, identify, and categorize them in ways that are useful for policy and practice.

In addition, there is an important need not only for more process and outcome evaluations, but for evaluations that use consistent and rigorous measures with relevance across a variety of jurisdictions and studies. The extent to which research is being conducted that powerfully exposes both the strengths and weaknesses of restorative community justice will largely determine our ability to design and implement truly restorative policies and programs. Furthermore, the extent to which such research can and does (1) define consistent outcomes measures for "restoratives," (2) generate protocols that can be applied across jurisdictions, programs, and other individualized boundaries, and (3) provide results that can be generalized across jurisdictions, programs, and other individualized boundaries will determine the extent to which restorative community justice survives as a viable future for the justice system.

Conclusion: Dangers and Opportunities

An interesting conceptual framework within which to consider the restorative community justice approach lies within the Chinese character for conflict. This character is made up of two other Chinese images: one representing danger and another representing opportunity. The criticisms of the restorative community justice model presented in this volume suggest dangers that, if left unheeded, will inevitably lead to its demise. On the other hand, they also present invaluable opportunities for critical reflection, thought, and (ultimately) action. The concerns cited here have the potential to either devastate or give rise to some of the most exceptional advances within the restorative community justice movement. Figure 14.1 explores some of these dangers and opportunities.

The dangers we have focused on in this chapter center around the "myth" of community, the power imbalances and inequity in restorative community justice processes, the inflexibility of process, and deficiencies in social structure. Each of these concepts offers a corresponding opportunity to examine existing policies and procedures in order to develop strategies that better represent restorative values and meet the needs of multiple stakeholders.

Figure 14.1

Dangers	Opportunities
▼ Failing to define, demarcate, and distinguish "community," resulting in inconsistent, unmanageable, and unprincipled practices.	▲ Identifying "communities of care" or other self-defined groups that coalesce around important issues (e.g., crime) and thus empower members to become involved in, and responsible for, one another's lives.
▼ Rigid and/or exclusive processes that impose a "one size fits all" approach on diverse persons, communities, cultures, or situations.	▲ Developing flexible and integrative processes that can truly resolve differences by redefining stakeholders and fully involving participants.
▼ Making assumptions based on inadequate and inconclusive research.	▲ Developing and implementing rigorous and responsive research protocols that can be applied across jurisdictions and programs.
▼ Condoning systems that ignore power imbalances, inadequately protect rights, and disregard inequities.	▲ Cultivating forums wherein individuals are empowered to participate and speak out as equal coproducers with government of a responsive justice system.
▼ Ignoring the potential for system cooptation and government domination of restorative community processes.	▲ Producing formal and informal systems that can be differentially invoked depending on the needs and choices of the participants.
▼ Seeing restorative community justice as a panacea that will resolve social ills and inequities.	▲ Generating opportunities for healing, reparation, and open relationships based on understanding of other cultures, experiences, and lifestyles.

For example, to Ken Polk, and several other authors (e.g., Arrigio and Scheher, 1998; Immarigeon, 1999; Pranis, this volume; Zellerer and Cunneen, this volume), a danger of restorative and community justice is that it inadequately addresses social justice concerns. Though such a challenge is important, where else in the criminal justice system, or in efforts to reform it, is much being done to make a dent in inequality, racism, and the like? By itself, restorative community justice will not transform society. However, simply by virtue of demanding that those impacted by a crime be actively involved in its response (Van Ness and Strong, 1997), restorative community justice presents an opportunity to move away from the "individualizing" tendencies of punishment and treatment-oriented approaches that invariably reduce complex issues to either a clinical or control problem of the offender (see Bazemore, 1999b). In other words, it presents a possibility for identifying and engaging stakeholders as previously untapped resources in building viable and socially just responses to crime.

Clarifying these inherent dangers and opportunities can help determine the future of the restorative community justice vision. A danger rarely presents itself without a corresponding opportunity. If no opportunities seem present in the face of overwhelming liability, there are two possible explanations. First, the costs (i.e., dangers) inherent in that particular policy or practice may be too high, overriding any current or potential benefits from further cultivating that strategy. The other, more likely possibility is that opportunities are not immediately visible. Opportunities to create innovative policies or processes generally arise when decisionmakers recognize that existing strategies are not working. For example, victim-offender mediation and family group conferencing have arisen from the failure of current adversarial models to address the needs and interests of victims and offenders in the justice process (see Achilles and Zehr, this volume). Restorative practices have been designed to address the insufficiencies of current practices that leave victims, communities, and offenders alienated from the justice process. When properly implemented, restorative practices enable participants to coproduce a reliable and responsive justice system.

While it has come a long way, restorative community justice is still relatively young. As Mark Carey suggests, perhaps its current processes can be likened to the psychological states of infancy or perhaps in some areas, adolescence. It has not yet reached adulthood and should not be expected to have the corresponding maturity of a fully grown process. The current state of restorative community justice should not be seen as a definitive model; rather, it is best understood within a continuum of progress (or perhaps several continua representing different dimensions) wherein some elements are more mature than others.

The biggest mistake at this point would be to see restorative community justice as a panacea that can right all the wrongs of prior justice approaches. Instead, comments and critiques such as those presented here are better viewed as critical contributions within an evolutionary process. Most laypersons and scholars alike would agree that nothing built in a day is likely to withstand the test of time. Restorative community justice is no exception. We do not question whether the concept has value for the long run; our hope is that this volume has made a contribution to the birth of a justice system for the future that heals rather than harms, that prevents rather than reacts, and that transforms rather than reforms its constituents.

Discussion Questions

1. Why do Schiff and Bazemore suggest that it is premature to conclude that restorative justice has "failed"? What do they believe is a more appropriate way to view the current state of development of restorative justice?

2. How do these authors respond to Crawford and Clear's concern about including too many stakeholders in the restorative process? About seeing communities as rigid and inflexible and resistant to change?

3. Does restorative justice add to or ameliorate human rights abuses perpetrated on indigenous and other minority populations?

4. Are Polk's concerns about structural inequalities that inhibit the ability of restorative community justice to have any significant impact on young people valid? What do Schiff and Bazemore suggest is an appropriate response to Polk's concern?

5. What are some of the important issues that these authors feel have been overlooked by the critiques presented in this volume?

6. Why is the relationship between danger and opportunity important in understanding the critiques presented by authors in this volume?

References

Arrigo, B., and R. Schehr (1998). "Restoring Justice for Juveniles: A Critical Analysis of Victim-Offender Mediation." *Justice Quarterly* 14:629-666.

Bazemore, G. (1999a). "The Fork in the Road to Juvenile Court Reform." *The Annals of the American Academy of Political and Social Science* 564:81-108.

Bazemore, G. (1999b). "Restorative Justice and Earned Redemption: Communities, Victims & Offender Reintegration." In *Civic Repentance*, edited by A. Etzioni, 45-96. Lanham, MD: Rowman and Littlefield.

Bazemore, G. (1999c). "After Shaming, Whither Reintegration: Restorative Justice and Relational Rehabilitation." In *Restorative Juvenile Justice: Repairing the Harm of Youth Crime*, edited by G. Bazemore and L. Walgrave. Monsey, NY: Criminal Justice Press.

Bazemore, G., and C. Griffiths (1997). "Conferences, Circles, Boards, and Mediation: The 'New Wave' in Community Justice Decisionmaking." *Federal Probation* 61(2):25-37.

Braithwaite, J. (1994). "Thinking Harder about Democratising Social Control." In *Family Conferencing and Juvenile Justice: The Way Forward or Misplaced Optimism?*, edited by C. Alder and J. Wundersitz, 199-216. Canberra: Australian Institute of Criminology.

Braithwate, J. (1998). "Restorative Justice." In *The Handbook of Crime and Punishment*, edited by M. Tonry, 323-344. New York: Oxford University Press.

Braithwaite, J., and C. Parker (1999). "Restorative Justice is Republican Justice." In *Restorative Juvenile Justice: Repairing the Harm of Youth Crime*, edited by G. Bazemore and L. Walgrave, 103-126. Monsey, NY: Criminal Justice Press.

Christie, N. (1977). "Conflicts as Property." *British Journal of Criminology* 17:1-15.

Crawford, A. (1997). *The Local Governance of Crime: Appeals to Community and Partnerships*. New York: Oxford University Press.

Cullen, F.T. (1994). "Social Support as an Organizing Concept for Criminology." *Justice Quarterly* 11:527-559.

Feld, B. (1999). "Rehabilitation, Retribution and Restorative Justice: Alternative Conceptions of Juvenile Justice." In *Restorative Juvenile Justice: Repairing the Harm of Youth Crime*, edited by G. Bazemore and L. Walgrave, 17-44. Monsey, NY: Criminal Justice Press.

Griffiths, C.T., and R. Hamilton (1996). "Spiritual Renewal, Community Revitalization and Healing. Experience in Traditional Aboriginal Justice in Canada." *International Journal of Comparative and Applied Criminal Justice* 20:285-310.

Hirschi, T. (1969). *Causes of Delinquency*. Berkeley: University of California Press.

Hudson, J., B. Galaway, A. Morris, and G. Maxwell (eds.) (1996). "Introduction." In *Family Group Conferences: Perspectives on Policy and Practice*. Monsey, NY: Criminal Justice Press.

Immarigeon, R. (1999). "Implementing the Balanced and Restorative Justice Model: A Critical Appraisal." *Community Corrections Report* 6:35-47.

In re Gault, 387 U.S. 1 (1967).

In re Kent, 383 U.S. 541 (1966).

Hunter, A.J. (ed.) (1985). "Private, Parochial and Public Social Orders: The Problem of Crime and Incivility in Urban Communities." In *The Challenge of Social Control: Citizenship and Institution Building in Modern Society*, edited by G.D. Suttles and M.N. Zald. Norwood, NJ: Aldex.

Morris, A., G. Maxwell, J. Hudson, and B. Galaway (1996). "Concluding Thoughts." In *Family Group Conferences: Perspectives on Policy and Practice*, edited by J. Hudson, A. Morris, G. Maxwell, and B. Galaway, 221-234. Monsey, NY: Criminal Justice Press.

Pearl, A., D. Grant, and E. Wenck (1978). *The Value of Youth*. Davis, CA: Dialogue Books.

Pittman, K., and W. Fleming (1991). "A New Vision: Promoting Youth Development." Washington, DC: House Select Committee on Children, Youth and Families, Academy for Education and Development.

Polk, K., and W. Schafer (1972). *Schools and Delinquency*. Englewood Cliffs, NJ: Prentice Hall.

Pranis, K. (1998). "Building Justice on a Foundation of Democracy, Caring and Mutual Responsibility." Unpublished paper. Minnesota Department of Corrections (March).

Pranis, K, and D. Bussler (1998). "Achieving Social Control: Beyond Paying!" Minneapolis: Minnesota Department of Corrections.

Riestenberg, N. (1999). *Restorative Measures in the Schools*. Roseville, MN: Minnesota Department of Children, Families and Learning.

Rose, O., and T. Clear (1998). "Incarceration, Social Capital and Crime: Implications for Social Disorganization Theory." *Criminology* 36:471-479.

Sampson, R., S. Rodenbush, and F. Earls (1997). "Neighborhoods and Violent Crime: A Multi-level Study of Collective Efficacy." *Science* (August):277.

Schiff, M. (1998). "Restorative Justice Interventions for Juvenile Offenders: A Research Agenda for the Next Decade." *Western Criminology Review* 1(1) [online]. See *http://wcr.sonoma.edu/v1n1/schiff.html*

Stuart, B. (1996). "Circle Sentencing: Turning Swords into Ploughshares." In *Restorative Justice: International Perspectives*, edited by B. Galaway and J. Hudson, 193-206. Monsey, NY: Criminal Justice Press.

Ticiu, M. (2000). "In-School Behavior Intervention: Quarterly Progress Report." St. Paul: Minnesota Department of Children, Families and Learning.

Umbreit, M. (1999). "Avoiding the Marginalization and Mcdonaldization of Victim Offender Mediation: A Case Study in Moving Toward the Mainstream." In *Restoring Juvenile Justice: Repairing the Harm of Youth Crime*, edited by G. Bazemore and L. Walgrave. Monsey, NY: Criminal Justice Press.

Van Ness, D., and K.H. Strong (1997). *Restoring Justice*. Cincinnati: Anderson

15
Exploring and Shaping the Future

MARA SCHIFF
GORDON BAZEMORE

By now it should be apparent to readers that restorative community justice is a viable model from which practice, policy, and influence are likely to continue expand. As discussed in Chapter 1, the growth in interest and implementation of restorative community justice programs in the past decade has been of a scale that would surprise even some of its strongest advocates—given the concomitant expansion of policies associated with the more dominant "punitive paradigm" (Cullen and Wright, 1996). There is, in this sense, clearly a future for community restorative justice; the question is what kind of future. How long will this new way to thinking about and responding to crime survive and what form will practice and policy take?

There has been relatively little speculation to date about answers to this question. Even less consideration has been given to how current visions for restorative community justice and strategic emphases that guide implementation efforts may propel the current movement toward one future model or another. At a recent North American session on strategies for implementing restorative justice convened by the Open Society Institute, a group of restorative justice scholars and practitioners—including Howard Zehr, John Braithwaite, Kay Pranis, Barry Stuart, and Ellen Halbert—considered different visions and futures for restorative community justice and how these may be linked to current movement strategies. It was Walter Dickey of the University of Wisconsin who first suggested that without careful attention to strategy, restorative justice was vulnerable to becoming the "alternative to incarceration movement of the twenty-first century." While Dickey's prognosis for the movement was the most pessimistic, others, such as

Braithwaite, suggested that it might be possible to examine opposition movements in other sectors (such as the environment, women's rights, labor, etc.) for clues as to how certain strategies may produce a stronger, more sustainable movement. Participants suggested various versions of possible pessimistic or optimistic futures for restorative justice that would depend upon current strategic choices.

One important point of difference in the future vision for the new movement may depend on whether restorative justice and community justice are perceived as one reform paradigm, or separate (albeit compatible) frameworks. We began this book by suggesting that the differentiation between restorative and community justice hinges on three distinctions. These three distinctions are: (1) a case versus community focus, (2) reactive versus preventative interventions, and (3) formal versus informal strategies. We then suggested that a better way to consider these two approaches would be to concentrate not on their points of divergence but on where they converge and seek common ground. We stated our own belief that these distinctions are, in fact, being replaced with a new concept—restorative community justice—that better characterizes the values, intent, and principles of the vision to which we (and other advocates) are referring.

Throughout this book, chapter authors have alternatively referred to either "restorative" or "community" justice as they deemed appropriate to the context of an example or argument. We have not attempted to impose some artificial consistency throughout by editing out all references that do not employ our own term. Rather we believe the occasional use of both terms to describe the same phenomena provides further evidence of convergence rather than divergence (e.g., Bazemore, 1997; Braithwaite, 1998; Karp, this volume). While some authors (e.g., Crawford and Clear, this volume) suggest important differences between the two, we feel that the real power lies in identifying where these visions complement, strengthen, and enhance one another. In other words, rather than spending energy concentrating on disparities, we would rather spend it generating a new, more integrated, and cohesive model.

Though the future is uncertain, we suspect that the union of restorative and community justice as an alternative paradigm is a viable possibility. Whether and how these terms are remembered at all 50 years from now is anyone's guess, and the arguments between the two are likely to become obscure. Many of the criticisms made by the authors in this volume (detailed in Chapter 14) apply almost equally to restorative practices and to community justice practices. The promising prospects that have been identified by some seem most likely to be achieved in an integrated model. In thinking about possible futures for the new movement (or movements), we attempt to consider common concerns and invite readers to create their own alternatives while trying to imagine how the future of the system will look 100 years from now.

Justiceworlds in the Year 2075

In the following sections we have created four possible versions of a scene occurring on a college campus in North America about 75 years from now. The setting is an archive or museum (formally known as a library) in which original copies of books are made available to students doing historical research. Because most books needed for such research are available to them on computer systems built into all homes and college dorm rooms, students visit archives only for the purpose of conducting research on obscure topics.

In each scene, a student is immersed in a book, with several more scattered about the desk. All the books focus on the criminal justice system, and all were written in the late twentieth or very early twenty-first century. Each book focuses on something called restorative and/or community justice, and examines some aspect of those perspectives. The students, each in the context of a different "justiceworld," are having distinctive, though equally puzzled reactions to what they are reading.

Justiceworld 1:
Restorative Community Justice: The Alternative to Incarceration Movement of the Twenty-First Century

Joe is perplexed. He has come upon a series of books, all approximately 75 years old (give or take a few years) and all referring to something called "restorative community justice." He wonders what that means. These books discuss a justice system approach in which victims and offenders meet and discuss the crime, where victims and communities have a voice in determining the outcome of criminal events, and where the government plays a limited, mostly supportive role for a predominantly community-driven justice system. This seems inconceivable. Having read books by Van Ness and Strong (1997) and Braithwaite (1989), Joe is now reading one edited by Bazemore and Schiff, which is a compilation of articles written by what seem to have been the leading scholars and practitioners of this restorative community justice model.

The concepts mentioned in this book are peculiar; they are foreign to the justice system Joe knows. This system is completely government-driven, with no role at all for victims or communities. In fact, the idea itself seems preposterous—what would such people *do* in a courtroom or any decision-making process? What does crime have to do with individuals or communities? It is, after all, an offense against the state and thus the state is responsible for its redress. In fact, the majority of people Joe knows have had some interaction with the justice system, and it is rare to reach age 25 without having spent at least some time in jail, on probation, or under community control. This is true for men and women alike, although it seems to occur slightly less often for women. In Joe's "justiceworld," no one really thinks that state control is such a big deal because pretty much everyone has experienced it on some level or another. It is easy to offend; simple offenses such as graffiti, disobeying traffic signals, a run-in with someone in the supermarket, or even littering can result in a court appearance.

In the justice system Joe knows, any form of offense is intolerable, whether it be simple or complicated, violent or moderate. Most offenses result in some form of state control, and more serious offenses, when they occur, are always prosecuted and typically result in incarceration. In fact, to a large degree, people prefer the risk of state intervention to the intolerably high violent crime rates that were experienced in the latter part of the twentieth century.

In the current system, due process is secondary to what are considered to be the crime control needs of the larger society, and Joe finds it hard to understand perspectives such as Zellerer and Cunneen's (this volume) suggesting that indigenous and other minority group human rights might take precedence over crime control. Moreover, he cannot understand a proposition such as Stuart's (this volume) that considers "flexibility of process" as something for which to strive. Like Zellerer and Cunneen's concerns, such flexibility flies in the face of the uniformity the system has fought for decades to establish and maintain. While he finds some merit to the concept of active and passive responsibility as described by Braithwaite and Roche (this volume), he cannot see its relevance or understand how or why such a concept would be applied outside of a state-driven system.

Although Joe's "justiceworld" does include a massive treatment (i.e., rehabilitative) system, he (like most of his fellow students and teachers) has not thought to question the assumptions of the dominant punitive system—despite its clear linkage with a dramatic increase in incarceration in the past half-century. He cannot make sense of the implicit and explicit questioning of punishment in some of the contributions (Bazemore and Dooley, this volume; Braithwaite and Roche, this volume), or the concern for victim or other stakeholder satisfaction as an outcome (Van Ness and Schiff, this volume). The restorative community justice approach that this book seems to advocate is enigmatic to him, because it bears no relation at all to the system under which he has grown up, nor the one he has been studying in all his criminal justice courses.

Justiceworld 2:
Less than Meets the Eye: Restorative Community Justice as the New Diversion

Tanya looks around at the pile of books and papers that surround her. She is taking a course on "Alternative Justice Approaches" and is studying something called restorative community justice. Tanya is puzzled because restorative justice and community justice are described in several of the old manuscripts as models for systemic reform encompassing entire justice systems and the communities that surround them. Apparently, the vision of these early reformers was that restorative conferencing processes and problem-solving agencies could be system-wide, community-driven responses to crime. This seems ludicrous when she looks at twenty-first century adaptations of what was then called restorative justice and/or community justice.

In her day, what were called restorative justice practices in these early writings are viewed as part of something called "community resolution." Such processes as victim-offender dialogue, now called "mediation," are still occasionally referred to as restorative justice, but this generally involves only one meeting with a juvenile offender and his or her family; victims are almost never involved. Although she has never heard of a community policing program or community prosecution unit, Tanya's "justiceworld" is full of agencies with community affairs or community liaison units that mostly address citizen complaints against them. She wonders if these bear any relationship to what was referred to as "community justice."

Tanya's professor has given several examples of programs that still employ some of the practices about which she is reading. What seems to have occurred, however, has been a proliferation of what some early reformers called "fast food" restorative justice options on the front end of the criminal justice system (Umbreit, 1999). These are mostly uniform, "one size fits all" programs in which the needs of victim, offender, and community—viewed as primary by the early reformers—are basically irrelevant.

These and a sea of other "prevention" programs are now widespread, and her professor has told the class that they function in a way similar to what were called "diversion" programs in the twentieth century. The only apparent difference is that early diversion programs seem to have handled a much greater proportion of *criminal* cases. According to her professor, the current formal criminal justice system now covers many of the functions that used to fall under other social services and public works agencies. The resolution programs really just extend the formal system rather than serving as true community alternatives. In fact, they take very few referrals from courts or prosecution; instead, they serve primarily as a referral source for families, schools, and other agencies dealing with minor youthful misbehavior and conflicts that were once handled informally in community groups and institutions.

Funded with criminal justice dollars, like diversion in the previous century, community resolution is rarely a true alternative to court or other formal decision-making procedures. These programs clearly "widen the net," and although no one has used this term in 50 years, it can clearly be demonstrated that youths in those programs often soon find their way back into the punitively oriented criminal justice system. However, this is pretty much what everyone expects will occur anyway so little effort is made to circumvent it.

Tanya has read some of the twentieth-century writers who clearly advocated a community capacity-building approach as a way to create a more meaningful and effective response to crime (Bazemore and Dooley, this volume; Braithwaite, 1998; Braithwaite and Roche, this volume; Pranis, this volume). The restorative justice programs she has studied in class, however, rely exclusively on professional mediators and therapists rather than citizen volunteers, as such programs were originally designed to do. Unlike the community-building and problem-solving orientation envisioned by some writers of the past century (e.g., Clear and Karp, 1999), community resolution strategies rely on early intervention programs to identify "problem" young people and refer them to specialized remedial and therapeutic assistance. Courts, prosecution, and police agencies have more cases and control than ever; indeed, they are very "accessible," but the vision of having community members involved in sentencing or other criminal justice functions has long since been abandoned as unrealistic and unworkable (Clear and Karp, 1999; Pranis and Bazemore, 2000).

Tanya reads the articles by Karp and Walther (this volume) and Maxwell and Morris (this volume), and wonders what all the fuss was about concerning "victim offender dialogue," "reparative boards," or "family group conferencing." The findings of late twentieth- and early twenty-first-century researchers that such processes apparently resulted in a greater sense of "stakeholder satisfaction" is now pretty much conventional wisdom—but no one really cares very much. The thought of these approaches serving as an *alternative* to court and "building community capacity" to respond to crime seems a bit ridiculous to Tanya. While resolution programs seem concerned with seeing that offenders make reparation to victims and seek to avoid the adversarial process of the courts, little or no personal attention is paid to victims and their needs, and actual "problem solving" generally targets only the offender and his or her problems.

Justiceworld 3:
Parallel Systems: Community Restorative Justice as More Than Meets the Eye

Jeff sits in the library, working on the final paper for his "Contemporary Criminal Justice" class. His topic is to describe and analyze the origins of the current justice system wherein parallel, equally strong and viable, formal and informal systems characterize the justice approach. In his class, Jeff has been studying how what was once a fairly marginal and disconnected group of informal practices known as restorative community justice became institutionalized as a system of nonadversarial, less professionalized options.

As he understands it, this process began as an effort to establish alternatives to formal court decisionmaking (particularly diversion and sentencing/disposition). These alternatives expanded and were later incorporated into prison and other correctional sentences within juvenile residential programs, as well as parole at the "deep end" of the criminal justice system. Gradually, they also became the standard means of addressing harm and conflict in schools and neighborhood settings. As this occurred, criminal justice systems were slowly transformed from the formal government-controlled legalistic model with a wide range of ancillary, system-expanding "alternatives" to a bifurcated model that now includes an equally strong informal, community-driven alternative at each point in the justice process.

Jeff has learned from his various criminal and juvenile justice courses that there is a formal and informal alternative available at each stage of the justice process and participants are empowered to choose their venue at each stage. The choice must be by consensus of all parties, and generally there is agreement. Jeff is surprised to learn that in the previous century—at least in Western countries—few persons charged with a crime actually admitted responsibility and most were, in fact, encouraged *not* to do so. Today, however, admission and apology are common responses, and everyone assumes that those hearing cases in one or another informal restorative community justice process will generally be fair and compassionate. This is largely because in the informal sector the decisionmakers are neighbors, family, and friends rather than justice system professionals.

What Jeff is familiar with is a system wherein each stage of the process is guided by the interests of the participants. A hearing to determine the appropriate venue is the first event that occurs at the beginning of each stage [i.e., following arrest, before any possible court involvement, at sentencing (if court has been elected), and following any adjudicatory agreement]. At each key decision point in the process, the parties select the type of decision-making approach that best suits their individual and collective needs, and this is reviewed by a restorative community justice panel comprised of both community members and justice professionals. The parties themselves, in conjunction with the panel, determine the next step. This, to Jeff, is both normal and logical, and it is hard for him to envision it working any other way. In fact, the satisfaction of the parties, as discussed by Van Ness and Schiff (this volume), is the typical yardstick used to assess the success of the process. He is a bit surprised to learn that it had ever been any other way.

Jeff has been reading the literature from the period in which the informal model was developing, and is working to understand how the "separate but equal" justice system approach evolved. He has already read most of the primary literature from the era, including Howard Zehr's *Changing Lenses* (1990), John Braithwaite's *Reintegrative Shaming* (1989), Daniel Van Ness and Karen Strong's *Restoring Justice*, and Todd Clear and David Karp's *Community Justice* (1999). He is now on Gordon Bazemore and Mara Schiff's *Restorative Community Justice* (2001), and is learning about some of the justice models that existed at that time as well as some of the criticisms of the restorative community approach.

Jeff notices that this book seems to focus on the integration of restorative and community justice, which had been perceived as separate up until then. He also notices that a lot of the literature of this period seems to address integrating the victim and the community into the justice process and "reintegrating" the offender back into the community. This all seems a bit odd to him, as he cannot imagine how (or why, for that matter) a system in which victims and communities are not included would work. For example, he finds Achilles and Zehr's (this volume) critique of how victims were typically treated as hard to imagine in light of the current system's dependence on victim participation to drive the informal alternative model. Moreover, Zellerer and Cunneen's (this volume) piece on human rights and indigenous justice seems slightly antiquated, given the full and active involvement of such cultures in both informal and formal system processes. According to his professor, this was achieved by the use of consensus-based circle decision-making processes in all negotiations between indigenous nations and nonaboriginal system representatives. The distinctions between what was called community justice and restorative justice appear not to have been very important because all these ideas have been brought together in the informal justice sector.

In Jeff's "justiceworld," the state continues to have a role in the justice process—both as a referee and monitor of the now extensive informal justice system, and when guilt is contested and a trial is necessary. Crime, though, is no longer viewed as a problem requiring only "expert" solutions. Although the informal sector handles 80 to 90 percent of all criminal cases in North America, both sectors seem stronger and more coherent than in the previous century. The justice system of 2075 is not perceived as adversarial and competitive but rather as a place to redress harms and mend relationships; an adversarial process of sorts is reserved for cases in which guilt is contested. Even after this process is underway, numerous restorative options are available at any point during fact-finding or sentencing and are utilized in more than one-half of the cases that begin in the formal system.

Though Jeff realizes that all this would have been inconceivable 100 years ago, his professor has explained that most accountability for crimes in the previous century was established in a strange, quasi-formal process called plea-bargaining, which was abolished well over 50 years ago in most states. Today, when parties disagree about the level of offender responsibility, community forums hear the case and make adjustments in offender obligations based on victim, offender, and other community input. This is no longer a bargain between defense and prosecution. Instead, attorneys and other court representatives are encouraged to participate in order to identify how the needs of victim, community, and offender would be best served.

Most of the work of the court and attorneys is focused on helping community restorative programs ensure that participants are in no way coerced, and on advising clients of their rights to avail themselves of more formal decision-making options when they feel an agreement was excessively onerous. Community processes do not recommend incarceration but may recommend reparative obligations and caps on periods of incapacitation pending completion of these. Community groups involved in restorative programs generally choose to stay in touch with, and provide support for, incarcerated offenders and their victims. Informal restorative processes are also available inside even the most restrictive prison settings and have become a primary means of resolving disputes within these facilities.

Jeff has grown up in a society in which most of what was processed formally as crime in the 1990s is now dealt with by community-driven processes in schools, workplaces, faith community institutions, neighborhoods, and housing developments. He is especially puzzled by the contributions in Bazemore and Schiff's book that question the capacity and willingness of community members—including crime victims and offenders—to participate in justice decisionmaking focused on repairing harm; in his world, this is not perceived an imposition, it is simply something everyone does.

Justiceworld 4:
Restorative Community Justice: The Maximalist Vision

Gretchen is perplexed by some of the books scattered around her. She is studying the origins of the current justice system for her "Justice System Foundations" class, and she has come across something interesting. She has found some books, written in the late twentieth and early twenty-first century, that discuss restorative community justice. What is confusing is not the topic of the books, nor the majority of the content. What she cannot figure out is what all the fuss was about. She has found a number of books discussing different aspects of restorative community justice, from its theoretical underpinnings to its processes and outcomes, to a variety of criticisms about the validity and practicality of the model.

She reads with interest Crawford and Clear's article (this volume) about the boundaries of community and the difficulties in assessing precisely who and what constitutes "community." This seems a strange dilemma to her because no one is much concerned with that anymore; communities are self-defined, citizens are expected to participate, and generally they wish to do so. In fact, it is unusual to find someone not interested in taking part. People recognize that the extent to which they are involved will determine the extent to which their communities "work." It is rare that someone will elect not to participate because this will limit the extent to which they can count on others to support them.

In Gretchen's "justiceworld," courts no longer exist and she has some trouble deciphering the court process to which the literature refers. The current unified restorative community justice system has numerous options for resolving conflict and addressing the harm of crime at every point in the community or justice system in which a response to crime occurs. These vary along a continuum of formal to informal, depending on the willingness of offenders to acknowledge responsibility for crimes and, most importantly, depending on the individual needs of offenders, victims, and their communities. There is no separation between the formal and informal. Gretchen's experience is that "justice" is almost completely neighborhood-based. Although there are formal rules of procedure (especially for determination of responsibility for crime when guilt is contested), citizens—guided by paid professionals— carry out all stages of the justice process and make key decisions. Gretchen has read that early citizen decisionmaking was limited to the jury, which seemed to her a very weak and ineffective use of community members' time and energy, especially when compared with the modern forums in which citizens have significant discretion to make decisions with the support and guidance of professionals.

From Gretchen's experience, it is difficult to identify a "criminal justice system" in the twentieth-century sense of this term. Rather, specialists work with citizen volunteers and paid coordinators in various functional areas (e.g., neighborhood patrol, conference coordination, victim support). The latter are elected for one-year terms from the pool of citizen volunteers. This pool includes all citizens, and everyone at any given time will be involved in some justice function, with most citizens rotating between various roles. Although there are national organizations that convene conferences and discuss revisions in outdated legal codes, justice is local and driven by citizens who participate in processes like community policing, community courts, and restorative conferencing models of decisionmaking. Paid justice professionals act as coordinators and conveners of volunteers, who may be engaged in neighborhood watch and local problem-solving, a restorative panel or conference, working with offenders on community service projects, assisting victims, or any of a number of other roles consistent with some of the practices that first gained some popularity in the late twentieth century.

Neither judges nor legislative bodies are involved in sentencing. A small portion of their job, and of the job of attorneys such as prosecutors, involves the 3 to 4 percent of cases in which guilt/responsibility is contested. Some of these professionals have a role in monitoring citizen decisionmaking about obligations for fairness and efforts to address the needs of all parties. Judges and prosecutors spend equal time convening citizen forums concerned with victims' issues and groups concerned with youth socialization and development. In fact, many jurists use their free time to initiate or hear cases aimed at institutions that continue to perpetuate inequality and oppression.

Indeed, the majority of litigation in Gretchen's "justiceworld" is attached to social justice issues. Its target is either public institutions or private businesses who pollute the environment, put children at risk, exploit workers, provide inadequate housing, and so on. A recent wave of lawsuits has been launched against schools that appear to be failing to prepare young people for careers that are consistent with the communitarian focus of the larger social justice agenda. As Pranis, Polk, and other writers suggested was necessary, community justice groups realized early on that restorative community justice could not be limited only to micro processes focused on the needs of individual victims, offenders, and neighborhoods.

For Gretchen, Stuart's article about circles and the extent to which they are informed by principle seems, frankly, to simply state the obvious. The idea that processes should be determined by the needs of the participants rather than the mechanics of some program model seems self-evident; how else could it possibly work? In fact, Gretchen is perhaps most puzzled by the idea that hundreds of special programs in the past century seemed mostly to provide ways for judges and other decisionmakers to "get rid of" a case while doing nothing to solve underlying community-level problems. The idea that indigenous and other minority community members might be either excluded or oppressed by justice processes seems preposterous: What would be the point of a justice system that was unresponsive to the needs of its constituents? And why would there be any concern about including victims and communities? Is there some other way it might work? And what's the big deal about satisfaction? How else would you assess the extent to which "justice" is being delivered? The systemic restorative community justice approach is an integral part of the justice model under which Gretchen has grown up, and she finds it hard to imagine that at one time punishment and isolation was the norm, rather than the exception.

A Model for the Future

"There is nothing so practical as a good Utopia."
Lode Walgrave

The scenarios presented above offer four distinct visions of the future. These visions are obviously fanciful, oversimplified, and perhaps overstated case studies of the worst and best futures for criminal justice, and how restorative community justice might shape such futures. However, it is important to consider what elements might result in scenarios like Justiceworlds 1 or 2, and what might produce models like Justiceworlds 3 and 4.[1] To what extent is current policy driving all of us toward Justiceworld 1, and to what extent is the restorative community justice movement setting itself up for a rapid demise or trivialization as in Justiceworld 2 (where little is done to advance the values and principles envisioned by some of the writers in this volume).

The first scenario, Justiceworld 1, describes a future in which restorative community justice is merely a faded vision of the past of which no useful shard remains. In the second, Justiceworld 2, something like restorative community justice is still practiced, but only in small, isolated programs that suck conflict *up* from the community to professional systems rather than *down* from the courts into community-based structures. In Justiceworld 3, parallel systems allow formal and informal processes to work side-by-side to provide an extensive menu of options for victims, offenders, and their communities of support, while also exerting an enormous influence on informal, community-based social control and socialization. Finally, Justiceworld 4 offers another idealized vision in which anything other than an integrated, full-fledged restorative community justice model is a distant memory, all but forgotten by justice system students, practitioners, researchers, and policymakers.

As distinct visions, each Justiceworld (or any alternative version of the future) implies that different strategic responses to current problems of crime and justice may, over time, result in dramatically different criminal justice systems. Doing nothing is probably the most direct route to Justiceworld 1. An emphasis on expanding restorative justice simply through case-driven programs that rarely consider the implications of policy responses for larger justice bureaucracies (or for how such events affect the social context in which they occur) may lead to Justiceworld 2. Each scenario offers some insight about possible outcomes given our current and potential responses to the strengths and weaknesses of the restorative community justice model. Many of these strengths and weaknesses are raised by the contributors to this volume (see Chapter 14). The continuum of future criminal justice systems implied by these scenarios suggests that the current criticisms of restorative community justice may have greater or lesser significance depending on how they are managed by policymakers and practitioners.

Essentially, restorative community justice advocates have a choice. They can see criticism and critique as either a hindrance to be avoided or an asset to be uncovered; it all depends on the "lens" through which they observe (Zehr, 1990). The lens we choose is an optimistic (though not rose-colored) one; it perceives criticism as a crucial vehicle for strengthening and supporting an emerging strategy. While we celebrate the empowering successes of effective interventions, we also believe it is important to share information about those successes in terms that can effectively counter news stories that continue to foster distrust, pessimism, and fear. The criticisms presented in this volume are vital for developing a system that emulates Justiceworlds 3 or 4, and they should be taken seriously to the extent that the problems they highlight may otherwise move us more in the direction of Justiceworlds 1 or 2. The difference will be made not by our thoughts about the model but by our resultant actions.

Conclusion

> I believe we were put on this world to reach out to others. And that doesn't just mean to the good people."
>
> Pat Robinson, mother of a murdered teenager,
> victim advocate, offender educator.

> So we make mistakes—can you say—you (the current system) don't make mistakes . . . if you don't think you do, walk through our community, every family will have something to teach you . . . By getting involved, by all of us taking responsibility, it is not that we won't make mistakes . . . But we would be doing it together, as a community instead of having

it done to us. We need to find peace within our lives . . . in our
communities. We need to make *real differences* in the way people act and the way we treat others . . . Only if we empower
them and support them can they break out of this trap.
                    Rose Couch, Community Justice Coordinator,
                        Kwalin Dun First Nations, Yukon, Canada.

This volume has been designed to be an objective account of the
potential and the limitations of the emerging movement we have
called restorative community justice. Social scientists naturally rely
heavily on research and theory, and the practices and policies of
restorative and community justice should rise or fall based on empirical evidence of their effectiveness. Theory development should inform
rigorous research that tests or further expands theories and guides the
development of new ones.

Social reforms, however, especially those as ambitious as the ones
being pursued by advocates of restorative community justice, are not
driven primarily by data and theory but rather by practice and policy—
and trial and error. The engine that drives, and then sustains, the
progress of restorative community justice reforms is the collective, mostly frustrating experience that crime victims, offenders and their supporters, and community members and groups have with the current
criminal justice system. Restorative community justice is fueled by the
personal emotions of individuals who have experienced firsthand this
system as well as the alternatives described in this volume. These
groups and individuals share a vision about the possibilities for a different response to crime, and their excitement grows in potency as
neighborhoods, communities, justice system professionals, and other
government officials become allies in mobilizing and redirecting criminal justice attention and resources toward the new vision.

This volume has emphasized the scientific, skeptical, and decidedly
analytical and nonemotive side of the movement around community
and restorative justice. It has given voice primarily to researchers and
professional practitioners of restorative justice. However, we wish to
conclude by dedicating this book to those crime victims who suffer from
their experiences with the current system but continue to find hope and
healing paths—especially to those like Pat Robinson and other survivors
who give back more to others than could ever be imagined; to those
countless offenders and their families who acknowledge the harm
they have caused to others and who work to redress the damage to victims and community and then also seek to give back more by helping
others avoid their mistakes; and to those staff and volunteers in
restorative community justice who, like Rose Couch, struggle against
great odds to make sure the community's voice is heard and to seek to
build something better than was there before the crime occurred.

Discussion Questions

1. Briefly describe the four possible alternative scenarios that might characterize the future of restorative justice.

2. Which scenario do you think is most likely for the future and why? Is there some other scenario that you think may better represent the future of the restorative community justice model?

3. According to these authors, what will determine the extent to which the future looks more like Justiceworld 1, 2, 3, or 4? Do you agree with their assessment? What do you think will be the most important factor in determining the future of the justice system?

4. If it were up to you, which Justiceworld model would you choose? Why? How would you go about ensuring that your model predominated?

References

Bazemore, G. (1997). "The 'Community' in Community Justice: Issues, Themes and Questions for the New Neighborhood Sanctioning Models." *The Justice System Journal* 19:193-228.

Braithwaite, J. (1998). "Restorative Justice: Assessing an Immodest Theory and a Pessimistic Theory." In *Crime and Justice: A Review of Research*, edited by M. Tonry. Chicago: University of Chicago Press.

Braithwaite, J. (1989). *Crime, Shame and Reintegration.* Cambridge, England: Cambridge University Press.

Clear, T., and D. Karp (1999). *The Community Justice Ideal: Preventing Crime and Achieving Justice.* Boulder, CO: Westview Press.

Couch, R.C. (1995). "quote." In *Circle Sentencing: Mediation and Consensus— Turning Swords into Ploughshares*, edited by Barry Stuart. Yukon, Canada: Territorial Court of the Yukon.

Cullen, F.T., and J.P. Wright (1996). "The Future of Corrections." In *The Past, Present and Future of American Criminal Justice*, edited by B. Maguire and P. Radosh. Dix Hills, NY: General Hall.

Pranis, K., and G. Bazemore (2000). "Engaging the Community in the Response to Youth Crime: A Restorative Justice Approach." Monograph, Washington, DC: U.S. Department of Justice, Office of Juvenile Delinquency Prevention.

Van Ness, D., and K. Strong. (1997). "Restorative Justice Practice." Monograph. Washington, DC: Justice Fellowship.

Umbreit, M. (1999). "Avoiding the Marginalization and McDonaldization of Victim Offender Mediation: A Case Study in Moving Toward the Mainstream." In *Restoring Juvenile Justice: Repairing the Harm of Youth Crime*, edited by G. Bazemore and L. Walgrave. Monsey, NY: Criminal Justice Press.

Zehr, H. (1990). *Changing Lenses: A New Focus for Crime and Justice.* Scottdale, PA: Herald Press.

Biographies

The Editors

Gordon Bazemore is currently a Professor of Criminal Justice at Florida Atlantic University. His primary research interests include juvenile justice, youth policy, community policing, corrections, and victim issues. He is the author of many articles, book chapters, and monographs, and has directed several recent evaluations of juvenile justice, corrections, and policing initiatives. He has also completed a project funded by the Office for Victims of Crime (U.S. Department of Justice) to study judges' and crime victims' attitudes toward victim involvement in juvenile court.

Mara Schiff is an Assistant Professor of Criminology and Criminal Justice at Florida Atlantic University. Her research and publications focus on restorative and community justice, corrections, and juvenile justice. Schiff has worked for government, academic, and nonprofit organizations since 1981, concentrating on criminal justice policy planning and research. She is Co-Principal Investigator (with Gordon Bazemore) of a nationwide research project on conferencing in restorative justice. She has been involved in a variety of community-based projects to promote and implement restorative justice locally through victim-offender dialogue, delinquency prevention, and other neighborhood justice initiatives.

Other Contributors

Mary Achilles is Victim Advocate for the state of Pennsylvania. She spearheaded the development of an integrated system for the delivery of services to crime victims between the Board of Probation and Parole and the Department of Corrections. Achilles is a member of the Coalition of Pennsylvania Crime Victims Organizations, Vice-Chair of the

Victim Services Advisory Committee of the Commission on Crime
and Delinquency, and on the board of directors of the National Organization for Victim Assistance.

John Braithwaite is a Professor in the Centre for Restorative Justice,
Research School of Social Sciences, Australian National University. He
is also Chair of the Regulatory Institutions Network, of which the Centre for Restorative Justice is a part. He is the author of the seminal 1989
book, *Crime, Shame and Reintegration* (Cambridge University Press).

Mark Carey is the Deputy Commissioner of Community and Juvenile
Services in the Minnesota Department of Corrections. He has more than
20 years of experience in the correctional field serving as a counselor,
probation/parole officer, planner, and consultant. He taught juvenile
justice at Rochester Community College, and has written a variety of
articles and two books.

Todd Clear is Distinguished Professor at John Jay College of Criminal
Justice, City University of New York. Clear has published extensive-
ly on topics of correctional policy and justice system reform. His
work has been recognized through several awards, including those of
the Rockefeller School of Public Policy, the American Probation and
Parole Association, the American Correctional Association, and the
International Community Corrections Association.

Adam Crawford is Professor of Criminology and Criminal Justice
and a Deputy Director of the Centre for Criminal Justice Studies at the
University of Leeds (UK). He recently co-edited a book (with J. Goodey) on integrating the victim perspective within criminal justice, which
brings together contributions by leading international researchers on
issues of victims of crime. He is currently part of a research team evaluating the national pilots of restorative justice reforms introduced by
the British government under the Youth Justice and Criminal Evidence Act 1999.

Chris Cunneen is Associate Professor and Director of the Institute of
Criminology at the University of Sydney Law School. He has worked
with a number of Australian Royal Commissions and Inquiries, including the Stolen Generations Inquiry and the National Inquiry into
Racist Violence, aboriginal organizations such as the Aboriginal and
Torres Strait Islander Commission (ATSIC), the National Committee
to Defend Black Rights, and the federal Human Rights and Equal
Opportunity Commission. He has written widely in the areas of juvenile justice, policing, indigenous issues, and hate crime.

Michael Dooley is a Correctional Program Specialist with the Academy Division of the National Institute of Corrections. Prior to joining the Academy, Dooley worked with the Vermont Department of Corrections and with the Vermont Bureau of Justice Assistance to accomplish an organizational restructuring of correctional services in Vermont. His work has included the development of several alternative sanctions programs and the community-driven restorative justice program.

David Karp is an assistant professor of sociology at Skidmore College in Saratoga Springs, New York, where he teaches courses in criminology, deviance, and social issues. He conducts research on community-oriented responses to crime and is currently engaged in a qualitative research study examining Vermont's community reparative probation boards.

Gabrielle Maxwell, a psychologist and criminologist, is currently a Senior Research Fellow at the Institute of Criminology at Victoria University of Wellington (New Zealand). Much of her research has focused on restorative justice and the New Zealand youth justice system. She has written articles evaluating the New Zealand system in terms of meeting its objectives and the extent to which family group conferences are effective in reducing reoffending in New Zealand and internationally. She is presently engaged in a major study on achieving effective outcomes in youth justice in New Zealand.

Allison Morris is Professor in Criminology and Director of the Institute of Criminology at Victoria University of Wellington (New Zealand). She studied law at the University of Edinburgh and criminology at the University of Cambridge and Columbia University. She has carried out research on the juvenile justice system in Scotland, England, and New Zealand. She is presently engaged in a major study on achieving effective outcomes in youth justice in New Zealand.

Kenneth Polk is Professor of Criminology at the University of Melbourne (Australia). He received his Ph.D. from UCLA and was Professor of Sociology for many years at the University of Oregon before moving to Australia in 1985. His most recent research has been in the area of violence and homicide. Much of Polk's early research and writing centered on issues of juvenile delinquency.

Kay Pranis is a Restorative Justice Planner with the Minnesota Department of Corrections, where she provides education about restorative justice to the criminal justice system, other agencies, and the general public. She also assists groups interested in implementing the principles of restorative justice in their communities through system change and community empowerment. Pranis has presented papers and workshops on restorative justice in the United States, Canada, and Australia. She is currently involved in the development of peacemaking circles in U.S. public processes.

Declan Roche is a doctoral student in the Law Program, Research School of Social Sciences, Australian National University. He works part-time as a restorative justice conference facilitator in New South Wales and has worked as a judge's associate and Law School lecturer.

Barry Stuart, a Yukon Territorial Court judge, was chief negotiator in the Yukon Comprehensive Land Claim. His positions have included Chief Judge, Yukon Territorial Court, and Principal Legal Counsel/Senior Policy Analyst with the Central Planning Office in Papua, New Guinea. Stuart has also taught at Dalhousie Law School and Osgoode Hall Law School and is a founder of Mediation Yukon, the Canadian Environmental Law Association, and numerous other organizations. He has taught courses on mediation and consensus processes.

Daniel Van Ness is Vice President of Prison Fellowship International and director of its Center on Justice and Reconciliation. He has been involved in criminal justice issues for more than 20 years, as a lawyer, a criminal justice reform advocate, and a teacher. During his 11 years with Justice Fellowship, Van Ness focused on restorative justice and directed lobbying activities on sentencing reform and victim rights issues in the United States. After leaving Justice Fellowship, he spent two years in Malta helping the government restructure its correctional system. Van Ness is the coauthor (with Karen Heetderks Strong) of *Restoring Justice* (Anderson, 1997).

Lynne Walther works with the Central Restorative Justice and Community Development Team of the Vermont Department of Corrections. Her roles with the Community Reparative Probation Program have included project management, curriculum development and training, quality assurance, and volunteer management. Walther helped develop the Burlington Community Justice Center and is currently working on a statewide project to bring restorative initiatives to elementary and secondary schools.

Howard Zehr joined the graduate Conflict Transformation Program at Eastern Mennonite University in 1996 as Professor of Sociology and Restorative Justice. He is currently serving as Interim Director of the program. Prior to that, he served for 19 years as director of the Mennonite Central Committee U.S. Office on Crime and Justice. He has been called the "grandfather of restorative justice" in Van Ness and

Strong's *Restoring Justice* (Anderson, 1997). Zehr lectures and consults internationally on restorative justice and the Victim Offender Reconciliation Program (VORP), which he helped pioneer.

Evelyn Zellerer is an assistant professor in the School of Criminology and Criminal Justice, Florida State University. She first became interested in restorative justice through her research on violence against women and indigenous justice in Canada. Her work focuses on gender, race, and justice from an international, cross-cultural perspective. She is currently working on a project that examines the implementation and evaluation of a restorative project for young offenders.

Index

CPSIA information can be obtained at www.ICGtesting.com
Printed in the USA
237814LV00003B/7-12/P